Seven Doors to Islam

Seven Doors to Islam

Spirituality and the Religious Life of Muslims

JOHN RENARD

University of California Press

BERKELEY   LOS ANGELES   LONDON

University of California Press
Berkeley and Los Angeles, California

University of California Press, Ltd.
London, England

© 1996 by
The Regents of the University of California

Library of Congress Cataloging-in-Publication Data

Renard, John, 1944–
    Seven doors to Islam : spirituality and the religious life of Muslims
/ John Renard.
        p.   cm.
    Includes bibliographical references (p.   ) and index.
    ISBN 0-520-20095-0 (alk. paper). — ISBN 0-520-20417-4 (pbk. :
alk. paper)
        1. Religious life—Islam.   2. Islam.   I. Title.
    BP161.2.R47   1996
297'.4—dc20   95-45130
                                                                  CIP

Printed in the United States of America
9 8 7 6 5 4 3 2 1

The paper used in this publication meets the minimum requirements of
American National Standard for Information Sciences—Permanence of
Paper for Printed Library Materials, ANSI Z39.48-1984.

To Oleg Grabar for sharing his love of the arts of Islam

Contents

List of Illustrations

Preface

Welcome to this house with seven doors. It has its secrets, as most houses do; but this house is unusual in that it is built of seven rooms, one within another. To reach the innermost space, you must pass through each of the first six in succession. And as you move from one room to the next, you ascend a flight of stairs, arriving at last not only at the center but at the uppermost floor as well. Here is a wondrous and mysterious place where dwells the spirit of an ancient and perhaps unfamiliar way of learning and thinking. Enter and sample the riches of the Islamic spiritual and religious tradition as well as its literature and its arts and architecture.

ISLAMIC SPIRITUALITY AND RELIGIOUS LIFE

The multivolume *World Spirituality: An Encyclopedic History of the Religious Quest* associates spirituality with the discovery of one's core, with openness to the transcendent dimension, with the experience of ultimate reality, and with the methods and progress of a journey from the discovery of the core of one's being to the ultimate arrival at the journey's goal.[1] The present study emphasizes the importance of experience and of the relationships among human beings, and between human beings and God, as Muslims have understood them.

But Muslims, like Christians or Buddhists, are not all the same. Within the Islamic tradition one must therefore distinguish among many subtraditions of spirituality, which can be defined in a variety of ways: sociologically, along sectarian or institutional lines, noting, for example, how members of various Sufi organizations develop unique styles; doctrinally, according to school of thought within or across social or organizational boundaries, noting differences between, say, the majority Sunni and minority Shi'i views; or culturally, observing how some practices vary from Morocco to Indonesia and yet still can be called Islamic.

As its starting point, this exploration takes a working definition of the term *spirituality:* it is that dimension of a religious-cultural tradition that focuses on the unfolding experience of a relationship, expressed both individually and communally, between the person and the source and goal of that person's existence.

But what about the term *religious life?* What does it mean in this context? I use the term to encompass the whole range of pious practice and creative endeavor that is inspired by and fosters spiritual growth. The study of religious practices is often considered the province of anthropology. However, I am less concerned with ritual behavior as such, than with how Muslims have communicated, recorded, and displayed, both textually and visually, the beliefs and convictions underlying those practices. In other words, spirituality both grows out of and gives rise to religious living.

Approaching Islam in this way naturally affects what is included in or omitted from this survey. On the one hand, its seven chapters will scan a broader spectrum of materials than studies of Islamic spirituality typically include; on the other, these chapters do not survey those highly technical sources customarily associated with theological and legal scholarship. Although theology and law are crucial elements in any study of Islamic religious tradition, the writings of professional theologians and jurists have generally had little direct influence on the everyday lives of the vast majority of Muslims.

APPROACHING THE SOURCES

Any attempt to cast a net around the expansive reality of Islam's spiritual traditions, as expressed both verbally and visually, may seem presumptuous. But a study of a broad spectrum of materials from an equally broad array of cultural settings can help define and give substance to such a notion as Islamic spirituality by drawing concrete connections among the varied literary and visual arts that Islamic spiritual traditions have inspired from Morocco to Malaysia, from Albania to Zanzibar.

Most studies in Islamic spirituality have taken one of several forms. Literary investigations focus on a single work or on the writings of a single author, situating the central topic within the context of region, nation, or language, and relating it to other writings within that setting. Historical approaches typically detail the contribution of a school or outline broader movements such as Sufism (the Muslim mystical tradition). Largely theological or philosophical analyses chiefly discuss religious and mystical themes in relation to their intellectual antecedents. Anthologies have likewise typically followed thematic lines, perhaps supported by an interest in grouping entries according to compatibility of thought or affinity within schools. I propose a hybrid method, more synthetic than analytic, even eclectic, whose ultimate purpose is to show the thread of Islamic spirituality discernible across the length and breadth of the Islamic world.

My assumptions are that for educational purposes at least, surveying a broad range of materials is useful, that nonverbal data are as significant in unfolding the story of Islamic spirituality as are written sources, and that the various shapes and uses of literary and visual artifacts can provide links between and among the different places and peoples that make up the world of Islam.

The seven chapters of this work must be read in succession. Later discussions necessarily presuppose familiarity with earlier material, and the topics are arranged in order of ascending importance and difficulty—broadly speaking—within the traditional Muslim understanding of Islamic spirituality.[2]

ACKNOWLEDGMENTS

I wish to acknowledge the valuable assistance of the Graduate School of Saint Louis University; of the Mellon Faculty Development Fund of the College of Arts and Sciences, by way of partial funding for the writing of this book; and of the Eugene Hotfelder Professorship in the Humanities for its gift of time and resources with which to complete this project.

To Professor Ahmet Karamustafa of Washington University in Saint Louis, Professor Stephen Humphreys of the University of California at Santa Barbara, and Professor Carl Ernst of the University of North Carolina, I owe particular thanks for their helpful comments on an early draft.

To Dr. Thomas Lentz of the Freer Gallery and Mr. Peter Brenner of the Los Angeles County Museum of Art, I send my appreciation for assistance in obtaining the cover photograph. And to the following museums I am grateful for permission to reproduce works from their collections: Saint Louis Art Museum, Metropolitan Museum of Art in New York, the Freer and Sackler galleries of the Smithsonian, Harvard University's Fogg and Sackler museums, and the Egyptian National Library in Cairo. Unless otherwise credited, all photographs are by the author.

Thanks to Rachel Berchten for her superb copyediting, and to Michael Spath for final proofreading and indexing.

My special thanks go to Mr. David Vila of Saint Louis University for his research and editorial assistance in preparing a final manuscript. His careful attention to the details of every draft has been an invaluable gift.

Finally, I thank my wife, Mary Pat, for her extra patience and good humor during times when my preoccupation with this project left me short of both.

1 Foundations
Prophetic Revelation

Islam, the youngest of the three Abrahamic faiths, grew out of a revelation to and through a prophet. The seed of that divine speech germinated, through Muhammad's recitation (*qur'an*) of it, into the scripture known as the Qur'an. Three aspects of the foundations of Islamic tradition occupy our attention in this chapter. First, I look at the Qur'an, the center of the whole tradition, as both text and source of inspiration for the calligraphic arts and the arts of book production. After a background sketch, I describe several principal ways that Muslims have interpreted the sacred word in the literary forms known collectively as Qur'anic commentary, then discuss the range of scriptural themes that bear directly on Islamic spiritual life as I have defined it. Second, I examine the significance of an extensive collection of literature known as Hadith. The term *hadith* embraces three distinct bodies of textual material: reports of the words and deeds of Muhammad called Prophetic Hadith; a much smaller collection of sayings attributed to the imams of Shi'i Islam; and a still smaller group of Sacred Hadith (*ahadith qudsiya*; s., *hadith qudsi*), sayings attributed to God but held distinct from Qur'anic revelation. Third, I explore several dimensions of the experience of Qur'an and Hadith—in literature, in speech, and in the visual arts, emphasizing the ways that the "living" Qur'an instills a palpable sense of the divine presence.

QUR'AN IN ISLAMIC SPIRITUALITY

In this chapter and throughout the book, I emphasize the experiential, relational, and developmental elements in Islamic spiritual discourse. The Qur'an is central to that discourse and to the formation of Islamic spiritu-

Figure 1. (*Opposite*) Scripture in stone: sections from Suras 36 and 48 on the entry facade of the Ince Minare madrasa (1260–1265), Konya, Turkey. The architect, Keluk ibn 'Abdallah, may have been a convert from Christianity. Thanks to Sheila S. Blair for identifying the texts.

ality. Three aspects of the scripture are especially critical to an understanding of its foundational role: the unfolding of the Qur'an as the uniquely Islamic revelation, the scripture's key spiritual themes, and the varieties of scriptural interpretation.

Sacred Scripture

Muslims believe that God has, since the beginning of time, actively communicated with and through all of creation in a variety of ways. Foremost, God communicates in the very act of creating, by suffusing the universe with divine signs. More intimately, God communes with each animated being by infusing those same signs into every individual. God has established, moreover, a history of revelatory communication embodied in a succession of prophets, beginning with Adam. Through that unbroken chain of spokespersons, God has continued his self-revelation through another sign, namely, that of the verses of the scriptures given to the principal prophetic intermediaries.

Some of these prophets (*anbiya'*) have been raised to the status of messengers (*rusul*) as well, in that God has delivered sacred books through them. The most prominent messengers are Moses, to whom God gave the Torah; David, whose scripture the Qur'an calls the *zabur* (Psalms); Jesus, who delivered the *injil* (Gospel); and Muhammad. The verses of a scripture are called *ayat* (signs). God is also said to reveal signs "on the horizons" (that is, in creation) and within the individual human being (as suggested in the honorific title *ayatullah*, "sign of God").

God's ongoing and intimate relationships with the prophets and messengers provide the fundamental paradigm of divine-human interchange. It has become a commonplace of Muslim religious discourse on the subject to insist that at no time have the personalities of the messengers influenced the message delivered. That is not to say, however, that God does not engage these conduits of divine revelation on an intensely personal level, or that the messengers do not in turn respond to the divine initiative in a fully human way. For example, when God commissions Moses to come to the mountaintop, Moses hears the divine voice and responds with the request, "O Lord, let me see You that I might look upon You." God declines, saying, "In no way can you look upon Me; fix your gaze instead on the mountain. If it holds firm in its place, then you can cast your eye on Me." But when God manifests his glory to the mountain, it crumbles to dust, and Moses nearly dissolves in astonishment. When he recovers, a transformed and humbled Moses says to God, "Glory to You! I repent before You and am foremost among believers" (Q 7:143).

In the Qur'an the relationships between God and the major prophetic figures are described piecemeal. Since the scripture's primary purpose is not biographical, one gets only occasional glimpses of the more personal dimensions of the prophets' responses to their encounters with the revealing God. One finds recurrent themes in stories of the prophets' experiences of the divine initiative. Prophets feel both awe and dread in God's presence. Often they are terrified of embarking on their missions, but they can count on divine protection in the face of sometimes violent resistance to the message they bring. Theirs is overwhelmingly an experience of transcendence and power, but also of a divine justice softened with mercy and forgiveness.

Especially in the case of Muhammad and his communication of the Qur'an, one perceives the progressive nature of God's self-revelation and of its gradual transforming effect on the human prophet. The scripture recounts that Muhammad's critics complained loudly that if this revelation were authentic, it would surely have come all at once. He is told not to back down when they confront him with their desire for a flashier, more externally compelling revelation granted in a single stroke (Q 11:12–13). On the contrary, the Qur'an suggests, human beings are not able to bear all the truth at once; the divine pedagogy accommodates itself to humanity's short attention span and unreadiness to hear the whole of the demanding message immediately. God says to Muhammad, "We will teach you in stages so that you will not forget, except as God wills; for God knows the apparent and the concealed" (Q 87:6–7). Muhammad himself is enjoined not to attempt to hasten the process by anticipating the message and thus preempting the divine initiative: "Do not move your tongue in anticipation of it (the revelation); indeed, its composition and reciting are up to Us. But when We have recited it, then you recite it in imitation; moreover, it is also for us to clarify it" (Q 75:16–19).

So critical is this progressive, unfolding dimension of the Islamic understanding of the divine-human relationship that it has been enshrined in the interpretative principle that distinguishes between the way two different kinds of texts function in the Qur'an. Sometimes a revelation given earlier appears superseded or replaced by a later revelation given under slightly different circumstances. Muslim interpreters say that the earlier text has been replaced (literally, "abrogated," *mansukh*) by a superseding (literally, "abrogating," *nasikh*) revelation. To resolve apparent internal inconsistencies or contradictions, exegetes search for evidence that suggests how one text can be seen as nullifying or reframing another revealed earlier. These interpreters conclude that either the abrogated verses are considered no longer binding or of diminished force, or that a slightly varied revelation made under different circumstances has to be understood differently than the earlier revelation. For example, the early Muslim community prayed facing Jerusalem. Not long after the journey known as the Hijra (emigration) brought the community from Mecca to Medina (622 C.E.), an abrogating Qur'anic revelation informed Muhammad and the faithful that God would "turn you to a direction that will satisfy you. Direct your face toward the mosque of the sanctuary [the Ka'ba in Mecca]; wherever you may be, turn your faces in that direction" (Q 2:144; the text is visible above the niche of Sultan Hasan's *madrasa*—literally, "place of study"—in Fig. 7).

The notion that within the Qur'an, God tailors particular revelations for specific circumstances is striking. If God adjusts revelation, the divine communication, as he sees fit and according to the capacity of the recipient, does that mean that God has had a change of mind? Or perhaps that the revelation leaves human beings a good deal of room to bargain? Not quite. The implications of this remarkable idea might have had a far greater effect had early Muslim scholars not developed interpretative devices that were so precise that they discouraged interpreters from taking advantage of the divine flexibility. Some of Muhammad's critics evidently tried to do just that, as this text suggests (God is speaking): "When Our clear signs are put before them, those who are not hopeful of meeting Us say [to Muhammad], 'Bring us a different Qur'an, or alter this one.' Tell them, 'Changing it is not left to my whim, for I follow only what is revealed to me; and I fear an overwhelming day of retribution should I disobey my Lord'" (Q 10:15).

Nevertheless, Qur'an interpreters tend to emphasize that God's intention is not to increase the burden revelation places on the believer but to lighten the load. One pioneer of Islamic religious jurisprudence, Shafi'i (d. c. 820), makes an important point. He notes that although God initially instructed Muhammad to keep vigil and recite the Qur'an for about half the night, God abrogated that requirement by acknowledging that such an expectation might be too strenuous. A new revelation instructed the Prophet: "Therefore recite as much of the Qur'an as will be more convenient for you. God knows that some among you may be in poor health, some traveling in search of God's bounty, and some engaging in battle in the cause of God" (Q 73:20).[1]

Interpreting Qur'an

Two questions help to understand the many ways Muslims have read their scriptures. Through what sorts of lenses have Muslims seen the divine message? And how has the ancient historic scripture helped Muslims make sense of their lives in the present? Several major interpretative styles have arisen over the centuries, each in response to particular kinds of questions Muslims have put to their scripture. Jurists, philosophers, political theorists, theologians, mystics, grammarians, and historians—all have approached the Qur'an looking for specific themes and pronouncements germane to their interests. One common English technical term for this complex process of scriptural interpretation is *exegesis*, a Greek word that denotes "to lead or draw out" meaning.

Islamic exegetical tradition has developed a distinction between two categories of interpretation, *tafsir* and *ta'wil*. As the twelfth-century Iraqi scholar Ibn al-Jawzi (d. c. 1200) explains, the two terms were originally used almost synonymously to refer to Qur'anic interpretation, but they gradually came to designate significantly different approaches:

> Those educated in the religious sciences have held various views on whether the terms *al-tafsir* and *al-ta'wil* have the same meaning or two different meanings. A group whose proclivities were linguistic held the view that the two meant the same thing. This is the opinion of the generality of earlier exegetes (*mufassirun*). A group with primarily legal interests were [*sic*] persuaded that the two terms differed in meaning. They defined *al-tafsir* as "moving something out of concealment into full view" and *al-ta'wil* as "shifting discourse from its conventional signification to some allusion which may even neglect the literal sense of the utterance."[2]

By the middle of the thirteenth century, ta'wil was associated almost exclusively with a more mystical type of exegesis that, in the words of the Andalusian-born mystic Ibn 'Arabi (d. 1240), "varies with the state of the listener, his moments in the stations of his mystical journey [*suluk*] and his different degrees [of attainment]. As he reaches higher stations, new doors are open to him through which he looks upon new and subtle meanings."[3]

This distinction paralleled the idea that the sacred text has both an outward, obvious meaning and an inward, less apparent significance. That notion in turn arises out of the Qur'an's own statement (in Sura 3:7) that it contains both clear and unambiguous verses (*muhkamat*), and verses whose meanings are not quite so obvious (*mutashabihat*), and whose ta'wil only God knows.[4] Some of the major commentaries assert boldly that the former were revealed to abrogate the latter and thus remove all ambiguity, but the need to inquire into the ambiguous or metaphorical verses remained a significant theme in Islamic intellectual history.

The Islamic science of scriptural interpretation is both technical and subtle. The purpose of this discussion is not to become immersed in the science of exegesis but to emphasize its centrality to all spiritual pedagogy. Interpreting the Qur'an is not merely an academic exercise and a practical service to the community of believers, but it is in itself a devotional act. Accordingly, a saying attributed to Muhammad advises that only "one whose right hand does good and whose tongue affirms the truth while his heart is upright" is fit to engage in scriptural interpretation.[5]

Muslim commentators have likened tafsir to a woman's unveiling her face for her spouse or to dawn's removal of darkness's veil from the night sky. Tafsir elucidates such questions as the immediate historical context of the revelation, its dating either in the Meccan (610–622) or Medinan period (622–632), its status as either a clear or ambiguous verse, its weight as either an abrogating or abrogated verse, and its applicability as either general or specific. All these matters pertain to a text's exoteric or outward meaning and application, and its transmission. Tafsir is sometimes related to various levels of knowledge. Texts convey truths that are plainly evident to speakers of Arabic or fundamental and universally binding moral norms or solely the province of religious scholars or known only to God.

Muslim scholars distinguish between two broad categories of tafsir. One is based on traditionally attested materials (*tafsir bi'l-ma'thur*). Sources for this kind of tafsir are generally arranged in a hierarchical order. The Qur'an is placed first, then Prophetic Hadith, followed by the sayings of Muhammad's Companions (the first generation of Muslims), then of his Followers (the second generation), and finally material from Jewish and Christian sources. The second category, inherently more controversial, is known as "interpretation by personal judgment" (*tafsir bi'r-ra'y*), based on the scholar's opinion and learned argument, which begins to cross into the realm of ta'wil.

Every religious tradition must concern itself not only with passing on its heritage intact but also with adapting that heritage to changing needs and circumstances. When a more conservative approach proves lacking in flexibility and applicability, a mode of inquiry more responsive to actual human experience will inevitably rise to the occasion. Developments in ta'wil represent just such an accommodation, for "it has been through ta'wil that Muslim scholars and mystics were able to bring the Qur'an into the hearts, imagination, and total life experience of the masses."[6] These developments have, however, remained under the ever critical eye of more cautious interpreters and have often been condemned outright as unjustifiably innovative, tendentious, or even heretical.

Two branches of esoteric Qur'an interpretation deserve specific mention here. Sufi, or mystical, exegesis began as a distinct approach as early as the eighth century, with the first full-scale commentaries dating to the late ninth and early tenth centuries. A number of classical authors developed a new literary genre sometimes referred to as allusions (*isharat*).[7] This new kind of ta'wil went beyond the bounds of earlier understandings of esoteric exegesis in that the mystics allowed much greater latitude to interpretation based on personal experience. Sayings of the great mystics naturally became an important source for interpretation and came to be considered nearly equal in authority to sayings of Muhammad.

By a process of imaginative metaphorical association, the mystical interpreter unites certain key expressions from the Qur'an with imagery arising from the unconscious, producing evocative allusive expressions of the mystic's personal engagement with the scripture. The mystical interpreter reads the scripture with particular attention to any suggestion of God's immanence and of the possibility of an intimate divine-human relationship. As Gerhard Böwering describes it, speaking of the ninth-century mystic Sahl at-Tustari, "The process of reception of Qur'an recitals and reaction to their impact upon the Sufi's mind primarily implies the auditive energies of the Sufi and results in Sufi speech, sometimes manifested in ecstatic utterance. This auditive and oral process is transposed onto the plane of written record . . . where a succinct Sufi statement is jotted down next to a Qur'anic phrase."[8]

The mystical imagination finds allusive connections with the scripture. For example, the scriptural Verse of Light reads,

> God is the Light of the heavens and the earth; His Light is like a niche in which is a lamp, and the lamp is within a glass, and the glass is like a shining star kindled from a sacred olive tree neither of the East nor of the West, whose oil nearly glows though fire touch it not: light upon light; God guides to His Light whom He will. And God coins similitudes for human beings, and of everything God has knowledge.
>
> (Q 24:35)

One mystical reading of the text goes like this:

> The likeness of His light (refers to) the likeness of the light of Muhammad, since it is deposited in the loins like (in) a niche. . . . By the lamp He meant his heart and by the glass his breast. It is as if it were a glittering star because of the faith and wisdom that is included in it. It is kindled from a blessed tree, that is to say from the light of Abraham. Its oil wellnigh would shine, that is to say the prophethood of Muhammad wellnigh would elucidate mankind prior to his (actual utterance of) speech like this oil.[9]

The second branch of ta'wil has emerged from within the Shi'i community. Shi'i Muslims now make up about 10 percent of the total Muslim population. They began to form into a separate community within Islam in the early seventh century, shortly after Muhammad's death. A difference of opinion arose as to whether Muhammad had formally designated a successor before he died. The majority asserted that he had not, and that it was up to the elders of the community to choose a leader. A minority held that Muhammad had indeed designated his cousin and son-in-law 'Ali. Soon this minority, called Shi'i, became convinced that a legitimate successor to Muhammad must be from the family of the Prophet and be so designated by his predecessor. That interpretation of early Muslim history has naturally influenced the classic Shi'i interpretation of the Qur'an.

For Shi'i Muslims, the underlying meaning of the scripture relates especially to the ways God has continued to be present and active in the world through the mediation of the family of the Prophet, as embodied in a succession of descendants known as imams. A principle of Shi'i exegesis is that "the Qur'an must always be shown to have relevance or applicability to some persons or situations."[10] Shi'i interpreters read the scripture with a view to demonstrating how knowledge of the esoteric sense can relate virtually every text to some aspect of the life and teaching of one or more of the imams. The sayings of the imams have thus acquired an authority nearly equal to those of Muhammad himself as sources for the interpretation of the Qur'an.

In addition, some of the symbolic and often expressly allegorical Shi'i exegesis sees references to the imams and the family of the Prophet sprinkled throughout the Qur'an. Consider, for example, the case of the Qur'anic Verse of Light quoted above. A quintessential example of a Shi'i approach attributed to the sixth imam, Ja'far as-Sadiq (d. 765), interprets the text allegorically. The exegesis bears some clear initial similarities to the Sufi interpretation just mentioned but then veers in a distinctively Shi'i direction. Ja'far says that God's light is Muhammad, who is like a niche that contains the light of knowledge that is inherent in the office of prophecy. The reference to the lamp's containment in the glass means that Muhammad's prophetic knowledge passed from Muhammad into the heart of 'Ali, the first imam. Ja'far finishes his explanation this way:

> (The words) *the glass as it were a glittering star, kindled from a blessed tree, an olive that is neither of the east nor of the west,* according to as-Sadiq, are coined in reference to the Ruler of the Believers, 'Ali ibn Abi Talib, who was neither a Jew nor a Christian. (Regarding God's words:) *Whose oil wellnigh would shine, even if no fire touched it,* as-Sadiq says: The knowledge would wellnigh issue forth from the mouth of the knowing one of the family of Muhammad (that is, 'Ali), even if Muhammad had not spoken it. *Light upon light,* as-Sadiq says (means): Imam to Imam.[11]

Christian readers might see here an analogy to the way their tradition has found countless references to the Christ buried in the text of the Hebrew scriptures, and often interprets figures of the Hebrew scriptures as acting out of faith in the Christ.[12]

Scriptural Themes

One of the principal difficulties non-Muslims encounter in reading the Qur'an is in their search for a focus to help them trace the scripture's basic message. In the preceding section on Qur'anic interpretation I note that what one sees in the Qur'an depends a great deal on what one is looking for, yet it is essential to bear in mind that the Qur'an, like all sacred texts, seeks to communicate an experience. One way to draw a bead on the essential part of that experience is to read the Qur'an as both a sourcebook of prayer and as a prayer in itself.

As a sourcebook of prayer, the Qur'an lays the conceptual and practical foundations for all subsequent developments in the history of Islamic spirituality. (I speak of the scripture as a word spoken by God and addressed to human beings.) As a prayer in itself, the Qur'an becomes a divinely initiated word addressed to God in return. Prayer is also a theme in the sacred text, both a divine instruction in how humans ought to respond to God and a concrete prophetic example.

From earliest times, Muslim scholars distinguished between revelations that occurred during the Meccan period and those that occurred in the Medinan. They concerned themselves with establishing a chronological sequence in the delivery of the book's 114 chapters called suras. In more recent times, scholars have further broken those two periods into subperiods, early, middle, and later, for example. That sequence bears significantly on the concept of an unfolding revelation as implied in the concepts of abrogating and abrogated verses, since only a text known to be later can be said to abrogate another earlier text.

The implications of establishing a clear chronology are less momentous in the search for themes such as prayer, but one can still garner important insights into the nature of Islamic prayer by attending to the contexts in which examples appear in the Qur'an. Early texts concerning night vigil and recitation offer important clues to the development of the various forms of Islamic prayer. References to prostration and to various daily times for prayer also occur in early suras. For example, a sura dated to about the year 615–616 says:

> Therefore glorify God when evening comes and when you awake; for to Him belongs praise in the heavens and on the earth; and in late afternoon and as dusk begins to fall.
>
> (Q 30:17–18)

Such suggestions of what eventually developed into the five daily prayers receive more detailed attention in later suras, especially those of the Medinan period, when the growing Muslim community needed increasing communal discipline and instruction.

Examples of personal prayer, or what would come to be known as the prayer of invocation or supplication (du'a'), also abound in the Qur'an. During the middle and later Meccan periods, when Muhammad was experiencing growing opposition from influential members of the Quraysh tribe, stories of previous prophets and the enmity of their peoples toward them become crucial to the scripture's message. Those prophets serve as models of prayer, suggesting both when and how one ought to address God from the heart. The years 615–622 were times of particular hardship for the small Muslim community, and the prayers of the pre-Islamic prophets reflect and comment on that experience. Abraham's extended prayer at the core of Sura 14 is a prime example. He intercedes for the people of Mecca:

> My Lord, make this city secure, and protect me and my children from worshipping idols. My Lord, truly have they misguided many people. One who follows me is with me, but the one who rebels—but You are the Forgiving, the Merciful. . . . My Lord, cause me and my descendants to be given to regular communal prayer (salat), O our Lord, and receive my supplication (du'a'). Our Lord, be forgiving to me and my parents and all believers on that Day of Reckoning.[13]

From the Medinan period comes another, more generic prayer that seems to express the sentiments of a more firmly established community of believers:

> Our Lord, not in vain have You created this, may You be glorified! . . . We have heard the call of one inviting to faith, 'Believe in Your Lord,' and so we have believed. Our Lord, forgive our sins, cover our evil deeds, and let us die among the righteous. Our Lord, give us what You have promised through your Messengers and let us not be put to shame on Resurrection Day.[14]

Among the various essential attitudes the Qur'an recommends, the following deserve special mention: attentiveness, intention, striving, and gratitude. The theological equivalent of the attitude of attentiveness is uncompromising monotheism—belief in and acknowledgment of one God only, called *tawhid* in Arabic. Its opposite is carelessness, laziness, a spiritual torpor born of self-absorption, an insidious and destructive form of denial. Attentiveness means seeing things as they really are, with the eyes of faith; it means discerning in creation and in oneself, as well as in the revealed scripture, the signs of the Creator and Revealer.

Without that mindfulness and heedfulness no divine-human relationship is possible. Directly related to that attentiveness is right intention (*niyya*). Any unthinking or mechanical action loses its fully human character and hence produces no spiritual benefit. Explicit intention precedes all fully human acts.

At the center of the human condition lies the need to struggle, to strive against one's baser tendencies and against the spiritual entropy born of the heedlessness that is endemic to the human race. This is the core of that most misunderstood of Islamic themes, *jihad*. The Arabic root *Ja-Ha-Da* (with the three consonantal root letters in uppercase) means "to exert oneself." Believers must struggle against whatever stands between the self and its origin and goal, and strive to overcome injustice and oppression. Battle against the fiercest of all enemies—the enemy that resides "between one's two sides," as a hadith puts it—ancient tradition calls the Greater Jihad. Combat against outward foes is known as the Lesser Jihad.

What could possibly motivate the hard work of rigorous spiritual discipline? One often hears Islam characterized as a religion of submission, whose adherents operate largely out of fear of a cold, capricious deity. While the Qur'an's emphasis on divine majesty and power has indeed sometimes given rise to a resigned fatalism, the scripture in no way recommends passivity. Prayer for forgiveness occurs often in the Qur'an, but a sense of gratitude to God is at least as significant a motive for ethical action as is fear of punishment: "God has given you all you have asked for; and were you to attempt to add up the kindnesses of God, you would fall short. Indeed, humanity is prey to injustice and ingratitude" (Q 14:34).

All positive virtues flow from the awareness that God is the beneficent and unstinting source of all good, who expects that those most blessed will in turn share their gifts most generously with others. To attain the experience of gratitude, one must be purified of any delusions of grandeur or self-sufficiency, as well as of selfish motivation in giving. The term that came to mean "almsgiving," *zakat*, derives from a root meaning "to purify oneself."

> If you give alms in public, for others to see, it is well; but if you conceal your alms, and give them to the poor, it is better for you. . . . Whatever of good you spend in alms shall be for your souls and you should not spend except out of longing for the face of God.
>
> (Q 2:271–72)

Gratitude ultimately flows over into praise of God, an attitude that suffuses both the Qur'an and ordinary Arabic speech. The Arabic term for thanks (*Sh-u-K-R*) is often said to be the direct opposite of that most ungrateful of acts, acknowledging a deity other than God—a sin called in Arabic *Sh-i-R-K*, a word composed of the same consonants as *Sh-u-K-R*, only slightly transposed. These interior qualities of attentiveness, intention, striving, and gratitude have implications for human action.

The human spirit does not suffer isolation gladly; it naturally seeks expression in relationships to other persons and to the world. Generosity, personal responsibility, and diligence in the Lesser Jihad are manifestations of healthy engagement of the individual with his or her surroundings. Generosity is the outward result of inner gratitude: one can be truly generous only to the degree that one acknowledges God's primacy in giving.

> Give to kin, to the poor and the traveler what they need; that is best for those who seek the face of God. . . . What you give in the hope of profiting at the expense of other people will gain you nothing in God's sight; what you give as purifying alms [*zakat*] as you seek the face of God—that will produce abundant return.
>
> (Q 30:38–39)

All beneficence thus points not to the individual, who serves really as a broker, but to God. Generosity in turn is linked to a heavy emphasis on social responsibility (see, e.g., Q 2:177). The scripture condemns those who hoard their wealth in the hope that it will save them from their mortality (Q 104:1–3). Equally condemned are those "who do not treat the orphan with dignity nor encourage each other to feed the poor . . . [and who] greedily devour their inheritances" (Q 89:17–19).[15]

One of the Islamic ethical and theological issues most discussed over the centuries, from the earliest times, has been the tension between divine omnipotence, and human responsibility and moral freedom. In attempts to preserve God's transcendent sovereignty from any dilution, parties to the debate have sometimes gone to the extreme of virtually denying human freedom. On the other side, an overriding concern to safeguard individual moral responsibility has led some to the opposite extreme of suggesting that God's choices are limited by principles of absolute justice. As we have seen, one can interpret the Qur'an in many ways; but, on the whole, it maintains a paradoxical balance. God's power knows no bounds, but human beings both enjoy a wide array of options and must shoulder responsibility for their choices. Again and again, the scripture makes it clear that "God does not change a people's condition until they change the thoughts of their own hearts" (Q 13:11).

That responsibility leads to another outward dimension, willingness to engage actively in the hard work of stewardship over creation. Islamic tradition calls acceptance of the divine charge of accountability for the shape of things here on earth the Lesser Jihad. One cannot authentically enter into this often mundane striving without first joining the battle within, the Greater Jihad. In practice the struggle involves acting on one's convictions about everything from the environment to human rights to electing the local school board. Muslim authors speak of the *jihad* of the pen, of the tongue, and, more recently, of the ballot box. Wherever human beings work for peace and justice, there is *jihad*. There is also the *jihad* of the sword. As a last resort, when all other means have been exhausted, *jihad* may also include the use of force; but violent means are carefully hedged with prohibitions against terrorism, mistreatment of prisoners, and wanton destruction of natural resources. War against an aggressor is justifiable because "aggression is more despicable than killing" (Q 2:193).[16]

HADITH IN ISLAMIC SPIRITUALITY

These thematic aspects of Qur'anic spirituality—attentiveness, intention, inner discipline, gratitude, generosity, personal responsibility, and the struggle for justice—represent only a small sample of the important issues the scripture offers for consideration. Many similar themes, presented in a different form, lie at the heart of Islam's second documentary wellspring, Hadith. The three principal developments in hadith literature are the massive collection known as Prophetic Hadith, the smaller body of hadith attributed to the Shi'i imams, and the little treasury of gems called Sacred Hadith.

Sayings of the Prophet

Next to the Qur'an, Islam's most important documentary source is known collectively as Prophetic Hadith (*al-ahadith an-nabawiya*). As literary source, Prophetic Hadith consists of thousands of reports of Muhammad's words and deeds as transmitted by generations of Muslims, beginning with firsthand accounts from among the Prophet's Companions, the first generation of Muslims. Each report comprises a chain (*isnad*) of transmitters, each individual listed by name, all the way back to the first witness; and a body (*matn*) of text that may run from a few words to several pages in length. On a library shelf, the main authoritative collections, called the Six, along with a number of minor works and several anthologized selections, would add up to fifty or sixty sizable volumes.

Scholarly compilers of these works employed several very different methods for organizing the material. A cursory glance at tables of contents of two or three of the major collections offers a fair impression of the prevalent themes and of those most germane to the study of Islamic spirituality Hadiths cover everything from minute details for the performance of ord nary ritual to the conduct of daily business to the most intimate secrets of the believer's heart and hearth. One that pertains to *jihad*, a tradition included in at least four of the authoritative collections, reports that Muhammad once said, "The most excellent Jihad is to speak a word of truth in the presence of a tyrannical ruler."[17]

Leafing through a several-volume set of hadiths can be a most rewarding experience, like panning for gold. The collections are full of surprises and small nuggets that can give the prospector a sense of the humanity of the people to whom these reminders of Muhammad mean so much. Some talk of prayer and of how God takes the initiative:

> 'Ali reported God's messenger as saying, "When the middle night of [the eighth lunar month of] Sha'ban comes, spend the night in prayer and fast during the day, for in it God most high comes down at sunset to the lowest heaven and says, 'Is there no one who asks forgiveness so that I may forgive him? Is there no one who asks provision so that I may provide him? Is there no one afflicted so that I may relieve him?'"[18]

There is also a great deal of wry wit sprinkled amidst the more serious matters, as in this earthy reminder of the importance of attentiveness at the moment the muezzin issues the call to one of the five daily ritual prayers. Muhammad's Companion Abu Hurayra, an active transmitter of hadiths, repeats these words of the Messenger:

> When a summons to prayer is made the devil turns his back and breaks wind so as not to hear the call being made, but when the summons is finished he turns around. When a second call to prayer is made he turns his back, and when the second call is finished he turns around to distract a man, saying, "Remember such and such; remember such and such," referring to something the man did not have in mind, with the result that he does not know how much he has prayed.[19]

Many Muslims explain that the sayings of Muhammad are, like the Qur'an, revealed by God; but in this instance, the revealed message is couched in the Prophet's own words rather than those of God. For that reason the hadiths are second in authority, so that, for example, one cannot rely on a hadith to abrogate a scriptural injunction. In case of an apparent conflict between Qur'an and a hadith on a particular issue, one accepts the scriptural text as definitive.

Sayings of the Imams

Second in importance and in sheer numbers to Prophetic Hadith comes a body of reports attributed to the succession of spiritual descendants of the

Prophet known to Shi'i Muslims as imams. In the two main branches of Shi'i Islam—the Imami, or "Twelver," and the Isma'ili, or "Sevener," communities—these persons vary in number, either twelve or seven. Shi'i Muslims were virtually unanimous in their acceptance of the authority of the first six imams, down to and including Ja'far as-Sadiq, whose interpretation of the Verse of Light is cited above. Ja'far designated his older son, Isma'il, as his successor. When Isma'il died before his father, around 760, a crisis arose. Ja'far designated a younger son, Musa; but a significant number of people refused to transfer their allegiance, claiming that Isma'il remained the legitimate seventh imam through his ongoing spiritual presence. For that faction, the line of imams officially ended with the seventh, Isma'il. Meanwhile, those who acknowledged the leadership of the newly designated Musa formed the nucleus of the community for whom the line of imams would end only with the twelfth. In the view espoused by the vast majority of present-day Iranians and over half of the inhabitants of Iraq, the twelfth imam entered a state of lesser concealment or occultation in 874. Until 940, the last imam communicated through a series of four intermediaries. When the last spiritual representative died without appointing a successor, the imam entered into greater concealment, a state from which Twelver eschatology says he will eventually emerge to usher in a new age.

Traditions ascribed to the imams (al-ahadith al-walawiya) supplement, rather than replace, the Prophetic sayings that are uniquely seminal in the Sunni community. These hadiths function in Shi'i tradition as a historical projection of the authority and voice of Muhammad through his extended family. They are "not only a continuation but also a kind of commentary and elucidation of the prophetic Hadith, often with the aim of bringing out the esoteric teachings" inherent in them.[20]

The most influential and numerous of these materials are those attributed to Muhammad's cousin and son-in-law, 'Ali, as anthologized in a tenth-century Arabic collection called *The High Road of Eloquence (Nahj al-balagha).*[21] Only a portion of the work consists of hadiths in the narrower sense used here; much of the collection is homiletical and epistolary. A sample of the spiritual wisdom attributed to 'Ali speaks of the negative way of knowing God:

> Praise belongs to God, whose laudation is not rendered by speakers, whose bounties are not counted by reckoners, and whose rightfully due . . . is not discharged by those who strive. Grand aspirations perceive Him not and deep-diving perspicacities reach Him not. . . . The first step in religion is knowledge of Him. The perfection in knowledge . . . of Him is to confirm Him. . . . The perfection of confirming Him is to profess His unity. . . .

> The perfection of professing his unity is sincerity . . . towards Him.
> And the perfection of sincerity towards Him is to negate attributes . . .
> from Him, because of the testimony of every attribute . . . that it is not
> that which possesses the attribute and the testimony of everything that
> possesses attributes that it is not the attribute.[22]

Four other tenth- and eleventh-century collections encompass a broader selection of traditions, and are parallel in authority, for Shi'i Muslims, to the six basic anthologies of Prophetic Hadith mentioned earlier. In addition, at least three other anthologies, including one completed during this century, function as important sources. Materials traced to 'Ali's sons, Hasan and Husayn, and to subsequent imams, have sustained great popularity and authority throughout the centuries among Shi'i Muslims. Among these traditions one finds, as among Prophetic Hadith, a sprinkling of those utterances of a separate category known as Sacred Hadith.

Sacred Sayings

Still another collection of texts represents sayings attributed to God, not to Muhammad or one of the imams. This Sacred Hadith remains distinct from the divine utterances that make up the Qur'an and is of decidedly secondary—some Muslims would even say tertiary—authority. Many of these traditions appear as separate sayings or are integrated into Prophetic Hadith in the standard editions, as in the hadith cited above, in which God descends to the lowest heaven and calls out to humankind. Others are considered extracanonical but have nevertheless achieved wide popularity. Sacred hadiths are most significant in the present context for the light they shed on the emotional tone of Islamic spirituality. The sayings tend to emphasize God's immanence and accessibility, and highlight the possibility of a loving relationship between creature and Creator. Precisely because some sacred hadiths seem to lean too far toward divine immanence, thus compromising God's transcendence, many Muslims have considered them spurious. They represent, nevertheless, some of the most beautiful and popular crystallizations of an important dimension of the Islamic spiritual genius.

In one of the most famous sacred hadiths, transmitted in several slightly different versions, God describes how supererogatory devotion establishes the most intimate bond between a servant and the Lord.

> My servant continues to come near to me by piety beyond what is
> required, so that I love him; and I show my love by becoming the eye with
> which my servant sees, the ear by which he hears, the hand with which
> he grasps. And if my servant approaches a hand's breadth, I go toward him

an arm's length; and if he approaches an arm's length, I go forward the
space of outstretched arms; and if he comes toward me walking, I go toward
him running. And if my servant should bring to me sins the size of the
earth itself, my forgiveness will be more than equal to them.

Other sacred hadiths are usually briefer but express sentiments equally
lovely and convictions equally moving. God says, "Heaven and earth cannot contain Me, but there is room for Me in the heart of the believer"; "I
was a hidden treasure and I wished to be known; so I created the world";
and "I am in the midst of those whose hearts are broken for My sake."[23]
Such sayings convey a deep conviction that, as the Qur'an says, God is
"closer than the jugular vein" (Q 50:16).

EXPERIENCING QUR'AN AND HADITH

To analyze the textual and visual products of a religious tradition from the
perspective of an outsider requires careful study. To move beyond observation toward a more penetrating insight into the ways believers experience
the tradition through those textual and visual expressions requires a great
deal of imagination as well. Here I examine some ways in which Muslims
encounter and express their tradition through text, recitation and meditative listening, and works of art—all of which celebrate the sacred message.

Sacred Literature

Questions about the degree to which a sacred text shares characteristics of
such conscious literary productions as the novel, biography, lyric poetry, and
so forth have not surprisingly raised much controversy in a number of global
religious traditions. Many believers, regardless of their religious affiliations,
reject the suggestion that one might subject their scripture to a literary
analysis. The conclusion that the revealed word communicates through literary devices is unacceptable. They fear that any overt identification of the
divine speech with mere human convention removes the transcendent
meaning from the sacred text. To associate a scripture directly with the human imagination reduces revelation, they fear, to a fleeting creative impulse.

Still, virtually every religious tradition based on a scripture has devised
ways of straddling the fence, of affirming that its scripture is of divine origin even as it represents in itself an enormous concession by God to the
limitations of human communication. Islamic tradition has found the balance between transcendence and immanence in its two most sacred sources,
Qur'an and Hadith.

Early Islamic tradition developed the notion of the Qur'an's inimitability (*i'jaz*). Initially a theological concept intended to safeguard the divine content of the revealed scripture, the notion of inimitability gradually came to be interpreted in literary terms. This began a long history of investigation and criticism of the Qur'anic text as an Arabic masterpiece, with careful attention to the ways in which it surpasses all other works in that language. One difference between literary and theological approaches to scriptural interpretation is particularly important here. Literary interpreters presume *formal* continuity within the Qur'anic text until their study convinces them to the contrary. Theological interpreters are more concerned with unity of content than of form: "Under the assumption of [formal] continuity, one looks for links and connections between verses and pages, and only upon failing to find any does one concede that the text is discontinuous. But a typical Muslim theologian or lawyer searches for theological or legal content in the Qur'an, and, as soon as he finds such content, focuses on it, often in disregard of the context."[24] From the theological perspective it matters little whether the scripture manifests literary seamlessness. What theological interpreters presume in the text is that it represents a unified message. Exegetes must then demonstrate how the divine message fits together, as in the examples of the various styles of tafsir and ta'wil discussed earlier.

Muslims never approach the Qur'an as though it were a product of the literary imagination, of course. It is always a communication from God and therefore incomparable. But God is speaking to human beings in one of their languages and in doing so makes use of the various idiomatic and rhetorical devices that language uses to communicate clearly and evocatively.

When one reads the Qur'an with special sensitivity to its literary characteristics, a number of features become evident. First, a commentary that attends to the subtleties of the Qur'an's use of specific terms and idioms can highlight for the non-Arabic reader subtle colorations not available in most translations. The same may be said of frequent use of wordplay and terms chosen apparently for their multiple meanings. Much of the vivid imagery of the Arabic original does, nevertheless, come through in other languages, especially in the case of the more obvious use of figurative speech, such as the extended similes of the Verse of Light or the more metaphorical Verse of the Throne (Q 24:35–40 and 2:255). The latter reads in part:

> God—there is no deity but He; the Alive, the Eternal. Neither slumber nor sleep overcomes Him. To Him belongs all that is in the heavens and on the earth. . . . His throne stretches across heaven and earth; and dominion over them does not tire Him, for He is the Exalted, the Magnificent. (See Fig. 2.)

Stirring images such as this and those of the Verse of Light have given

Figure 2.   Tile niche (early fourteenth century) from Kashan, Iran, combines visual imagery of the Verse of Light (the lamp within the niche) with the text of the Verse of the Throne around the outside and within the niche. New York: The Metropolitan Museum of Art, Rogers Fund.

impetus to much potent personal response from Muslims over the centuries. Verbal imagery has the power to move people, and Muslims have always acknowledged the unique literary qualities of the Qur'an as integral to the overall experience of divine eloquence.

Important aspects of the emotional mood of the Qur'an emerge through its use of humor, satire, and irony. Humor and satire are not dominant devices, but they are evident and effective. The latter is easier to detect and interpret than the former. Numerous dramatic scenes abound in irony and paradox; the story of Joseph, occupying the whole of Sura 12, uses many of these devices. One of the most ironic scenes in the scripture describes the moment Joseph's brothers arrive at the Egyptian court and are granted an audience with the brother whose true identity remains unknown to them. Joseph contrives to keep his brother Benjamin behind by hiding a goblet in his sack and then having his soldiers feign a search for the missing cup. The brothers then are not only willing to believe that Benjamin is a thief but even allude to "another brother"—they refer to Joseph—they once had who was also a thief. Joseph is playing something of a practical joke on his brothers and is in no great hurry to let them off the hook. But he shows far more leniency to them than they deserve (Q 12:58–93).

This story also presents the best example of extended narrative in the Qur'an, though one can find dozens of briefer but equally arresting passages throughout the scripture. With the notable exception of the Joseph story, Qur'anic narration of a particular prophet's tale almost always occurs intermittently. Each episode or reappearance of the prophet either reinforces a particular theme in Muhammad's preaching or illuminates an event in his experience as prophet.

The use of dramatic dialogue is another important literary characteristic of the Qur'an. Some, such as the conversation between Moses and Pharaoh, recur in different contexts, not unlike the segments or retellings of a prophetic narrative account. As a device, dialogue therefore also serves as a thread of conceptual continuity through the scripture. Dialogue also facilitates another literary feature, namely, characterization. Something of the uniqueness of principal prophetic figures emerges in their verbal exchanges, especially with their adversaries. The most important dialogue occurs between a prophet and either his people or God, but there are also many examples of one-on-one conversations between human beings.[25] In one encounter, Pharaoh addresses Moses and his brother Aaron, and asks:

> Who, Moses, is the Lord of you two? He [Moses] said: Our Lord is the one who has granted to each being its features and then guided it. [Pharaoh]

said: Then what about previous generations? [Moses] replied: That
knowledge is with my Lord in a scripture; my Lord is never in error and
never forgets. He it is who has fashioned the earth as a carpet unrolled for
you. He has given you ways you may travel, and has sent down water from
the heavens.

(Q 20:49–53)

The Qur'an uses several exchanges between Moses and Pharaoh to underscore the gulf between faith and unbelief, qualities the two figures represent.

A number of other striking and, at first glance, puzzling rhetorical devices are readily discernible even in translation. Several figures of speech
surviving in the scriptural text as remnants of pre-Islamic usage are often
called oath-takings (technically known as asseverative clauses), conditional
clauses, and soothsaying. (The Qur'anic texts themselves are not pre-Islamic,
but they make use of communicative devices frequently employed by
speakers of Arabic prior to the rise of Islam.)

Used most in the earlier, more poetic suras, such devices reinforce a point
dramatically. They heighten tension by bringing the audience to a peak of
expectation, revealing at last the kernel of the message. Sura 81 is a fine example of the conditional clause technique. This chapter comprises a series
of thirteen short, explosive phrases, all but one beginning with the Arabic
words for "when . . . and when" (*idha . . . wa idha*) and all ending in the
same rhyme (in Arabic, *-at*). Each clause describes a condition (the first six
are physical; the latter six, spiritual) that shocks and seems, to the nonbe-
liever at least, quite impossible. Foretelling a rude awakening for the heedless, the sura alludes to a future day of reckoning, heralded by an unimag-
inable train of apocalyptic events:

> When the sun is folded up,
> and when the fading stars fall away,
> and when the mountains disappear,
> and when camels ten months pregnant are abandoned,
> and when free-roaming creatures are corralled,
> and when the oceans turn to tidal waves,
> and when the souls (of all people) are divided (good together, evil together),
> and when the baby girl buried alive is asked for what sin she was murdered,
> and when the Scrolls are unrolled,
> and when the heavens are revealed,
> and when the infernal conflagration blazes,
> and when the Garden becomes closer . . .
> THEN the individual will know the import of his or her deeds.[26]

The expression "when hell freezes over" is perhaps the closest parallel now in common use. Here the magnitude and seeming impossibility of the events described arrest the attention of the hearer or reader, and encourage serious reflection on human destiny and responsibility.

Soothsaying and oath-taking devices are related to each other in that both swear by, or call to witness, natural occurrences to emphasize a particular point. Like the conditional-clause device, these adjurations build in a series. The difference between the two is that in soothsaying, the speaker swears specifically by beings whose Arabic names are feminine in form in a series of rhyming images, and that the passage closes with a line of resolution that does not rhyme with the previous ones. The form is evidently a remnant of the practice of pre-Islamic seers called *kahins*. A sample of such a text is Qur'an 100:1–6, whose simile is extended and embellished:[27]

> [I swear b]y the coursing chargers panting, striking fiery sparks, and rushing forward on a dawn raid, raising billows of dust and scattering the gathered [foe]—indeed human beings are ungrateful to their Lord.

Soothsaying in this context differs from the oath-takings only in its poetic form, not in its function.

In English translation these soothsayings are difficult to distinguish from the more ordinary asseverative, since the gender of Arabic words does not ordinarily survive in English. The asseverative, which takes no account of the gender of the object by which the speaker swears, is more readily identifiable. Characteristically its speaker swears by contrasting pairs of natural phenomena, such as day and night, sun and moon, as in Sura 91:1–10:

> [I swear b]y the Sun, brilliantly shining, and the Moon as she follows him; by the Day reflecting (solar) brilliance, and the Night covering it over; by the Heavens wonderfully made, and the Earth spread abroad; by the Soul well-proportioned, and its awareness of good and evil—indeed, one who purifies it succeeds, and one who corrupts it fails.[28]

Finally, refrains appear in a number of texts. Sura 55, for example, presents a litany of divine blessings punctuated with the dramatic question "Which, then, of the blessings of your Lord will you deny?" And in Sura 77, there is the equally arresting warning "Woe on that Day to those who refuse the truth," interjected repeatedly.[29] Refrains like these focus the hearer's or reader's attention on some aspect of human response to God's deeds, in view of accountability at Judgment Day.

From a literary standpoint, most hadiths take one of several forms: pithy saying, brief dialogue, instruction, commentary on the meaning of a Qur'anic text, or apparently straightforward narrative varying in length from several lines to several pages. Proverb-like sayings such as "The truthful and trustworthy merchant is the companion of the prophets, the righteous, and the martyrs"[30] enshrine nuggets of moral wisdom. Some sayings are apparently responses to specific questions Muslims asked the Prophet, and in some instances those responses take the form of mnemonic reductions of some essential teaching to a cluster—typically, three, four, seven—of easy-to-remember elements, similar to sayings collected in rabbinical works. For example, Muhammad advises that Muslims avoid the "seven noxious things." When asked what they are, Muhammad enumerates: Setting up a partner with God (idolatry); magic; killing a person declared inviolate by God without just cause; devouring usury; consuming the property of an orphan; deserting in battle; and slandering chaste women who are believers but who act indiscreetly.

Many hadiths are cast in the form of a give-and-take between one of the Companions and the Prophet. For example, Hudhayfa approaches Muhammad with a concern for the evil he fears might overtake him: "O Messenger of God, once we were in the age of paganism and evil, then God brought this good age to us. Will evil follow upon this good?" Muhammad answers, "Yes." Hudhayfa comes back, "And will there be good after that evil?" The Prophet replies, "Yes, but there will be smoke in it." Hudhayfa asks about the nature of the "smoke," and Muhammad explains, "People will follow a way of life that is not mine and give guidance that is not mine, so you will recognize some good in them as well as some evil."[31] This is an example of a narrative created around an alleged meeting between a widely known transmitter of hadiths, Hudhayfa, and the presumed source of all hadiths, Muhammad. In this instance Hudhayfa has not only transmitted the words of Muhammad but has also provided a narrative frame within which to report them, namely, a brief conversation.

What purpose do such conventions serve? One view is that by depicting Muhammad involved in all sorts of ordinary daily actions, narrative elements "create an atmosphere of the presence of a beloved hero. . . . In the context of some of those activities small miracles are performed, as when the amount of water miraculously increases for him in the ritual washing before prayer. Indeed, all the hadith about prayers create some sense of intimacy and friendly presence, as when he prays with a child near him or avoids waking a sleeping cat after praying."[32] Sometimes more elaborate full-scale stories unfold in a hadith, such as the accounts of Muhammad's Ascension to heaven, which are punctuated by his conversations with various prophets as he makes his way upward through the heavens. In the final analysis, even if one assumes that every hadith quotes the Prophet accurately and faithfully, one may also reasonably assume that the transmitters exercised varying degrees of literary creativity in passing along the Prophet's utterance.[33]

Memory and Recitation

In the earlier consideration of scriptural themes I note that the Qur'an not only functions as a sourcebook of prayer but is itself the central prayer in the daily life of Muslims. That second dimension focuses on the notion of remembrance as a key to understanding the scripture as living prayer and as divine word now addressed back to God. The Arabic verb *Dh-a-K-a-R-a* and its various modifications, based on the root *Dh-K-R*,[34] convey a range of meanings. They include at least these four: that which reminds one of something; the act of remembering; the ongoing state of mindfulness or of spiritual presence; and the physical action of speaking that results in an audible mentioning of something.

Since human beings are by nature forgetful, the Qur'an serves as "that which reminds" them of their true origin and goal, and Muhammad's role is preeminently that of a "reminder." In Sura 87:9–15, God enjoins the Prophet (italicized words indicate translations of derivatives of the root *Dh-K-R*):

> *Remind*, therefore, if *reminding* is useful. The Godfearing will *be mindful*, while the one in direst straits will remain at a distance—that one will suffer the great Fire in which one neither lives nor dies. The one who is already purified flourishes and *calls to mind* the name of his Lord and offers prayer [all italics mine].

The phrase "offers prayer" is a translation of a word whose root came to be associated with the five daily ritual prayers known collectively as *salat*. The early Meccan text just cited suggests three meanings of the root *Dh-K-R*: the act of reminding, that of which one is to be mindful, and the state of mindfulness. The Qur'an developed these themes further during the middle Meccan period. In those later texts *qur'an* and *dhikr* are virtually synonymous, and *dhikr* is linked with the prayer of invocation (*du'a'*) and with patience (*sabr*, a virtue the Qur'an associates strongly with the prophet Joseph).

In texts from the last Meccan period, during which Muhammad experienced growing intolerance from the ruling Quraysh tribe, it becomes even more clear that mindfulness is the attitude that separates believers from unbelievers. Out of mindfulness arises the requisite interior attitude for prostration before God, and for praise, according to Qur'an 32:15. The association between dhikr of the heart and ritual prayer reaches its peak in the Medinan suras, as exemplified by Qur'an 62:9:

> You who have faith, set aside your trades and hurry to the remembrance [dhikr] of God when you are summoned to ritual prayer [salat] on Friday.

Mindfulness is therefore the soul and ritual prayer the body of a believer's grateful surrender (*islam*) to God.[35] Subsequent developments in Islamic tradition gradually came to distinguish among dhikr, salat, and du'a' as forms of prayer.

Against this backdrop, one can more readily appreciate the importance of both memorizing and reciting Qur'an, of both receiving the word and addressing it back to God. With respect to the revealed scripture these are the two sides of the coin of mindfulness, as beautifully suggested in this hadith: "There are no people assembled in one of the houses of God to recite the Book of God and study it together but that the *sakinah* (divine tranquility) descends upon them. Mercy covers them, angels draw near to them and *God remembers them* [italics mine] in the company of those who are with Him."[36] To learn the entire scripture by heart has always been a distant ideal for Muslims, and some still reach that goal. Another hadith says that anyone who has memorized a third of it possesses a third of prophecy; two-thirds of it, two-thirds of prophecy; the whole of it, the whole of prophecy, "except that no revelation is sent down" to that person.[37]

People who have memorized the Qur'an and are trained to recite it publicly have traditionally occupied a special place in Islamic societies. To them God has entrusted the ultimate treasure for safekeeping. Their impact has been so great that, as a group, these people and their religious responsibility have been the subject of much commentary and are mentioned in scores of hadiths. In more recent times, committing all the Qur'an to memory has become more and more the exclusive province of professional reciters specially trained in the arts of the two styles of recitation, measured (*tartil*) and embellished (*tajwid*). The social and religious importance of such public recitation, especially in more traditional Muslim societies, cannot be overestimated. The sound of Qur'an recitation remains one of the most entrancing, moving experiences in Muslim daily life, and it continues to sustain in Islamic spirituality an oral and aural substrate stronger perhaps than in any other global religious tradition.

As an art entirely separate from that of music performed for purposes of entertainment, Qur'an recitation creates its own unique atmosphere, even as it rests on a distinctive system of training. Though reciters are not usually professional scholars, effective vocal interpretation of the text naturally presupposes some familiarity with the tradition of tafsir. The simpler tartil style tends to be used for private occasions as well as during the five daily ritual prayers, and is ideally suited to assisting individuals to memorize the text. Tajwid, far more demanding and elaborate, serves a more public function in radio broadcasts, competition in recitation, and the communal Friday noon ritual prayer. It calls for spontaneous creativity and develops a high dramatic intensity. If one listens to a sura recited first in tartil, then in tajwid, the differences in cadence and feeling will be immediately apparent.[38]

The sheer massive energy in scholarly and practical discipline that Muslims have committed to the Qur'an and its living transmission is itself a marvel of Islamic spirituality. Muslims desire most of all to take the scripture into themselves, to receive it in a remarkably holistic manner, to be enveloped by its physical presence. God's word is not merely a book; it is an integral, sensible experience. The look of intensity on the face of an accomplished reciter and of responsive feeling on the faces of hearers epitomizes the impact of recitation. The recited Qur'an has an extraordinary power to move people to a sense of awe and longing. Kristina Nelson sums up the chief criteria for an effective performance: "The affecting recitation is that which the reciter recites with heartfelt and present enthusiasm, true concentration of the mental faculties, and readiness of the soul, not languidly or listlessly. Perhaps the hadith 'Recite the Qur'an as long as your hearts are united with it, and when you differ then arise from it' is a command to this reciting, for it calls for reciting as long as the heart is accepting and the mind alert, and the soul responsive, and if not, postponement is best."[39]

One way to appreciate the power of listening and recitation for Muslims is to liken the experience to the sacrament of the Eucharist or Communion with which many non-Muslim readers are familiar. To pronounce the Qur'an devoutly is to have the Word on one's tongue and thus to receive it most profoundly. Among the various specific qualities Muslim tradition associates with praiseworthy and meritorious recitation, the notion of *huzn* captures it best and most completely. It is a kind of bittersweet sadness, not a morose grief born of guilt, but a profound and moving intimation of one's frail, mortal humanity in awe before the transcendent God.[40] Several texts in the Qur'an allude to the emotional response its reception can elicit, even, according to one text, from non-Muslims. That text refers to the similarity between Muslims and humble, devout Christians: "when they attend to the revelation revealed to the Messenger, you will see their eyes overflow with tears as they understand the truth" (Q 5:86). A sense of awe and humility accompanied by intense feeling are the hallmarks of listening to the scripture or of reciting it (see also Q 17:107–9). Muslims have often apparently disregarded the texts' original reference to non-Muslims, choosing to interpret them as referring to a universally desirable response to the divine revelation, and as a kind of incontrovertible proof of the inherent power of God's speech.[41]

Seeing the Word

Muslim artists have dignified even marginally religious objects in virtually every medium, from the largest building to the smallest clay vessel, by associating them with divine revelation and Prophetic wisdom. Non-Muslims frequently think of Qur'an and Hadith as books first and foremost. For Muslims, however, the words of God and Muhammad are a living presence, an atmosphere as pervasive as the air they breathe. The chief ways in which Islamic tradition has embodied that living presence overlap to some degree: epigraphy, calligraphy and illumination, and the creation of a range of related objects of practical as well as ritual and symbolic significance.

Epigraphy includes the application of inscriptions to buildings, tombstones, mosque lamps, prayer carpets, and a wide variety of other objects whose content is religious or whose function is sacred. Inscriptions on religious buildings appear typically on facades; around portals (see Fig. 1); around the drums, bases, and oculi of domes; on the qibla wall (indicating the direction toward Mecca); and around the mihrab (the niche in the qibla wall). Mosques, theological colleges (madrasas), residences for members of dervish orders (khanqah or tekkes), and shrines or mausoleums are the architectural functional types that most often receive extensive epigraphic treatment. Inscriptions are frequently placed out of easy reading range, and in many cases they are so visually complex as to be legible only to the specially trained reader. Still, building planners almost always choose their texts either according to a new creative design or in accord with long-established convention.

Some structures, such as the Taj Mahal (see Fig. 24), exhibit epigraphic programs of such intricacy as to remind one of the sculptural and stained-glass iconographic arrangements of cathedrals like Chartres and Notre Dame. Qur'anic texts speaking of death, judgment, resurrection, and forgiveness are placed in dramatic and tightly coordinated sequence, beginning at the arch around the monumental entry portal and culminating in the burial vault beneath the Taj Mahal's central domed chamber. Within the tomb, for example, one finds: "Blessed is He who holds the sovereignty, for He is powerful over all things! He it was who created death and life in order to test you, to see which of you will be most upright in deeds; and He is the most powerful, the all-forgiving" (Q 67:1–3). All the texts used in and around the Taj Mahal represent thematically a textual integration that complements the visual and architectural integration of this artistic and religious masterpiece. According to one interpretation, the whole ensemble suggests an image of the Throne of God (alluded to in the Verse of the Throne), borne aloft by four angels at the far end of the heavenly plain of Judgment and Resurrection.[42]

One frequently used text is the basic creed, or *shahada* (witnessing): "There is no god but God, and Muhammad is the Messenger of God." A distinctively Shiʿi version, often used around a niche or on prayer rugs, alerts the viewer immediately that the building or object was created for a Shiʿi patron or public. That version adds a third phrase, "and ʿAli is the intimate friend of God." (See Fig. 3.) Two other inscriptions used most frequently on both buildings and objects are the Verse of the Throne (Q 2:255) and the Verse of Light (Q 24:35). The former appears often around mosque and mausoleum domes, and around the borders of mihrabs (see Fig. 2) and prayer rugs. The verse also appears on numerous everyday objects as a protection against evil. The Verse of Light occurs on enameled glass mosque lamps, on mosque and madrasa facades, and on qibla walls. Texts dealing with death and forgiveness occur regularly on tombstones and mausoleum walls, for example, in the Taj Mahal. A favorite short text, also often used on burial cloths for coffins, is: "Every soul shall taste death. We put you to the test with both good and evil as a trial, and to Us you shall return" (Q 21:35; cf. also, 3:185 and 29:57; see Fig. 11).

Some texts, however, have become conventional in certain settings merely on the strength of the occurrence of a catchword or phrase, even though the original meaning of the verse scarcely applies in its new visual setting. A prime example is the use of Qurʾan 3:37: "Every time Zakariya [father of John] went to her [Mary] in the mihrab, he found that she [already] had sustenance." Turkish mosques frequently locate the text over the niche of the mosque, even though in the Qurʾan the term *mihrab* evidently refers to a structure quite different in form and function from that of the mihrab in the qibla wall of a mosque. Hadiths occur far less often in epigraphy than do Qurʾan texts, and they are, in that respect, more telling when they do appear. A hadith such as "One who prays converses intimately with his Lord," or "One who believes in God and His Messenger and observes ritual prayer and the fast of Ramadan, God will provide entry to the

Figure 3. Fatimid votive niche (1094), mosque of Ibn Tulun, Cairo. Text of the shahada in horizontal panel just above the niche includes the distinctively Shi'i phrase "and 'Ali is the Friend of God."

Garden," emphasizes the religious function of the structures on which it appears.[43] Other popular texts include short formulas such as "Sovereignty belongs to God," "God alone lives eternally," "Praise to God," and "God is supreme," which frequently appear on the exterior drums of mosque, madrasa, and mausoleum domes in Iran and Central Asia, for example.

Calligraphic styles figure prominently in the creation of epigraphic inscriptions, and if they are understood from the perspective of style and formal qualities, one might say calligraphy encompasses epigraphy. (I use the term *calligraphy* here to refer specifically to texts written with pen or brush, on paper or similar media.) Designers have created over a dozen major styles of script, including several used almost exclusively for languages other than Arabic, that use the Arabic alphabet (such as Persian, Turkish, and Urdu). Crafting a beautiful Qur'an or a collection of favorite hadiths has been among the loftiest of devotional activities. Learning to write Qur'an has long been an essential ingredient in literacy education across the globe, especially but not only among Arabic speakers.[44]

Directly related to calligraphy in this restricted sense are the arts of illumination that create geometric and floral decoration as embellishment for the visual setting of the Qur'anic or Prophetic word. Illumination evolved along with the early decorative Arabic scripts, initially in the form of small bosses, medallions, and panels used to separate verses and suras. Eventually the panels used as sura headings developed into intricate combinations of floral and geometric background and setting for calligraphic indications of the sura's title, the number of verses, and the place of its revelation (Mecca or Medina).

In more lavish productions, these panels provide an opportunity for the illuminator to demonstrate imagination and creativity in the invention of design shapes and combinations. Along with more decorative panels within the text came the practice of making the opening sura and the beginning of the second sura an elaborate two-page spread. Artists also began to create separate decorative two-page frontispieces, typically including the text of Qur'an 56:77–80 in upper and lower panels: "This is a noble Qur'an in a hidden book; let none but the pure touch it; it is a revelation from the Lord of the Universe." The text thus came to serve as a talismanic device to warn off the unworthy. Such a use assumes that the word *pure* refers to ritual purity. But that interpretation virtually disregards the verse's original context, where *pure* apparently refers to the origins of the Qur'an, and therefore to its legitimacy and authority, not to its ritual function.[45]

Finally, one can identify a number of objects whose form and function relate directly to the calligraphic arts. Inspired at least indirectly by Qur'an and Hadith, these include brass pen boxes. Engraved and often inlaid with silver and gold, these boxes testify to the lofty calling and social prestige of those who have created Islam's sumptuous religious manuscripts. The most important examples come to us from the Middle East and south Asia. Earlier works, mostly from the twelfth and thirteenth centuries, are typically covered with geometric and floral patterns, sometimes serving as background

Figure 4. Brass pen box inlaid with silver (thirteenth century), Egypt or Syria. Testimony to the calligrapher's elevated place in society, the box is inscribed in plaited Kufic script with images of courtiers. New York: The Metropolitan Museum of Art, Gift of Joseph W. Drexel.

for a historical or proverbial inscription. In addition some have figural images, most often from the visual vocabulary of astrology (human figures or nonhuman symbols of the planets or zodiacal signs) but occasionally also from that of court life (such as musicians and hunters). (See Fig. 4.)

Another group of related objects that have received explicit artistic attention are book covers, principally in tooled and embossed leather or lacquer. From a formal point of view, these objects are related to the arts of illumination. Their designs usually consist chiefly, or only, of geometric and floral patterns, often modeled on those of central-medallion carpets (a design popularly associated with so-called Persian or Oriental rugs) and found also on front and end pages in Qur'an manuscripts.

Two other kinds of objects that bear Qur'anic epigraphy and have ritual functions are Qur'an boxes and stands. Muslim artists have produced elegant storage places for the scripture, in a wide range of shapes and sizes. Mostly of wood, the boxes are sometimes carved and lacquered, sometimes covered with engraved and inlaid sheet metal, sometimes inlaid with ivory or exotic hardwoods. Their shapes range from simple squares to tall, gable-roofed rectangular cabinets to elaborately architectural polygons with spherical or ogival domes. These boxes are of different sizes, reflecting variant traditions in Qur'an production, some including as many as thirty separate compartments for Qur'ans written in as many volumes (one for each major liturgical division of the text). Sometimes these boxes have a reading stand built in above the storage place. There are also beautifully carved portable folding stands (*kursi* or *rahl*).[46] (See Fig. 5.)

The foundational texts, their performative or oral significance, and the visual arts they have graced or inspired provide an entrée into a religious

Figure 5.   Wooden Qur'an stand (1360), Turkestan.
The name "Allah" appears four times in the upper
panel. New York: The Metropolitan Museum of Art,
Rogers Fund.

tradition of enormous breadth and richness. They express something of Islam's conviction of the divine initiative in establishing an ongoing relationship with humankind. Muslims have acknowledged and cultivated that relationship through the ritual and liturgical texts and objects that, in turn, speak of their religious devotion.

2   Devotion
Ritual and Personal Prayer

By the term *devotion* I mean all the elements of personal investment—energy, feeling, time, substance—that characterize Muslim communal and individual response to the experience of God's revelation and involvement in human affairs as described in the first chapter. I use the term *ritual* to denote a range of religious actions with which Muslims express their response in faith to what they believe are God's ways of dealing with them. These actions include those prescribed by the rubrics of Islamic communal practice and those left to the discretion of the participants or canonized by local custom, or both.

In Islam there are two large categories of religious practice, one comprising regular observances programmed by its liturgical calendar. Each major observance has its times and seasons through the lunar year. The literature of the Five Pillars and of the Friday sermon, as well as some arts and architecture, is directly related to regular religious observance.

Various kinds of additional devotion include forms of communal and individual prayer not regulated by religious law, as well as the full range of rites of passage and popular practice associated with matters of everyday life and special occasions particularly important within specific segments of the world's Muslim population. Sermons for every occasion are a variety of pulpit literature, and some aspects of architecture and the arts are associated with popular or devotional preaching. Many textual and visual sources are related to ritual and devotional activities that, while often regulated by a calendar or season, are optional in that Islamic law does not strictly require them. In a given cultural context these activities may indeed be expected of everyone as though they were juridically obligatory, but they fall in the category of custom rather than that of divinely revealed duties.

Rituals help members of social and religious communities negotiate moments of special significance. These may be times of grief or of joyous cel-

Figure 6.   (*Opposite*) Indian calendar poster with caption "Du'a'Boy" (1994), showing the Ka'ba and Muhammad's tomb; 786 is the numerical value of the Arabic letters in the phrase "in the name of God." Qur'an is open to 33:33, a reference to ritual purity. Courtesy of Carl Ernst.

ebration, of intense struggle or of liberation from spiritual or psychic en-slavement. As rites of passage, religious rituals give structure to the other-wise threatening and often chaotic experience of change. Acts of devotion mark a temporary excursion from the ordinary into the extraordinary, whether they are prescribed in religious law or are merely what people "have always done" in a particular cultural setting.

The notions of sacred time, sacred space, and the state called liminality are useful in describing the goal of these excursions. (Derived from the Latin word *limen*, "threshold," the term *liminality* suggests a dramatic change in one's condition.) When religious persons mark off and intentionally enter upon a ritual undertaking, they must commit themselves to a change of mind and heart. They signify this commitment by certain physical and behavioral changes, such as donning special garb, leaving daily tasks aside for a time, and performing specific bodily actions prescribed by the ritual in question. Such controlled change (sometimes called separation) introduces the par-ticipant into a state of liminality. In that state the individual is cut loose from the accustomed moorings of everyday life—relationships, job, status—to drift for a while in sacred time and space. The devotee thus enters into a con-dition of heightened receptivity to the powerful symbolism of the ritual. Lim-inality is a vulnerable state, but the participants' realization that others have also chosen to take the risk makes the prospect less forbidding. Supported by a mutual sense of community, devotees can give each other permission to express feelings they might otherwise keep controlled or safely hidden.

Various kinds of ritual differ in both content and emotional tone. Some provide catharsis through tears born of sympathy with the suffering of some spiritually potent figure; others offer release through ecstasy or trancelike states. Some suggest an emphasis on the need to attain and maintain a state of purity; others focus on the task of cleansing an individual or community from the curse of some ritual impurity. Whatever the specific tenor of the experience, the participant must at the end make the transition from limi-nality back to the ordinary. To this "reaggregation" the individual, ideally, brings a self slightly different from the self that had earlier willingly sub-mitted to the potential danger and power of the ritual.[1]

ON THE LITURGICAL CALENDAR

About the Five Pillars

The Islamic tradition has specific ways of communicating to believers the appropriate ways to express their faith by means of ritual actions. The most familiar summary characterization of Islamic religious belief and practice is that they rest upon the Five Pillars. The five are: profession of faith (sha-hada), "I confess that there is no god but God, and Muhammad is the Mes-senger of God"; pilgrimage (*hajj*) to Mecca during the prescribed days of the twelfth lunar month, given sufficient health and means; ritual prayer (salat) five times daily toward Mecca; almsgiving (zakat); and fasting (*sawm*) between sunrise and sunset during the ninth lunar month, Ramadan. One cannot reduce the spirit and life of a complex global community to a clus-ter of religious practices. Still the metaphor of the Five Pillars is more than a mnemonic convenience, so long as one remembers that it is merely a sum-mary. Through these rituals the tradition has communicated to its adher-ents the importance not only of basic practical observance but also of the spirit that must breathe life into that practice.

Some casual observers dismiss Islam's ritual and devotional life as dry and mechanical, hardly worthy of the name "religion" because it seems lit-tle more than a collection of external actions performed robotically. In re-ality, Muslims are no more or less likely than anyone else to participate sin-cerely and vitally in the religious life of their tradition. One of the most important concerns governing the performance of the basic Islamic rituals is the intention of the worshiper. Islamic sources accord great importance to individual attentiveness and heartfelt presence in religious observances generally.

Written sources describe intention on at least two levels. First and min-imally, one must actually pronounce one's intent to perform each specific ritual action, including ablution, prostration, and the oral profession of faith. But prior to the enunciation of intention one must cultivate a more basic interior attitude of receptivity or "presence of the heart." Once classic text describes the attitude more fully:

> The "intention" involves place and time and method and ideal. We ask Thee for the purity of those places, the observance of those times, for faultlessness in that method, and for full realization of that ideal. We ask Thee for due fulfillment of the obligation and for right purpose, and for a desire for the Countenance of God Most High. Now the place of "inten-tion" is the heart; its time is at the beginning of the actions of the prayer-rite, its method is a binding control of the heart and of the members. It is built up of four elements, purpose, determination, desire, and act of will, all of these united in one idea. And the "intention" has two aspects, first the direction of the heart in the rite with full awareness, and secondly single-heartedness towards God out of longing for the reward that He has to give and desire for His Countenance.[2]

One of the most influential works dealing with these matters is *Revivi-fication of the Sciences of the Faith (Ihya' 'ulum ad-din)*, by Abu Hamid al-Ghazali (1058–1111). A four-volume work organized into forty books, *Revivification* is a compendium of Islamic spirituality ranging from the most elementary to the most advanced mystical pedagogy. Even when he is proceeding through fairly detailed descriptions of how to perform a ritual action such as the daily prayer, Ghazali never fails to attend to the requisite underlying attitudes. He cites the Qur'anic prohibition against approaching the ritual prayer while intoxicated (Q 4:43): "O you who believe, do not approach the ritual prayer while you are intoxicated; [wait] until you can comprehend what you are saying." Ghazali interprets the text by observing, "Some say that 'intoxicated' means inebriated by many anxieties, while others say it means drunk on the love of this world. According to Wahb [a famous traditionist], the meaning is obviously a caution against worldly attachment, since the words 'until you know what you are saying' explain the underlying reason. Many are those who pray without having drunk wine, yet do not know what they are saying in their Prayers!"[3]

Among the most widely disseminated and least consulted textual sources for the study of Islamic spirituality are the unpretentious manuals of religious education one finds on the shelves of mosque bookstores the world over. At the most basic level, they instruct the believer in the fundamentals of ordinary ritual. They offer directions on how to perform the ablution before prayer, where to place the hands during salat, what invocations to say while circumambulating the Ka'ba (a roughly cube-shaped structure traditionally said to have been built by Abraham) during pilgrimage to Mecca, and how to tell when sunset occurs during Ramadan. These concerns come under the heading of basic catechesis, the sort of instruction given to children or to new converts or to Muslims who wish to return to active observance after years on the periphery of the community.

In their function of religious education, these sources stand on a continuum with a larger body of literature. At one end, the texts are written for as diverse a public as possible. Close to the midpoint of the continuum are works whose range narrows to include, for example, individuals training to become professional Qur'an reciters or to fulfill other functions whose responsibilities require specific instruction. At the other end are works addressed to a still more selective constituency, members of religious fraternities and mystical adepts.

Even the most rudimentary religious education invariably addresses issues far deeper than the superficial rubrics of ritual performance. There are, of course, manuals dedicated almost exclusively to teaching believers the raw structure of ritual practice, but they presume that one already brings at least the inchoate stirrings of a genuine desire to seek God. Muslims call the whole complex of ritual and devotional acts deeds of worshipfulness (*'ibadat*, which could also be translated as "signs of servanthood"). All acts that describe or acknowledge the human posture of a servant before a divine master are thus distinguished, in Islamic religious law, from those that regulate relationships between and among human beings (*mu'amalat*).

The manuals ground every required or recommended practice in the Sunna, Muhammad's example. Even when an individual can find no profound personal significance in, say, kissing the Black Stone (a bowling-ball-sized object, possibly of meteoric origin, set in a silver collar in a corner of the Ka'ba) or placing the hands in a particular position during salat, the action nevertheless rests on solid authority and precedent. It is not merely that an unnamed someone at some unknown date began a practice that stuck. Each practice draws its sacralizing power from the custom of the Prophet himself. For example, tradition ascribes to Muhammad dozens of the intermittent prayers worshipers might say while performing the various movements of the salat (standing, inclining, sitting on the heels, prostration, etc.). One manual observes that when Muhammad performed the prostration he used to say, "Before Thee I prostrate myself, in Thee I believe, to Thee I am surrendered. My face is prostrate before Him who created it and moulded it and pierced for it (the openings of) hearing and sight. Blessed be God the Best of Creators."[4]

William Chittick has translated three thirteenth-century Persian instructional texts that likewise evidence the centrality of right intention.[5] Their probable author, a certain Nasir ad-Din, lived in the central Anatolian city of Konya and was a fellow townsman and contemporary of the original "whirling" dervish, Jalal ad-Din Rumi (d. 1273). All three short and charming works lay out the fundamentals of Islamic faith and practice from slightly different angles and with varying levels of subtlety and sophistication. One is a gem dedicated to conveying "command of a few preliminaries of the intellectual and practical pillars of Islam, the knowing of which is mandatory for the seeker."[6] Nasir ad-Din wrote *The Easy Roads of Sayf ad-Din* (*Manahij-i sayfi*) for a Turkish convert who had asked for guidance through the fundamentals. Leading his supplicant down five "roads," Nasir ad-Din begins with the rudiments of faith and then moves on to the particulars of practice (purification, ritual prayer, fasting, and the personal prayer of supplication). The work is remarkably similar in content to Ghazali's *Beginning of Guidance* (*Bidayat al-hidaya*), an Arabic introduction to the faith written some two centuries earlier.[7] Nasir ad-Din explains the spiritual meaning of the ablution prior to ritual prayer:

When the person finishes the ablution and aims to say the ritual prayer, he should turn away from all things to the extent possible. He should make his heart present and be aware of the tremendousness and majesty of God. He should understand that he will be talking intimately with the Sultan of sultans. Since he has purified the parts of himself where creatures look with outward water, he should also purify the place where God looks—which is called the "heart"—with the water of turning toward God, repenting, and asking forgiveness. If he does not do this, he is like someone who wants to bring the sultan into his home. He cleans the outside of the house, but he leaves the inside of the house—the place where the sultan will sit—full of filth. We seek refuge in God from that! "God looks not at your forms, nor at your works, but He looks at your hearts."[8]

While the instructional manuals prepare worshipers to participate more fully in the community's canonical rituals, other materials record some of the kinds of religious communication that occur within those rituals themselves. One such genre preserves the preaching associated with the Friday salat.

From the Pulpit

Literature of the pulpit (*adab al-minbar*) refers specifically to collections of sermons delivered in a mosque by famous preachers (*khutaba*'; sg., *khatib*). I divide the literature into two categories, liturgical preaching and popular preaching. In the case of the sermon the principal difference between the two is functional rather than formal. The shape and content of a sermon preached during the Friday midday congregational prayer may be virtually identical to that of a sermon delivered on the occasion of a holy person's birthday or in commemoration of some signal historical event. The ritual context of the Friday sermon sets it apart by virtue of its obligatory status in religious law.

The literature of the pulpit also functions as a bridge between Qur'an and Hadith, and institutional texts (see chapter 5). The Friday sermon always takes place in a mosque. Through its mandatory mention of the name of the legitimate political authority, the sermon has historically often been an expression of formal institutional allegiance. Throughout Islamic history, however, liturgical oratory has also been a prime vehicle for disseminating revolutionary sentiments. In either case, the Friday sermon has been potent both as a symbol and as a form of discourse.

Liturgical oratory is called *khutba* in Arabic. In its broadest meaning, however, khutba refers to any sort of public address. Typically, Islamic tradition has not distinguished neatly between sacred and secular activities in general; nor does Arabic preserve a distinction parallel to that between generic speech and religious sermon. Nevertheless, the oratory that has come to be associated most of all with the Friday midday congregational prayer has taken on a number of distinctive formal features.

After the call to prayer, timed to mark the sun's passing its zenith, the khatib rises from his place on the steps of the pulpit (*minbar*) and faces the assembled worshipers. The classic form includes four distinct segments: an introduction; the body of the address, divided into two separate sections; and a conclusion. An initial thanksgiving (the anaphoric exordium) opens with praise and thanks to God, followed by a first-person profession of faith and recollection of Muhammad's prophetic mission, and a prayer for blessings upon Muhammad and for the well-being of the congregation. A brief moral exhortation (*maw'iza*), sometimes in the form of a litany, closes the exordium.

The main section of the khutba typically develops a distinctive central theme often related to a religious observance or some important event, although some addresses merely continue in a general vein of moral exhortation. Islamic liturgical oratory differs from the classic Christian homily, in that the mosque preacher does not set out principally to elucidate a passage of scripture, though the Qur'an does play an important role. The preacher will quote the Qur'an often, as proof text or as rhetorical device, and sometimes uses a text as his theme. Only on rare occasions does the speaker set about an exegetical elaboration of a text, which typically occurs in gatherings dedicated to the study and discussion of a particular text.

In the body of the address, the mosque preacher seeks to persuade his listeners of the need to change, to point to which areas of life might need changing, and to instruct them in distinguishing between desirable and reprehensible options. With an invocation to God, the first movement closes, and the preacher sits down for a minute or two. The second part returns to the main theme but more briefly, as if to reinforce the message. Finally, the address concludes with a reference to God's glory, sometimes in litany form. After the preacher comes down from the pulpit steps, the congregation performs the regular liturgical prayer (salat), engaging in only two cycles of prostration rather than the more usual four. For major observances, such as the breaking of the Ramadan fast ('Id al-fitr) and the Feast of Sacrifice during Hajj season ('Id al-adha), the ritual prayer comes before, rather than after, the address.[9]

Pilgrimage is a good example of a theme of great importance to preachers on Fridays that fall during the formal pilgrimage season (days 8–13 of Dhu'l-hijja, the twelfth lunar month). Symbolically taking on the role of Muhammad, who delivered the inaugural pilgrimage sermon in 632, the preacher virtually reenacts the journey for his congregation. As he leads his listeners through the various ritual locations in and around Mecca, the preacher describes the inner experience of the pilgrim. Texts of sermons clearly reveal a sense of deep insight into the spiritual significance of pilgrimage, not only for those actively participating in it but for those sharing in its benefits from afar as well.

The major themes of the sermon are duty, community, several important matters of economic justice, and the transformation following a feeling of liminality that the pilgrim experiences. The preacher begins with Qur'anic reminders that the pilgrimage is a divinely ordained duty for all able-bodied adults who have the funds and a safe means of transportation (Q 3:97). God never burdens people with more than they can carry (Q 2:286); and if times are hard now, God will surely provide the appropriate circumstances for pilgrimage at some later time.

Muslims who do make the pilgrimage have the responsibility of bringing back blessings and charity for their community. One of the great benefits the preacher describes is the feeling of coming together in harmony and equality with other Muslims from all over the world. In a sermon originally preached in Arabic, pilgrims are exhorted to become aware of the expanse of Islam and to feel supported in their faith, "saying [to God] with one voice that softens hearts and seeking the favor of the knower of the hidden: Here I am, at your service; all felicity and blessing are in your hands." The opportunity to visit the sacred sites associated with Muhammad helps believers become more grounded in their faith. And the benefits of learning the customs of other people while traveling also expand the pilgrim's sense of wider community.

Issues of economic justice enter into the experience as well. When pilgrims go to the holy land, whatever money they spend there improves the lot of the poor of the land: "he who spends on the Pilgrimage a dirham, it is as if he has spent a thousand dirhams." On the other hand, a pilgrimage accomplished with ill-gotten gains is worthless. To any person who lavishly spends money made from theft of plunder, God says, "You are not here. You are not at my service. Yours is not felicity and your Pilgrimage is thrown back on yourself."

This typical sermon closes with the theme of personal transformation. Of those who have undertaken the struggle of pilgrimage, God says to his angels:

> "you are seeing [none] except my worshippers. They left the comfort of their homes and they came to me whether riding or on foot. They filled the land with, 'There is no god but God,' and 'God is great.' . . . Bear witness I

shall smooth the way for them with a hospitable reception [on Judgment Day]; I shall entrench their successors [on earth] and I shall place them in paradise." Oh ye who have neglected the Pilgrimage and carry a heavy burden of sins, hurry to the Pilgrimage of the sacred house of God. . . . There is a people on whose hearts is written faith and on whose works [is written] mercy and [God's] favor. While they were paying their last respects by circumambulations [of the Ka'ba] and resolving on a return, they were impelled by yearning [to visit Medina] [as seen] by the rapidity of their walking to the [home of the] chosen Prophet. There [in Medina on Judgment Day] they will be encompassed by the light (grace) of Muhammad and they will be included in the prophetic blessing. The Messenger of God said: "He who makes the Pilgrimage and does not speak obscene speech and does not commit obscene acts, his sins are taken away and he emerges as he did on the day his mother gave him birth." And he, may God's prayers and salutations be upon him, said: "The Pilgrimage of good faith, there can be no reward for it but paradise."[10]

Predictably Muslim preachers find the ultimate model in the sermons of Muhammad. Next in importance are those of the Prophet's immediate successors, the four Rightly Guided Caliphs. A sermon from the first caliph, Muhammad's aged father-in-law, Abu Bakr, demonstrates several other prominent themes that reveal important emotional dimensions of Islamic spirituality. This selection emphasizes the need to live this life with an eye on the next:

I enjoin on you the fear of God in His unity, and that you praise Him as He deserves, and that you mix desire with fear, and importuning with requesting, for God praised Zachariah and his family, when He said . . . "They used to vie in good deeds and call upon Us, out of longing and fear." Then know that God has bound your souls with His truth, and therefore has taken your oaths, and has purchased from you what is small and transient for what is large and eternal. This is the Book of God, given to you, whose wonders do not pass away and whose light is not extinguished: so believe it, and accept the advice it gives, and draw enlightenment from it against the day of darkness. Then know that your comings and goings in the morning and evening are in a fixed term, knowledge of which has been hidden from you, and if you are able to do something that may not be accomplished unless you are doing it for God, then do it, for you will certainly not be able to do it except for God. Strive in gentleness, and [beware of being] a people who fixed their terms for others and forgot their own souls: and how many of you will be like them. So make haste and be saved. Verily, behind you is a questioner whose course is swift, so make haste.[11]

Sermons and pilgrimage, along with all the other central ritual deeds that help Muslims organize and interpret their religious lives, do not occur in a vacuum. They presuppose a world of spaces in which the actions take place and a host of objects that facilitate their performance. Architecture and the arts provide that physical context.

Art and Architecture

Two broad distinctions are useful in a discussion of the visual expressions of required religious rituals. First, one can distinguish between the more formal, elite, or "official" arts associated directly with the performance of ordinary observances, and the more popular arts through which people associate themselves, publicly or privately, with the performance of those actions. A good deal of the more popular art might also be called folk art; it often functions in a magical-protective fashion. Second, a distinction between religious and sacred can help clarify further the nature of the material in this and in subsequent chapters. Religious art is so identified by its content or subject matter, whereas sacred art is identified by its function in the context of worship. In other words, an image of an angel (in an illustrated manuscript, for example) is religious, but not sacred. A tile mosaic created to adorn the niche of a mosque, on the other hand, belongs to the sacred arts because of its immediate connection with liturgical worship.[12]

Mosque architecture is the primary sacred art in that its chief function is to create a space for prayer. There have been important examples of mosque architecture funded by local patronage or even grass-roots financing. But historically the finest works have been built, out of economic necessity, by royal or government commission. Various distinctive architectural styles developed across the Islamic world, so one can make only a few useful generalizations about formal features. The typical mosque has a minaret, a cylindrical or polygonal tower from which the call to prayer emanates. Interior space is generally left as open and unobstructed as possible to accommodate uninterrupted rows of worshipers lined up elbow to elbow. Many mosques, especially those known as Friday or congregational mosques, have some sort of minbar from which the preacher addresses the congregation; the minbar is usually located to the right of the mihrab. (See Fig. 7.) Ascending its steps with back to the congregation, the preacher then turns to face the assembled worshipers either on a step or on the upper level, which is often covered by a small cupola.

Another of the mosque's principal functions is to communicate fundamental spiritual values in a unique way. Anyone who has ever taken a careful look at a Gothic church has likely been impressed by the various ways in which the building communicates, telling stories in stained glass and sculpture. The more elaborate Gothic creations, such as those of Chartres and Notre Dame, exhibit extraordinarily sophisticated coordination among

Figure 7. Mihrab and minbar of the Sultan Hasan madrasa (1356–1363) in Cairo. A text about the proper direction for prayer (Q 2:144) is inscribed on the wall above.

their rose windows, lancet windows, and portal sculptures. Seen as a whole, the physical arrangement and decorative program of the cathedral presents a coherent theological interpretation of history and human life. It offers the viewer a cross section of the history of Christian spirituality. Visitors to a cathedral know immediately that the building is saying something, even if the precise content of the message is not immediately apparent.

A Mosque's visual message is more subtle and complex precisely because mosque architecture does not communicate in the narrative style of stained glass or in the more blatantly symbolic mode of programmatic sculpture.

Still, the mosque does speak grammatically and in a distinctive idiom, especially through its Qur'anic inscriptions. But how does one learn this language without pictures? By learning the vocabulary and syntax of architectural space. Although the concept of architectural semiotics—the way a building communicates nonverbally and by its very spatial quality—is too vast to delve into in any detail here, the field can provide some important insights. The external features of orientation and siting, and the internal features of spatial composition and ornamentation—all contribute to the mosque's message.

Orientation is the most distinctive feature of the mosque. All mosques face Mecca, a sacred center of the universe, whereas the cathedral ideally looks toward the rising sun. In the traditional Christian church, all worshipers everywhere face in the same direction, rather than toward a fixed geographical point. Unlike the cathedral, the mosque, with its mihrab and qibla wall, focuses the congregation's visual attention, not on a sacred action occurring within the structure, but on a spiritual center beyond the qibla wall. Perhaps more than any other Islamic institution the mosque embodies the tradition's emphasis on forming community. For sheer scope, of course, no ritual practice matches the annual pilgrimage to Mecca as a celebration of shared humanity; but on a more modest scale, the mosque also fosters community.

Siting is an important external consideration as well. Naturally the practical matter of what sort of property is available at a given time has often limited a builder's options. There are many examples of mosques whose facades are aligned with an existing street or other public space, but whose courtyard and prayer hall is built at an angle, rotated from the axis slightly, in order to be oriented to Mecca (such as the Mosque of al-Aqmar in Cairo or the Royal Mosque in Isfahan). The Sulaymaniye Mosque in Istanbul stands, as do several other important imperial foundations there, on one of the seven hills of that Rome of the East. In this case the choice of site not only makes the building complex stand out on the city's skyline but clearly makes a statement of power as well.

A number of Islam's greatest mosques have been located not merely out of concern for accessibility, visibility or availability of real estate. Some, such as the great mosques of Cordova and Damascus, are located on the sites of earlier structures belonging to other religious traditions. Both sites were formerly occupied by Christian churches and Roman temples. The Dome of the Rock in Jerusalem, located over what was once Solomon's Temple, is a special case since it is not technically a mosque. In some instances the siting clearly makes a statement about the supersession of Islam over the earlier religious and political dispensations. Such a statement seems to override any concern that an observer might take it as a validation of the earlier tradition's identification of a particular site as holy.

Among the mosque's internal features, spatial organization and the use of calligraphic inscriptions are particularly significant. Good mosque architecture sets a mood—as does all successful architecture—and creates a space conducive to the noncompetitive, coordinated effort of one people surrendering in unison to the one God in whom they believe. Most important in this context are the interrelationships among the various functional spaces within the larger compositional design of the mosque. Since Islamicate architecture has developed in many regions over many centuries, of course, one needs to exercise caution in making generalizations. Every cultural setting puts its own distinctive stamp on religious expression, no matter how powerful the sense of belonging to a global community of belief and practice.

Larger mosques normally include facilities and space for ritual purification; a vestibule area or perhaps a courtyard that can serve as overflow prayer space if the crowd is very large; and the prayer hall proper, with the niche and pulpit its only truly essential visual and functional elements. Roger Joseph mentions several key features to consider when assessing the semiotics of a mosque. They include "codes establishing relationships based on spatial designs, geometric patterning, rhythmic sequences, oppositions between high and low, the structuring of polygons, and other systematically assembled elements." Interpretation of nonverbal codes in an architectural space is tricky, but it is an important and much-neglected source of cross-cultural understanding. Joseph theorizes, for example, that a mosque's "repetitive fragmentation" has the effect of "deemphasizing any single item which might draw attention to its uniqueness. Space within the mosque is unpunctuated; it is like the *dhikr* chants of occult recollection—repeated over and over in an effort to shut out the external world of distractions and tunnel into the singular world of unity with God."[13]

Most important, however, is the role of inscriptions as part of the decorative and interpretative program. Among the connections between Qur'anic calligraphy and architecture, I underscore two features of architectural calligraphy: the content of the text and its placement within the architectural space in relation to specific formal (such as facade, courtyard, and dome) and functional features (such as the mihrab and minbar). But beyond that, calligraphy constitutes the single most significant iconic communicator in the visual repertoire of the mosque designer. Even if an inscription is not legible, its mere presence delivers a powerful message.[14]

A madrasa is a second major functional type of religious architecture. The madrasa has traditionally provided advanced instruction in the religious sciences of theology and jurisprudence. Major foundations across the Islamic world have often combined mosque and madrasa in architectural complexes along with other educational and social functions, such as medical facilities, lower-level schools (of Qur'an and Hadith), public kitchens, and social service agencies.[15]

Smaller, decorative objects include a host of items associated with regular liturgical observances. Prayer carpets reproduce, in two dimensions and on a small scale, the sense of the sacred space of the mosque as well as its cosmic orientation toward Mecca. Carpets and mosques alike are places of prostration (*masjid*), and the niche shape that is the prayer carpet's central design element recalls the mihrab in the wall facing Mecca of every mosque.[16] (See Fig. 8.) Among the finest products of the glazer's art, graceful enameled mosque lamps are often inscribed with the Verse of Light. (See Fig. 9.) Brass candlesticks, engraved and sometimes inlaid, flank the niches of major mosques across the Islamic world. To these one can also add articles such as illuminated manuscripts, book covers, Qur'an stands, and pen boxes in connection with the Qur'an.

Religious in content but no longer sacred in function, the illustrated handbook for pilgrims is an example of elite art. Manuscripts like the *Openings of the Two Sanctuaries*, that is, Mecca and Medina (*Futuh al-haramayn*) and *Guidebook to Blessings* (*Dala'il al-khayrat*) often include exquisite pictures of the holy places. Texts of this sort enjoyed continued popularity until well into the nineteenth century. Their images offer the equivalent of aerial views of the sacred sites' topography and internal features, often showing the interrelationships of a site's secondary features, such as the place near the Ka'ba from which the Prophet is said to have been taken on his Night Journey. Many depict a combination of ground plan and elevation of each place—that is, one sees the site as though simultaneously from above and from ground level. Particular features within each site appear in stylized drawings, often with an identifying caption. A picture of the sanctuary of the Ka'ba in Mecca, for example, usually shows the Station of Abraham and the Well of Zamzam in addition to the black cubic-shaped Ka'ba. Images of Medina typically indicate the tomb of Muhammad's daughter Fatima as well as that of the Prophet.

Sacred sites depicted include, first of all, those associated with the greater and lesser pilgrimages (hajj and *'umra*, respectively). In addition to the sanctuary of the Ka'ba in Mecca, artists often depict the various ritual stations in the valley of 'Arafat outside Mecca, which are all associated with either Abraham or Muhammad. There is the Mount of Mercy, where Muhammad

Figure 8. An early seventeenth-century Mughal prayer rug in which the original imagery of the lamp within the niche has given way to a stylized floral design, India. New York: The Metropolitan Museum of Art, Bequest of Joseph V. McMullan.

Figure 9.   An enameled glass mosque lamp of the
kind that appears in early prayer rugs and in decorative niches (c. 1350), Syria. The upper section
bears words from the Verse of Light: "like a niche in
which there is a lamp." The goblet shape within the
three circular blazons indicates that the donor held
the rank of cupbearer to the Mamluk sultan. New
York: The Metropolitan Museum of Art, Edward C.
Moore Collection, Bequest of Edward C. Moore.

delivered his farewell sermon in 632, and the three Satanic pillars at which
pilgrims toss stones to commemorate Abraham's rejection of the Devil's suggestion that he avoid God's command to sacrifice his son. A beautiful sixteenth-century Turkish scroll shows fifteen topographical scenes of the holy
places, including a number of sites in Jerusalem but without extended text,
like an ancient filmstrip travelogue of the pilgrimage route. Production of
such scrolls began at least as early as the thirteenth century.[17]

Several variations on this theme occur in south Asian pilgrimage accounts
produced as recently as the 1970s. With regard to their literary qualities,
Barbara D. Metcalf observes that "[t]he *hajj* accounts turn out not to be an
isolated genre, a continuation of a static medieval form, but rather a genre
that develops in ways broadly similar to the modern novel and autobiogra-

phy ... [and] biographies of the Prophet Muhammad. . . . The accounts should be read as part of an enduring yet shifting constellation of three poles: changes in society generally, changes in concepts of individuality, and changes in the interpretation of central religious symbols."[18] Although the literature is worthy of attention on its own merits, a number of these works also include visual illustrations. Thanks to changes in book production, the nineteenth- and twentieth-century images no longer belong to the category of elite arts, but they do retain the medieval works' use of stylized plans and elevations of the sacred sites.[19]

Wall tiles showing the plan of the Ka'ba sanctuary depict the same central subject but serve a different function, in a different medium and on a larger scale. These may have provided a meditative focus or visual recollection of the goal of pilgrimage and the orientation of prayer.[20] Popular art of pilgrimage includes both two- and three-dimensional souvenirs of the journey to Mecca. Small models of the Ka'ba reportedly sold as mementos to departing pilgrims by street vendors in Mecca are mentioned in travelers' memoirs of the late seventeenth century.[21] Islam, like virtually every major religious tradition, has also made ritual use of miniaturized architecture. (See Fig. 13.)

On the walls of ordinary houses all over Egypt, one can still see colorful two-dimensional mementos of the sacred journey to Mecca. A lively tradition of domestic mural painting has preserved a formulaic combination of inscriptions and images of the Ka'ba and of the Prophet's mosque. Images usually show the various modes of travel to the holy places, typically including planes, trains, ships, camels, and often depict the pilgrim on a prayer carpet. These murals serve a protective purpose in addition to certifying publicly and proudly that the house's inhabitants are due the special status and prestige accorded to those who have accomplished the hajj and received the honorific title of *hajji*. It is especially significant that family and friends of the pilgrims execute the paintings while the travelers are away, so that the dwelling undergoes its ritual transformation even as its inhabitants do. Paintings often include the text of Qur'an 3:97: "God enjoins upon people a hajj to the House [i.e., Ka'ba], if they are able to do it."[22]

Finally, sacred pilgrimage sites are a frequent theme in calendar art. The picture entitled *Du'a' Boy* (Fig. 6) shows both the Ka'ba in Mecca and the green dome of Muhammad's tomb in Medina. The Qur'an on the kursi is open to Sura 33:33, which reads: "God desires to remove from you defilement, People of the House [i.e., the family of Muhammad], and to make you entirely pure." This text was originally addressed to the Prophet's wives, enjoining them to be faithful not only to their larger religious obligations but also to their more quiet and hidden prayer and recollection of God. In Islam sincerity and pure intention must always have priority over ostentation.

DEVOTION BEYOND DUTY

Prayer

I discussed earlier Qur'an's unfolding teaching on prayer and on the relationships among the various forms of prayer. Now I turn to postscriptural developments in the many popular forms not integrally connected with liturgical prayer. Just as the term *khutba* has come to mean, in ordinary parlance, religious and mostly liturgical oratory, so a number of Arabic terms originally of broader meaning have come to signify specific types of prayer. The word *du'a'* is a good example. Originally from a root that means "to call or invite," the term now usually refers either to extraliturgical prayer in general, sometimes also called free prayer, or to the prayer of supplication or petition. As a component in Islamic devotional literature, supplicatory prayer comes to us principally in the form of collections attributed to famous persons. A prime example is *The Complete Book of the One Who Constantly Prostrates Himself in Prayer (As-Sahifat al-kamilat as-sajjadiyya)*, attributed to the Shi'i imam Zayn al-'Abidin (c. 658–713).[23] (See Fig. 10.) In addition to integral collections, anthologies have been compiled to provide Muslims with a handy source of texts to rely on when words do not come easily. Abu Hamid al-Ghazali, the eleventh-century theologian, offers a representative sample of such a source in book 9 of his *Revivification of the Sciences of the Faith*. In a chapter entitled "Prayers Transmitted for Every Occasion of Human Life," Ghazali offers this advice, quoting a prayer that was a favorite of Muhammad's:

> So when you go out to the mosque, say: "O God, make a light in my heart and a light in my tongue. Make a light in my ear; and make a light in my eye; make a light in back of me and a light in front of me; make a light above me. O God give me light." . . . If you go out of the house for a need, say: "In the name of God, My Lord, I take refuge with You that I should not wrong nor be wronged, or that I should not be foolish nor be fooled. . . ." [On looking in the mirror, say:] "Praise be to God, Who has given moderation and uprightness to my person and has given nobility and beauty to the form of my face, and to Him Who has made me one of the Muslims."[24]

Lest his reader wonder what good supplication could possibly do if God already has the individual's destiny set, Ghazali adds the assurance that "revocation of an affliction by supplication is itself a part of Preordination. Sup-

Figure 10. A painting depicting the fourth Shiʻi imam, Zayn al-ʻAbidin, son of the third imam, Husayn, on pilgrimage at the Kaʻba, from *Silsilat adh-dhahab*, by Jami, folio 66a (1549–1550), Iran. Washington, D.C.: Courtesy of the Sackler Gallery, Smithsonian Institution.

plication is a cause for the revocation of the affliction and the procurement of mercy, just as a shield is a cause for the rejection of an arrow and water is a cause for the growth of a plant."[25]

Associated with duʻaʼ is the term *dhikr*, whose root denotes "remembrance and mindfulness." The term also refers to a category of prayer not always neatly distinct from duʻaʼ in form or content. One might characterize dhikr (recollection) as simple praise and acknowledgement of God's sovereignty without specific request for a grant from the divine largesse. In *Revivification of the Sciences of the Faith*, Ghazali cites many beautiful hadiths that recommend dhikr as a constant practice, an ongoing way of being before God. In one hadith, when a Companion of Muhammad's asks him what act is most meritorious, Muhammad replies that it is to "die while your tongue is moistened" with the remembrance of God. In another, Muhammad says, "God spreads His shade upon seven people on the Day when there is no shade but His [i.e., Resurrection Day]. Among them is a man [i.e., any person] who [remembered] God privately and whose eyes overflowed [with tears]."[26] Dhikr, however, eventually became associated with both individual and communal activities characteristic of mystical fraternities called Sufi orders.

A spiritual and devotional movement known generically as Sufism traces its origins to Islam's earliest generations. The term *Sufism* has come to refer to the Islamic mystical tradition, but some further background is useful. As early as the time of Muhammad, certain individuals had developed reputations for exceptional and distinctive piety. Over the next century or so, informal circles began to form around men and women known for their sanctity. The term *Sufi* came to be applied to some of those individuals, perhaps in connection with their wearing rough garments of wool (*suf* in Arabic). Initially the circles used the humble dwellings of their spiritual leaders as meeting places, but some groups soon grew to need larger facilities. With increasing size came more formal and permanent structures. In time the once informal and temporary circles began to outlive the holy persons around whom their members had originally gathered, and it became more common for the founding figure to appoint a successor to the leadership. By the twelfth century, a network of organizations dedicated to the pursuit of personal and communal piety was spreading across the Middle East. Each order, called literally "path" (from the Arabic *tariqa*), developed its distinctive forms of ritual and devotional practices. Members of the Sufi orders receive a specific word or phrase expressly chosen by the *shaykh*, the spiritual guide and leader of the order, for that person to repeat. Used in that way, dhikr fosters a quality of presence of the heart. As in the prayer called the rosary, the repetitious words or phrases provide a controlled distraction.

As a communal practice, dhikr has also been linked to group prayer services that involve chanting a dhikr along with some form of ritual movement or dance. Repeated words or phrases include, for example, "ya Allah" (o God); "Allahu akbar" (God is supreme); "Allah" (which drifts away till only its last soft *h* fades out), followed by "hu" (he [i.e., God]). The creedal phrase "La ilaha illa Allah" (There is no god but God) and invocations of God by any of his ninety-nine names—as in "ya Rahman" (o Merciful One) or "ya Sabur" (o Patient One)—are also commonly used.[27] These ceremonies have also been known by the general term *audition* (*sama*ʿ). The sound of a large group chanting in unison can be quite moving.

The plural form of *dhikr, adhkar,* refers to supplication and thus is virtually synonymous with the plural of *du ʿa*ʾ, as in the work of Ghazali mentioned above. When a number of these adhkar are strung together, the resulting form is called a litany (*wird,* also *hizb*). Here, as always, Islamic traditional sources hasten to explain that the physical action of pronouncing a dhikr or any other form of vocal prayer has a metaphysical counterpart that corresponds to nearly every human faculty. In the following text, to make clear the original connotation of recollection and remembrance I have reinserted the word *dhikr* where the translator had chosen *worship* as its equivalent: "The [dhikr] of the eyes is weeping; the [dhikr] of the ears is listening; the [dhikr] of the tongue is praise and laud; the [dhikr] of the hands is distribution and giving; the [dhikr] of the body is effort and accomplishment; the [dhikr] of the heart is fear and hope, and the [dhikr] of the spirit is surrender and satisfaction in God."[28]

Another variation on the theme of personal prayer occurs in the form of *munajat,* sometimes translated "intimate conversations," "whispered prayers," or "prayer within the heart." Although munajat are often difficult to distinguish from duʿaʾ in written texts, Islamic tradition has steadfastly maintained a distinction in the titles of important works. A number of famous and beloved collections of prayers are titled *Munajat,* among them, the final section of Zayn al-ʿAbidin's *Complete Book.* These lovely Arabic prayers, all in prose, represent one of the earliest of these collections. One prayer asks:

> O God, carry us in the ships of Thy deliverance, give us to enjoy the pleasure of whispered prayer to Thee, make us drink at the pools of Thy love, let us taste the sweetness of Thy affection and nearness, allow us to struggle in Thee, preoccupy us with obeying Thee, and purify our intentions in devoting works to Thee, for we exist through Thee and belong to Thee, and we have no one to mediate with Thee but Thee![29]

The short Persian prayerbook of ʿAbdallah Ansari of Herat (d. 1089), called *Intimate Conversations* (*Munajat*), is among the most celebrated and widely disseminated collections of munajat. Ansari's disciples compiled his prayers, a mix of poetry and prose, from other works of his, producing a book that has been popular and influential over the centuries. His *Intimate Conversations* may have provided a model for a type of wisdom literature made famous by the Persian author Saʿdi of Shiraz (d. 1292) in *Rose Garden* (*Gulistan*). In addition, according to Wheeler Thackston, "[A]s a genre, the *munajat* gained in popularity after Ansari and even became an essential part of the Persian epic romance, taking its place between the sections on God's unity and on the Prophet."[30] Ansari prays in short bursts: "O God, When you had the flame of separation, why did you kindle the fire of hell?"; "O God, What you sewed I put on; what you poured into the cup I drank. Nothing has come of that for which I myself have striven"; and "O God, Although people think You are distant, You are nearer than the soul—yet You are more sublime than any token that may be given of You."[31] Ansari's prayers are so appealing because they are both brief and substantial, at once intense and soothing in their capacity to put the heart's deepest intimations into clear, simple words.

Rites of Passage

The Five Pillars are not the only religious practices timed by a liturgical calendar. This section will discuss the literary sources associated with several broad categories of popular practice: commemorations of key events in the life of Muhammad; the observance of birthdays or death dates of the Friends of God; the phenomenon of visitation (*ziyara*) to the tombs of holy persons; and the Shi'i memorialization of the martyrdom of Husayn.

Every year on the eve of the twelfth day of Rabi'u 'l-Awwal, the third month in the lunar liturgical calendar, Muslims in many countries celebrate the birthday of Muhammad. The same day marks his death as well. In some areas, such as Saudi Arabia, the event receives no formal acknowledgment as an occasion of special ritual significance, since some people consider such observances an inappropriate aggrandizement of the Prophet. A number of exquisite literary works form the textual foundation for the occasion, and some texts have been integrated into ritual observances. One such work, the poem of the *Noble Birth* (*Mevlid-i sherif*), written about 1410 by the Turkish poet Sulayman Chelebi, has remained an essential text for communal recitation not only on Muhammad's birthday but on death anniversaries as well. Here is the section in which celebrants respond to the news of his coming into the world:

> Welcome, O high prince, we greet you!
> Welcome, O mine of wisdom, we greet you!
> Welcome, O secret of the Book, we greet you!
> Welcome, O medicine for pain, we greet you!
> Welcome, O sunlight and moonlight of God!
> Welcome, O one who is not separated from God!
> Welcome, O nightingale of the garden of Beauty!
> Welcome, O friend of the Lord of Power!

Welcome, O refuge of your nation!
Welcome, O eternal soul, we greet you!
Welcome, O cupbearer of the lovers, we greet you!
Welcome, O darling of the Beloved!
Welcome, O much beloved of the Lord!
Welcome, O mercy for the worlds!
Welcome, O intercessor for the sinner!
Welcome, O prince of this world and the next!
Only for you Time and Space was created.[32]

Numerous Swahili works, some composed as late as this century, attest to the popularity of the material. Typically such works amount to translations or versifications from earlier Arabic prose works, sometimes with considerable variation introduced by the Swahili author. Jan Knappert has translated several of these *mawlid* (pl., *mawalid;* literally, "birthday") pieces. They offer excellent examples of modifications of earlier Arabic texts as well as of important Swahili poetic meters. An unusual aspect of most mawlid prose and poetry is that they do not stop with descriptions of the wonders that attended Muhammad's birth. They merely begin there, continuing through a condensed narration of the Prophet's entire life. Sometimes they end with his death, but they almost always include sections extolling his noble physical and spiritual attributes. One example will suggest the wondrous atmosphere the poetry seeks to create. In the beginning, the text says, when Muhammad's mother, Amina, conceived the child, all the herd animals of the Quraysh spoke most eloquently and said, "The pregnancy of the Prophet has set in here today, the appearance (on earth) of our lord has come near." Every month as the new moon appeared they would say together with the angels, "His appearance on this earth (means) every happiness." As Amina neared labor, four indescribably beautiful women came to be with her. Two were dark-eyed heavenly maidens called houris; the other two were Mary, mother of Jesus, and Pharaoh's wife Asiya. Of the moment of birth the text says, "The Confessor, the fully lit moon, appeared, who was perfect in his perfection, with every beauty. . . . O thou informed of every secret, peace is with thee. O thou who were sent out of mercy, peace is for thee. O thou who art loved, thou hast loved thy Lord, prayers and peace-wishes descend upon thee eternally."[33] The intensely personal, familiar tone in which the speakers address the Prophet is a hallmark of the mawlid genre.

Muhammad's Night Journey (*isra'*) and Ascension (*mi'raj*), usually commemorated on 27 Rajab, has likewise provided occasion for distinctive ritual observances over the centuries. In East Africa, for example, the day of fasting occurs after a three-night recitation of Najm ad-Din Ghayti's prose version of the story, first in Arabic and then in Swahili translation.[34] The tale recounts Muhammad's experiences en route from Mecca to Jerusalem, and from the Dome of the Rock through the seven heavens, where he meets a number of the major prophets and converses with them. He then descends into hell to witness the tortures of the damned. In a popular Swahili version we find this image of Muhammad's progress under Gabriel's guidance:

> After that they went on and saw a vast plain, and (heard) a pleasant voice, and (perceived) unequalled smells. Gabriel said: "Listen, Messenger-Prophet: The voice of Paradise that speaks to God most Generous." (The voice said:) "Lord, I want many people, I long for them. I am great beatitude, I wait for those who will come . . . when?" God told him: "Yours is every faithful person, women and men for whom you claim great happiness." After that they went and saw a plain of heat, and heard the ugly voice of Munkar, like donkeys, and perceived unpleasant smells (which) he endured, being a man of patience. Gabriel said: "It is the voice of hell." It said: "Lord, I am plagued with excessive heat; I want the immoral people, my people of the fire." The Lord answered: "Every oppressor is yours, the women and the men who rebelled against the Mild Lord."[35]

These episodes also figure prominently in many mawlid works. I make a distinction here between narrative versions of the experience now integrally part of a ritual observance, and those mostly poetic and usually shorter settings of the tale that come under the heading of praise poetry.[36]

An aspect of popular practice analogous to commemorations of Muhammad's birthday are celebrations of the birthdays of numerous holy personages. Sunni and Shi'i Muslims alike in a number of countries observe these occasions (mawalid) of such figures as members of Muhammad's family, his daughter Zaynab for one, or of founders of religious orders, such as the twelfth-century Friend of God (Wali Allah) 'Abd al-Qadir al-Jilani or the immensely popular thirteenth-century Egyptian Ahmad al-Badawi of Tanta. Panegyric poetry, similar to the mawlid texts in honor of Muhammad, and pilgrim manuals supplement long-standing local tradition in the performance of the rituals. Often the observances last for several days or a week, with the celebrants becoming increasingly fervent and emotionally involved as the days draw on. Farmers come to Cairo from all over Egypt to commemorate Lady Zaynab's mawlid. They gather in virtually every available mosque and madrasa, and throng the narrow streets of the old city around her mosque for a full week. (See Fig. 32.)

Dozens of rites of passage are part of Muslim life across the globe. Bestowing a name on a child, haircutting and sacrifice of an animal on a child's seventh day, circumcision, marriage, and funerals are among the more im-

Figure 11. Funeral bier awaiting burial, outside the Sulaymaniye Mosque (see Fig. 19), Istanbul, draped with a cloth bearing the text of Qur'an 29:57. Note the niche design on the right pedestal. The mosque's own cemetery is just behind the wall in the background.

portant. Here I discuss only the literature of the funeral rite, since it is associated symbolically with several of the other practices to be discussed shortly, namely, the commemoration of martyrdom and visitation to sanctified burial places.

Jurisprudence treatises are the first line of textual material on funeral practice, building of course on Qur'anic references and hadiths reporting Muhammad's views on the matter. I consider here the tone of the observance rather than the rubrics followed, for attitudes toward death say much about a tradition's sense of the individual's relationship to God. A special salat marks the passing of a Muslim from this life (see Fig. 11). The line "Every soul shall taste death; then unto Us you will be returned" (Q 29:57) establishes the tone. The prayer service includes a commendation of the departed one to God by proclaiming four times God's dominion over all things—"Allahu akbar" (God is supreme)—along with other prayers for both the deceased and the mourners. A striking feature of the ritual is the final instruction to the deceased as to how to deal with the two formidable interrogating angels, Munkar and Nakir, whose task is to test the dead Muslim's faith one last time. An example from an Urdu primer suggests that the mourners say to the deceased:

> Remember the Covenant . . . which is the witness that there is no god but God and that Muhammad is the Apostle of God . . . and that thou art well satisfied with God as (thy) One Lord and with Islam as (thy) religious practice and with Muhammad as Apostle and Prophet. This is the first abiding place of the abodes of the other world and the last abiding place of the abodes of this transitory world. . . . Let them not (the two angels) disturb thee . . . for they are only creatures, a part of God's creation. And when they ask thee, "Who is thy Lord and who is thy Prophet and what is thy *imam* [prayer leader], and thy religion, and thy *qibla* [prayer direction], and thy brethren?" Then say, "God is my Lord and Muhammad my Prophet, the Qur'an is my *imam* and the Ka'ba my *qibla*, and all the believers and Muslims are my brethren."[37]

Help from the community of believers enables the deceased to pass this crucial test, thereby alleviating the loneliness of the tomb, mitigating the sense of constriction the dead feel, and assuring an easier passage from this world to the next.

Another popular devotional parallel to the canonical ritual practice of pilgrimage is journeying to shrines or tombs associated with local holy personages. Considerable literature in several major languages belongs to a genre of pilgrimage manual devoted to the practice of visitation (ziyara). That genre, called *ziyaratnama*, in turn belongs to the broader category of travel literature. When Muslims travel to the tomb of Muhammad in Medina upon completion of the greater or lesser pilgrimage to Mecca and its environs, they are engaging in ziyara. For many Muslims, this is the only acceptable instance of this noncanonical practice; but that is by no means the end of the matter. Muslim theologians have debated at length the acceptability of ziyara; some, such as Ibn Taymiya (d. 1328), have gone so far as to condemn even the visit to Muhammad's tomb. Ibn Taymiya's views have exercised a formative influence on theological underpinnings of Islam in present-day Saudi Arabia. In his *Book Setting out the Straight Path over against the Denizens of Hellfire (Kitab iqtida' as-sirat al-mustaqim mukhalafat ashab al-jahim)*, Ibn Taymiya notes that the Prophet forbade any act that might have the effect of turning a grave into a holy sanctuary. The process begins, he says, with people claiming a certain place is the station of a prophet or tomb of a Friend of God, "the claim being substantiated with a report, the identity of whose narrator is anybody's guess, or a vision, whose true nature is not known. The next step is to turn such a spot into a mosque. Thus it becomes a distinct idol which is worshipped apart from God: *shirk* [idolatry] grounded in *ifk* [lie]!"[38]

At the other end of the spectrum of theological opinion, one finds a variety of sources that favor ziyara. Sunni and Shi'i texts alike not only praise the practice but also explain in great detail how one does it properly. Here is a sample of the prayer recommended to a pilgrim upon visiting the tomb of 'Abd al-Qadir al-Jilani in Baghdad (see Fig. 15) on his anniversary, 11 Rabi' ath-thani, the fourth lunar month:

> Peace be to thee O King of the age, O Imam of the place, O wielder of the command of the Merciful, O heir of the Book and representative of the Apostle of God, O thou whose benefit is heavenly and earthly, O thou to whom all the people of the time are his family. Thou through whose petitioning help comes down, through whose blessing supplication is efficacious.[39]

For Shi'i Muslims, the chief focus of the practice is the tomb of the protomartyr, Husayn, in Karbala, Iraq. Tradition says that in the year 680, Husayn, son of 'Ali and Fatima, was making his way with a small band of the family of the Prophet toward an engagement with the Umayyad caliph Yazid, whom Husayn regarded as an evil usurper. Yazid meanwhile had dispatched an expeditionary force to intercept the Shi'i band near Karbala, south of Baghdad. In the face of enormous odds, against the vastly superior power of the Umayyads, the valiant Husayn refused to surrender. In the end he and most of his little band were slaughtered, and Husayn's tomb became a goal of pilgrimage, as did those of all the other martyr-imams.

Shi'i authors have produced numerous works whose function parallels that of the manuals of instruction for Muslims who make the hajj. One mid-fourteenth-century compendium of material for these rites of commemoration, the *Complete (Book of) Visitation (Kamil az-ziyara)*, by Ibn Qawlawayh of Qum (a city in Iran noted for educating religious scholars), offers several alternative ways of performing the visitation. It includes specific recommended prayers to say at each key point in the ritual. The text emphasizes the role of the ritual and its prayers in integrating the pilgrim into the larger Muslim community and the larger world under divine dominion, as mediated by Husayn, whose life and death sum up the values and aspirations of believers. Addressing Husayn, the pilgrim prays:

> I testify that you are the purity of the pure and pure of purity. Through you, the land is pure. The earth where you are is pure and your sanctuary is pure. I testify that you ordered and called for justice, and that you are the

vengeance of God on His earth so that He may arouse the feelings of all His creation because of you. The blessings of God be with your spirit and your body. You are the sincere one, the truthful one and confirmer of truth. May God destroy those who destroy you with their hands and tongues.[40]

Originally centered on Husayn, the ritual has gradually broadened to include the whole family of imams and all their fellow martyrs. When Shi'i pilgrims visit the tombs of other imams, such as that of the eighth imam, Riza, at Mashhad, they keep the image and story of Husayn in mind.

An example of the enduring popularity of the pilgrim manual is the *Treasury of Death Anniversaries* (*Makhzan-i a'ras*) of an eighteenth-century Indian Sufi named Muhammad Najib Qadiri. Ziyara typically takes place in the context of the *'urs,* literally, the "wedding," commemorating the death of a holy person whose soul is thus married to God. Ritualizing the mystical marriage of a Friend of God ordinarily occurs on a date believed the anniversary of the holy person's death. Ceremonies include the travel to the tomb, circumambulation, and prayer for intercession. This work discusses proper timing and ritual for visitation. For example, upon entering the tomb the pilgrim circumambulates it either three or seven times. After bowing low to the foot of the grave, the pilgrim stands to the right of the grave and says, "Peace be unto you, people of 'There is no god but God.'" After scattering roses or other floral decorations on the tomb, the pilgrim, either sitting or standing, recites a series of texts from the Qur'an. These include the *Fatiha* (the first sura) and the Verse of the Throne, followed by Suras 99 and 102 said once each, and Sura 112 recited either seven or ten times. Ziyara is especially efficacious on Friday, and it is better to visit in the morning than later in the day.[41]

In this case, as in virtually all matters surrounding the practice of ziyara, the pivotal theological issue is intercession. Islamic tradition has often debated two related questions: whether anyone can intercede with God for the individual believer; and, if so, who can intercede and to what degree. Much discussion hinges on the interpretation of the clause in the Verse of the Throne that says, "[N]one can intercede with Him except by His permission" (Q 2:255). The issue has been debated throughout the history of Islamic thought. On one end of the spectrum one finds a tendency to reject (exemplified by the Wahhabi movement of pre-modern Arabia) any belief or practice that might tend to raise a human being above merely human status: hence, no intercession is possible. That position presumes that God clearly has not given anyone such permission. Every individual faces God alone at the final accounting. On the other end, popular practice has endowed many Friends of God with the power to put in a good word with the Almighty and perhaps produce thereby a miraculous answer to prayer. Somewhere in the middle is the acceptance of some basic intercessory capability on the part of Muhammad alone but only at judgment and only for the most sincerely repentant. Both these last positions assume, for practical purposes, that the sacred text would not have mentioned permission at all if it was not an actual possibility. On balance, however, the tradition strongly discourages the hope of a deathbed conversion.[42]

One famous annual but not strictly canonical observance occurs in still traditional enclaves of Twelver Shi'i Muslims. During the first ten days of the first lunar month, Muharram, Shi'ites commemorate the death of Muhammad's grandson Husayn at Karbala. A climactic event in that commemoration is the *ta'ziya,* a play depicting the sufferings of pre-Islamic prophets and reenacting Husayn's martyrdom. Husayn thus stands in a long line of holy persons who have experienced rejection—and much worse—at the hands of their unbelieving people. But, as the text of the play emphasizes in many ways, their suffering redeems all who are well disposed, and in the end their forgiveness softens the hardest of hearts. In Husayn's case, the martyr intercedes even for his murderer, the vile Shimr, an agent of the tyrannical Yazid.

At the end of one version of the story, Muhammad announces to Husayn at resurrection time, that God has told the Prophet to give Husayn the key of intercession. Muhammad then instructs Husayn to rescue from hellfire all who have ever shed a tear for this martyr or helped his cause or performed pilgrimage to his shrine or composed a poetic lamentation for him. Husayn responds by addressing all sinners: "O my friends, be relieved from grief, and come along with me to the mansions of the blest. Sorrow has passed away, it is now time for joy and rest." As they throng into Paradise, the grateful sinners sing out, "God be praised! by Husayn's grace we are made happy, and by his favor we are delivered from destruction. By Husayn's loving-kindness is our path decked with roses and flowers. We were thorns and thistles, but are now made cedars owing to his merciful intercession."[43]

Sermons for Every Occasion

Sermons preached for special occasions outside the formal midday Friday prayer in the mosque share the same basic form as the Friday khutba. Except for the relationship between theme and special occasion, one can rarely discern an obvious difference between liturgical and devotional preaching.

A separate discussion of the noncanonical sermon emphasizes the importance of ritual context in understanding the meaning of the address, whatever its theme.

Very often the theme of a sermon preached on Friday is determined by that day's proximity to a special but noncanonical commemoration, such as that of Muhammad's birthday or his Night Journey and Ascension as discussed earlier. Some examples of issues that preachers have treated during the month of Rajab are as follows: First, was Muhammad's Night Journey and Ascension a spiritual and physical experience, or solely a spiritual one? That is, did God transport Muhammad bodily on this journey, or did the Prophet experience the journey inwardly? Second, why did Muhammad descend to Jerusalem rather than directly to Mecca? This is not idle theological speculation; one can readily understand the political significance of interpreting these issues in the late twentieth-century Middle East. Muhammad's relationship to Jerusalem is crucial to a religious legitimation of Palestine as an Islamic land.[44]

Another variety of material stands functionally midway between the mosque address and the forms dedicated to telling stories of holy persons. A class of public figures whose profession was either to give moral exhortation (the *wu''az,* "professional exporters") or to tell stories (the *qussas,* "professional raconteurs") were influential across the Middle East, especially during medieval times. Theirs was the quasi-official task of religious education of the unlettered masses. Like their colleagues, the professional Qur'an reciters, these itinerant preachers were sometimes targeted for harsh criticism by religious officials, the *'ulama',* those more rigorously trained in the Islamic traditional sciences (exegesis, hadith, and jurisprudence). As a result, a number of important documents recommended that these preachers cultivate strict personal discipline to avoid the pitfalls of arrogance and pride that can attend celebrity status.

The twelfth-century theologian Ibn al-Jawzi wrote *The Book of Professional Storytellers* (*Kitab al-qussas wa 'l-mudhakkirin*) as a manual for young preachers. He traces the origins of popular preaching to the Sunna, Muhammad's example. Ibn al-Jawzi identifies the practice as a legitimate religious science and extols its potential for good, granted that one engages in it responsibly. Both Ibn al-Jawzi and Abu Hamid al-Ghazali are concerned at least as much with the requisite interior dispositions as with the external manifestations. (The two are not in agreement on all matters, however, and Ibn al-Jawzi severely criticizes Ghazali for basing his work on too many unsound hadiths.)

Ibn al-Jawzi defines the three functions of public preaching: the narration and interpretation of stories of the past (*qisas*); reminding (*tadhkir*) people "of the blessing God has bestowed upon them, urging them to render thanks"; and "instilling fear that softens the heart" (*wa'z*). This final element is related to a formal component of the Friday sermon, namely, the segment devoted to moral exhortation (maw'iza). Ibn al-Jawzi holds practitioners to the strictest discipline, insisting that preaching "is to be carried out in accordance with the principles of asceticism by means of a woolen garment, an emaciated body, the consuming of small quantities of food, thus distracting the mind away from the body and preoccupying it with the excellences of the spirit."[45] In other words, those who hold so lofty a responsibility need to guard against anything that might tempt them to become absorbed in themselves and forget their ultimate purpose. For virtually every deep human need, popular Islamic rituals provide a response that helps Muslims to celebrate, grieve, commemorate, and acknowledge their feelings and convictions. These rituals occur within a temporal and spatial context that is exemplified in Islamic art and architecture.

Art and Architecture

In everyday life it is unlikely that Muslims across the globe often make the tidy distinction between prescribed and popular practices. The distinction is useful as an organizational device, however, and is based on significant differences suggested in the literary and visual sources themselves. In architecture the primary function of various kinds of structures is either funerary or reliquary. Funerary architecture is much more common than reliquary, but the association of sacred relics with holy places deserves a mention here. For example, a nineteenth-century dervish in the Ottoman Turkish city of Erzincan was in charge of the construction of a new facility. He reports how his shaykh traveled to Istanbul and returned with a hair of the Prophet's beard to be installed there. The dervish writes:

> In the end the dergah [Sufi meeting place] appeared, by the favor of the Prophet, like a sun of truth. . . . For the hair from the beard of the Prophet a place was made like a little dome with glass sides, in the center of the mosque on the ceiling; and the hair was put in a coffer made of iron and placed in its special place in the dome with a big long ladder. When it became necessary to take it down, this poor soul would put the ladder in place, ascend, open the coffer with two keys, take the inner case on my head and bring it down. In the same way, I would take it back up and put it in its place. On this account, I give special thanks and praise to God that I have repeatedly taken the case containing the blessed whisker of our Lord the Most Gracious Beloved, on whom God grant blessing and peace, on my head and transported it down and up.

The newly completed dergah opened on 12 Rabiʿu ʾl-Awwal, Muhammad's birthday, and the author describes the festivities at some length.[46]

By far the most numerous sacred places are the graves of Friends of God. Because of their associations with persons of great spiritual power (*baraka*), burial sites often take on the secondary function of shrine. Some become shrines immediately, some do so years later. There is a de facto, though not officially published, hierarchy of such holy places. The more important the person, generally, the grander and the better maintained the monument. For Shiʿi Muslims the most important are the tombs of the martyr-imams and members of their families. The most famous are the tomb of Riza, the eighth imam, in Mashhad, Iran, and shrines associated with ʿAli and his son Husayn at Najaf and Karbala in Iraq. These elaborately decorated structures function as sanctuaries within which devotees can express their grief over the loss of the holy ones; many leave behind as a type of votive offering some symbol of their deepest needs and prayers. Around the tomb of Imam Riza, for example, is a silver framework on which pilgrims tie small ribbons or pieces of paper. More recently, devotees have displayed similar signs of piety at the tomb of Ayatollah Khomeini.[47]

In theory Sunni Islam does not allow for the cultivation of sacred sites built around mere mortals. According to some regional traditions, in fact, the ideal is to bury the deceased, wrapped in a simple shroud, in an unostentatious grave. The only structural requirement is that "bodies are buried in a recumbent posture at right angles to the *qibla* in such a way that they would face Mecca if turned on their side."[48] But in actual practice, Sunni Muslims, too, have historically developed and attended to hundreds of such holy places throughout the Islamic world. To these sites pilgrims make ziyara for special observances of events in the holy person's life, as well as for the purpose of requesting restored health, success in marriage or employment, and fertility. A tomb of an important Friend of God has often formed the nucleus of an extensive necropolis.[49] Just as often, the revered person's grave becomes a starting point for the foundation of a religious institution or complex, such as a madrasa or residential facility for members of a religious fraternity.

In Ottoman Turkey numerous sites dedicated to the rituals and residences of members of dervish orders have also included a prominent funerary and commemorative function. The founder of the organization (tariqa), and often the spiritual leader's successors as well, are buried within the structure, either in a separate room or in a space continuous with that used for communal prayer rites. In the former case, visual communication between the spaces occurs through windows through which dervishes can cast a glance into the funerary chamber. In addition, windows often open into the shrine room from the street, so that passersby can make a visitation without actually entering the burial place.

Visitation of holy persons' tombs as practiced in connection with dervish orders in Turkey has followed much the same etiquette as that observed by individuals meeting with a living shaykh or other member of the order. Approaching only on foot as a sign of respect and self-effacement, the pilgrim crosses the threshold, right foot first, after making gestures of homage and requesting the dead person's permission to enter. A visitor then stands at the foot of the tomb before circumambulating it three times, and departs by backing out of the space and repeating the various gestures of respect observed on entering. Common motives for such veneration include requests for favors such as healing or intercession, or sanctifying individual rites of passage such as circumcision or marriage. Votive offerings have spanned a wide range, from renovation of the tomb to sacrifice of various animals whose meat is then given to the needy to supplying necessary furnishings such as prayer carpets or lanterns to small gifts of oil for the shrine's lamps. Baha Tanman, speaking of Turkish practices, concludes that "the basic source of the structural relation between tomb and tekke [dervish residence] is to be sought in the human instinct, the desire common to members of every society to be close to their loved ones and to perpetuate this proximity through their spiritual presence beyond the tomb. . . . In the Islamic Sufi tradition, this tendency merged with belief in the power of the saints to intercede with God on behalf of their followers and with the belief in their power to bestow graces and favors."[50]

Monumental funerary architecture created by and for Muslims presents an immediate religious problem. It appears to violate flagrantly an early ban on all structures over burial places, as expressed in the hadith literature. Still, one has to account for the phenomenon in religious terms, since the people who have created the works claim to have done so, at least in part, for religious reasons. Significantly, Islamic tombs seem to function religiously as images of Paradise and as shrines.

Building a roof over a tomb evokes the paradisiacal attribute of shade, alluded to by Ghazali in a hadith cited earlier; tomb towers and lofty domes also suggest elevation from earthly limitations. In some instances the shapes employed suggest further symbolic associations. The fluted tile drum and conical vault over the tomb of Rumi (see Fig. 12), for example, is a visual allusion to reeds that grow in a stream bed. Rumi calls the soul a

Figure 12.   Tomb of Jalal ad-Din Rumi (thirteenth century),
Konya, Turkey. Note the fluted tile of the drum and conical
vault. The grave markers shown in Figure 33 are located in
the same building, just to the left of the domed chamber.

reed flute that longs to return to its original home, whence it has been
plucked. Some textual sources link various building plans (square or cylindrical with protruding angles as in a multipointed star, for example, or polygonal shapes) directly with imagery of Paradise and firmament. In some instances the shapes are particularly significant by virtue of the numbers of
sides, as in eight- or twelve-sided forms with their allusions to multilevel
celestial gardens (called the eight paradises) and zodiacal imagery. As for
more explicit symbolism, the use of mihrablike shapes as doorways suggests a deliberate reference to the deceased's transition to another realm or

plane of existence; and literary sources link various dome designs (after which entire structures take their names—*gunbad, qubba, turba*) with images of Paradise and the heavens. Finally, the choice and location of inscriptions, especially of texts from the Qur'an, further reinforces the religious interpretation of the tomb as an image of Paradise.[51] (See also Figs. 24, 26, and 31.)

In addition to these architectural forms, Muslim artsts have developed many types of smaller items. Funerary art spans a range of objects and ornamental themes meant to mediate the presence and blessing of the saintly figure as well as to decorate. In Turkey, for example, the tomb of a Sufi *pir* ("elder"; hence, "spiritual guide") or a former shaykh often bears various insignia of the orders, such as distinctive headgear; panels showing the names of the great figures along with those of Muhammad and the first four caliphs; and images of the order's banner. Qur'anic texts on life's transience and images of Mecca and Medina also appear in these settings. So do scriptographs (in which calligraphy forms the outline of the face of some holy personage) and pictographs (in which calligraphy forms the outline of an animal, plant or object) with the individual's name either incorporated into his headgear or above it. Other visual embellishments include panels or pictures of dervish equipment such as the begging bowl, staff, ax, or mace. Sometimes actual objects believed to have belonged to the deceased person, such as a mantle or rosary, are placed on the cenotaph (the coffin-shaped empty marker located above the actual grave).[52] (See Fig. 33.)

Though Shi'i Muslims make up only a small proportion of the global community of Islam, they have produced a great deal of visual source material related to commemoration of the saintly departed. A unique type of architectural decoration has developed in more recent times in association with the Shi'i observance of Husayn's martyrdom. For centuries a censure of public depictions of the scenes of the protomartyr's story relegated illustration to a variety of folk art called Karbala painting. During the nineteenth century, Iranians began to create narrative murals on the facades of the structures (sg., *takiya*) in which they reenacted the tragedy of Karbala, site of Husayn's martyrdom.[53]

On a smaller scale, processional models of the tomb-shrines of Shi'i imams have been a standard ritual device in communal observances in various Muslim countries. When one cannot circumambulate the actual shrine, a miniature model allows celebrants to carry the holy place among themselves. Vernon Schubel describes the Pakistani use of replicas of tombs called *rowza* or, in the case of Husayn, *ta'ziya* (the same term used to refer to the plays commemorating the imam's martyrdom). These models are displayed in the visitation house (*ziyaratkhana*), so that people who visit that building can make a surrogate pilgrimage to the martyr's tomb by visiting the miniature of it. The models are made from a variety of materials, from paper and wood to more permanent and expensive materials. Those of lesser quality are destroyed after the observances of the month Muharram, by being thrown into the sea or buried; the better constructed ones are either kept in their visitation places year round or brought out once a year for procession.[54] (See Fig. 13.)

One final type of funerary object deserves mention here, the decorative burial container called the *tabut*. An example is the large, exquisitely carved wooden box rediscovered in the Cairene Mosque of Husayn in 1939. It dates from the later years of the Fatimids, an Isma'ili Shi'i dynasty during whose regime the head of the martyr Husayn was brought to Cairo and enshrined there. The tabut's extensive Qur'anic inscriptions make it a fine exemplar of work by Isma'ili Shi'i artists. The texts that adorn it refer subtly and indirectly to certain central Shi'i tenets, including several that are distinctively Isma'ili. For example, several references to "you people of the house" recall the Shi'i emphasis on the family of the Prophet as uniquely favored. Another text, revealed to Muhammad while 'Ali was praying, suggests to Shi'i Muslims proof that 'Ali was indeed the Prophet's legitimate successor: "Your friend [*wali*] is only God, and His Messenger, and the believers who perform the prayer" (Q 5:55). References to the seven days of creation, along with the appearance of a decorative seven-pointed star, one can associate specifically with Isma'ili thought; the same may be said of several prominent references to *jihad*, one of the Seven Pillars of Isma'ili teaching. The seven include fasting, pilgrimage to Mecca, almsgiving, and daily ritual prayer, in common with Sunni Muslims. Isma'ilis add devotion to the imams (*walaya*), ritual purity (*tahara*), and *jihad*.[55]

Pilgrimage manuals of the sort discussed earlier often include sacred sites that are the goal of noncanonical pilgrimage. Illustrated books of this kind come from all over the Islamic world. Travelers visit the holy places out of personal piety, or because such visitations have either become virtually inseparable from the major pilgrimage to Mecca, or because local tradition recommends it. Images include stylized plans of the Prophet's mosque in Medina, where his tomb is located, and of the Dome of the Rock in Jerusalem, the goal of Muhammad's Night Journey and the place from which tradition says he ascended to heaven.

As suggested earlier, these illustrated works function ostensibly as guidebooks for actual travel, but their images also take the viewer to the holy places in memory or imagination. A still more symbolic function may be

Figure 13.   Processional models of tombs of Shi'i martyrs (1980s), Rawalpindi, Pakistan. Photograph by David Edwards.

that of a cosmological atlas, locating all the major sanctuaries of divine power symbolically on a map of the spiritual universe. Schematized drawings, both in plan and elevation, of the "Garden" of Medina, site of Muhammad's tomb and that of his daughter Fatima, have apparently served as particularly important meditative devices, allowing the reader of the *Guidebook to Blessings* to travel inwardly.[56]

Illustrated manuscripts, whose cost renders them almost exclusively royal or elite, rarely include images of more popular ritual practices. However, folksy pictures of Buraq, the winged quadruped upon which Muhammad is said to have made his Night Journey and Ascension, are popular in many parts of the world. These depictions of the human-headed creature function symbolically as reminders of a key event in Muhammad's life, commemorated on 27 Rajab, the seventh lunar month. They also serve as talismanic protection; festooning vehicles from huge trucks to pedicabs, the Prophet-bearer's image protects driver and cargo.

Islamic popular iconography covers a broad range of themes in virtually all the major artistic media. With one or two notable exceptions, such as images associated with Husayn's martyrdom, most art produced in connection with noncanonical ritual functions as symbol rather than narrative. Depictions of objects, sometimes quite stylized and abstract, such as the

Prophet's sandal or Buraq, serve as reminders of the whole story of a sacred person or event. But often that very symbolic power also invests images with an almost magical quality that endears them particularly to millions of townspeople and villagers whose world, despite the corrective measures of teachers of official Islam, remains inhabited and animated by countless spiritual forces with which these folk must contend to survive. Imagery of the prophets and Friends of God figures prominently in that struggle.

Even a cursory glance at the rich devotional life of Muslims quickly dispels any impression that Islam is a dry, anemic tradition. The varied sentiments expressed in prayers and in countless evocative and charming images reveal the vividness and vitality of Islamic devotion.

3 Inspiration
Edification and Ethics

Islam's vitality as a spiritual tradition depends much on the example of those who have walked the road before, individuals whose courage, conviction, and dedication have raised them to the status of models. These embodiments of the tradition's core values live on in the stories and visual images that have appealed to broad masses of Muslims across the globe for many centuries. Some figures deemed worthy of religiously heroic status—prophets, Friends of God, imams, and martyrs—have been enshrined in their final resting places and endure in classics of literature and art.

Heroic figures survive cycles of popularity, neglect, and revival. Debunking and demythologizing may chip away a coat of lacquer or dull the luster of an older generation's image of some paradigmatic person. For a while that exemplar might all but fade from memory, but the need for models of laudable human behavior runs deep. Successive generations invariably revive the most durable personifications of those values, reinterpreting and adapting them to changing circumstances.

Textual material falls into two large categories, life stories and wisdom literature. In the first I locate hagiographical texts, stories that highlight the wondrous or miraculous in a holy person's life. They are a source of inspiration at every level of society and religious sophistication. I begin with a look at the role of prophets and Friends of God as heroic paradigms, and at some of the principal literary forms that have borne the tradition. Some hagiographical sources recount the lives of individual figures at length; others group together in one volume briefer lives of many outstanding figures.[1]

Wisdom literature is also of two types. One is called the mirror for princes. Although rarely so self-consciously religious as the other forms considered here, it represents a significant aspect of the Islamic spiritual tradition. Just

Figure 14.   (*Opposite*) A painting from a late sixteenth-century Turkish book of stories of the prophets, *Qisas al-anbiya'*, by Nishapuri, showing Muhammad on a minbar in a mosque, with 'Ali, Hasan, and Husayn on the right. The flaming nimbus indicates the lofty status of these holy persons. New York: The Metropolitan Museum of Art, Rogers Fund.

as the mirror genre poses a moral challenge for those in power, several other literary forms address the ethical issues that ordinary folk must confront every day.

In this chapter I discuss the principal ways that Muslims have experienced these exemplary figures, namely, through performance and the visual arts. Vocal artists continue to enthrall audiences with the arts of storytelling, and visual artists have created heroes to delight the eyes of both popular and elite constituencies. Although I have already introduced some of these figures, here I emphasize the ways in which they have stood for a human potential at least marginally within the reach of the ordinary person.

EXEMPLARY MODELS

Prophets and Friends of God

Classic hagiographical sources tell stories of two different kinds of religious figures. Tales of prophets, beginning with Muhammad's life story (*sira*), recount how over the ages God has communicated with humanity through specially appointed spokespersons. Another body of literature tells of how other holy persons, whom the Islamic tradition calls Friends of God, have served special purposes over the centuries since the age of the last prophet.

Holy persons have functioned as intercessors and mediators, and in popular spirituality they have helped people to identify and gain access to the wellsprings of grace, blessing, and power. Muslims acknowledge how God manifests his power and presence through chosen persons, but there is more to the role of these embodiments of sanctity: they also serve as inspired examples. The stories of Muhammad's wondrous qualities, of the imams' redemptive suffering, and of the benevolent approachability of other holy persons function not only as assurances of divine providence but also as reminders of the spiritual potential to which God invites humankind.

Heroic tales abound in all cultures and societies. Muslim writers have produced an extraordinary wealth of testimonies to spiritual aspiration and struggle. Their works range from anecdotes of the more mundane and light-hearted picaresque hero to paeans to the sorrowful otherworldly martyr. Folk heroes and heroines, often of pre-Islamic origin, model bravery, strength, cleverness, and a host of inborn virtues deemed necessary for success in this life. They achieve their human potential without necessarily appealing to a higher power. Royal heroes model courtly values like romantic love, high-minded chivalry, and a refined wisdom that goes with experience of the wider world. Like their folk counterparts, the royal heroic figures do not necessarily act with explicit consciousness of the presence of divine power in their lives. That is where religious heroes differ from folk and royal paradigms.

Religious heroes live and move in a world ordered according to a divine plan. They exist only to reflect and point out God's signs and presence in creation. When they conquer they do so by God's leave and power; and even when they lose in time, as rejected prophets or martyrs for justice, they win in eternity. Religious heroes function as custodians of hope against terrible odds, testifying to the virtual certainty of ultimate victory. Their life stories bear witness to the reality of a transcendent dimension in human experience. Most of all, prophets and Friends of God represent the best of religious and cultural ideals in accessible form, perhaps too far away to attain fully but not so far as to discourage an attempt.[2]

Throughout the world, in a score of major languages, Muslim authors have devised or employed a broad range of literary forms for communicating values and inspiring their fellow Muslims to greatness. Interpretation of their various modes of communication is a complex matter. Carl Ernst makes an important observation about the Sufi biographical tradition in India, raising a caution much needed in the study of hagiographical material in virtually all Islamic contexts. Ernst notes that one cannot always make a tidy distinction between political and religious biography. "In classical Islamic literature, the lives of Sufi saints are often found in local biographical works devoted to the notable of a particular city. Books of lives of the saints frequently have an explicitly political context, signaled by a dedication to a sultan or other powerful political figure. . . . Implicit political motives can also be inferred by reference to contemporary events or by comparison with other hagiographic texts ostensibly describing the same period." Mystical and royal historiographies, Ernst concludes, exist in a symbiotic relationship.[3]

In this context I note a crucial connection between spirituality and a distinctively Islamic interpretation of history that is based on a Qur'anic paradigm. The Arabic scripture emphasizes humanity's invariably hostile response to God's messengers. That emphasis provided early Muslim historians a lens through which they interpreted certain painful events in their community's past. This pattern of events has always raised difficult questions for reflective Muslims, questions similar to those Christians and Jews have asked as they reflect on their histories: Where is history heading? Does God have a long-range plan for this people? Will God deal kindly with humanity in the end? Members of all three religious communities have answered such questions by appealing to patterns that emerged from their readings of the salvation history they discern in their scriptures.

The historian Steven Humphreys observes that "[a]mong early Muslims, the soul-searching provoked by the dialectic of scripture and historical experience crystallized in the form of an almost universally shared myth, one which we can call the myth of Covenant, Betrayal, and Redemption." This sequence of events occurs repeatedly: God establishes a primordial relationship of trust; selfish and heedless people violate the trust; and God sends a new prophet to mend the relationship and reestablish the revealed order. Although Humphreys discusses the matter from the point of view of its formative influence on Islamic historiography, the issue is of decisive importance for the study of spirituality as well. Humphreys argues that the myth of Covenant, Betrayal and Redemption ceased to function as a historical paradigm after about the middle of the tenth century, the age of the great historians Tabari (d. 923) and Mas'udi (d. 956).[4] However, the paradigm has retained its vitality over many centuries as an important theme in the literature of Islamic spirituality. One can argue that it is even making a comeback in some contemporary revivalist, also called Islamist, discourse and preaching. These broad cultural and theological issues can help, in part, to explain why Muslims have always been fascinated with the stories of religious heroes, for heroes are the instruments of divine renewal and symbols of hope for the future.

Individual Life Stories

Surely the most famous of all examples of the genre known as biography or life story (sira) is that of the Prophet Muhammad. Ibn Ishaq's pioneering work in Arabic, available to us in its ninth-century revision by Ibn Hisham, launches dispassionately into its subject matter. With the simple statement "This is the book of the biography of the apostle of God," the author unrolls a lengthy genealogy designed to trace Muhammad directly back to Adam.[5] A rare sample of the author's own attitude to his material occurs in his treatment of Muhammad's Night Journey and Ascension. He says that various transmitters of material contributed their points of view to the formation of the account, so that the result is a patchwork. He regards the story as "a searching test and a matter of God's power and authority wherein is a lesson for the intelligent; and guidance and mercy and strengthening to those who believe." Leaving open the possibility that the event might be interpreted as primarily a spiritual, rather than physical, experience, Ibn Ishaq continues, "It was certainly an act of God by which He took him by night in what way He pleased, to show him His signs which He willed him to see so that he witnessed His mighty sovereignty and power by which He does what he wills to do."[6]

Ibn Ishaq's lengthy and complex work is full of stories and reports of Muhammad's sayings and deeds, often in several variations—a far cry from what readers of modern biography have come to expect. Every now and then, largely due to the poetry that appears throughout the work, one gets a sense of the author's feelings for his subject. For example, at the very end, Ibn Ishaq cites these moving verses by Hassan ibn Thabit (d. c. 659), wrung from the experience of loss:

> Tell the poor that plenty has left them
> With the prophet who departed from them this morning.
>
> . . . .
>
> He was the light and the brilliance we followed.
> He was the sight and hearing second only to God.
> The day they laid him in the grave
> And cast the earth upon him
> Would that God had not left one of us
> And neither man nor woman had survived him!
>
> . . . .
>
> By God, no woman has conceived and given birth
> To one like the apostle the prophet and guide of his people;
> Nor has God created among his creatures
> One more faithful to his sojourner or his promise
> Than he who was the source of our light,
> Blessed in his deeds, just, and upright.
>
> . . . .
>
> O best of men, I was as it were in a river
> Without which I have become lonely in my thirst.[7]

That early sira inspired a number of later emulations. A thirteenth-century version by Abu 'l-Hasan al-Bakri served as the foundation for the fourteenth-century Turkish work by Mustafa Darir, whose text would later provide the occasion for one of the most lavishly illustrated religious books ever produced by Muslims. Darir's patron wanted "a work which would contain quotations from the Qur'an, and extracts from tales of saints and heroes, tales which would not only teach their readers gratitude, patience and the praise of God, but which would, in themselves, be a form of prayer."[8]

In Southeast Asia, Malay tradition adopted an Arabic term that means "narrative" (*hikaya*; pl., *hikayat*) to refer to shorter works dedicated to the tale of a single prophet, holy person, or heroic figure. Several works of this kind focus on Muhammad's life as a whole or retell selected episodes or highlight thematic elements from it. Individual episodes include Muhammad's meeting with Iblis (a name derived from the Greek *diabolos*, the devil), his teaching his daughter Fatima, his preaching to various groups, and his conduct of various military encounters. Thematic elements include Muhammad's "light" (*nur*) or his miracles, such as splitting the moon. Anyone who reads *The Story of the Light of Muhammad* (*Hikayat nur Muhammad*) can look forward to wonderful benefits, according to the text. All the merit of reading the Torah, the Psalms, the Gospels, and the Qur'an, as well as of making pilgrimage, await the reader of this one text. To read this wondrous story, night or day, is to share in the merit of martyrs.

Another popular narrative focuses on Muhammad's miraculous splitting of the moon. In the *Story of the Prophet's Miracles* (*Hikayat mujizat nabi*), we find Abu Jahl, Muhammad's implacable enemy, attacking the Prophet. He charges that Muhammad is obviously inferior to the earlier prophets, since he cannot work wonders as they did. Noah's ark became airborne, Abraham's enemy Nimrod failed to burn the prophet in his fire, Moses turned his staff into a dragon. What can Muhammad do, if anything, Abu Jahl taunts the Prophet. Muhammad is asked to come to a meeting of all Meccans, whereupon the ruler of the city issues a challenge: "Call down the moon and bid it recite the creed that there is no god but Allah and you are His Prophet; bid it circle the Ka'ba seven times and entering your right sleeve come out from your left sleeve; bid it split in two halves, one to the east and the other to the west, and then return whole to the sky." When Muhammad easily accomplishes the wonder, the ruler naturally embraces the faith, and Abu Jahl is put to shame.[9]

The Malay hikaya form also became a vehicle for retelling the lives of virtually all the other major prophets—Moses, Joseph, and Solomon most prominently—and a few minor ones as well. Some narratives derive from earlier Persian or Arabic works, but much material also comes from less identifiable folkloric sources that often account for a distinctively local coloration. A further extension of the genre in Southeast Asia has made it a vehicle for recalling the exemplary lives of Muhammad's Companions, the first generation of Muslim notables, and of his family, whose stories are especially important to Shi'i Muslims. A miraculous atmosphere suffuses most of these tales, and the stories go far beyond the details of Qur'an and Hadith in their embellishment.[10]

In addition to the individual stories of prophets, Muslim hagiographers have produced some important works on the lives of Friends of God, those often colorful characters whose personalities and teachings have attracted numerous disciples both while and after they lived. Among Islam's mystics, a number of historically important persons have been the subjects of longer works dedicated to a single personality, among them, Abu 'l-Hasan ad-Daylami's sira of the mystic Ibn Khafif (d. 982); a biography of his spiritual descendant, Abu Ishaq al-Kazaruni (966–c. 1033), who founded a community of Sufis; and a hagiography devoted to Abu Sa'id ibn Abi 'l-Khayr (967–1049).

Ibn Khafif's disciple Daylami (d. c. 1000) produced a life of his master from Shiraz, Iran, in Arabic. The work was later translated into Persian and revised substantially by Ibn Junayd in the early fourteenth century. Founder of a famous Sufi residence (*ribat*) in Shiraz, Ibn Khafif was a true ascetic, for whom asceticism (*zuhd*) meant "distancing the heart from riches and the hand from goods. True asceticism consists in indifference to the world and finding peace in setting it aside."[11] His biography offers a model of stringent self-discipline and denial of even legitimate pleasures. Rigorous fasting was one of his hallmarks; even so, he is said to have lived well past ninety. Ibn Khafif's life story, therefore, like that of most famous Sufis, offers a paradigm for a relatively narrow segment of society. The aspects of his life, and those of other Friends of God and mystics, that ultimately offer the most important kinds of inspiration are the attitudes that lie beneath the actions. Complete trust in God was one of Ibn Khafif's most basic values, a value that Islamic tradition recommends to all believers.

Abu Ishaq al-Kazaruni was one of Ibn Khafif's more famous disciples. His life story was set down in 1327, nearly three centuries after the death of its subject, and is among the older large-scale Sufi biographies. Over five hundred pages in a modern edition, it is also one of the more complete works of its kind. *The Paradise of Spiritual Guidance in the Secrets of Eternity* (*Firdaws al-murshidiya fi asrar as-samadiya*) is divided into five books with varying numbers of chapters. The first book surveys the shaykh's life span, from birth to death, giving special attention to his education and travels, his personal habits and qualities. In the second the biographer considers Kazaruni's more elevated characteristics, such as his wondrous deeds (*karamat*), including an excursus on various aspects and degrees of sainthood and attendant marvels. An analysis-anthology of the shaykh's characteristic modes of teaching—through such devices as anecdotes, allusions, advice, question-and-answer sessions, and the use of poetry—makes up the third book. An account of Kazaruni's testament and a discussion of his treatment of selected tenets of Islamic belief conclude the work.

Two key features of Kazaruni's ethical legacy are his zeal for the spread and defense of Islam against outside forces and his deep concern for the poor. He was a sort of chaplain to the warriors who did battle on the frontier with Byzantium during the late tenth and early eleventh centuries. He made perhaps his greatest contribution in founding the first of many residential and social institutions called *khanqahs.* Numerous others were founded by Kazaruni's disciples, spreading his practical social concerns across Iran and into Turkey.[12]

One recently translated biography is the story of one of Kazaruni's contemporaries, Abu Sa'id ibn Abi 'l-Khayr, entitled *The Secrets of God's Mystical Oneness* (*Asrar at-tawhid*). Though the tone of this late twelfth-century work differs from those of the biographies described above, it follows an organizational pattern similar to that of Kazaruni's sira. It begins with an account of the shaykh's early life and studies. Most of the hagiography of Abu Sa'id consists of stories of the mystic's wonderworking and teaching, along with some of his poems, prayers, and letters. The final section treats Abu Sa'id's testament and death.

The author, Muhammad ibn-i Munawwar, was a grandson of the shaykh. He depicts his colorful, footloose subject as a hero for all who have suffered the heavy hand of an authoritarian Islamic officialdom. Abu Sa'id was anything but a stern ascetic, although in his youth he had been known to go to extremes. For example, for seven years after his parents' deaths he ate only twigs and brambles in the desert. Another story tells how for seven years Abu Sa'id did not cease to repeat the name of God, night and day, so that at last every cell in his body began to call that name. His reputation for saintliness grew to such a point that people once walked behind his donkey to collect its dung, so that they might avail themselves of at least that indirect contact with the saint. He moderated his more austere tendencies considerably as he grew older; in fact, the change suggested by anecdotes about his middle years is so dramatic that he hardly seems the same man.

Ibn-i Munawwar reveals an important reason for composing a work on his grandfather. After reminding his reader of the crucial role of prophets in the divine communication, he explains the lofty didactic and inspirational merits of the lives of the next echelon in sanctity, Friends of God. He suggests that even God would find it impractical to send prophets in every age, but that the uninterrupted presence of Friends of God is entirely feasible. These "possessors of miraculous powers and masters of the mystic stations" are sent

> so that by means of their spiritual states, their sayings, what they do and what they refrain from doing, they may turn men at large from the world of appearance to the world of higher meaning. Thus, men will realize that beyond this world of forms is another world for which man has been created, that man is in this world to gather provisions for the journey to the other world and to prepare . . . for . . . arrival there and, that even if

man cannot attain to the rank of the spiritual angels, he may achieve elevation above the rank of beasts and animals.[13]

The author explains that while the shaykh ("may God illumine his final resting place") lived, and even for a while after his death, enough followers knew his teachings by heart to render a written account unnecessary. The passage of time and of those who knew the teacher personally, as well as invaders' wholesale destruction of his town and memorabilia, convinced the author of the need to preserve the shaykh's exemplary tradition. Ibn-i Munawwar continues his reflection on the purpose of the work:

> Indeed, it is known and confirmed that as time marches forward, men's aspirations are increasingly beset with faults. The traveler on the mystic path becomes more scarce, religious science is no longer available to everyone, and pious actions are as rare as the philosopher's stone. Yet, in no less wise do the words of that outstanding man of religion, unique in his age, give delight to the ears of the true believers and provide pleasure for the hearts and souls of those who aspire to follow the mystic path.[14]

At this point the author's focus has begun to move from the broader function of inspiration of the wider public toward the more specialized spiritual instruction meant for a more select group. But Ibn-i Munawwar does not want the broader public to dismiss the subject of his work as beyond their reach. Acknowledging that the goal of advanced spiritual development probably eludes the grasp of most ordinary folk, he nevertheless maintains that all persons are capable of a desire for growth. The grace to move on will almost certainly follow that desire, and that is what counts ultimately. To support his view, Ibn-i Munawwar then quotes with a touch of wry wit the apparently proverbial saying, "Though I can't afford to buy the sugar heap, / In any case I'll shoo away the flies." The belief that divine mercy descends when one recalls individuals of great devotion makes reading sacred biography a significant religious act.[15]

Collected Lives

Two types of literature have treated the stories of a number of prophets and holy persons in succession, thus producing anthologies of heroic sanctity. The first comprise a genre called stories of the prophets; the second, the collective hagiography, amounts to something closer to a biographical dictionary.

Books entitled *Stories of the Prophets* (*Qisas al-anbiya'*) include most notably the Arabic works of Tha'labi (d. 1036), Tarafi of Cordova (977–1062), and Kisa'i (c. 1200); a Persian work of Ibn Khalaf of Nishapur (eleventh century); and books by various Turkish authors from the early fifteenth century on. Numerous other works composed largely in imitation of earlier ones have appeared in virtually every major Islamic society. The pioneers of the genre include vignettes of as many as several dozen prophetic figures, meant to provide a sweeping view of divine providence since creation. Their material belongs to the larger category of religious folklore, the treasure trove of storytellers all over the Middle East for millennia. (See Fig. 14.)

Tha'labi's work tends to follow the style of tafsir, and the material is arranged in a way more suited to a sourcebook for storytellers and popular preachers than for public or private reading. Tha'labi quotes the Qur'anic verse "All of the accounts of the messengers we have narrated to you [Muhammad] that We might strengthen your heart with them" (11:120). Among the five wisdoms hidden in the stories of former prophets, he lists an important ethical benefit. To everyone from Muhammad himself to the humblest person, stories like these issue a summons and challenge to moral betterment. Tha'labi regards the stories of the prophets' lives chiefly as vehicles for teaching about God. Kisa'i sees a similar value in the tales, observing in the prologue, God charged his creatures "with no more than they could endure and burdened them with no more than they could bear; and He urged them to discern and taught them by example, that they might know that God is capable of everything and that God's knowledge encompasses all things."[16]

These works are not merely classical writings now found only in rare-book collections. Individual and collected lives of prophets (and to a lesser degree also of Friends of God) enjoy continuing popularity among Muslims all over the world. Bookstalls on the streets of Cairo still offer copies of Tha'labi's *Stories of the Prophets*.[17] Contemporary writers still find a market for retellings of the old stories. The contents of one recent book, entitled *Prophets of God (Anbiya' Allah)*, by the Egyptian author Ahmad Bahjat, comprises the classic catalogue of prophets: Adam, Nuh (Noah), Hud, Salih, Ibrahim (Abraham), Lut (Lot), Isma'il (Ishmael), Ishaq (Isaac), Ya'qub (Jacob), Shu'ayb (sometimes associated with the biblical Jethro), Yusuf (Joseph), Ilyas (Elijah), Idris (possibly the biblical Enoch), Ayyub (Job), Yunus (Jonah), Musa (Moses), Harun (Aaron), Khidr (Khizr), Dawud (David), Sulayman (Solomon), 'Uzayr (Ezra), Zakariya (Zacharia), Yahya (John the Baptist), 'Isa (Jesus), and Muhammad. Among his sources Bahjat lists a number of the classic works mentioned earlier (including Tha'labi), along with several modern works, such as Husayn Haykal's famous *Life of Muhammad (Hayat Muhammad)*. Bahjat acknowledges that many books on the subject have been written but says that what is new in his work is the mode of communication, the point of view, and a unique feel for the meaning of each story, tending toward Sufi sensibilities.[18]

Not only in the Arabic-speaking Middle East but wherever Muslims live, these stories have been and remain important vehicles of religious education and edification. Modern parallels to classical hikaya are available everywhere in Southeast Asia, for example. There, too, one can find comic-book versions of the lives of such notables as 'Abd al-Qadir al-Jilani. Lives of the prophets are increasingly popular among Muslims in the Americas as well, from Toronto to Tucson, from Boston to Barbados. A cursory glance through the catalogues distributed by mosque bookshops and other vendors of Islamic materials reveals a full selection of readings, from pamphlets to hefty tomes and multivolume sets.

Early in Islamic history, religious scholars developed a literary form whose purpose was to provide a ready reference to the personal credentials of many hundreds of individual Muslims, the collective hagiography or biographical dictionary. The new genre responded to the need to assess the veracity of those responsible for transmitting Hadith from generation to generation. If any individual named in the chain of transmission (*isnad*) of a hadith was known to be less than credible for any reason, the hadith was deemed less than authentic. Implications of this science of Hadith criticism for jurisprudence are enormous. The legal concerns that gave rise to these works of the science of men (*'ilm ar-rijal*, understood as "individual persons," most of whom were indeed males) have their rough analogy and counterparts in the realm of spirituality.

The genre called *tabaqat* shares the basic form of the biographical dictionaries originally devised to verify the trustworthiness of transmitters. The term originally meant "classes" or "categories," but came to mean "generations." Ibn Sa'd's (c. 784–845) sketches of individuals among the first two generations of Muslims is one of the first of its type. The tabaqat developed along with the growth of new spiritual circles and fraternities. Unlike the earlier dictionaries, the tabaqat not only verified an individual's trustworthiness but also traced spiritual lineages and offered edifying anecdotes. Under the pens of seekers and adepts, the form became a vehicle for recording both the spiritual genealogies and the wondrous deeds of holy persons, mystics, founders of orders and their dynasties. Abu 'Abd ar-Rahman as-Sulami's (d. 1021) *Generations of the Sufis* (*Tabaqat as-Sufiya*), devoted mostly to the sayings of famous Sufis, was later expanded and translated into Persian by 'Abdallah Ansari of Herat. Sulami applied Ibn Sa'd's method to the Sufis by associating each individual whose life he recounts with the transmission of one hadith, thus situating the Sufis among the ranks of the pillars of the faith.[19]

Variations on the genre are called remembrances (*tadhkira*) and exploits (*manaqib,* also "miracles or wondrous deeds"). They share to some extent the earlier works' concern for mystical lineage but place greater emphasis on the power of their stories to edify and inspire. Sometimes their organizing principle is either a single geographical area or a particular religious confraternity. Farid ad-Din 'Attar's (d. 1220) Persian *Remembrances of the Friends of God (Tadhkirat al-awliya')* developed the form to a fine art.

'Attar based his prose work on Abu Nu'aym al-Isfahani's (d. 1037) ten-volume *Ornament of the Friends of God (Hilyat al-awliya')*. 'Attar's candid preface lists his wide-ranging motives in composing the book, some purely self-interested: he hopes the work might afford him a measure of lasting fame, and that the saints might rain down their blessings on him and intercede for him before God. Then 'Attar enumerates the benefits of contemplating holy lives. Even people incapable of incorporating fully into their lives the advice of the Friends of God can benefit from a certain increased spiritual fervor and diminished self-centeredness. Exemplary lives can strengthen readers' resolve, persuade them that God's mercy is not beyond their reach, and encourage them to keep the next life ever before their eyes.

Most of all, 'Attar envisions his book as a way of keeping a candle burning in an age spiritually dark and devoid of salutary example. He concludes with the kind of endorsement of his book that all authors dream of eliciting from their reviewers, but 'Attar is praising the inherent excellence of his subject matter rather than his own skill as an author: "One may say that there does not exist in all creation a better book than this, for their [i.e., the Friends of Gods'] words are a commentary on the Qur'an and Traditions, which are the best of all words. Any one who reads it properly will perceive what passion must have been in the souls of those individuals to bring forth such deeds and words as they have done and said."[20]

From south Asia come a number of important works of the genre, especially from the fourteenth century on, written mostly in Persian and Urdu. Mir Khwurd (d. 1368), a Sufi of the Chishti order, provides in his *Biographies of the Friends of God (Siyar al-awliya')* an interpretation of the lives and sayings of early Chishtis, especially of Nizam ad-Din Awliya'. Mir Khwurd was determined to avoid giving undue attention to the shaykh's miracles, thereby maintaining an air of nonsensationalist objectivity. He apparently found one story impossible to resist, however. It seems that a flying camel would stop by the shaykh's room every evening, take him to Mecca where he could perform his devotions at the Ka'ba, and bring him home in time for breakfast.[21]

Noting that such Sufi hagiographical collections often served as tools to legitimate political regimes, Ernst describes the continued popularity of the literary form through the Mughal dynasty and into the twentieth century. He writes of the more recent Urdu works, "These modern works preserve many of the features of medieval imperial historiography in their exaltation of the kings buried in Khuldabad [a Sufi necropolis in central India], and they add to it both the element of hagiographic legend and the modern concern with Sufi saints as missionaries of Islam."[22]

The biographical segments of Ibn 'Arabi's thirteenth-century work *The Spirit of Holiness in the Counseling of the Soul* (*Ruh al-quds fi munashahat an-nafs*) and *The Precious Pearl* (*Ad-Durrat al-fakhira*) are of a slightly different temperament. That Iberian-born author recounts stories of individuals who had profoundly influenced his own spiritual development during his thirty years in what is now Spain. Part 1 of *The Spirit of Holiness* describes Ibn 'Arabi's profound disappointment at the degenerating condition of Sufism; and as a counterbalance, he offers sketches of fifty-five Sufis he has known who still embody appropriate values and demeanor. The second work (whose full title runs *The Precious Pearl Concerned with the Mention of Those from Whom I Have Derived Benefit in the Way of the Hereafter*) in its present form represents a synopsis of an originally much fuller account of 42 biographies, 26 of which also appear in *The Spirit of Holiness*.

Four of Ibn 'Arabi's subjects are women. Nuna Fatima bint ibn al-Muthanna lived in Seville, and she merits a significant mention in both of these biographical anthologies. Ibn 'Arabi says that although she was ninety when he first met her, the two struck up an important relationship. The biographer describes the following sequence of events toward the end of her life:

> Although God offered to her His kingdom, she refused, saying, "You are all, all else is inauspicious for me." Her devotion to God was profound. Looking at her in a purely superficial way one might have thought she was a simpleton, to which she would have replied that he who knows not his Lord is the real simpleton. She was indeed a mercy to the world.
>
> Once, on the night of the Festival, Abu 'Amir, the muezzin, struck her with his whip in the mosque. She gave him a look and left the place feeling very angry with him. In the morning she heard him calling to prayer and

said, "O my Lord, do not rebuke me that I was affected by one who calls Your Name in the darkness of night while other men sleep, for it is my Beloved who is mentioned on his lips. O God, do not censure him because of my feelings against him."

The next morning the jurists of the locality went, after the Festival prayer, to convey their respects to the Sultan. This muezzin, full of worldly aspiration, went in with them. When the Sultan enquired who the fellow might be, he was told it was only the muezzin. Then the Sultan asked who had allowed him to come in with the jurists and ordered him to be thrown out, which he was. However, after someone pleaded with the Sultan for him he was let off, although the Sultan had intended to punish him. Fatima heard about this incident and said, "I know about it, and if I had not prayed for leniency for him he would have been executed." Her spiritual influence was very great indeed. After this she died.[23]

The Turkish writer Shams ad-Din Aflaki's (d. 1356) *Wonders of the Mystics* (*Manaqib al-'arifin*) provides a good example of a hagiographical work dedicated to the key members of a single tariqa, the Mevlevi. Numerous short episodes in the lives of Rumi, his family and his followers make up Aflaki's work. He began writing in 1318–1319, almost half a century after Rumi's death, and completed it in 1353–1354. Typical of its marvels is a short section on Rumi's experience of intimacy with God when he was only seven years old. Every morning the boy used to recite Sura 108 of the Qur'an: "Indeed We have granted you great abundance. Therefore turn to your Lord (in prayer) and offer ritual sacrifice. Whoever despises you has no future hope." The words would bring tears to the boy's eyes. Then one day God promised to appear to Rumi visibly, at which the boy fainted. As he returned to his senses, he heard a voice informing him that he had been brought beyond the stage of struggle with his lower self and elevated to mystical vision. At that Rumi promised to dedicate himself to God all his days "in the firm hope that they who followed him would also attain to that high grade of favour and excellence."[24] Rumi remains an important Friend of God whose life story has offered inspiration to countless Muslims over the centuries.

WISDOM LITERATURE

The stories of the exemplary models are a less direct form of moral guidance than that offered by the ethical challenge of two types of wisdom literature. This literature has long been a significant element in virtually every major religious tradition. I use the term *wisdom literature* to refer to texts that reflect specifically on what it is to be human, focusing on appropriate conduct as defined by a particular religious tradition. These texts can take the form either of short, memorable proverbial sayings or fuller treatises in prose or poetry or combinations thereof. In Jewish tradition, wisdom literature is generally associated with such books of the Bible as Proverbs, Wisdom, Ecclesiastes, and Job, and in particular with King Solomon. Muslims consider their own scripture as the source of wisdom as well; but as a genre Islamic wisdom literature is mostly nonscriptural. Islamic sapiential materials span a broad range, from lengthy works that address the duties of rulers of the Muslim community to shorter and more colorful essays in popular religious morality. A literary genre important in various Muslim societies, the mirror for princes is an example of the practical application of ethical norms in the craggy realm of politics and public life.

Pointers for the Powerful

The mirror for princes takes the notion of ideal behavior and applies it within a political context. In these mirrors, moral advice is based on a model of exemplary conduct that holds those in positions of public authority and responsibility to a high standard. The genre provides a transition between edifying biographies of holy persons and the wisdom literature that recommends a certain moral code to the wider public. Many famous and influential Muslim authors have been willing to expose themselves to the rough and tumble world of public service. Though they may have considered themselves first of all seekers after the deepest religious truths, and were never directly involved in political office, they acknowledged their responsibilities as citizens and took the risk of posing the challenge of Islamic spiritual values to the high and mighty.

Authors of the stature and influence of Ghazali, for example, created in these works an image of the model sovereign, the just ruler. In some cases these works draw parallels between prophetic and kingly authority, always noting, of course, the crucial differences between kings and prophets. For example, whereas God provides a prophet power in the form of evidentiary miracles, the king's power derives from God-given intelligence and justice. Oppression of the people and exploitation of the powerless is a sure sign of a sovereign's lack of political and religious legitimacy.[25] These works were "intended to edify and they pointed society to an ideal—the ideal, it is true, predominantly of the official classes. In part, their works were also a protest against the evils of contemporary society and its failure to reach that ideal. Mirrors thus, in some measure, aimed at the remedy of contemporary political evils."[26] Mirrors for princes offer us, in short, a glimpse of an Islamic spirituality of political action.

As a genre, the mirror for princes developed in Arabic early in the Islamic era and belongs to an even more ancient Middle Eastern literary type. As Persia became more and more prominent in the fortunes of the central Islamic world, political theorists, philosophers, and theologians writing in Persian contributed significantly to the growth of the genre.[27] Sometimes in separate treatises and sometimes in segments of larger works, the authors counsel their rulers about responsibility; about the harsh realities of government that may cause the sovereign to do violence or to lie; and about resisting the temptation to imagine that life's ultimate purpose resides in the exercise of temporal power rather than in seeking life hereafter. They recommend the essential virtues of intelligence, knowledge, fear of God, and the capacity to inspire awe. A sovereign must avoid, on the other hand, impetuosity, weariness, and inappropriate familiarity with women. But the overriding theme is the exercise of justice.

A small sample of the advice these works offer the sovereign is found in the *Treatise on Government* (*Siyasatnama*) of Nizam al-Mulk (d. 1092), the chief *wazir* (minister) of the Saljuqid sultan of Baghdad.[28] The author asserts confidently that "[n]o king or emperor can afford not to possess and know this book, especially in these days, for the more he reads it, the more he will be enlightened upon spiritual and temporal matters." Nizam wrote in the hopes of reforming rule in the Saljuqid realm. As the following selection, from a chapter entitled "On recognizing the extent of God's grace towards kings," suggests, the Saljuqids had established the political office of sultan to parallel the seriously weakened office of caliph, which was now relegated to matters of religious leadership:

> Of a certainty the Master of the World (i.e., the Sultan) should know that on that great day he will be asked to answer for all of God's creatures who are under his command, and if he tries to transfer (his responsibility) to someone else he will not be listened to. Since this is so, it behooves the king not to leave this important matter to anyone else [e.g., the caliph.—Ed.] and not to disregard the state of God's creatures. To the best of his ability, let him ever acquaint himself, secretly and openly, with their conditions; let him protect them from cruel tyrants, so that the blessings resulting from those actions may come about in the time of his rule, if Allah wills.[29]

Nizam's most famous protégé, Ghazali, also wrote a book of advice for rulers. His *Counsel for Kings* (*Nasihat al-muluk*) was first written in Persian and later translated into Arabic. Its theological context sets it apart from others of the genre. Ghazali emphasizes that only a sovereign who has assimilated the most profound spiritual values can rule justly. Here the author shows his partiality to the ideals of Sufism, recommending serious discipline in prayer and fasting. Ghazali is also practical but without a trace of cynicism; he therefore recommends just rule as essential to a monarch's enlightened self-interest:

> May God grant to His Majesty . . . a clear eye, whereby he may see this world and the next as they (really) are, and so take pains in matters appertaining to the next world and in this world treat mankind well; for a thousand or more of God's creatures are his subjects. If he governs them justly, they will all be intercessors for him at the Resurrection, and he will be secure against rebuke and punishment; but if he governs them unjustly, they will all be his adversaries, and the position of one who has so many adversaries will be very, indeed terribly, dangerous. When intercessors become adversaries, the case is hard.[30]

His first wish for the ruler recalls a hadith in which Muhammad asks God, "Show me things as they really are." This saying is not found in the standard collections but has enjoyed great popularity among Sufis.

Ghazali's entire work is salted with aphorisms and anecdotes. One chapter is devoted to reporting the aphorisms of the sages, including those attributed to pre-Islamic figures as well as to prophets and Friends of God. They frequently take the form of question and formulaic, easy-to-remember answer. Someone once asked the pious Malik Dinar whether there was anything for which human beings would unhesitatingly give their lives. He replied, "Three things are dearer than life: religion, spite, and relief from hardship."[31]

A mid-twelfth century anonymous Persian work called *The Sea of Precious Virtues* (*Bahr al-fawa'id*) offers an interesting variation on the theme, for it belongs to "neither the administrative nor the philosophical current of mirror literature, but to what might be called the homiletical tradition." Unlike the other mirrors mentioned, which draw from a broad range of cultural antecedents, this one uses nearly all Islamic sources. According to the book's translator, Julie S. Meisami, it "paints a vivid picture of its times as seen from the viewpoint of a group little represented in mirror literature: the pious, orthodox class, possessing a religious rather than a secular education, and putting values enjoined by the Shari'ah [revealed Islamic law] and its sources above humanistic or philosophical considerations."[32] This work is a composite of several other genres; it includes maxims and biographical sketches as well as extended sections on how to observe various Islamic rituals. Many of the author's examples come from anecdotes about famous Sufis, but the focus is on values related to the Greater Jihad (against the lower self) rather than on lofty mystical qualities. For example, the young prince might do well to reflect on this tale attributed to the Sufi Ma'ruf Karkhi (d. 815):

> A prophet complained of poverty several times and lamented. God sent him a revelation: "How long will you lament and weep; are you not thankful that I have saved you from unbelief? Were you an unbeliever, though the whole world were yours, what would be your state tomorrow? I did not give you a prophet's robes so that you might worry about your daily bread. If (kings) seized world dominion from their friends, for the sake of friendship, I would never have given a drink of water to an unbeliever in this world. This world is worth neither the recompense of the believer nor the punishment of the unbeliever."[33]

In a more direct vein, the author recommends that a good king must observe ten rules, all of which he bolsters with reference to Qur'an and Hadith. A sovereign must pray and read scripture each morning; make at least a small gift to charity; resolve to do some good, as though each day were his last; deal directly with his Muslim subjects however humble, and treat them with kindness, always striving to make them content; do and command justice for salvation's sake; take regular counsel with the religious scholars; and see that his staff acts fairly.[34] *The Sea of Precious Virtues* is a gold mine of information about the place of religious values in the medieval Islamic Middle East.[35]

Morals for the Masses

An expansive array of more popular literary works are related to the mirror for princes genre in that they spell out the behavioral and ethical implications of the exemplary conduct described earlier in this chapter. Popular wisdom literature parts company with the mirrors, however, in that in general its message is intended for a much wider public and represents a spirituality for the laity. The content and method of these texts is distinct from those ethical treatises of a more technical philosophical or theological nature, such as Nasir ad-Din Tusi's (d. 1274) *Nasirean Ethics* (*Akhlaq-i Nasiri*).[36] Wisdom literature, as defined here, includes two principal genres, aphorisms and composite forms that integrate prose and poetry.

Before discussing several examples of the fully developed forms, I set the phenomenon of Islamic wisdom literature in its broadest possible context. To that end, I return to the origins of the Islamic understanding of wisdom as found in the Qur'an and Hadith. Dimitri Gutas cites a saying of Muhammad's to the effect that no person "can devote himself to the worship of

God for forty days without the springs of maxims [*hikam*] arising out of his heart and overwhelming his tongue." He notes further the apparently ancient associations among wisdom (*hikma*) as knowledge enacted (i.e., practical, concrete learning), legal judgment (*hukm*), and the notion of ethical admonition as embodied in maxims (hikam). Subsequent uses of the term *hikma* in medieval Arabic sources suggest further development in its connotations of guidance for appropriate behavior; of a quality requisite in all truly educated persons and bureaucrats, and perhaps all the more desirable in the ruling class; and of general moral exhortation.[37]

Though works of this sort may seem secular in tone when contrasted with the literature discussed in earlier chapters, their importance and influence in the wider scheme of Islamic spirituality is considerable. Most of the material I have included in this category comprise two distinct genres. The first is the pithiest of all teaching devices, the aphorism, a memorable saying of some famous teacher. These quotable one-liners are similar to proverbs, except that an aphorism is usually associated with a named source, whereas proverbs are typically anonymous. As for their origins, Gutas observes that "the unit of revelation is predominantly the short, eloquent verse, aesthetically pleasing and easily remembered and reproduced, and having distinct formal affinities with wisdom literature. Hadith literature also derives naturally from this conceptual framework; the *hadiths*, without *isnad* originally, are the wisdom sayings of the Prophet."[38]

Aphorisms from Muslim shaykhs have come down to us principally through two literary channels. Some survive only among the miscellaneous sayings gathered by the authors of manuals or compendiums; in a few instances, these represent all that remains of the patrimony of a given shaykh. Others live on in lovingly edited collections of utterances attributed to a single teacher. The Indian Shaykh Baba Farid's (c. 1174–1265) five hundred aphorisms, assembled by Mir Khwurd, provide a good example of the type:

> Do not regard the ignorant as among the living.
> Avoid the ignorant who pose as though they were wise.
> Do not utter a truth which resembles a lie.
> Do not sell what people do not wish to buy.
> Do not make a statement based on supposition.
> Treat a calamity as the consequence of greed.
> Be grateful but do not compel others to be grateful to you.
> Seek a pretext to perform a good work.
> Always keep the doors of peace open in war.
> Fear the man who fears you.
> Do not forget religion in the company of state dignitaries.

Consider the dervish who seeks riches as covetous.
Annihilate the enemy by discussion and captivate the heart of friends
 by hospitality.
Acquire knowledge through humility.
If you wish to make the whole world your enemy, be arrogant.
Protect religion through knowledge.[39]

Chapter 7 investigates another aspect of the wise aphorism, for the form has also functioned both for less practical purposes and at a higher level intellectually and spiritually. Gnomic utterances also called hikam, more complex in content and often composed in rhymed prose or poetry, are an important source for knowledge of more subtle interpretations of mystical experience.

The second genre is the sapiential work that combines prose and poetry, anecdote and moralizing reflection. It is represented prominently by Sa'di of Shiraz's *Rose Garden* and Abd ar-Rahman Jami's (d. 1492) emulative *Abode of Spring (Baharistan)*. These works are distinct from didactic or mystical/romantic epics, partly because of major formal differences, and partly because they function at different levels of pedagogy. In Persian literary tradition this genre is called *andarz* (precept or instruction), some of which shows the passage of material from the mirror for princes genre into more popular form.[40]

Sa'di arranged his *Rose Garden* in eight chapters, each treating a more or less discrete topic. He integrates short poetic compositions of his own with anecdotes (hikaya) that exemplify either a particular aspect of society or some ethical or religious principle. His chapters treat the manners of kings; the behavior of dervishes; the excellence of contentment; the advantages of silence; love and youth; weakness and old age; the results of education; and the conduct of one's social life. The last chapter consists almost entirely of aphoristic maxims.

Sa'di does not punctuate the maxims with the narrative sections so characteristic of his earlier chapters, but he includes many already proverbial sayings from Arabic and Persian tradition. When he quotes an Arabic proverb, he usually gives the original and follows it with a Persian translation or paraphrase. Sometimes the wisdom derives directly from a prophet:

Moses, peace be upon him, advised Qarun [the rebellious Israelite who trusted only in his massive wealth], "Do good as God has done good to you." He heeded not, and you have heard of his recompense [the earth swallowed him and all his gold].

Sa'di follows up with the moral:

That person who does not collect the gold and silver coins of goodness, ends up worth no more than dinars and dirhams. If you wish to enjoy this world and the next, be generous to people as God has been generous to you.[41]

Sa'di's chief works were written for a broad segment of literate society. As a result, the headings of his chapters are similar to the progression of stations and states the Sufi teaching manuals use to describe and evaluate spiritual progress. Sa'di is the shaykh of an educated populace, offering a spirituality for the laity, so to speak, whereas the more technical works of spiritual instruction offer guidance for those with more specialized needs.

Some two centuries later, the poet Jami wrote an imitation of Sa'di's work built around the nine rose gardens that constitute the *Abode of Spring*. Jami observes that "justice without religion is better for the order of the universe than the tyranny of a pious prince." But the best rule of all is that of a just believer. He tells the story of how the second caliph, 'Umar, heard a complaint from a Jew that the governer of the Iraqi city of Basra refused to pay him a debt. Since the Jew had no paper at hand, 'Umar wrote a note to the governor on a fragment of pottery: "Those who complain of you are many; those who speak well of you are few: beware of giving rise to complaints— or else quit the throne of power." After he had signed the note, the caliph sent the plaintiff off to Basra. Upon reading the note 'Umar had signed, the governor immediately did homage to the Jew and paid his debt. Jami then quotes a wry proverb about the exercise of power, "When the lion loses tooth and claw, he must suffer the blows of limping foxes."[42]

ENCOUNTERING THE EXEMPLARS

Books have long been powerful tools for exhorting people to strive for lofty ideals, but mass literacy is a relatively recent development in most of the world. Over the centuries the vast majority of Muslims have learned their tradition's values without reading. What they have learned first from their families has been reinforced by listening to people with a gift for bringing the past to life, and by looking at the vivid renditions of Islam's models, fashioned by artists both popular and sophisticated.

Storytelling as Entertainment

In the ancient arts of stylized, recitative storytelling, as well as in the more elaborate musical narrative forms, exemplary figures continue to come alive for communities of Muslims all over the world.

In chapter 2, I situate the role of the professional storyteller in the context of popular preaching and exhortation. In *The Book of Professional Story-tellers*, Ibn al-Jawzi describes the important role storytellers have played in Muslim societies. Any group that exercises such influence can, he admits, fall prey to various problems. Ibn al-Jawzi deals with those difficulties head-on in an attempt to make it clear that, for all their human failings, story-tellers perform an essential service.

He lists six reasons why earlier generations of Muslims had criticized and hated storytellers. Muslims, he notes, have traditionally been careful not to introduce practices not sanctioned by the Prophet himself. Early Muslims even questioned the writing down of the Qur'an, because Muhammad had not done so. Another reason is that many popular stories about the peoples of old, especially those about the children of Israel, were often unreliable—in contrast to the total authenticity of the Qur'anic revelation. For example, stories of how David deliberately contrived to have the husband of Bathsheba killed or of how the prophet Joseph let himself be seduced by Zulaykha are manifestly untrue because no prophet would have acted thus. More impor-tantly, such stories are dangerous, for they persuade people that if a prophet sinned that way, perhaps they should not be concerned about their own fail-ings. Ibn al-Jawzi sums up the remaining reasons:

> The fourth reason is that there were stories in the Qur'an and exhortations among the traditions of the Prophet which rendered superfluous stories whose authenticity was not certain. The fifth reason is that some people who introduced into religion that which did not belong there told stories. Furthermore, they inserted into their stories elements which corrupted the minds of the masses. The sixth and final reason is that the majority of *qussas* did not search out what was true, nor were they on their guard against error by reason of the meagerness of their knowledge and their lack of fear of God. And so, therefore, those who despised these excesses came to despise storytelling. However, when the learned man gave exhortation, and those who knew the difference between what was authentic and what was corrupt narrated stories, there was no loathing.[43]

In other words, Ibn al-Jawzi is convinced that the benefits of the storyteller's art outweigh the dangers, assuming that the storyteller is a person of in-tegrity, and that listeners exercise good judgment as they absorb the tales. The principal virtue for the professional storyteller is sincerity: one must always practice what one preaches. One must not succumb to the lure of popularity and put on airs as a result of this important vocation and the gifts that support it. Storytellers must remain ever conscious of their origins among the people. Their task is to keep alive in the minds and hearts of a broad public the words and deeds of Islam's religious heroes, for the power of example in ethical formation is enormous.[44]

Visual Arts as Education

Pictures created to illustrate a live story performance have a long history in various cultures across the Islamic world. They have taken the form of scrolls or posters big enough for a small crowd to see but small enough to be portable, and have been used extensively in Iran.[45] From a functional perspective these images form a bridge between narrative as public entertainment and reading stories for personal enjoyment and edification. I make a distinction between folk and popular arts on the one hand, and the more elite arts on the other; and I use the term *folk art* to characterize artifacts produced by individuals not formally schooled in their art, usually constructed of basic natural materials and often of unpolished execution, such as the domestic pilgrimage murals described earlier. Popular arts, objects of broad appeal and accessibility, are often produced by highly skilled individuals rigorously schooled in an artistic medium. These works include the murals painted on structures used for the ta'ziya ritual.[46]

Multimedia presentations are hardly a modern invention. Muslim storytellers have often used visual aids, notwithstanding the widespread impression—even among Muslims—that Islamic tradition forbids images of human beings. An excellent example of a tradition of popular art still alive especially in the Arab Middle East and North Africa is that of under-glass painting. Themes for most of these paintings come from the vast repertoire of heroic lore and epic saga that has continued to form the kernel of much popular storytelling the world over. Most of the characters are folk heroes, such as 'Antar, Abu Zayd al-Hilali, 'Abdallah ibn Ja'far, and such famous female counterparts as 'Abla and Yamina. Many paintings in this genre, however, come from stories of religious figures, including Muhammad; 'Ali and his two sons, Hasan and Husayn; and the widely popular Friend of God 'Abd al-Qadir al-Jilani. Among these works, three types are distinct: images of religious heroes; representations of some attribute or character intimately connected with the personage's story; and symbolic, nonrepresentational images, sometimes utilizing calligraphic designs, that are associated with a particular religious figure.

Pictures of 'Ali engaged in combat against the demon of woeful countenance known as Ra's al-Ghul are among the most prominent North African examples of the first type. Here Muhammad's son-in-law displays the essential trait of the religious hero, willingness to engage the forces of evil and injustice. 'Ali usually dispatches the demon with a stroke of his forked sword, Dhu 'l-Faqar (the cleaver), which he inherited from Muhammad. The sword provides a natural iconographic clue to the hero's identity.

Images of 'Ali and his sons, Hasan and Husayn, have been particularly significant for Shi'i Muslims; but they have received special attention also within the Sunni community in various regions. North African tradition, particularly in Tunisia, regards 'Ali as a high exemplar for youth. He was "the first adolescent to have embraced the new religion without ever having previously bowed to any idol or worshipped a deity other than God."[47] 'Ali is moreover the father of two sons who model ideal behavior for young people. Before they were martyrs, Hasan and Husayn were children of a heroic father. And as youthful martyrs, the two embody innocence and purity standing firm in the face of evil. On lacquered mirrors and boxes from Iran, as well as on under-glass paintings from further west, the trio often appear seated frontally, with 'Ali in the middle holding his sword across his lap.

The renowned Friend of God 'Abd al-Qadir al-Jilani also appears in under-glass paintings. A favorite episode depicts the hero taming a wild lion. More than mere fable, the scene speaks to its viewers of the power (baraka) of a holy person over brute force. In addition, and perhaps more important, the victory of the Friend of God over the lion models the crucial theme of the Greater Jihad, the struggle against one's own baser tendencies and passions. The lower self, or *nafs*, is sometimes likened to a wild beast.[48]

In the second category stylized and abstract representations of objects or beings are often associated with some religious hero's story. All over the Islamic world one finds pictures of Buraq, the winged human-faced quadruped upon which Muhammad made his Night Journey from Mecca to Jerusalem and his Ascension from Jerusalem through the seven heavens and the netherworld. The image itself recalls the story of the Prophet's wondrous adventure; but it often functions also as a protective device. Such talismanic functions are often difficult to separate neatly from those of devotional ritual and spiritual edification.

The term *pictograph* has been used to describe some of the objects in the third category, because it uses calligraphy to outline an animal or plant. For example, calligraphic texts referring to 'Ali as "Our Master, the victorious Lion of God" are molded, like wire-frame images, into the shape of a lion. Such calligraphic forms appear in media other than under-glass painting all over the Islamic world.[49]

Abstract symbolic designs intimately associated with the Prophet are related to pictographs. Actual images of Muhammad do not appear in the under-glass paintings, but one fascinating symbol of the Prophet's life and presence has maintained some popularity: the image of his sandals, and that image is in turn associated with footprints. Sometimes occurring in under-glass painting and in other media, such as manuscript painting, the sandals function both as talismanic devices and as reminders of the whole of the Prophet's exemplary life story. The Arabic word *sira* (used earlier to refer to Muhammad's earliest literary biography) derives from a root whose literal meaning is "progress or journey," a notion the image of a sandal or a footprint readily recalls. Many mosques and shrines, especially in south Asia, claim to possess footprints of Muhammad.[50]

Another genre of popular imagery occurs in the form of revolutionary poster art. The most prominent examples thus far studied as a group come from Iran during the Khomeini era (especially through the 1970s). Some emulate the style of classic Persian miniatures but are blown up to a size suitable for posting on walls in public places. The posters draw their fundamental themes from Qur'anic and postscriptural stories of the prophets such as those discussed earlier in this chapter. These visual productions clearly serve a predominantly political purpose, but they use evocative religious imagery to bolster their claims to political legitimacy and to undermine that of the incumbent regime—in this instance, that of Muhammad Riza Shah Pahlavi.

Many of the posters juxtapose images of Ayatollah Khomeini with images of a deposed shah in such a way that the Iranian Muslim viewer cannot escape certain scriptural associations. For example, Khomeini is a modern-day Moses; the shah, a new Pharaoh. The staff of the new Moses has become a fire-breathing dragon about to scorch and devour the godless monarch. Although visual materials of this genre do not inspire in the same way that, for example, biographies of prophets and holy persons do, they nevertheless belong on a continuum with those life stories. Both provide vivid examples of the conviction that a provident God has sent spiritual models and exemplary leaders in timely fashion throughout history. The posters depict Iran's recent revolution "as an Iranian and Islamic event, and its context is Iranian history in its sweep from the legendary past to today. It is taking place in a God-centered society in which the rules are divinely given and men are governed by a regent of God."[51]

Finally, a type of calendar art popular especially in south Asia recalls the exemplary role of prophets and Friends of God in two ways. Some actually depict the holy persons, either individually or in groups—sometimes gathering in a single image personalities from far-separated times and places.

Others suggest the ongoing presence of these paradigmatic figures indirectly by showing pictures of the holy sites associated with them. (See Fig. 15.)

The media and forms change at a different level of artistic production and patronage, but there is a great deal of functional continuity. In this category one encounters a wide range of illustrated manuscripts, objects that are both expensive to produce and of limited availability. Many of the kinds of texts discussed earlier in this chapter have inspired patrons and painters to create marvelous visual accompaniment, but the purpose of the images is not always easy to determine. One aspect of their function is fairly clear from the outset. Images in expensive books enhance and beautify the written text; they are not substitutes for it. Pictures produced in glass or on murals, or even to a great extent as poster art, do not presuppose a written text at all. They speak for themselves through symbolism or recall a whole story with a set of powerful associations or illustrate a dramatic performance. Although the theme of an image may be obviously religious, its function is not necessarily sacred. Furthermore, an important difference exists between the function of devotion and that of inspiration and edification. The life story of Muhammad and other works dedicated entirely to the stories of exemplary figures may be illustrated; however, mirrors for princes are illustrated very rarely, if ever.

One of the most extraordinary illustrated manuscripts produced anywhere by a Muslim is the sixteenth-century Turkish *Life of the Prophet* (*Siyar-i nabi*). The six-volume version of the fourteenth-century text includes over eight hundred illustrations, most of which depict a veiled Muhammad entirely surrounded in a flaming nimbus. Its story begins with the signs and portents attending the announcement and expectation of Muhammad's birth, and proceeds visually through dozens of events in his life. Scores of fabulous occurrences, in which Muhammad engages beings from does to dragons, punctuate the narrative of historically verifiable events in the life of the early Muslim community. Made for a royal patron, these images are meant to beautify an already magnificent work of calligraphy and to entertain. But the pictures just as clearly communicate a dimension of a spiritual tradition that sees its loftiest values embodied in an exemplary person. The miniatures, far more than mere ornamentation, offer clues to the feeling their painters and patron had for their subject: a sense of awe and wonder when Muhammad mediates extraordinary happenings, of tension when the Prophet and his community are in peril, and of deep sadness and loss when Muhammad and his family die and grieve.[52]

One cycle of stories from Muhammad's life has received special attention in an early fifteenth-century manuscript of the *Book of the Ascension*

Figure 15. Indian calendar poster (1994) showing five pilgrimage sites: the Ka'ba; Muhammad's tomb; the tomb of Mu'in ad-Din Chishti, founder of the Chishti Sufi order, Ajmer, India; the holy places of Jerusalem—the Dome of the Rock and the Mosque of al-Aqsa; and the tomb of 'Abd al-Qadir al-Jilani, Baghdad. The Arabic text above is the shahada, and below are the names "Allah" and "Muhammad." Courtesy of Carl Ernst.

(*Mi'rajnama*), from Herat (in what is now Afghanistan). Approximately four dozen charming miniatures show Muhammad, face unveiled and wearing his emblematic green robe, moving through the various key moments in the experience of Night Journey and Ascension. In Jerusalem he accepts the invitation of the various prophets assembled at the al-Aqsa Mosque to lead them in prayer. As he makes his way through the various strata of heaven, he meets each prophet in his assigned level. He witnesses in amazement such wondrous phenomena as the cosmic rooster, the ultimate arbiter of the timely call to prayer, a creature so huge that its feet protrude beyond the bottom edge of the miniature's frame. The images of the torments of the damned in hell are exceedingly vivid; lovers of European painting may find them reminiscent of works by Hieronymus Bosch. As for the influence of the stories themselves, one scholar has theorized that their imagery is so similar to that of Dante's *Divine Comedy* that one can hardly resist

Figure 16.   Mid-sixteenth-century Iranian painting of Adam and Eve being driven from Paradise on the dragon of deception and the peacock of pride, from *Fal nama*. Washington, D.C.: Vever Collection. Courtesy of the Arthur M. Sackler Gallery, Smithsonian Institution.

suggesting that the Islamic material may have fueled the fourteenth-century Italian's imagination.[53] (See Fig. 35.)

Many images of religious themes adorn the pages of various versions of the genre of stories of the prophets. Among the frequently depicted figures are Adam, Noah, Abraham, Moses, Joseph, Solomon, and Jonah. Adam usually appears with Eve, either as the two are expelled from the Garden (see Fig. 16) or arranged across the page with their progeny. Noah and the ark are often shown, and I know of no other scene in which Noah appears. Abra-

Figure 17.   Late sixteenth-century Turkish painting from a book of stories of the prophets, *Qisas al-anbiya'*, by Nishapuri, showing Jesus raising Lazarus. New York: The Metropolitan Museum of Art, Purchase, Francis M. Weld Gift.

ham's two most important scenes are his victory over the fire into which the evil king Nimrod threw him, and his preparation to sacrifice his son just as God intervenes by angelic messenger.

Moses plays a number of visual roles, occasionally from the episodes of his encounter with Pharaoh, but more often in peripheral scenes—encountering an infidel, berating a shepherd—whose ancient textual antecedents are difficult to trace. Joseph appears in perhaps more images than any other prophet. Solomon usually sits on his throne, often side by side with Bilqis, the queen of Sheba, but almost always surrounded by the jinn (creatures of smokeless fire) and by members of all the animal kingdoms, whose languages the king speaks. The fabled encounter with a whale provides virtually the only visual setting for Jonah. The Arabian prophet Salih, extruding a camel miraculously from a mountain, occasionally appears; David makes chain mail as his ravishing song (the Psalms) renders the iron soft to his touch; and Jesus is depicted as a child with Mary, or raising Lazarus. (See Fig. 17.)

In these first three chapters, a pattern has begun to emerge. What begins in oral form (Qur'an and Hadith, forms of prayer, stories) is soon written down for the sake of accuracy and preservation. Then over a period of perhaps centuries, a layer of commentary on the written sources (tafsir, manuals of prayer and ritual, elite literature on heroic figures) appears in order to reinterpret the tradition for changing circumstances. As the written commentary becomes more elaborate and less accessible to the average person, parallel forms of oral and visual commentary (popular preaching and the folk arts) continue to make the tradition available to a broader public. In the next several chapters a change is evident.

In later chapters I investigate aspects of Islamic spirituality that presuppose either greater knowledge of the subject or more refined grounding in the religious sciences, or both. First, although the written materials I examine in these chapters still often rest upon an oral substrate, an increasing proportion of them are conscious literary creations from the outset. These works were not written to preserve, protect, and propagate an older strand of tradition; more immediate concerns and different needs motivated their creators. Second, most of these materials, both literary and visual, were produced by and for a social or religious elite. The public to whom these works are addressed was small. I show how authors of these sources are increasingly sophisticated in the ways they read, interpret, and apply these earlier works that I have discussed in the first three chapters. I now turn to the aesthetic dimension of Islamic spirituality.

4   Aesthetics
From Allegory to Arabesque

Although various aesthetic aspects of the literary and visual sources of Islamic spirituality have already surfaced, an explicit consideration of the role of beauty in word, picture, and architecture is important for several reasons. It offers an opportunity to ask why certain modes of human communication are more effective than others in conveying religious values. In addition, an appreciation of aesthetic qualities facilitates a deeper understanding of the emotional dimensions of a spiritual tradition. Feeling, mood, and intensity are important but often neglected aspects of religious experience. Last, a study of the aesthetic aspects of Islam's textual and visual sources brings to the fore the roles of imagination and creativity in the communication of religious values.

Revelation and artistic inspiration go back a long way, but theirs has been an often tempestuous love-hate relationship. The Islamic tradition has drawn an exquisitely fine line between divine initiative and human effort, between genuine spiritual experience and simple self-deception, between verbal and visual imagery and the transcendent reality to which they allude. This study of religious aesthetics attempts to trace that line. In chapter 1, I introduce the classic distinctions between categorical and ambiguous Qur'anic texts, and between outward and inward meanings. Here those insights raise deeper questions of the relationships between form and meaning, between the hidden and the manifest.

The literature and art I explore in this chapter exhibit clear thematic, formal, and functional affinities with material treated in other chapters. But two additional elements essential to the creation of high quality arts—namely, deliberate artistic production and elite patronage—change the focus in a subtle but important way. The expense and effort required to pro-

Figure 18.   (*Opposite*) The crested hoopoe (middle right) addresses all the assembled birds about setting out on their journey to find the Simurgh; a painting illustrating the beginning of 'Attar's allegorical *Mantiq at-tayr*. The text was written in Herat in 1483 under Timurid patronage, but the illustration was added in the early seventeenth century under Safavid patronage. New York: The Metropolitan Museum of Art, Fletcher Fund.

duce or own many of the works treated here, or to do both, means that they have been created by and available to relatively narrow segments of society. Though highly refined poetry has enjoyed wide popularity in some cultures, often the highest-quality illustrated manuscripts have been within reach of only the wealthiest. Still, the more elite works form an important element in the story of Islamic religious life. In addition, Islamic spirituality has found expression in a wide range of popular and folk poetry that has often flourished alongside of the less accessible forms. Before turning to the principal poetic genres and the visual arts associated with them, I survey the origins and history of Islamic religious poetry.

LITERATURE AND SPIRITUALITY

In chapter 2, I introduce the Arabic term *adab*, where the phrase *adab al-minbar* means the "literature of the pulpit" and refers in a general way to the form and functions of religious discourse (khutba) in its various ritual contexts. But the term has a wider range of meanings. In this chapter *adab* denotes the whole spectrum of fine or artistic literary production, as distinct from the writings of jurists, theologians, historians, and geographers, for example. *Adab* in the present context therefore means literature as literature, and it includes a plethora of prose and poetic forms.

Three considerations have influenced my choice of textual sources. First, strictly speaking, not all poetry (*shi'r*) belongs to the category of adab. Some finely constructed and powerful poems have originated in spontaneous creative impulse; in many cases their creators probably did not intend that the fruits of their inspiration should eventually be written down. Some of this material is popular or folk poetry. Second, although adab encompasses prose as well as poetry, I consider poetry almost exclusively, with a nod in the direction of rhymed prose and several works that interweave poetry with prose. Third, I deal only with those types of adab that promise deeper insight into Islamic spirituality.[1]

Religious Poetry

Refined or elite literature has long been a significant part of Muslim cultures, though it did not enjoy pride of place during Muhammad's lifetime and those of first and second generation Muslims. Pre-Islamic poets exercised an important function in Arabian society, but the advent of Islam brought with it a reassessment of poetry's value. Muhammad's critics, the scripture records, dismissed the Prophet as a mere poet, scarcely worthy of credence beyond what one might accord any tribal bard, however eloquent. The Qur'an even seems to condemn outright the practice of poetry, as in this text: "Those who wander malevolently follow the poets. Do you not see how they loiter absentmindedly in every valley? How they say one thing and do another?" (26:224–26). The scripture makes a notable exception for three poets who turned their art to the defense of the new faith. But because the tone of the earliest poetry was often adversarial and polemical, it was employed "for special occasions."[2] Meanwhile, Muslims came to regard the Qur'an itself as the inimitable standard and epitome of literary eloquence.

Under the Umayyad dynasty (661–750), religious poetry flourished among nascent dissenting factions, such as the Shi'a and the secessionist Khawarij,[3] as a weapon against what was to become Sunni Islam. A dominant theme of mourning over martyrs suggests a religious development of the time-honored pre-Islamic opening scene of weeping over the campsite traces of departed friends. In the words of Imru' al-Qays, author of one of the famous seven odes known as the *Suspended Ones* (*Mu'allaqat*), "Let us stop and lament at the remembrance of the beloved and of our resting place, on the edge of the desert between Dakhul and Haumal." These odes evoke extraordinarily vivid images of nature; for example, in the *Mu'allaqa* of Labid, the speaker recalls:

> The tent marks in Minan are worn away,
>   where she encamped
> and where she alighted,
>   Ghawl and Rijam [place names] left to the wild,
>
>   And the torrent beds of Rayyan
>   naked tracings,
>   worn thin, like inscriptions
>   carved in flattened stones,
>
> Dung-stained ground
>   that tells the years passed
> since human presence, months of peace
>   gone by, and months of war,
>
>   Replenished by the rain stars
>   of spring, and struck
>   by thunderclap downpour, or steady,
>   fine-dropped, silken rains,
>
> From every kind of cloud
>   passing at night,
> darkening the morning,
>   or rumbling in peals across the evening sky.[4]

The great pre-Islamic poems represent the earliest polished examples of a poetic form called the *qasida,* usually translated as "ode." These mono-rhyming works are medium length, sometimes up to 120 lines, longer than the love lyric called the *ghazal* and shorter than narrative epic poetry. The classic genre begins with a section (*nasib*) in which the lover expresses a longing for the departed beloved, as in the *Mu'allaqa* of Labid. Then the poet describes the subject's quest and concludes with the lover boasting iron-ically of how he has succeeded in exiling her from his memory. Muslim po-ets transformed both the themes and the three-part structure of the qasida form, adapting the genre to specifically religious and mystical purposes. An-other important early theme, that of a "pristine Islamized Bedouin love that was far removed from the polluted urban sexuality," developed in poems and tales originally popular among the 'Udhra clan. Reminiscences of this Arab version of platonic love, recommended by a number of famous ascetics, are found in later lyric and romance poems.[5]

During the long tenure of the Abbasid caliphs (750–1258), new genres of religious poetry developed in Arabic while Persian grew into an impor-tant vehicle for some of the world's finest mystical verse. Early ninth-century themes of ascetical self-denial, personal discipline, and flight from the world soon yielded to more genuinely mystical sentiments. The Iraqi poet Rabi'a al-'Adawiya (d. 801) boldly explores the hitherto forbidden ter-ritory of reciprocal, though perhaps not precisely mutual, divine-human love. She prays,

> O God, the night has passed and the day has dawned. How I long to know
> if Thou has accepted my prayers or if Thou hast rejected them. Therefore
> console me for it is Thine to console this state of mine. Thou hast given me
> life and cared for me, and Thine is the glory. If Thou want to drive me from
> Thy door, yet would I not forsake it, for the love that I bear in my heart
> towards Thee.[6]

Following Rabi'a's lead, Arabic-speaking mystics developed new genres of poetry. Descriptive poems adapted a language formerly confined to ver-bal depictions of an outer world, to portraits of the seeker's inner cosmos and of the ideal lover. From this point, mystical verse grew in two very dif-ferent directions more or less simultaneously. First, more technical poems evolved as a means of refining the developing lexicon of terminology now needed to analyze mystical experience with greater precision. Full of arcane wordplay and subtle allusions, this genre was naturally available only to ini-tiates. Meanwhile, a genre of popular poetry in simpler and more attractive language made the intuitions of the mystics more accessible while inject-ing a new element of feeling into the religious expression of ordinary folk.

The martyred mystic Hallaj (d. 922) wrote some of the most famous of such verses; the sentiment is lofty, and he uses a somewhat technical vocabulary, but his language is relatively straightforward and simple.[7] In one poem, Hallaj addresses God:

> I saw my Lord with the eye of my heart, so I asked, Who are you? He said, You.
> And there is no "where" apart from you, and no "where" where you are.
> Imagination can conceive no image of you, so how can imagination know where you are?
> You are the One that encompasses every "where" on the way to "no where," so where are you?
> So in my passing away (fana') even my dying to self (fana') has vanished (fana'), and in my loss of self (fana') you are found.[8]

After reaching a high point during the early tenth century, Arabic mystical poetry declined in both quality and quantity until the thirteenth century when its literary and intellectual sophistication was revived. Poetry of the shorter lyric form known as the ghazal spoke intimately of the lover-beloved relationship. From the religious confraternities (tariqas), with their total dedication to pivotal founding figures, came poems that emphasize the affinity of the founder and his legitimate successors with the "light" of Muhammad. Two of the thirteenth century's most influential Arabic religious poets were the Egyptian Ibn al-Farid (d. 1235) and the Andalusian-born Ibn 'Arabi.[9]

Though Ibn 'Arabi is better known as an author of tightly woven, and often arcane, mystical treatises than as a poet, his collection of poems entitled *The Interpreter of Desires* (*Tarjuman al-ashwaq*) offers a fine example of an adaptation of classical language and themes for mystical purposes. Ibn 'Arabi appends to each poem a commentary on its esoteric meaning, to insure the reader's understanding. The poet-commentator refers to himself in the third person, much as the Iberian Christian mystic John of the Cross does when he glosses some of his own poetry. Recalling the tone of the pre-Islamic ode with an unmistakable allusion to Imru'al-Qays, Ibn 'Arabi writes:

> Halt at the abodes and weep over the ruins and ask the decayed habitations a question.
> "Where are the loved ones? Where are their camels gone?" (They answer), "Behold them traversing the vapour in the desert."

Ibn 'Arabi then comments that the poet is answering the voice of God that calls from his heart. The former abodes of the loved ones are the stations at which mystical journeyers pause in their quest; here the poet must weep, since he cannot remain in the company of those travelers. Their former resting places are "decayed" because those who once dwelt there are gone. Camels are the spiritual aspirations that bear the mystics away, and the vapors are the hints that entice the seeker to press on.[10]

Ibn 'Arabi further spiritualizes the classic imagery into a description of the soul's journey:

> My longing sought the Upland and my affliction the Lowland, so that I was between Najd and Tihama [Arabian place names].
> They are two contraries which cannot meet: hence my disunion will never be repaired.
> . . . .
> The camels, footsore from the journey, long for their homes and utter the plaintive cry of the frenzied lover.
> After they have gone my life is naught but annihilation. Farewell to it and to patience!

In the attached commentary Ibn 'Arabi explains that the Upland represents God enthroned. The two contraries represent the struggle between the physical and spiritual sides of humanity. And in a slight variation on his interpretation of the first text, the camels here are the noble thoughts that bear good words toward God's throne. Finally, Ibn 'Arabi, like Hallaj, refers to the passing away of his passing away.[11]

As Arabic spiritual poetry was nearing the apogee of its renaissance, Persian was already coming into its own as a vehicle of polished mystical expression at the eastern fringes of the Abbasid caliphate. Persian poets refined forms already in use: the distinctively Persian form known as rhymed couplets (*mathnawi*); the older Arabic qasida and ghazal; and the shortest of poetic genres, the quatrain (*ruba'iyat*). The major poets who wrote in Persian are Sana'i of Ghazna (in present-day Afghanistan, d. 1131), 'Attar, Rumi, and Jami.[12]

As Persian mystical poetry neared its zenith, poets in far-flung lands had begun to adapt to Islamic spiritual purposes the dozens of regional and local tongues of post-Abbasid Muslims. The most important of those vernacular languages came to be the various Turkic dialects of central Asia, along with several south Asian languages (such as Urdu, Sindhi, Bengali, Panjabi), as well as Malay and other Southeast Asian languages (especially of Indonesia, today by far the most populous Islamized nation on earth). In addition to importing and adapting forms originally developed in Arabic and Persian, these poets used distinctive local genres. The writing of mystical poetry in the vernacular languages was an important factor in the spread of Islamic religious concepts and terminology well beyond the Middle East.[13]

Metaphor

Muslim scholars early on began to debate the degree to which one may—or must—interpret as metaphors the numerous examples of anthropomorphic or other figurative speech in the Qur'an. Some argued that it is best simply not to ask questions at all about the scripture's references to God's face or hands, or any other attribute to which ordinary human experience provides the only analogy. They argued that God chose to describe the divine reality in these terms, and that it is not up to human beings to second-guess or speculate. Others insisted that since such anthropomorphic features clearly compromise God's transcendence, one has no choice but to understand them in a purely metaphorical way. Thus, the terms *face, hand,* and *throne* merely suggest the divine omnipresence, power, and sovereignty. Those who rejected speculation replied that in spite of the expressed concern for divine transcendence, this dalliance with metaphor runs the risk of infidelity to the sense of God's mystery. That was the beginning of a long and lively exchange of views about the uses of language as a vehicle for communicating the ineffable.[14]

According to an Arabic proverb, "Metaphor is a bridge to ultimate reality." Islam's various literary traditions, beginning with those of Arabic, Persian, and Turkish, and growing to include dozens of other languages, have developed an enormous range of metaphors with which to hint at the divine-human relationship. In the following kaleidoscopic overview, I allow images to blend into one another as if in a stream of consciousness, for that is indeed the feeling the reader often gets from the primary sources.

God and the human being are beloved and lover, a metaphor that in turn generates a whole complex of others. The nightingale cannot get enough of the beloved rose, but its thorns keep the lover at bay. Finding separation too cruel, the lover will nevertheless go to any lengths to elicit a response from the beloved—even if only an angry "Get away from my doorstep," even if only to have his or her head (polo ball) whacked downfield by the beloved's arrogantly raised eyebrow (polo stick).

The beloved is the flame into which the loving moth crashes and burns; that image in turn merges either with that of the raw beloved becoming cooked, or with that of the green fruit becoming ripe. God is the pilgrim's goal, and the journey, a mi'raj, an ascending alchemical transformation of base matter into precious metal. To arrive at one's true and original home, one must be willing to leave one's present secure dwelling, that is, to make a hijra after the example of Muhammad; that in turn transforms life into a *jihad*, a continual struggle for victory over one's inner tendencies to self-centeredness.

God is wine, and the lover cannot but become intoxicated; but the hapless drunk then becomes a pariah, scandalously preferring tavern to mosque. It is true that drunkenness blurts out stark realities that sobriety will not suffer; but sobriety's penchant for control and fear of ecstasy can leave one trapped in oneself. God is the ocean in which the seeker either willingly drowns or becomes a fish; but still the soul's fire blazes unquenched.

In garden and desert, palace and ruin, mountain and valley, the seeker goes from feast to fast, light to darkness, expansion to contraction, birth to death, annihilation to survival, and then back again. Behind the imagery lies a wealth of insight into the dynamic quality of religious experience, the subtle circular relationship between human longing and divine initiative or response, and the gradual unfolding of the kind of self-knowledge that leads to intimate knowledge of God.

Allegory

Stories of both historical figures and fictional characters form an integral part of Islam's spiritual heritage. Narratives of important persons, particularly Muhammad's, can educate and entertain. Beyond the paradigmatic purpose of narrative, however, lies the conscious elaboration of its more symbolic dimensions. Allegory explicitly links the various elements of a narrative to the elements of another order of meaning. For example, the parable of the sower in the Christian scriptures (Matt. 13:1–23, Mark 4:1–20, Luke 8:4–15) narrates the actions of a farmer at planting time. Some seed he sows falls on rocky ground; some falls by the wayside and is eaten by birds; some falls among the weeds that choke the seedlings; and some falls on good soil where it produces abundantly. The first part functions as a teaching story. But all three evangelists then explain why Jesus taught in parables and reveal the parable's allegorical meaning (allegoresis). The seed is the word of God; the rocky ground represents those who refuse to hear at all; the weeds are the cares of ordinary life that keep one from carrying out the demands of the word.

In the didactic mathnawi *The Garden of Ultimate Reality* (*Hadiqat al-haqiqa*), Sana'i of Ghazna tells the ancient and popular story of the blind men and the elephant. Then he adds an element of allegoresis. Once upon a time a king marched his vast retinue through a city of blind people. In the vanguard of his army strode a huge elephant. When the townspeople heard about the awesome beast, several went out to explore its immense form.

Each touched a different portion of the pachyderm and came away with an idea as to the nature of the beast. When they returned to the city, their fellow citizens excitedly asked for a description of the elephant. The man who had felt the elephant's ear described the beast as broad and rough like a carpet; he who had explored the trunk said the behemoth was a long hollow instrument of death; while the man who had touched the legs explained that the elephant was a straight pillar. Because no one had experienced the whole animal, none could make sense of it. Sana'i then draws from the story a lesson on the futility of speculation about the reality of God. Alluding caustically to the hapless interpretive squabbles of the early schools of theology, he observes:

> One talks of "the foot," the other of "the hand," pushing beyond all limits their foolish words; that other speaks of "fingers" and "change of place" and "descending," and of His coming as an incarnation. Another considers in his science His "settling himself" and "throne" and "couch," and in his folly speaks of "He sat" and "He reclined," making of his foolish fancy a bell to tie around his neck. "His face" says one; "His feet" another; and no one says to him, "Where is thy object?" From all this talk there comes altercation, and there results what happened in the case of the blind men and the elephant.[15]

Of course, just as a good comedian does not need to explain a punch line, an apt allegory rarely follows itself with footnotes about its various referents and levels of meaning. The reader usually has to look for less obvious indications as to the allegorical key to a story.

Allegory, both subtle and blatant, is an important feature of the literary communication of Islamic spirituality. Neat examples of allegory and allegoresis may be found, such as those just cited from the Gospels and Sana'i, but it is not so much a discrete literary form as a structural device and a way of thinking. Hence one finds strong traces of allegory in both prose and poetry, in mystical as well as in ethical and theological works, in Qur'anic exegesis as well as in fictional narrative.

As Peter Heath observes, allegory operates on two levels at once: "While its literal levels are intended to be comprehensible and attractive to a broad spectrum of readers, its symbolic levels direct restricted levels of meaning . . . to select groups or individuals. Thus aiming to be simultaneously democratic and elitist, the genre rests on an aesthetic contradiction."[16] Less complex forms such as fables and proverbs are generally employed in popular literature, but allegory more often serves the purposes of elite works. Allegory is meant, Heath suggests, to hold competing tensions in a harmonious balance in idealistic and sophisticated societies. It tends to increase in popularity when social conditions limit freedom of expression, and to recede as those conditions abate.

In Islamic thought, the Qur'an provides the key to allegory, in its distinction between verses that are clear and those that are ambiguous, and in its references to God as both the outward (*zahir*) and inward (*batin*). Allegory may be either compositional, a narrative with at least two levels of meaning, or interpretive, an exegesis of a narrative through the prism of some system of thought, whether or not the author of the narrative had any such point in mind. Hence, some narratives (like *Moby Dick*) may be interpreted allegorically, even though they are not technically allegories as such. In such a work, Heath explains, "narrative event, character development, and detail overshadow allegorical allusion . . . because [the work] lacks a readily identifiable and consistently foregrounded ideological program." In a true allegory, on the other hand the author places clearly before the reader a specific program that serves as a guide to the inner meaning of the story.[17]

PRINCIPAL POETIC FORMS

Although allegory as narrative structure often overlaps with poetic form, they are not synonymous. Islamic poetry has two formal and functional categories, didactic and lyric, whose form and thematic content are distinct. In general, lyric poems are shorter and more emotionally charged, focusing on the intricacies of an interpersonal relationship. Didactic poetry tends to use longer forms with more narrative elements and is often dispassionate in its treatment of themes.

Didactic Poetry

Didactic works differ from the inspirational works discussed in chapter 3, in that the teaching function remains diffuse and suggestive rather than direct and explicit. Poems of this type are often quite long. Although several forms may be said to perform a teaching function, I consider only the mathnawi genre. Major examples in Persian are works by Sana'i, 'Attar, Ilyas ibn Yusuf Nizami of Ganja (d. 1209), Rumi, and Jami. The term *mathnawi* means "couplets," and the form typically features half-lines, or hemistichs, whose endings rhyme with each other. A Persian invention, the mathnawi form originally served the needs of epic and historical narrative, most notably in the early eleventh-century Iranian paean to the nation's great heroes, Abu 'l-Qasim Firdawsi's (d. c. 1020) *Book of Kings* (*Shahnama*). Firdawsi set a standard emulated by many later poets commissioned to aggrandize warriors past or sovereigns present. Over the centuries important Turkish, Urdu, and Sindhi poets adapted the genre to different purposes, often borrowing thematic material as well as prosody, and putting their own stamp on it.

Religiously oriented mathnawis have three kinds of content: romantic, ethical, and mystical. Rumi's mystical work has a strong ethical dimension, and Nizami's romantic poems are full of mystical themes. Sana'i pioneered the use of rhyming couplets for didactic purposes in his *Garden of Ultimate Reality*. The tone of the classic religious mathnawis runs the gamut from the more explicitly spiritual (such as Sana'i, 'Attar, and Rumi) to the more subtly mystical (such as some of Nizami's).

Mathnawis are structured in various ways. Some organize material in a more or less continuous narrative, as in Jami's *Joseph and Zulaykha* (*Yusuf wa Zulaykha*) (see reprise). Some arrange diverse smaller forms, such as illustrative anecdotes and moralizing glosses, within a larger narrative framework, as in 'Attar's *Conference of the Birds* (*Mantiq at-tayr*), with its seven parts structured around the narrative of journey through seven valleys. 'Attar has his avian pilgrims traverse the various realms of inner spiritual experience, borrowing a metaphor from the traditional view of the external world as composed of seven regions or climes.

Nizami's *Seven Portraits* (*Haft paykar*) employs a similarly symbolic arrangement, but its structure suggests a more direct influence from astrology. The story follows King Bahram Gur from one wondrous pavilion to another, in each of which a princess from a different kingdom regales him with beguiling romantic tales, each on a different day of the week. Each palace's decorative scheme is dominated by one of the seven colors of a traditional artistic palette, and each is symbolically associated with one of the seven planets. Others, such as Rumi's *Spiritual Couplets* (*Mathnawi-yi ma'nawi*), seem to pursue a more spontaneous development, often not following an integral story line, but flowing from one topic to another and often doubling back in arabesque fashion.

One English translation of 'Attar's *Conference of the Birds* seeks to preserve the rhyming hemistichs of the mathnawi form. The setting is a gathering of all the world's birds and their deliberations as to whether and how to set out in search of their king, the Simurgh. (See Fig. 18.) A volunteer, the crested hoopoe, responds to the nightingale, who has just attempted to excuse himself from the arduous journey by saying he loves the rose far too deeply to risk separation from her:

> The hoopoe answered him: "Dear nightingale,
> This superficial love which makes you quail
> Is only for the outward show of things.
> Renounce delusion and prepare your wings
> For our great quest; sharp thorns defend the rose
> And beauty such as hers too quickly goes.
> True love will see such empty transience
> For what it is—a fleeting turbulence
> That fills your sleepless nights with grief and blame—
> Forget the rose's blush and blush for shame!
> Each spring she laughs, not *for* you, as you say,
> But *at* you—and has faded in a day."[18]

In these lines the hoopoe, which represents a kind of spiritual guide, counsels the nightingale about one way that the seeker can become distracted from the ultimate goal of life's quest.

Lyric Poetry

In the category of lyric poetry I include shorter, non-narrative forms that generally elicit a more intensely personal emotional response. Three principal lyric forms, whose chief subject is the lover-beloved relationship, are the qasida, the ghazal, and the ruba'iyat.[19]

Virtually all the great mystical poets employed the qasida form. Arab poets began early in the Islamic era to adopt the pre-Islamic genre as a vehicle for lavish praise of their royal patrons. Islamic panegyric largely borrows the formula of the pre-Islamic odes, highlighting the ruler's prowess and bravery in battle, along with his largesse, and adds some distinctively Islamic elements: "The ruler is not only just and resolute but the Guardian of the Faith and God's favorite, ruling by a special mandate from Him according to His dictates; the poet also sees to it that there are some Qur'anic allusions in his language."[20] The reader may decide whether or not the poet is merely laying a pious veneer over the "real" work of art to maintain an air of respectability.

Mystical poets gradually adapted the qasida form to praise God further, with elaborate reflections on the divine names and attributes. Each of the three structural segments of the early Arabic form has its unique tone and emphasis, offering the religious poet both a pattern to imitate and a challenge to meet in adapting and modifying the genre's purposes. The romantic prelude's (nasib) lamentation over the loss of longtime friends becomes a song of grief over distance from the divine beloved. This is allegorical thinking, even though the form does not utilize an allegorical organizing principle.

The second part of the classical qasida, the journey (*rahil* or *takhallus*, "disengagement") in search of the departed one, becomes an image of spiritual pilgrimage for example, to the Ka'ba of the heart. One discovers the poet's main motive in the ode's third section (*gharad*). In the classical form, the gharad can embrace any of at least seven themes, and occasionally it combines several of the following: love, description, praise, boasting, lampooning, panegyric, threnody, and wisdom saying.[21]

Recent studies have suggested that the tripartite structure of the classical Arabic ode reflects the three phases of the rite of passage, namely, separation, liminality and transformation, and return to community.[22] As adapted by mystics, the principal theme became some variation on the relationship of seeker to sought (God). Ibn al-Farid stands out as a master of the Arabic mystical ode; and Sana'i pioneered the qasida's adaptation into Persian.

Ibn al-Farid transforms the journey motif into that of pilgrimage to the Ka'ba, and then further spiritualizes the journey's goal into the ultimate Ka'ba, the divine beloved as paragon of beauty.[23] One of his most celebrated poems is the "Wine Ode" ("Al-Khamriya"). It develops the imagery of intoxication as a mystical theme, beginning with an allusion to the lament for the lost loved one. Ibn al-Farid refers to an eternally ancient wine that is divine love. An artifact called a drinking bowl gives Ibn al-Farid's visual imagery a material counterpart:

> In memory of the Beloved we quaffed a vintage that made us drunk before the creation of the vine.
> Its cup the full-moon; itself a sun which a new moon causes to circle. When it is mingled (with water), how many stars appear!
> But for its perfume, I should not have found the way to its taverns; and but for its resplendence, the imagination would not have pictured it.
> Time has deserved of it but a breath: it is unseen as a thing hidden in the bosom of the mind.

The poet then describes how the merest whiff of this vintage is enough to render even the casual passerby senseless. One whose palm is stained red by one drop of this wine will never lose the way, for the guiding star now shines from that hand. Many will fail to understand the one so intoxicated and may even condemn that person, but it matters little in the long view of life. For, Ibn al-Farid concludes:

> Joyless in this life is he that lives sober, and he that dies not drunk will miss the path of wisdom.

Let him weep for himself—he whose life is wasted without part or lot in wine![24]

Sana'i of Ghazna was an influential Persian religious poet, many of whose odes are best characterized as homiletical. They provide a link between poetry and liturgical and popular preaching, and underscore from a slightly different perspective the problem of aesthetic ambiguity discussed earlier in this chapter. Homiletic poetry supplies preachers with poetic imagery for illustrating their oratory. But the relationship between this type of poetry and religious oratory is complex. The hearer, steeped from childhood in the language and symbol systems of Islam, must decode the poetic allusions and translate them mentally into the religious concepts to which the allusion refers. For example, a passing allusion to some aspect of a prophet's story, such as the rod-dragon of Moses that God causes to devour Pharaoh's magicians, reminds the hearer of the whole of Moses' story with its emphasis on God's power and sovereignty (Q 7:100 ff.). A reference to Nimrod's fire recalls how God looks after Abraham even in the face of death (Q 21:60–70).

The homiletical qasida is characterized by more exhortation and less description than the standard classical ode. In one poem Sana'i outlines the spiritual journey. The seeker must move from ascetic control over self to awareness of the rose garden of realities beyond this world's mere appearances to the level of companionship in the mosque's rows with the great religious heroes wherein one becomes like a lover who abandons self entirely before the beloved's dwelling. The coded message in the second line of the quotation below is an allusion to a key episode in Abraham's life. According to Qur'an 6:76–79, God reveals his transcendence to Abraham by making the prophet understand that God is far beyond stars, moon, and sun—all of which eventually set. When Abraham accepts his own tendency to idolatry, he smashes the idols in the shop of his father, who makes a living by carving statues of them:

> Whatever you find, if it is not wickedness, it is religion: take it to your heart.
> Whatever you see, if it is not the Lord, it is an idol: smash it.
> When your heart and soul have become a leathern cloth under your feet,
>   dance upon it.
> When two forms of existence are united in your hands, try your hand.
> Rise through the rosegarden of searching truth; in the lane of religion
> You will see those who are living, though they have been killed, multitude
>   upon multitude.
> On one row you will see those wounded by a sword like Husain.
> On another row you will see those killed by a poison like Hasan.
> The pain of religion is in fact a pain full of tricks; you become like a candle:
> "When you fall ill, you only recover when they cut your throat."[25]

The poet then describes the parallel function of suffering in both religion and love. The imagery of the candle shedding tears of love as it burns has been a favorite of artists in bright metal as well as dark ink.

Another important adaptation of the qasida genre extols the exceptional qualities of the Prophet. During his lifetime, poets were already turning the classical genre's spotlight on Muhammad. Ka'b ibn Zuhayr (d. c. 630) wrote one of the earliest panegyrics of Muhammad; and Hassan ibn Thabit composed numerous verses that recount the Prophet's biography.[26]

After a hiatus of several centuries, the genre reemerged not long after the year 1000. It reached its peak, some critics believe, with Sharaf ad-Din Muhammad al-Busiri's "Mantle Poem" ("Burda") in the thirteenth century, one of many imitations of Ka'b ibn Zuhayr's poem of the same name. Launching the long ode with an adaptation of the nasib, nostalgic for happier days, Busiri (d. 1298) issues a warning against succumbing to desires of the flesh and then develops an elaborate description of Muhammad that has an epic flavor. Busiri's glowing encomium concludes with an autobiographical note:

> Him have I served by my panegyric, by which I ask pardon for
>   The faults of a life passed hitherto in poetry and serving [others].
> . . . .
> Whoever sells his future life for this transitory [world],
>   Will discover how he has been defrauded in the selling and the bargaining.
> Even though I commit a fault, yet unbroken is my covenant
>   With the Prophet, nor is my tie [with him thereby] cut.
> . . . .
> Far be it from him to disappoint one who hopes for his protection,
>   Or to let a client return from him unaided.
> Ever since I began to apply my thoughts to praising him,
>   I have found him the best of helpers towards my redemption.
> Riches from him never pass by a hand that is destitute,
>   Any more than the rain which makes flowers bloom on the hillocks.[27]

The poet insists that he writes out of sheer devotion rather than out of desire for the "flower of this world," that is, the hope of material gain that he suggests often motivates panegyrists.

Encomiums, or panegyric poems, can occur as part of a longer mathnawi as well as stand alone in the qasida or ghazal genres. Works praising the virtues of the Prophet are usually called na't (literally, "qualities, attributes"), a term that distinguishes works by content rather than by form. The distinction between panegyric (madih) and eulogy (ritha')—praise of the living and of the dead, respectively—does not apply in the case of the Prophet, since poets praised him with the same medium both while he lived and after he died. They did so because they thought of Muhammad as still alive spiritually even after his death.[28] Virtually every composer of religious mathnawis has included one or more na't sections as prologue to the work. Standard thematic elements include a recounting of the wonders of Muhammad's Ascension and an encomium of his heroic qualities. In illustrated manuscripts, painters often took the occasion to produce an image of Muhammad's mi'raj. (See Fig. 35.)

Among the shorter lyric forms several contribute significantly as sources of Islamic spirituality. The ghazal, often explained as deriving from the first segment of the qasida, the nasib, is the most important and widespread. The ghazal, roughly analogous to the English sonnet, is generally limited to fourteen or fewer monorhyming verses. Many Muslim poets have written ghazals in Arabic, Persian, Turkish, as well as in other languages; but perhaps none have been more popular or famous than Rumi and Hafiz of Shiraz (d. 1389).[29] In the following lines from Rumi's *Diwan*, the poet uses the imagery of wine, drunkenness, and the paraphernalia of the drinker, including the drinking bowl in the penultimate line, that recalls a favorite theme of Ibn al-Farid's. Rumi slides from one image to another, returning at the end to the metaphor with which he begins:

> Drunkards as a rule fall on one another, causing a great ruckus as they brawl.
> The lover is one up on the drunkard, for the lover keeps the same company.
>   Let me tell you what love is: falling into a goldmine.
> And what is that gold? [It makes t]he lover the Sultan of Sultans, safe from
>   death and beyond concern for a [mere] crown of gold.
> The dervish wears a cloak with a pearl in its pocket. What shame can door-to-
>   door begging bring?
> A drunken moon came along last night, letting his waist-garment slip to the
>   road, so tipsy that he did not notice his clothes had fallen.
> "O Heart," I said, "jump up and put wine in the soul's hand; the time has
>   come: it's time to scuffle;
> To consort with the orchard nightingale, with the parrot of the spirit to dive
>   into sugar." [Parrots love to eat sugar.]
> Bereft of the heart I've given away I have stumbled onto your road—and, by
>   God, I know no place else to fall.
> I broke your bowl, O my Adored, because I am drunk. Do not let me fall
>   drunk into danger from your hand.
> So now there is a new protocol and regimen [for drunkards to follow]:
>   breaking the drinking glass and picking a fight with the glassblower![30]

In content, feeling, and form this poem well represents the ghazal as adapted to mystical purposes.

The most compact form popularly employed by Muslim poets is the quatrain (ruba'iyat), composed of two distichs, with the first, second, and fourth hemistichs rhyming. Rumi composed several hundred of these short poems, and a number of others before and after him were equally gifted in the genre. The famous Sufi Awhad ad-Din Kirmani (d. 1237) communicates the intensity of his longing for God in these lines:

> Without the remembrance of you earthly life would be nothing,
>   without your love our hearts and souls nothing.
> If we miss one breath of your invocation (*dhikr*)
>   in the two worlds our reward would be nothing.
>
> From love of you passion enters every heart; without the remembrance
>   of you not a breath would rise from the soul.
> Do not sell me, do not pardon me, do not free me; though you have
>   countless slaves, you are my lord.
>
> Dawn again, and the thought of you opens me . . . then in every breath
>   your vision indwells my spirit.
> The odor of decay will never reach my soul
>   so long as your perfume is the wound of my senses.[31]

Quatrains like these serve as memorable condensations of intense feeling, each wrapped around a single sense-image cluster (such as odor/perfume) or mystical concept (such as dhikr, remembrance of the divine beloved).

Finally, an important poetic variant that developed far from the Middle East lends some geographical balance to this poetic map of the Islamic world. The Malay *syair* (from the Arabic *sha'ir*, "poet, one whose sensitivities are heightened"), a poetic form, played an important role in expressing a mystical side of Islamic spirituality as it developed in Southeast Asia. Using a quatrain structure with an a-a-a-a rhyme scheme (as distinct from the Persian quatrain a-a-b-a scheme), the syair is a medium length poem, created by stringing from ten to twenty (but most often thirteen to fifteen) quatrains together. The sixteenth-century Sumatran Hamza Fansuri crafted perhaps the earliest examples of the form as a vehicle for interpreting the mystical thought of Ibn 'Arabi. I locate the genre, as exemplified in Hamza's work, in the context of lyric poems because of its form, though one could argue that the tone and content of his verses qualifies them equally as didactic.

Of Hamza's thirty-two poems, a group of thirteen read like short exhortatory sermons, recalling in tone if not in form the homiletical odes of Sana'i. Hamza emphasizes the need to recite the Qur'an, for the scripture is the source of that salutary knowledge and wisdom that constitute union with God. His work is unusual and very important, even if not nearly as widely known as works by famous Persian and Arabic poets. Hamza provides a rare view of Muslim thought in Southeast Asia.

He begins one of his homiletical syair with a call to the community of

Muslims to seek out the mystical knowledge that Friends of God possess. Exemplified in the life of Muhammad, that knowledge leads to union with God. Hamza then uses two Qur'anic references as metaphors for mystical experience. The first, the confluence of the two seas, refers to the goal of Moses' journey in Sura 18, under the enigmatic guidance of a figure whom post-Qur'anic tradition came to identify as the prophet Khizr:

> He has mingled the two seas which meet
> Between which is a barrier which they do not overstep
> That here there is question of this knowledge
> Is evident to all knowers endowed with faith.
>
> These two seas are most amazing
> The barrier between them is constituted by the "light of the Beloved"
>   (*nur* [i.e., light of] *Muhammad*)
> As its outer meaning is all too obvious
> It is improbable in the opinion of the strangers (in this world).
>
> The words "the two seas" have a profound meaning
> They denote the meeting of God and the world
> That was the secret of the final Prophet
> Which sets the lovers aglow with an inextinguishable blaze.
>
> The two seas are shoreless
> Their waters are pure and very clear
> They are not situated in the eyes, the nose or the brows
> If you look for them there your head will spin.

Hamza's second scriptural allusion, to the "two bow-lengths," comes from the description in Sura 53:1–18 of Muhammad's mystical experience known as the Ascension. In that text, the expression "two bow-lengths off or nearer" appears to refer to the Prophet's encounter with the revealing angel. As with the reference to the two seas, Hamza also considers this allusion a figure of speech:

> The meaning of "two bow-lengths off or nearer" [Q 53:9]
> Is the meeting (of the servant) with the Lord most high
> The words "The heart did not falsify what it saw" [Q 53:11]
> Mean, "There was nothing but what it saw."
>
> "Two bow-lengths" is an allegorical term [*tamthil*]
> Of a lofty meaning and decisive weight
> The two seas referred to are of a supreme beauty
> Very few in number are those who are privileged to know them.[32]

Hamza was much influenced by the works of major Persian poets as well. One interesting theme is that of his recurrent allusions to 'Attar's *Confer-*

ence of the Birds. He speaks of the "naked bird," an image of the mystic freed of earthly attachments. Inebriated with the love of God, the yellow bird enjoys proximity to God's footstool. In a series of four poems, Hamza describes how the bird, of spiritual origin and mystical creed, begins at God's throne in the cage of God's house and journeys toward ultimate reality:

> Listen, oh [*sic*] stranger
> That bird is everyone of you
> You should gather this knowledge
> So that your being be exalted.[33]

The circumstances under which the works of these poets have survived vary. Some, like those of Rumi and Hafiz, have remained popular and accessible in modern editions. Others, like those of Hamza, have only been rediscovered recently by scholars, although the form of the syair has remained alive as a medium of oral expression in Southeast Asia.

This overview of poetic forms and functions yields two insights into the relationships between literature and Islamic spirituality. First, virtually all genres and themes of literature have become vehicles for the loftiest sentiments. Even the most secular forms, from drinking song to hunting poem to political praise to celebration of victory in battle, have served the religious imagination. Second, Muslim religious poetry testifies to the tenacity of the creative spirit. Over the centuries official religious, social, and other cultural pressures often demanded that Muslims repudiate modes of discourse that might threaten to compete with the divine revelation for the attention of the populace. Muslim poets have weathered many a storm. Notwithstanding the Qur'an's own evidently negative attitude to poetry, Muslims throughout the world have continued to use indigenous literary forms in writing Islamic poetry and to indigenize Islam through those forms.

ARABESQUE AND AESTHETICS

In *The Alchemy of Happiness* (*Kimiya-yi sa'adat*), Ghazali writes, "The beauty of a thing lies in the appearance of that perfection which is realizable and in accord with its nature. When all possible traits of perfection appear in an object, it represents the highest stage of beauty; when only part of them occur, it has that measure of beauty which appears in the realized degree of perfection."[34] Thus, Ghazali describes harmony, a quality Muslims have found in their arts on five levels: sensual, psychological, ethical, theological, and mystical. First, beautiful objects give pleasure to the senses. Second, formal linear harmony and the harmonious juxtaposition of color schemes can also satisfy psychological needs by supplying a sense of order and variety in the midst of what might otherwise seem a random and monotonous routine.

Third, Muslims have interpreted artistic harmony as a reflection of virtue. Only the pure of heart are capable of purity in artistic creation, and the harmony of the art can in subtle ways instill moral discipline in the viewer. Qadi Ahmad's sixteenth-century Persian treatise on calligraphers and painters, *Rose Garden of Art* (*Gulistan-i hunar*), cites two related proverbs: "The essence of writing is in the spirit" and "Excellent writing clears the eyes." He also quotes a saying that he attributes to Plato, "Writing is the geometry of the soul." The translator explains in the introduction that "[b]y maintaining that 'purity of writing is purity of soul,' . . . the medieval outlook made on the master calligrapher the same demands of asceticism as it did on members of the religious class."[35] Muslims have considered copying the Qur'an in exquisite calligraphy a devotional act worthy of spiritual merit.

Fourth, a combination of historical, mythical, and theological elements describe several Muslim views about the spiritual origins of the arts. Dust Muhammad, an older contemporary of Qadi Ahmad, wrote a treatise on painters. He reiterates there a long-standing Shi'i tradition that Muhammad's son-in-law 'Ali invented the first authentically sacred style of calligraphy. 'Ali thus bestowed on the Kufic script a religious legitimation by its association with a relative of the Prophet's.[36] Dust Muhammad also relates the tradition that the art of painting originated with the prophet Daniel.[37] Rumi provides further traditional lore about the myth of architecture's religious origins. He echoes ancient legends of how Abraham and his son Ishmael built the Ka'ba in Mecca, and of how Solomon constructed the Farther Mosque—the al-Aqsa—actually dating to the eighth century, at the southern end of the site of Solomon's Temple in Jerusalem.[38]

Tradition traces the origins of the arts—especially of calligraphy—all the way back to God, who wrote the celestial archetype of the Qur'an. Then, after fashioning the pen before any creature, God taught the Prophet "[b]y the Pen" (Q 68:1) what he had not known before.[39] According to Qadi Ahmad, creation itself is the divine calligraphy with which God "covered the pages of changing time with the black-and-white design of nights becoming days and days becoming nights." God, he continues, has "arranged the album of the revolving skies with the multi-colored pages of spring and autumn." Referring to God as the first painter, Qadi Ahmad justifies the art of painting as well as of writing. God created two kinds of pen: a vegetable type, the reed pen, and an animal type, the brush with its tip of hair.[40] Spiritual origins therefore account at least in part for the harmony of great religious art.

Finally, there is the mystical level. Carrying out the aesthetic implications of the classical distinction between outer and inner meanings, many Islamic writers have suggested that a work of art is always more than it appears. Ghazali writes that children and animals can experience form, but only the eye of the heart can perceive "inward form."[41] All things reflect divine beauty, says Rumi, for every visible form originates in the unseen world. God is Beauty itself, and from the "mine of loveliness" in which God dwells, "filings of beauty" fall into the possession of all creation.[42] Ibn al-Farid said that true pilgrims journey not to the physical Kaʻba at Mecca but toward the Kaʻba of Splendor that is God.[43] Rumi calls himself a painter whose images melt away in the presence of the divine beloved. God is the calligrapher who writes with the pen of the human heart. Every beautiful face is like a flawlessly executed copy of the Qur'an.[44]

Rumi comes as close as any classic Muslim author to describing a spiritual aesthetic when he says that no painter, no potter, no calligrapher creates a work of art for the sake of the work itself. One must regard all created form as a vehicle for appreciating the unseen beauty of the divine. The art historian A. Papadopoulo calls this point of view an "aesthetic of ambiguity," for the work does not coerce the viewer into attaching any one spiritual meaning to the form. The aesthetic of ambiguity suggests that the viewer cannot always say for certain which painters, for example, intended their scenes of lovers in a paradisal garden to be taken as visions of heavenly reality, and which wanted the viewer to see merely an earthly picnic.[45]

Unfortunately, relatively few Muslim artists have left their own explanations about how they viewed the spiritual or symbolic dimensions of their arts. When such documents do turn up, they are more fascinating for their rarity. One such work is the seventeenth-century *Manners of Practice* (*Adab al-mashq*) of Baba Shah Isfahani. The author delves into the technical aspects of the craft, to be sure; but his overall concern is with the deeper reach of the art. As a result, Baba Shah adds the invaluable perspective of a practitioner. He speaks of the requisite mastery of principles and of purity of intention, but then he begins to slide into the realm of mystical contemplation: "heedless of the pleasures of the world, he [the calligrapher] turns his heart toward practice, and the luminous sparks of the real beloved's beauty appear in his vision."

Quoting a verse of poetry about seeing the beloved's face everywhere, Baba Shah notes that when the calligrapher writes, "he reddens that paper with the bloody tears from the extremity of his love for that letter." He then describes three stages in the artist's development. Moving from the visual practice of studying a master's work to the pen practice of attempting to emulate the exemplar, the calligrapher advances to imaginative practice. Here the contemplation of God's beauty begins to suffuse the activity with life; no longer is the writing a mimetic craft but a spontaneous and genuine art.[46]

Visual Symbolism

Opinions on how best to interpret the essential Islamic message of visual arts vary widely, from an almost total denial of any symbolic content to a penchant for discerning symbols in the slightest curlicue and variation in color. Ironically, theories at both ends of the spectrum purport to derive their theological aesthetic from the same principle, namely, tawhid—the acknowledgment and assertion of God's uncompromised unity and transcendence. Each approach has both strengths and weaknesses, and each highlights important aspects of Islamic spirituality.

The minimalist approach argues that Islam's art, from architecture to miniature paintings to calligraphy, communicates not through literal or explicit symbolism, but only through implicit symbolism. I use a Byzantine icon as an illustration since it may be interpreted according to any of these three types of symbolism, and therefore exemplifies the two kinds of symbolism the minimalist view says Islamic art lacks. At the level of literal symbolism, the image communicates through specific iconographic clues, such as certain physical attributes or implements. For example, John the Baptist appears dressed in rough garments and is thus identifiable as an ascetic. He is also accompanied by a lamb. If the icon's symbolism is understood literally, the viewer might take John for a shepherd. But the lamb also operates at the level of explicit symbolism; Christian viewers already know that the lamb is an explicit referent for Jesus, the sacrificial Lamb of God. An icon can communicate through implicit symbolism as well. It can convey a sense of mystery through its use of nonrational colors, as in the case of a golden firmament, suggesting an otherworldly setting. The use of a strictly frontal view of figures, the intense and unbroken gaze, the lack of shadow, the sense of evenly suffused light as though the image were illuminated from within itself or from behind—all are what Lois Ibsen al-Faruqi calls implicit symbolism—symbolic content conveyed by means of indirect and subtle suggestion rather than a one-to-one correspondence between visual and nonvisual referent.

In Faruqi's minimalist view of Islamic symbolism, Islamic art communicates *only* through implicit symbolism. It does so out of the utmost care to avoid compromising God's unity and transcendence by even the slightest hint that any one visual form can fully portray any divine quality or attribute. Islamic art intimates, suggests, and, at most, alludes to transcendence, infinity, power, and majesty by its use of variations of vegetal and geometric arabesque, an infinitely repeatable pattern. Because the central realities so elude direct human apprehension as to be nonrepresentable, no visual creation can presume to point directly to them. Therefore, shapes, colors, or architectural features such as the dome or the niche have no explicit external referents. The dome is not a symbol of the firmament, nor is the niche in the back wall of the mosque a symbol of divine light, for example. Instead, all products of artistic creativity manifest such fundamental characteristics of arabesque as abstraction, modular composition, repetition, intricacy, dynamism, and successive combination—all of which imply or hint at the divine attributes of unity and transcendence.[47]

According to Faruqi, the qualities of arabesque pervade all visual forms and media. Even the human and animal forms found in miniature painting are variations on this theme. Faruqi suggests that Muslim miniature painters have never intended to portray the created world but rather meant to hint at the divine reality indirectly. Her conclusion is based on these features: multipoint (rather than single-point) conceptual (what one can "see" mentally all at once, rather than perceptual: what one would actually see) perspective; use of suffused light that results in lack of shadow and thus in a lack of any perception of mass in bodies or architectural shapes; and the denaturalization of human and animal forms (bodies without volume, for example).[48]

While the minimalist approach to symbolism has the merit of consistency and coherence, it presumes that all of Islamic art has been produced under the uniformly powerful influence of theological principles and does not take sufficient account of the presence of other factors. It tends, in other words, to be ahistorical and to force the issue of arabesque as the guiding principle, especially in its attempts to explain the figural art of miniature paintings.

At the other end of the spectrum are the maximalist theories founded on the pervasive influence of universal symbolic forms or archetypes, all ultimately to be taken as manifestations of the divine unity. Nader Ardalan's *The Sense of Unity: The Sufi Tradition in Persian Architecture*, Titus Burckhardt's *Art of Islam: Language and Meaning*, and S. H. Nasr's *Islamic Art and Spirituality* discuss the symbolic sensibilities that permeate Islamic cultures and the subtle influences that play a part in artistic creativity.[49] Their desire to view the arts as organic developments of a religious culture add an important perspective to the understanding of aesthetic questions.

Variations on the ancient theory of correspondences among cosmic realms or levels, along with shades of the Neoplatonic distinction between form and reality, characterize this approach. Ardalan, Burckhardt, and Nasr interpret shapes partly with reference to the theory of traditional geometries in which primal forms in the visible universe correspond with ideal forms in the uncreated realm. Hence, for example, the square represents earth; the circle, heaven; the cross (a quincunx composed of four points and center), the five elements (including ether); and so forth. When one interprets the meaning of an architectural composition, horizontal shapes must of course be taken together with their vertical counterparts. A ground plan may reveal shapes that suggest a mandala, but a mandala is fully significant only when understood as three dimensional.[50]

Faruqi classifies such an archetypal reading of shapes and forms as a theory of explicit symbolism. Where Ardalan sees symbolic shapes, Faruqi sees merely evidence of abstraction and modular composition. The maximalist view has the advantage of attempting to reconstruct an organic, all-encompassing cultural and intellectual context for the arts. That context functions in the maximalist position somewhat the way the religious or theological matrix serves the minimalist position. But, like the minimalist view, the maximalist also has serious limitations. This intensely idealistic approach presumes that the artist lives in and re-creates a seamless, perfect world, like that of the Neoplatonic forms. For that reason among others, the maximalist view is attractive and thought provoking; but it does not quite describe the ordinary experience of Muslim artists as religiously committed human beings living on terra firma. Both views are useful in that they seek to explain their subject from within, as it were, by discerning eternal principles at work within the heart of the artist and the soul of a global culture. But one also needs to account for many other factors that have come to bear on artists and cultures from without, while also taking seriously the relationships between creativity and experience, and accounting for the sheer physical reality of the work of art.

One of the most original and thought-provoking ventures into the enchanted forest of interpretations of Islamic art and its symbolism (or lack thereof) is Oleg Grabar's *Mediation of Ornament*. This work stands more or less in between the omni-symbolic view of the maximalists' and the minimalist view of Faruqi's. Grabar identifies, within the "visual order" that he calls ornament, a number of "visual characteristics as frequent enough to be typical of Islamic art." He defines *ornament* as an aspect of the broader category of decoration; it is "that aspect of decoration which appears not to have another purpose but to enhance its carrier."[51] One perceives in ornament attributes of several kinds: iconophoric, which has relatively clear and widely accepted referents (e.g., the hand suggesting the five members of

Muhammad's family in Shiʻi iconography); formal, consisting of color, shape, texture, but with no clear referent; expressive, as in the emotional tone of Michelangelo's *Pieta* or Caravaggio's *Deposition;* and optisemic (having to do with perceiving signs or phenomena as broad categories), including themes recognizable apart from any further iconophoric, formal, or expressive meaning (e.g., a human-headed quadruped that Islamic tradition then identifies as Muhammad's mount, Buraq).[52]

Grabar sees in Islamic ornament's abstraction and repetitiveness no inherent symbolism. Ornament mediates experience through calligraphy, nature (also called vegetal or floral motifs), geometry, and architecture. Grabar does not discern explicit symbolism in calligraphy, for example. He does, however, find a curious "ideological significance" in the contrast between the "visual brilliance but comparative senselessness" of an arresting tenth-century "blue Qurʾan" and the "absolute clarity and legibility" of the early eleventh-century Qurʾan attributed to the legendary master of calligraphy Ibn al-Bawwab. Grabar observes that "[i]t is in the realm of the minority and esoterically inclined world of the Fatimids and of Shiʻism in general that the blue Korans were executed, whereas the centers of the Sunni revival with its emphasis on the literalness and clarity of the divine message were the ones that fostered the new kind of precise writing."[53]

On the other hand, Grabar does not see in either mysticism or the Qurʾanic impulse sufficient cause for the development of Islamic calligraphy. Rather, the "true reasons must be sought much more profoundly within the fabric of classical Muslim life than within the mechanisms of the Revelation or of esoteric interpretations."[54] As he searches for the elements underlying the works of art, Grabar is momentarily tempted by the essentialist interpretations of both the maximalists and minimalists. His identification of Sunni revival with an "emphasis on literalness and clarity," for example, suggests a connection between doctrine and visual expression with which Faruqi and Nasr might concur. But Grabar prefers to find the key in the workings of Islamic societies rather than in the recesses of what he calls the "Islamic soul."

Faruqi's minimalist approach detects in all Islamic art the direct formative and controlling influence of a theological principle, tawhid. Translated into visual terms, strict adherence to tawhid and all its implications means that no artistic work can presume to make direct allusion to God's transcendent reality. Implicit symbolism can only hint obliquely at the divine. The maximalist view on the other hand finds explicit symbolism in virtually every facet of art and architecture, interpreting each facet as part of an organic cosmic system of color, form, and number. Artists assimilate the primordial archetypal realities as naturally, and perhaps as unconsciously, as they inhale air. And when they exhale creatively, they give physical expression just as naturally to those realities. Each approach begins with a system of thought that is regarded as undergirding all artistic expression, and then interprets a work of art in terms of that system. Grabar begins with the visual expression and works his way toward a systematic explanation, discerning symbolism in some manifestations but not in others. All three approaches are useful, but I believe the third offers the most realistic and balanced perspective.

Architectural Symbolism

Gulru Necipoğlu's approach to architectural symbolism also stands somewhere between the symbolic maximalists and minimalists. Her interpretation of the Sulaymaniye Mosque complex in Istanbul (see Fig. 19) is an illuminating example. Necipoğlu's purpose is "to demonstrate that culturally recognized symbolic and ideological associations do constitute a significant aspect of the Suleymaniye's multilayered architectural discourse."[55] Those layers are the functional, the connotative (myths and cultural associations), the formal (architectonic), and the "literal" (inscriptions). Sulayman the Magnificent (d. 1566) had his chief architect, Sinan, lay out a grand complex, centered around a mosque, including educational facilities serving every pedagogical level (from Qur'an and Hadith study to advanced tuition in religious law), a medical school, a hospital, a hostel, and a public kitchen. Taken together the various elements make "the religious complex a model of the world, signifying values and themes that are to be emphasized in the good life."[56]

Documents dating from not long after the sultan built his complex on one of Istanbul's highest hills suggest that the culture of the time attached a number of symbolic meanings to the structure. Likening the mosque to Paradise, the sources speak of the incomparable loftiness of its dome. The fountain at the center of its courtyard is likened to the celestial basin of Kawthar into which flow the waters of the four heavenly streams. Inside the structure, particularly on the dome and the qibla wall, inscriptional and visual allusions to the Verse of Light (Q 24:35) associate the sacred space with themes of firmament and celestial garden. But the mosque imitates Paradise indirectly, taking as its model the famous many-columned garden of Iram, whose creator, Shaddad, desired to emulate the celestial garden. Many of the Qur'anic inscriptions were evidently chosen to highlight the garden theme, transforming the portals, for example, into images of the gates of Paradise: One text, for example wishes peace to those who have persevered,

Figure 19.   The west facade of the Sulaymaniye Mosque
(1550–1557), Istanbul. Note the funeral platforms in the
right foreground (see Fig. 11) and the ablution facilities
along the wall beyond.

and welcomes them to the most excellent home (Q 13:24). Another acclaims
those in the state of purity and greets them, "Peace unto you; come into the
garden on the strength of what you have done" (Q 16:32). Still another de-
clares that God-fearing believers in throngs will find the gates flung open
to them (Q 39:73). And on the interior of the main dome is the text "God
it is who maintains the heavens and the earth in existence. Should they cease
to exist, no one could again revive them. Indeed He is the Clement and For-
giving One" (Q 35:41).[57]

The tombs of the sultan and sultana behind the mosque continue these themes, amplifying them by means of decorative and structural allusions to the Dome of the Rock in Jerusalem, the site of the ancient temple of the sultan's namesake, King Solomon. Sulayman associated himself with King Solomon in several other ways as well. He went to the enormous trouble of shipping construction materials from a temple site now in Lebanon (Baalbek) where, according to Islamic lore, the prophet-king Solomon built a palace for the queen of Sheba. These are complex symbolic associations whose implications are at least as political as they are religious; still, they offer important insights into the public expression of traditional Islamic values.

Turkish sources liken the Sulaymaniye Mosque to the Kaʿba, and the four columns that support its dome, as well as the four minarets, are viewed as reminders of Muhammad's four immediate successors, the Rightly Guided Caliphs: Abu Bakr, ʿUmar, ʿUthman, and ʿAli. Popular lore has it that the number of the minarets recalls that Sulayman was the fourth sultan after the conquest of Constantinople; and the total number—ten—of galleries or small balconies on the minarets reminds the viewer that Sulayman was the tenth sultan in the house of Osman, founder of the Ottoman dynasty. Sinan is reported to have told Sulayman on completion of the project that the structure would last till Judgment Day. Invoking images of a popular and influential mystic, Sinan assured the sultan that even if the martyred Hallaj were to return and shatter Mount Damavand (a peak in north-central Persia with powerful mythic associations), the dome would stand unscathed.[58]

A related spatial art highly refined in several Islamic societies is garden architecture. Formal garden settings lend themselves readily to the appropriation of Paradise imagery. As in the case of the Taj Mahal, elaborate garden compositions often provide a physical and metaphorical context for large funerary monuments. (See Fig. 24.) These compositions seek to reproduce visually the various Qurʾanic allusions to the heavenly garden. Watercourses, recalling the rivers of Paradise, form a central design element, usually dividing the space into repeating quadrant modules, so that the overall design resembles a mandala. Many important gardens delight the living as well. India's Mughal dynasty produced some of the most extensive compositions, often laid out in such a way as to remind one of a vast floral carpet.

A prime example from the western end of medieval Islam is the spectacular Court of the Lions at the Alhambra in Granada. Its function is not specifically religious, but the symbolism makes important religious connections. In the center stands a basin borne on the backs of twelve water-spouting lions, from which four courses channel water back and forth across

Figure 20.   The mid-fourteenth-century Court of the Lions in the Alhambra, Granada, Spain, showing the lion-borne fountain and the watercourses dividing the courtyard into quadrants.

the garden. (See Fig. 20.) Poetic inscriptions make clear references to Paradise. In addition, the lions not only recall zodiacal imagery but also the basin King Solomon constructed on the backs of twelve bulls in his temple in Jerusalem.[59] Whatever the garden's particular utilization, from funerary enclosure to vacation hideaway, this branch of the spatial arts draws heavily on imagery from Islamic religious cosmology.[60]

Painting and the Decorative Arts

Among the most spectacular visual creations ever produced in Muslim cultures are the miniature paintings that adorn exquisitely written manuscripts of didactic and mystical poetry. In form these works are sometimes similar to those that illustrate the written sources mentioned in earlier chapters, and to those found in texts whose themes are not explicitly religious. And, to some extent, these images serve the same functions of beautifying a book and entertaining the fortunate viewer. But because these manuscripts communicate a different kind of message than, say, the stories of the prophets or the pilgrimage manuals, their visual interpretations communicate at another level.

Here the image illuminates, but not merely as decoration, in the manner of illuminated or historiated letters in a medieval European manuscript. These images are the visual counterpart of the beauty of the literature. As such, they are not simply illustrations. This visual imagery complements and rounds out the experience of savoring the beauty of the verbal imagery, which reflects the popular conviction expressed in the hadith especially dear to Sufis, "God is beautiful and loves beauty." (See Fig. 38 and note relationship of text to image.)

Mention of figural imagery in connection with Islamic art frequently elicits one of two responses: either "I always heard Muslims don't do figures" (usually from non-Muslims); or "Whoever did these images, they were obviously not *good* Muslims" (often from Muslims). But, in fact, professed Muslims have produced an enormous amount of such work, and there is little evidence to suggest that either the artists themselves or the majority of their contemporaries considered them reprobates. In fact, the Qur'an does not explicitly forbid the making or use of images; and the hadiths on the subject are inconclusive at best. Still, the concept of Muslims as always and uncompromisingly iconoclastic persists.

How then might one interpret the visual data in light of the widely known concern among Muslims about the potential dangers of figural imagery? One can draw a distinction between sacred and religious art. Islamic sacred arts, those defined by their direct relation to worship and prayer, seem never to employ images of humans or animals, and rarely of products of human making, such as buildings. Religious arts, on the other hand, those defined by their inclusion of religious subject matter but used only outside cultic settings, often include anthropomorphic and zoomorphic imagery.[61]

Second, the representational and figural arts are also distinct. The term *representational* applies to any conscious portrayal of a living being, human or animal, as in a portrait, for example. Figural art, by contrast, refers to human and animal forms used in a reserved fashion and in such a way as to suggest strongly that the artist never intended to "create" or represent a living being. According to this distinction, traditional Islamic artists have often produced figural, not representational, art. From a religious perspective one can argue that figural art does not violate any stricture, on the grounds that the nonscriptural ban that has become widely accepted in Islamic traditional thinking refers to representational imagery. By making such a distinction, Faruqi includes miniature painting within the orbit of imagery that is acceptable within Islam. That is significant in this context if only because Faruqi was a Muslim searching for a religiously acceptable way of accounting for the visual data. She further qualified the notion of figural art, subsuming it under the category of arabesque. Just as calligraphic, geometric, and floral designs are highly abstract, Islamic miniature painting renders superficially anthropomorphic forms into abstractions.[62]

In the vast repertoire of Muslim religious painting, a number of visual themes and metaphors stand out. One that gained enormous popularity all over the Islamic world, but especially in Mughal India, is the theme of the prince taking counsel with a holy man, a theme reminiscent of the literary genre mirrors for princes. Scenes of intoxicated Sufis appear almost as frequently. (See Fig. 36.) These are sometimes set in a bucolic landscape outside of a town, where the ecstatic adepts can give free expression to their experience of inebriation with God's love and beauty.

Dancing and music, with or without the accompanying imagery of intoxication, offer another set of metaphors. Famous mystics are often pictured in illustrations for stories of how the mystic "discovered" the style of paraliturgical gesture and dance that has become a hallmark of his confraternity. A legend of how a casual walk through that area of the bazaar where metalsmiths tap out their wares with danceable rhythms, for example, provides a natural setting for images and stories of this genre. Friends of God appear often; painters depict them preaching to crowds of disciples or effecting some miraculous deed. Picnicking lovers offer artist and viewer alike yet another ambiguous device: are the lovers and their garden to be taken literally or regarded as a glimpse of life in Paradise?

In addition to paintings and drawings whose thematic content seems relatively straightforward, there are also images whose purpose is quite subtle and elusive. For example, one manuscript of mystical poetry contains marginal images that appear to depict scenes related to life in the various valleys through which Farid ad-Din 'Attar's birds travel on their pilgrimage to find their king, the Simurgh. Scenes that appear to show travelers, herdsmen, lovers, and scholars, for example, are in fact oblique allusions to the various stages in spiritual progress. In other words, images related to a famous and popular Sufi didactic mathnawi are superimposed on a later collection of lyric poems, thus serving as a kind of visual allegory.[63]

Especially in the Middle East, metalworkers have developed a wide range of objects that have often expressed profound spiritual sentiments, among them, the culturally and religiously important pen box and mosque candlestick. Other artifacts such as the oil torch (and the functionally related small candlestick, intended for private rather than institutional use) and the so-called dervish begging bowl have continued until relatively recent times to attract the attention of artists and patrons. By their evocative shapes and the frequent use of epigraphic poetry to comment on their meanings, these objects offer an unequaled opportunity to appreciate the interrelationships among visual form, textual interpretation, and function. Since metalwork has always been a costly medium, the objects produced represent understandably the taste and values of wealthier individuals; but the persistence of the themes suggests a broader base of popularity for the metaphors and the convictions they convey.

A much-loved product of the metalworker's art is the oil torch or similarly shaped candlestick. These elaborately decorated objects are usually of brass, sometimes inlaid with silver or gold. Like some beggar's bowls, they speak metaphorically, and often ambiguously, of the lover's longing for the beloved. Inscriptions from the great poets of earlier times, or of poetry composed specially for the object in question, play on the imagery of the burning heart and of the tears (wax) the candle sheds. Often the candle itself speaks, as in this text from Sa'di's *Orchard* (*Bustan*), with its punning reference to the unrequited love of the sculptor Farhad for the King's wife, Shirin (Sweet).[64] (See Fig. 21.) The moth is a favorite image of mystical poets for the lover who willingly loses self in the flame of divine love. The moth says to the candle,

> O my poor admirer,
> The honey which is my sweet beloved is burning down.
> When I see that the sweetness departs from me,
> Like Farhad, the fire flames from my head.

The artist who made the candlestick, Khwaja Ibn Mahmud, then adds a prayerful wish above his signature, "O God, may I die as a good man."[65]

Cylindrical or polygonal cast-brass oil torches (ranging from fifteen to thirty inches in height) often use similar imagery to describe the experience of love's longing and the searing pain of separation from the beloved. Inscribed ghazals by the Indian poet Amir Khusraw (1254–1325) give the torch eloquence. Around the uppermost part of the torch stand runs this Persian inscription:

> There is no time in which my soul from love of you is not burning.
> What breast is there which that artful glance does not burn?
> My own lamp does not burn at night because of my cold sighs.
> Even in my neighbor's house that lamp does not burn brightly.

A little lower a band of inscription reads:

> All night I burn with weeping, in darkness and in loneliness,
> For in this house no friendly one burns with me.

Figure 21. Brass candlestick from seventeenth-century Iran. Texts by Sa'di are inscribed in panels above the upper and beneath the lower metal joins. The Saint Louis Art Museum, Purchase.

You know of Khusraw's pain but make yourself not know—
I burned with envy, my beloved, when you set light to another.
You set light to another, and none but me is burning.

And the torch concludes with this less ambiguously religious sentiment:

The lamp that God lights up—Who blows it burns his beard.[66]

This light imagery, especially as interpreted from a mystical perspective, naturally recalls the Qur'anic Verse of Light: all light is ultimately a reminder of the divine presence in creation.[67]

Especially popular as an art form in Iran, the so-called beggar's bowl exhibits an extraordinarily wide spectrum of meanings and presents a diverting set of paradoxes. First, a beggar's bowl crafted of precious metals and covered with lavish decorative detail hardly conveys a sense of penury and utility. In addition, the primary identification of the bowl as a wine vessel might indicate that the poets' frequent references to the lover's intoxication with beloved are more—or perhaps less—than merely metaphorical, Islam's prohibition of wine notwithstanding.

But the richness of the bowl's imagery goes further still. Shaped like miniature boats, the bowls also remind the viewer of the crescent moon; and since they are often gold in color, they have become associated with the sun, while the wine in turn recalls liquid sunlight. Classic verses hint at the various meanings of the object: "From the sun and from the sky request your food and your tray: at the time of banqueting / The crescent-moon became an illuminated bowl for your feast"; and "Bring me a boat of wine, for without the Friend's face [often likened to the full moon] / Every corner in my eye has become an ocean from the grief in my heart." Other lines also apparently refer to the scenes of sailors depicted inside the object: "Inside the golden boat of the cup filled with an ocean of rubies [i.e., wine] / The exquisite imagery of its sailor(s) is silver-bodied." Thus, the full-moon-faced beloved cupbearer passes around the crescent moon full of the intoxicating beverage of rubies.[68]

Originally plainer objects called *kashkul* (literally, "tug shoulder," one who makes a request of another, hence, "beggar") were used by wandering dervishes as containers for whatever alms or food they might beg. Once again, both textual content and shape offer clues to meaning. More elaborate Iranian versions, dating from the sixteenth to the nineteenth centuries, bear a variety of inscriptions from Qur'anic, poetic, and occasionally hadith texts. The inscriptions suggest still further layers of meaning that are expressly religious, even if not always acceptable to mainstream Muslims. For example, use of the Verse of the Throne (Q 2:255), identifying the boat with the dome of heaven, along with texts inscribed on one bowl that clearly extol the virtues of actual intoxication, "leaves no doubt about the non-conformist background" of its owner.[69] Much less questionable references associate the object with charitable purposes as suggested by Qur'an 76:8–9: "And they feed the poor, the orphan, the prisoner out of love for Him, [saying] We feed you but to please God, requesting neither favors nor thanks from you."[70]

Some bowls are likened to the boat that carried Moses and Khizr toward the mystical goal of the "confluence of the two seas," as in the text of Sura 18 mentioned above in Hamza Fansuri's syair.[71] Others bear messages that suggest a more devotional purpose. One bowl, for example, conveys a wish for the Shi'i owner's successful voyage through life. It recommends that the owner

> [c]all unto 'Ali the manifestation of wonders
> O God may thy grace descend upon [then the first five imams are named]
> You shall find him your succor in calamity
> Every care, every sorrow shall be dispelled [then the remaining seven imams are named]
> Through your divine friendship, O 'Ali, O 'Ali, O 'Ali.[72]

A wide range of metaphors is expressed on the beggar's bowls.

Muslim artists and architects have spoken eloquently and evocatively, if sometimes also enigmatically, through their works. Unfortunately they have left almost no textual documentation as to either their methods or their intentions. Balanced interpretation of their visual legacy requires first a careful assessment of the monuments and objects themselves, including analysis of material, structure, style, and inscriptions. But these creations must also be related to their broader religious, cultural, and social contexts. In the absence of specific conceptual background provided by the creators themselves about, for example, the use of symbolism, the greatest challenge of contextual interpretation is how to relate the visual material to the thought world of the artists and builders without claiming to read their minds. Although some residual ambiguity as to the original meanings of a monument or work of art is inevitable, this overview hints at how the major aesthetic dimensions of the visual arts suggest Islamic purposes and values. Massive urban complexes and miniature masterpieces alike reveal something of the essential beliefs and convictions of Muslims, and evoke intriguing images of the societies in which they were produced.

5 Community

Society, Institutions, and Patronage

Previous chapters have explored Muslim identity, what sources of inspiration have united Muslims, and the foundations of their religious beliefs and practices. This discussion yields insights into what has fostered a sense of community, both local and global, among the world's Muslims. This chapter asks where have people formed societies readily identifiable as Muslim, and how have Muslims shaped and supported the institutions at the center of those societies?

Community is a delicate but durable bond that grows among people who discover that their core identities intersect with those of others. People find community and support, for example, in groups of individuals who cope with similar problems, who send their children to the same school, or who teach in the same department at a university. Shared experience, ethnic background, social purpose, citizenship, religious faith, and various combinations of these are among the more obvious bases for human community.

Matters of conviction, heart, and blood cannot be reduced to mere brick and mortar. But the full story of how human beings build community includes a chapter on how a community builds, and how it pays for what it builds. For some twenty years, members of the local Muslim community have gathered for prayer about two blocks from my office at Saint Louis University. As in a number of American cities, the Islamic Foundation here started out in what was once a business establishment. But things have changed. Not far from where I live, a new mosque has just been dedicated. Its architectural form sets it apart from nearby churches, and from the Hindu

Figure 22.   (*Opposite*) The monumental facade of Sultan Hasan's madrasa complex (1356–1363), in Cairo, with facilities for all four Sunni law schools. Inscriptions include Qur'an 24:36, just after the Verse of Light, referring to how that light (suggested by the star designs flanking the portal) illumines "[h]ouses that God permits to be raised and in which His Name is remembered and in which there praise Him morning and evening people whom neither buying nor selling distracts from the remembrance [dhikr] of God." The first half of this text also graces the facade of the Islamic Center in Washington, D.C.

temple just down the street. How that mosque arose there on Weidman Road is nearly as important a part of the story of the Saint Louis Muslim community as the joy its members experience when they gather under the copper dome. Saint Louis's new Islamic Foundation exemplifies the pattern of Muslim community building in a social setting where Muslims are a small minority. Grassroots, largely middle-class funding, here and in other North American cities, represents the principal type of financial support for Muslim development in such circumstances. In countries where Muslims form a majority of the population, large projects have often been, and in some cases continue to be, heavily subsidized by royal or government grants.

Millions of Muslims still live and practice their faith in tiny villages constructed of such ephemeral materials as adobe, thatch, and hide. But from early on, Islam's rapid spread soon made it a predominantly urban tradition. Since the mid-seventh century Muslims have wrestled with both the practical and theoretical questions of Islam's relationship to the societies on which the religion has exercised a formative influence.

SOCIAL AND HISTORICAL CONTEXTS

This section focuses on two sets of issues: first, the relationships between religion, society, and culture; and second, the roles of politics and economics in communicating religious values.

Religion, Society, and Culture

Three powerful but often elusive forces have shaped the material expressions of Islamic spirituality and religious life. First, the fundamental human need for community gives rise to many ways of gathering in common cause within the context of a religious belief system. Second, within Islam's varied cultural contexts, the aesthetic sense of taste and style further defines these ways as distinctively Egyptian or Indonesian or Turkish, and so forth. Third, sources of economic and political power provide the funding and the impetus required to shape those responses to the need for community into ever more concrete and readily identifiable forms.

In most societies, communities larger than biological family units eventually experience and express the need for a place to be together, a space suited to whatever they choose to do as a group. Virtually the world over, but especially in harsher climates, that usually means buildings bigger than houses. Some buildings begin as multipurpose structures and remain so, but more highly differentiated societies inevitably develop architectural forms either dedicated to one specific function (e.g., mosque) or limited to a few related functions (as in a mosque complex). Some religious architectural forms and functions serve the needs of a wide public (mosques), and others (funerary architecture) are accessible to a more limited public. Still others serve the needs of exclusive groups, such as Sufi orders. The distinction between public and private is reflected in the diverse functions of various religious institutions.

The wayside fountain (*sabil*), the fountain attached to a school for children (*sabil-kuttab*), and the theological college (madrasa) are among the more public institutions. Great urban mosque complexes have often included other public social facilities, such as hostels, hospitals, and soup kitchens. Several generally more private institutions are the primarily residential-ritual facilities known as the *khanqah, tekke,* or *zawiya.* These have been associated with exclusive religious confraternities; but in some instances they have combined public and private facilities within a single institution.

A wide diversity of material expressions of spiritual values exists throughout the Islamic world. In societies possessing highly evolved political structures and, in addition, located in regions with readily available building materials, the differentiation of functions within society has often meant the evolution of truly monumental architecture. In such large-scale structures the impact of taste that shapes the distinctive local and regional styles of Islamic architecture is most evident. Here I investigate several other masterworks of architecture from Egypt, Turkey, Iran, and India, pointing out some visual features that identify these buildings with particular cultural settings.

Money and Power

Peace negotiations between Israel and Jordan offer an excellent example of the symbolic connection between money and political power. As ruler of the Hashemite Kingdom, Jordan's King Hussein has been recognized in regional Islamic law as the custodian of the two most important Islamic holy places in Jerusalem, the Dome of the Rock and the al-Aqsa Mosque. In 1993, he exercised his authority in that connection by restoring, at a cost of several million dollars, the gold leaf decorating the Dome of the Rock. As a result of the negotiations, the state of Israel reinforced the king's regional status and prestige by officially recognizing Hussein as the executor of the deeds of endowment governing the upkeep of the holy places. Palestinian leaders vociferously protested the Israeli position, insisting that it unfairly undercut the authority of the Palestine Liberation Organization.

Within Muslim societies sources of funding for religious and cultural activities have generally been of three types. First, the pious endowment (*waqf*) is a legally regulated instrument whereby usually quite wealthy benefactors can both give to a charitable cause and reap some ongoing tax and income benefits from their largesse. An analogy is a donor's assigning a portion of an estate to a charity in return for a tax deduction and an amount of guaranteed income till death, at which time the remainder of the estate goes to the charity. This funding has come to assume institutional proportions. Second, outright and comprehensive foundational and support grants have come from rulers, the princely class, and the middle class. This money has generally paid for whole projects, designed, executed, and maintained in view of the possibility of full funding. Finally, religious and cultural institutions have been supported in a more piecemeal fashion by the smaller, occasional gifts of those who frequent the institutions.[1]

Several political-cultural settings have fostered extraordinarily rich developments in the construction of monumental architecture as well as in the depiction of religious and mystical themes, all more or less a direct result of the interests and tastes of wealthy patrons from the ruling class. Thus, power, money, and religion have interacted to shape cultural and social milieux. In view of the vast complexity of Islamic history, I narrow my discussion to power and patronage in the following dynasties: the Mamluk, which ruled Egypt and the southeastern quarter of the Mediterranean from 1250 to 1517; the Ottoman (1300–1921), successors first to the Byzantine Empire and then to the Mamluks; the Ilkhanid (1256–1385), Timurid (late fourteen century to early sixteenth century), and Safavid (1501–1722), rulers of Iran from the late thirteenth through the seventeenth centuries; and the Mughal, dominant power in the northern half of India through the sixteenth and seventeenth centuries. (Numerous other cultural contexts offer similar illustrative material; the contexts discussed here represent only a sampling of much greater wealth.)

The city of Cairo was founded in the year 969 by a Sevener Shi'i dynasty known as the Fatimids, who set themselves up as rival claimants to the universal authority of the Abbasid caliphs in Baghdad. Their new capital grew into a splendid walled enclosure divided into quadrants by the main axial streets. For nearly two centuries, Fatimid sovereigns funded dozens of masterpieces of religious architecture. Relatively little remains of their religious decorative arts (see Fig. 3). In 1171, with the dynasty feeling enormous external pressure from the Crusaders' Latin Kingdom of Jerusalem, the Fatimids called on the Kurdish leader Salah ad-Din (Saladin) for help. Salah ad-Din responded energetically, with his own dynasty, called the Ayyubids after his father, Ayyub, supplanting the Fatimids and ruling their lands until 1250. The Sunni Ayyubids in turn yielded power to one of Islam's most artistically inclined political entities, the Mamluk dynasty.

Taking their name from their original status as slave-soldiers and palace guard to the Ayyubids (*mamluk* in Arabic means "owned, possessed," hence, "slave"), the Mamluks cultivated the arts in virtually every medium. Under their patronage, artists produced some of the Islamic world's finest illuminated Qur'ans, Qur'an stands, and storage cases, as well as inlaid brass pen boxes for calligraphers (see chapter 1); enameled glass mosque lamps (see Fig. 9) and inlaid brass candlesticks to flank the mihrab (see chapter 2); and mosques, madrasas, khanqahs, mausoleums, and other religious architecture. As a center of cultural activity, Mamluk Egypt and greater Syria attracted artists and religious scholars from all over the world. Cairo became virtually a second Mecca, particularly for Muslims seeking refuge from political and social chaos elsewhere. Much of Mamluk social life revolved around architectural patronage, with neighborhoods invariably centered on the great complexes of mosque, madrasa, and shrine (see Figs. 7 and 29).[2]

From the mid-thirteenth through the fifteenth centuries, the Mamluk sultans promoted massive amounts of artistic production of both imperial and religious art. Although their motives for supporting imperial art are complex, they are not as difficult to explain as their patronage of religious art. Ira M. Lapidus suggests that Mamluk interest in the visual symbolism and imagery inspired by Islamic religious tradition was intensely personal and rooted in the individual rulers' experiences of life within the closed and austere system of Mamluk military tutelage: "They did not easily establish families and reproduce themselves. . . . The religious endowments were about the only useful thing the Mamluks could do with their accumulated wealth, apart from forfeiting it to the state upon death. . . . One feels that Mamluk patronage was aimed at overcoming the isolation and despair inherent in a glorious but brutalizing life; it was a way of entering the fellowship of ordinary human beings."[3] Quite possibly, individual rulers entertained genuinely spiritual motives for their philanthropy, and indeed much documentary evidence makes that very claim. Evaluating the patronage of the sultans from the perspective of their awareness of the public good, Grabar concludes that Mamluk architecture illustrates "the high Muslim ideal of an architecture of social service, supported by charity in the form of the economic and legal conditions of the waqf system and inspired by the ideological and religious reform of the Muslim system that began in the eleventh century and assumed many regional variants."[4]

The Ottoman Turks succeeded the Mamluks as rulers of the eastern Mediterranean shortly after they had compassed the end of the Byzantine

Empire with the fall of Constantinople in 1453. The sultan Sulayman was one of the most lavish of the Ottoman dynasty in his patronage of the arts, but he stood amid a long line of rulers who knew how to communicate their personal convictions through material culture.

In the older provincial capitals of Bursa, Manisa (near the Aegean coast of Turkey), and Edirne (formerly Adrianople, not far from the present-day Bulgarian border), as well as in Istanbul, the Ottoman sultans commissioned vast architectural projects. Like the Mamluks, the Ottomans favored the mosque complex as an emblem of royal power; but the Mamluk sense of empire had been considerably more modest than that of the Ottomans. Mamluk architectural complexes, while hardly diminutive, are generally contained within a single set of walls. Ottoman complexes are often sprawling groups of discrete structures arrayed around the central mosque (see Fig. 19). As one interpreter explains,

> On the one hand, the complex symbolizes the ideal Islamic city, Madina-i Fazila. It provides for worldly virtues and needs with its institutions: hospitals, schools, colleges, hamams [baths], hostels. . . . These are arranged around the mosque in the order of their spiritual significance, the commercial activities and stables placed on the peripheries. On the other hand, the universal and fundamental meanings are centered on the mosque itself, the northern court symbolizing active life, the mosque's interior symbolizing the spiritual realm . . . and the cemetery on the south which is the garden of the dead.[5]

Urban planning was surely the largest-scale concern of Ottoman patrons, but it was not their only accomplishment in the realm of the arts. They followed the practice of their earlier Iranian counterparts to the east, the Ilkhanids and Timurids, of establishing court studios employing large staffs of artists. Painters, gilders, calligraphers, bookbinders, and designers transformed the sovereign's wishes into the highest-quality illustrated manuscripts (see Figs. 14, 17, and 25) and luxury items in every medium. Specifically religious objects have served the devotional and ritual needs of both the architectural complexes and the usually more modest facilities dedicated to the memory of Friends of God.[6] All in all, the arts of Ottoman Turkey have earned a place among the world's most refined and sophisticated artistic traditions.

Chingiz (or Genghis) Khan (d. 1227) and the various Mongol hordes that have considered themselves his progeny are infamous, known for their implacable wrath and military prowess, not for their interest in the arts. However, some of the Islamic world's most enthusiastic patrons of the arts were equally avid claimants to a genealogical link with Chingiz Khan. Though

Chingiz Khan's religious background was a central Asian shamanism, some of his descendants embraced Islam as they moved westward across Iran and Iraq during the later thirteenth and early fourteenth centuries. Two of the most influential dynasties in the history of Iran, the Ilkhanids and the Timurids, are branches of the Mongol family tree. The former were among the political successors to the original waves of invaders who sacked Baghdad in 1258. The Ilkhanids were particularly strong in Iraq and northwestern Iran in the late thirteenth and early fourteenth centuries, especially supporting the arts in the cities of Tabriz, Qazvin, and Sultaniya.

Replacing a series of small, short-lived dynasties that had supplanted the faltering Ilkhanids, the Timurids established their power base in central Asia (now in the republic of Uzbekistan) in the latter half of the fourteenth century. Timur Lang (Tamerlane, 1336–1405) then made the ancient city of Samarkand his capital and soon projected his rule west across Iran and even menaced the Ottomans for a time. Timur's Chagatay Turkic ancestors had become Muslims generations earlier; and Sufi shaykhs came to assume the functions of religious authority that shamans had once provided for so many central Asian tribes. The fifteenth-century court of Timur's descendants in the city of Herat included greater Iran's most active patrons of the arts and architecture. Particularly under the patronage of Timur's son Shahrukh (1377–1447) and Sultan Husayn Mirza (r. 1469–1506), the arts of miniature painting flourished. The Timurid sultans supported some highly talented painters and calligraphers (see, e.g., Fig. 38), in addition to constructing splendid architectural works. Religious and spiritual themes enjoyed increasing popularity as subject matter for manuscript illustrations. Here, as at other royal courts, a good deal of patronage focused on the art of poetry, including prominently that of famous Sufi bards such as Jami, a leading figure in the Naqshbandi order. Illustrated versions of his works are among the most engaging that Persia's visual artists ever produced.[7]

As Timurid power waned in eastern Iran, the Safavids were gaining further to the west. Beginning where the Ilkhanids had once held sway, these scions of a Friend of God called Shaykh Safi ad-Din of Ardabil (1252–1334) established successive capitals in Tabriz, Qazvin, and finally Isfahan. Under the patronage of Shah Isma'il I (1487–1524), his son Tahmasp (d. 1576), and especially 'Abbas (r. 1587–1629), Safavid art and architecture achieved great refinement in both style and technique. Their studios of artists and architectural staffs further developed the methods and materials pioneered by earlier Iranian dynasties to produce some of the Islamic world's most exquisite miniature paintings (see Figs. 16, 18, 34, 35, and 36) and building complexes (see Fig. 23). The chief building material used in public and monumental architecture was baked brick, later enlivened by applying ceramic tile overlay with an increasingly varied palette and complex geometric, calligraphic, and floral decorative schemes.[8]

Meanwhile, in Afghanistan and northern India, a shoot from the stump of Timur appeared in the form of the nascent Mughal dynasty. The name "Mughal" recalls the importance of Mongol heritage in the dynasty's claims to legitimacy. Babur (1483–1530), the dynasty's founder, was sixth in the direct line from Timur, and his mother traced an unbroken lineage to Chingiz Khan. The city of Delhi in north-central India had been the home of important Muslim groups for three centuries when the second great Mughal ruler, Humayun (r. 1530–1556), claimed it definitively in the name of a new dynasty. Humayun was a contemporary of Sulayman the Magnificent, but it was his son Akbar (r. 1556–1605) who first made his reign the equal of the Ottoman in opulence if not in geographical expanse. Akbar's religious views were, from a more traditionalist Muslim perspective, eccentric to say the least; he was the most tolerant of religious pluralism of any of the Mughal rulers.

The Mughals inherited much from their Timurid ancestors in their taste in the arts. For example, variations on the Iranian double dome and vaulted alcove known as the *iwan,* often fronted by a rectangular facade called a *pishtaq* that provides an expansive decorative surface, are evident in Indian mosque and funerary architecture. Some Mughal religious architecture can be formally characterized as extroverted Iranian: take the classic Timurid/Safavid courtyard with its inward facing iwans and two-tiered arcades (see Fig. 23), turn them inside out, and the result is strikingly similar to the quadruple facades of Mughal tombs such as the Taj Mahal (see Fig. 24). But scarcely any Timurid or Safavid architectural works can compare with those of the Mughals in sheer quality. Mughal architects had much finer materials at their disposal; with red sandstone and white marble (see Fig. 31) available for building as well as decorating, they could produce monuments of exceptional polish. Akbar's son Jahangir (r. 1605–1627) and grandson Shah Jahan (r. 1628–1657) commissioned some of the world's most spectacular architecture, including the Taj Mahal.[9]

Political leaders, both the despotic and the democratically elected, must address questions of religious authority and legitimation in some way, if only to denounce them as unworthy of consideration. That is as true in the Muslim world as elsewhere. Some, such as certain descendants of Chingiz Khan, set an example for their own people, as well as for subject populations, by converting to Islam. Others, such as Saddam Hussein, not personally committed to Islamic values have taken pains to embellish their

Figure 23.   (*Top*) Interior of the central courtyard of the Safavid shah 'Abbas's Royal Mosque (1612–1637), Isfahan, Iran. Note the reflecting pool and the shadow of a minaret to the right of the iwan.

Figure 24.   (*Above*) The white marble Taj Mahal (1632–1654), Agra, India. The four iwans and double arcade face outward, with the main iwan looking toward the long reflecting pool (viewed from just inside the front gate). Unlike the tomb of Humayun (Fig. 26), which is set in the center of a large square enclosure, the Taj Mahal stands at the far end of a rectangular garden.

rhetoric with Islamic religious imagery to appeal to devout Muslims among their constituents. Still others, such as the Mughal Akbar and contemporary Indonesian rulers, have attempted to straddle the fence of religious allegiance by proclaiming open-ended tolerance, with Islam as the de facto norm. Whatever the preferred relationship between religion and power in a particular setting, textual sources hint at the expressed motivations behind various major institutional manifestations of Islamic spirituality and the functions their creators had in mind.

INSTITUTIONAL TEXTS

Two types of textual sources are important here. First come two kinds of text directly connected to buildings: the waqf or deed of pious endowment, and the foundational inscriptions that supplement our knowledge of the origins and purposes of individual structures. Waqf texts provide detailed information about the legal and practical concerns of donors, whereas foundational epigraphy, prominently displayed on facades, gives a sense of the public image the donor wanted to promote. The second type comprises a relatively large body of literature. A form of adab literature evolved as a vehicle for institutionalizing the ethical and disciplinary standards essential to good order in the formal organizations often called Sufi orders or confraternities. Adab texts served as charters or constitutions that not only gave group leaders a guide for solving day-to-day problems but also provided an important means of preserving an order's distinctive tradition from one generation to another.

Public Support

Readers familiar with Islam may be surprised at the prominence accorded here to the phenomenon of the waqf. The waqf document (*waqfiya* or *hujjat waqf*) provided a legal instrument by which a benefactor (*waqif*) could establish a property or foundation for a particular charitable cause, and could stipulate that any income accruing from attached shops or other sources of funds be used for the upkeep of the foundation. Although the occasion for many a waqf has typically been the construction and maintenance of a structure such as mosque, madrasa, or khanqah, a patron could also fund a sabil, a sabil-kuttab, or a *hawd* (drinking trough).

Many deeds of endowment exhibit a high level of social consciousness and responsibility. Endowments could underwrite a variety of causes by setting aside portions of income to bail out prisoners, support widows, ransom prisoners of war, free slaves, buy medical supplies for the indigent, pay funeral expenses for the destitute, and commission the reading of the Qur'an in the name of a deceased person. Some endowments also require that the document be read annually in the hearing of all those who enjoy its benefits, so that all might bear in mind their responsibilities to abide by the expressed values of the donor.[10]

Although initially this body of technical and often dry legal documentation seems unpromising, these public testaments provide a significant witness to an often neglected aspect of Islamic spirituality.[11] Two distinct formative influences have shaped the institutional manifestations of Islamic spirituality, namely, popular tradition and religious law. Tradition traces the origins of the waqf back through pre-Islamic times to the prophet Abraham. He became the paragon of hospitality, and through the tradition that he is the builder of the Ka'ba, his became the paradigm of the practice of endowment in perpetuity. Abraham stands amid a long line of prophet-builders. In literature mystical poets often associate prophets and religious figures with the origins of the religious arts. Prophets are sometimes referred to as Islam's preeminent architects, both literally and metaphorically. Solomon, for example, built the Jerusalem temple, enlisting the services of the jinn. And, metaphorically speaking, the prophets make of the whole world a cosmic sacred space by means of the *qibla* of their exemplary deeds, that is, the deeds of the prophets are so important ethically that all who seek to act rightly must turn toward them, just as people turn toward Mecca when they pray.[12]

Several significant aspects of the relationship between law and the societal expression of spiritual values must be examined. The link between widespread pre-Islamic practice and the apparent intent of Qur'anic guidelines appears to have raised problems for Muslim legal scholars. As the Islamic community spread west across North Africa to Spain, north into Iraq and Syria, and east into Persia and the subcontinent—all within less than a century of Muhammad's death—it encountered enormous ethnic, religious, and cultural diversity. Important strategic decisions had to be made about how to govern new subject populations. No longer could Muslim administrators enforce univocally the relatively small collection of specific injunctions contained in Qur'an and Hadith, for too many situations arose that were not addressed directly in either foundational source. In addition, most subject populations were already heirs to long-standing traditions of religious or customary law, or both. For a variety of reasons, administrative pragmatism not the least of them, jurists and judges in the provincial cities elaborated judicial principles and rendered court decisions rather differently than their counterparts in Mecca and Medina.

The institutional result of such regional variety was the growth of several schools of legal methodology known as *madhhabs*. Of the half-dozen or so that developed in the eighth and ninth centuries, four Sunni schools have survived into modern times: the Maliki, named after Malik ibn Anas (d. 795) of Medina; the Hanafi, named after Abu Hanifa (699–767) in Kufa, Iraq; the Shafiʿi, after a man by the same name (d. 810); and the Hanbali, led by Ahmad ibn Hanbal of Baghdad (780–855). Figure 25 depicts one of Abu Hanifa's renowned professional descendants, Abu Suʿud, conducting a session for younger legal scholars. Two Shiʿi schools, called the Mujtahidi and the Akhbari, have been influential especially in Iran and Iraq. However, many Muslims do not know or care about the schools to which they belong. Thus, Islam, like other religious traditions, has its specialists who busy themselves with the particulars. About as many Muslims are familiar with the intricacies of their sophisticated legal systems as Roman Catholics are with the statutes of Canon Law. It is sufficient to note here that the schools differ chiefly in the ways in which they apply the interpretative devices known as consensus (*ijmaʿ*) and analogical reasoning (*qiyas*) when Qurʾan and Hadith fail to offer immediate solutions to a problem at hand.

Relatively little is certain about the Islamic roots of the charitable endowment. The Qurʾan does not deal directly with the practice as such; nor does Prophetic Hadith provide a clear picture. Some Muslim jurists as early as the ninth century traced the origins of waqf to one of two events during the life of the Prophet. One theory holds that the first endowment occurred when a Muslim who died about 625 willed his property to Muhammad. The other view says that it took place when Muhammad advised his Companion and eventual successor ʿUmar to set aside for charitable uses land taken at an oasis called Khaybar.[13]

Abu Hanifa himself evidently sought to restrict the proliferation of pious endowments by placing severe conditions on their establishment. First, a waqf constituted no more than a simple one-time charitable donation, thus limiting its benefits to the lifetime of the donor. Alternatively, a waqf might be regarded as purely testamentary, that is, bestowing its benefits only after the donor's death. The intent of the restrictions was to keep bequests in line with the Qurʾan's insistence that no more than one third of the donor's estate be passed on to heirs. The scripture's concern is evidently to discourage the hoarding of wealth, in the interest of a more equitable distribution of resources among society's neediest.

Historically the first Islamic legal formulation of the principle of waqf is attributed to the Hanafi jurist Abu Yusuf (d. 798). He liberalized the definition of waqf to accord with an already widespread practice. He thus allowed

Figure 25.   An illustration showing the celebrated Turkish
Hanafi jurist Abu Suʿud teaching law in Istanbul, from *Diwan*,
by Baqi (c. 1550), Turkey. The different kinds of headgear
denote various social ranks and functions in sixteenth-century
Ottoman Turkey. New York: The Metropolitan Museum of Art,
Gift of George D. Pratt.

a donor to be the beneficiary during his or her lifetime, and to restrict testamentary benefits to members of the family line, at whose extinction the
benefits would go to the poor. Abu Yusuf's modification amounted to a tacit
acknowledgment that it would be practically impossible to root out the various forms of regional pre-Islamic customary practice still prevalent at the
end of the eighth century. He decided that they had somehow to be ratio-

nalized according to the principles of Islamic law. Abu Yusuf found precedent in the pious causes of the already ancient Byzantine legal system then in place in the newly Islamic lands of Egypt, Palestine, and Syria.

Since there are several schools of jurisprudence, each with its distinctive stipulations on these matters, there exist some related regional variations in the material manifestations of Islamic religious life, depending on the dominance of a particular law school in a given area. For example, the Maliki madhhab, once preeminent in Spain and still regnant across North Africa, allowed only for a reversible charitable bequest that would revert to the donor's nearest kin upon the extinction of the donor's direct line. It imposed that restriction because the indeterminate category of the poor did not constitute a legal entity and could thus not legally be designated as beneficiary of a bequest. George Makdisi argues that as a result one finds in Maliki domains relatively few instances of certain types of public religious institutions that are elsewhere largely or entirely dependent on waqfs for their inception and maintenance.[14] On the whole, however, Islamic law seems to have solved the beneficiary problem by identifying the endowed property as deeded to God, so that the fruits or proceeds of the bequest—not the property itself—could then be dedicated in perpetuity either to the upkeep of the property or to the needy.[15]

Even though a madrasa and a mosque might qualify equally as charitable endowments under the stipulations of a waqf, their legal status differs. As Makdisi observes, the principal difference lies in the control accorded a founder. Likening the founding of a mosque to the manumission of a slave, legal scholars argued that once a grantor founded a mosque, he or she relinquished control over it altogether. In the case of the madrasa, on the other hand, the founder "had virtually unlimited freedom in deciding the course of its existence. It is true, however, that once the instrument of waqf was drawn up and signed, and the foundation was thus brought into existence, the founder was forever bound by its contents. But up to that point his freedom of choice was limited only by the restriction that nothing in the foundation could be done which would contravene the tenets of Islam."[16]

Finally, an important feature of waqf documentation is that some pious endowments stipulate matters not only of administration but also of conduct and discipline to be observed by the beneficiaries. The residential facility for Sufis known as the khanqah provides a good example. With respect to administration, waqf documents regulate such matters as the shaykh's authority to screen applicants, assign quarters, control allotments of food and stipends, and provide means to fulfill the duty of pilgrimage to Mecca. The shaykh's spiritual obligations include guidance of individual Sufis, leading various ritual sessions, and deciding on scriptural texts for ritual use. In some instances the endowment requires specific prayers to be said over those buried in the institution's mausoleum, a privilege usually reserved for the founder and successive shaykhs. As for the requirements of institutional affiliation to a khanqah, some endowments allow nonresidents to enjoy limited membership benefits so long as they agree to spend all of each day in the facility abiding by its rules; others specify a set number of days residents may spend outside the khanqah.[17]

A fairly representative example of waqf documentation is the Mughal nobleman Wazir Khan's deed of endowment of the congregational mosque in Lahore, dated 1641. He begins by praising God for giving his servants the guidance to raise religious buildings, and blesses Muhammad for his encouragement of charitable projects. Upkeep is to be provided by income from the adjacent shops, residential facilities for rent, and services offered by a public bath and wells. After establishing that this endowment shall be permanent and inalienable, the donor says:

> Further, it is provided that the Imam-preacher attached to the mosque will be a person thoroughly skilled in the art of reading the Qur'an, and familiar with the rules of prayer; and the muezzin must be thoroughly familiar with the death ceremonies.
> Further, it is stipulated that twenty shops outside the eastern gateway, together with their upper stories, shall be for the exclusive use of the bookbinders and book-sellers of the books on Islam, free of rent in perpetuity.
> Further, it is covenanted that there shall be two teachers for the said mosque, for the purpose of giving instruction in the religious sciences. [References to staff salaries and use of income by beneficiaries follow.] . . .
> And whatever shall remain after defraying the expenses of the building, the servants of the mosque and other necessary expenses, such as providing for the overseer, the carrier of firewood [for the baths], the carpet-spreader and other rightful persons attached to the mosque shall be spent in maintaining the guests who come to the mosque; and a fixed amount shall be spent on such services in accordance to the rules of the Hanafi school.[18]

A related type of textual evidence is epigraphic, mostly in the form of foundational and other historical inscriptions on buildings; such texts also occur occasionally on smaller architectural features or decorative objects. Historical inscriptions typically include a litany of grand epithets especially dear to the founder of the institution, who is often the supreme ruler or someone of the princely class. These include such hyperbolic characterizations as: Inheritor of the Reign of Solomon, Alexander of the Age, Meteor of the Faith, Patron of Believers, Father of Orphans, and Protector of the

Downtrodden. Such blatant self-aggrandizement notwithstanding, the texts provide important insights into the spirit in which many fine works were funded. An inscription over the gateway of a fourteenth-century pre-Mughal Indian mosque offers a good example of one founder's stated motives in founding this place of prayer. This hadith is often used for such purposes, though usually in a shorter version:

> In the Name of God, the Merciful, the Compassionate. Verily the mosques are for God alone; invoke not therein anyone else with God. (Qur'an 72:18) And says the Prophet, peace be upon him, "Whoever builds a mosque for God, though it be as small as a sparrow's nest, for him God will build a house in paradise." This is by one who has been rightly guided and helped by Him.
>
> This auspicious congregational mosque and its buildings were constructed wholly and completely out of his own money from what God had given him through His grace and benevolence, merely for the sake of God the Exalted, during the reign of the learned and just emperor Muhammad Shah, son of Tughluq Shah the king—may God perpetuate his kingdom and sovereignty—by the feeble servant, expectant of the mercy of God, the exalted Daulat Shah Muhammad al-Butahari. May God enable him to achieve his object. And this took place on the 18th of Muharram 725 (= 4 January 1325).[19]

As in the above example, Qur'anic verses are typically incorporated into architectural epigraphy. Although many verses are frequently used for this purpose, one text (Q 9:108–110) stands out for its aptness in the case of mosque building, referring explicitly to the motivation of the builder. The text occurs in the context of Muhammad's dealings with some hypocrites among the bedouins late in the Medinan period, around the year 630. The Qur'an condemns the insincerity of those who swear allegiance to the Prophet one day and go back on their word the next. Some among the hypocrites evidently constructed a mosque in an attempt to fragment the Muslim community by drawing people away from Muhammad, claiming that their intentions were pure. Forbidding true Muslims from attending such a mosque, the text continues, "There is a mosque founded from the start upon pious intent; better for you to stand there, for therein are persons desirous of being purified; and God loves those who purify themselves" (Q 9:108). The text uses architectural imagery, referring metaphorically to the need for building interiorly, as well as on a footing of sincere piety and devotion. The passage ends with a warning that those who build on the unsure foundation of hypocrisy will ultimately find their hearts in ruins: "Is the better person the one who lays a foundation on devotion to God and what pleases Him? Or the one who builds on shifting sand? . . . The footing of those who build that way is never entirely sure and firm in their hearts, and at length their hearts are rent asunder."[20]

Patrons have also often funded the construction of portions of buildings or particular architectural features, such as mihrabs, minarets, or minbars. The item thus donated has the character of a votive offering (see Fig. 3). On the minaret of Gurganj in central Asia, for example, the builder placed this inscription, complete with unabashed mention of the founder's hopes for both temporal and eternal rewards:

> The amir, the sayyid, the just prince Abu 'l-'Abbas Ma'mun ibn Ma'mun Khwarazmshah ordered the construction of this minaret. He constructed it himself and supervised the laying down of the foundations, in humility toward religion and to approach God, may His mention be great, and with the desire for recompense in this world and the hereafter. This took place . . . August 1011.

The ruler's act of piety was especially apt, given his position on the map, for "in addition to its economic advantages at the end of the trade route to southern Russia and the north forest zone, [Khwarazm] was a bastion of Sunni orthodoxy and scholarship and the staging point for missionaries proselytizing in the steppes."[21]

The public face of Islam's religious institutions expresses important features of the relationships between religion and society. The desire to share wealth for ostensibly spiritual motives has been at least indirectly responsible for many of the social services available in more traditional Islamic cities. In addition, there is immense prestige attached to mounting a philanthropic project. Donors, whether royal or newly well-to-do, have often insured for themselves a place in public memory through charitable works. Some benefactors of public facilities have also established private facilities such as Sufi residences, sometimes availing themselves of the institution's spiritual resources by making retreat there or seeking the counsel of the shaykh. In the case of benefactions to Sufi orders, the patrons leave the stipulation of the rules of the order to be determined by the recipients of their largesse.

Private Discipline

Institutional disciplinary concerns include those that deal with organizational structure and administrative matters, and those that address issues of authority and behavior. The organizational structure of Sufi confraternities sometimes included several levels of membership, roughly analogous to the primary, secondary, and tertiary degrees of canonical membership in some Roman Catholic religious orders. For example, the first is often the men's group; the second, the women's; while a third welcomes interested laypersons who desire some affiliation short of full membership. Within the core (first order) of an organization are various types of administrative structure that distinguish among several levels of membership and authority. And at the level of the rank-and-file members, each confraternity typically has its own more or less distinctive style, mode of training, preferred rituals, and means of livelihood.

Established Sufi orders have generally distinguished among various ranks within their memberships. The Persian term *pir* (elder) often refers to the organization's founder; its Arabic equivalent, *shaykh,* denotes the founder's successor; in the Bektashi and Mevlevi orders the Turkish word *dede* refers to a senior member exercising local leadership; the shaykh in turn appointed a *khalifa* (caliph) as his successor, a kind of shaykh designate.

The Mevlevi order (from the Turkish term that derives from Rumi's honorific title, Mevlana, "our master") began in the central Anatolian city of Konya; the order branched out but generally maintained a centralized administration there. By the fifteenth century, Mevlevi organization had developed into six ranks (in ascending order): the sympathizer (*muhip*), the dervish, the elder (dede), the successor-elect of the shaykh, the shaykh himself, and the chelebi, who had authority over all the Mevlevi houses, with the main foundation in Konya. The various ranks were indicated by different headdresses. The wrappings added to the conical felt *sikke* cap were only for shaykhs, with white indicating the generality of shaykhs, green singling out descendants of the Prophet, and purple or black reserved for khalifas or the chelebi.[22] (See Fig. 33.)

Means of livelihood have varied among the orders. Some have allowed or even required their members to maintain ordinary gainful employment to support the community. Others have relied solely on alms. Still others have enjoyed sufficient income from endowments to free them from either commerce or charity. Opinions as to the suitability of the several methods have varied. In some instances Sufis have sought to maintain independence, for both spiritual and political reasons, by refusing to be beholden to any patron. Many Islamic theologians, like Ghazali, have considered commercial activities inappropriate for Sufis, but "the decision to lead the life of a dervish dependent only on charity or to support oneself by labor remained largely a personal one through the end of the nineteenth century" in the Ottoman empire.[23]

Another important structural aspect of Sufi orders that relates directly to authority has been a concern over proper lineage (*silsila,* "chain"; or *sha-*

jara, "tree"). Indices of legitimacy have been as important to religious institutions as to political ones. Founders and successors of the various confraternities invariably locate themselves on a family tree traceable back to Muhammad and his earliest Companions.[24] A shaykh would pass along his authority to a successor, thus insuring the continuity of spiritual power and authority; that continuity has often been given tangible expression in institutional burial places that hold the remains of all or most of an order's leaders. (See Fig. 33.) The spiritual trees of some orders became very complex. As the Christian tradition has its several branches of Franciscanism, for example, Islam has had its families of religious organizations. Sufi groups might be distinguished from one another by their relative emphasis on such practices as actual poverty, manual labor, or prayer rituals. Often, as in the Benedictine tradition, members of an order established subsidiary foundations more or less independent of the main branch.

The second important aspect of institutional discipline addresses questions of authority and personal behavior, and Muslims have dedicated a considerable body of literature to these matters. The term *adab* may refer to the literature of the pulpit or to the various genres of artistic literature associated with high culture, refinement, and education. These kinds of adab share some formal and functional features with institutional documents whose purpose goes beyond the didactic and inspirational to something like stipulation. In this context, however, the Arabic plural of the term *adab* refers to the comportment expected of a member of a Sufi organization. Since residential facilities for Sufis often served a wider constituency than that of more permanent residents (Christians might refer to a "cloistered" part of the institution), the line between public and private spirituality and discipline blurs. Many waqf documents include specific expectations as to the conduct (adab) especially of those unmarried residents who wish to use the endowed property more or less permanently. Not surprisingly, one such public concern relates to the assignment of living quarters and the degree to which Sufis might retain the rights to individual quarters if they are in the habit of traveling abroad for extended periods.

In short, the waqf sometimes functioned as a handbook of hotel management. One such text stipulates that a Sufi may travel within Egypt for no longer than a month at a time if he wishes to keep his cell; one who travels farther may expect upon returning to have the shaykh assign him to whatever room is available. In a regulation reminiscent of Saint Benedict's recommendation that "two stout monks" escort to the door unruly visitors to the abbey, this waqf says that any Sufi who "displays a behavior which is judged reprehensible and calls for his eviction from the khanqah shall be

expelled and shall not be allowed to return to it before traveling to a destination selected by the Sufi shaykh (*shaykh as-sufiya*), who also determines
the period of time for his repentance."[25] Even public documents therefore
are concerned to some degree with standards of conduct.

Most textual sources on institutional discipline, however, originate, not
from the outside (the deed of endowment), but from inside the religious organization itself. These sources include preeminently works of a type also
called adab, understood not in the sense of tuition in the literary arts but as
proper demeanor. Related to the mirror for princes and treatises on personal
ethics, such works seek to instruct aspirants in the mystical life and all
novices who have newly applied for membership in religious brotherhoods
in their basic duties and practices. Some are separate documents devoted entirely to the subject;[26] others are longer works with special segments on discipline.[27] Although aspects of several of these works appear to fall under the
rubric of spiritual pedagogy, there are important differences between institutional discipline and advanced pedagogy. Disciplinary sources deal with
those matters of behavior and daily activity that an individual of good will
might simply decide to comply with, or not. In matters of spiritual pedagogy, learning and assimilation of the teaching depends on far more—or
far less—than will power and obedience to one's superior.

Works of Sufi adab take their cue from the axiom that one's behavior
mirrors one's heart. Among the principal themes are these: interpersonal
relationships; eating, sleeping, personal hygiene, and clothing; and the conduct of spiritual exercises. Basic charity toward neighbors is not only recommended but presumed. A Sufi is generally counseled to marry but to do
so as a means of preserving chastity, and because Muhammad preferred marriage to celibacy. In addition, a Sufi is advised to keep the company of those
who will support his or her life choices and to avoid individuals who might
be inclined to raise doubts about them. A Sufi is instructed not to cultivate
the wealthy or those in authority, for ultimately God is the only company
needed. With regard to a Sufi's personal expression, one adab directive counsels, "He shall not say many words, and when he speaks he shall say only
that which is necessary. While speaking he shall not gesticulate, raise his
voice or make inappropriate movements. . . . While walking he shall neither strut not saunter, neither look to the right nor to the left, neither ahead
nor behind, but keep the head bowed down. . . . He shall likewise walk with
decorum so that at each step a good work be written down on his behalf."[28]

A Sufi ought to use only as little food, sleep, and material goods as necessary, and maintain health while avoiding vanity and excessive concern with
appearance. The patched frock (*muraqqaʿa*) or mantle (*khirqa*) is meant, in

part, to keep the seeker's sartorial priorities in order. Slovenliness is not to be mistaken for virtue, nor is fastidiousness. As a ritual object, the frock's conferral on the aspirant signals a level of spiritual progress and acceptance into the order. 'Abdallah Ansari's *Essentials of Sufi Conduct* (*Mukhtasar fi adab as-Sufiya*) mentions the significance of the mantle's color as a symbol of the seeker's progress on the path:

> If someone asks, which color should the frock (*khirqa*) be . . . I answer: if he has tamed his carnal soul (*nafs*) . . . with the sword of spiritual warfare and suffering . . . he shall wear a black or dark blue robe. . . . If he has repented of all transgressions, scoured his life's robe with the soap of contrition and ascetic exercise, and has cleansed the surface of his heart . . . he shall wear a white robe. If, in his striving, he has gone beyond the lower world, has reached the higher world, and has been filled with celestial energy, adorned with stars, he shall wear a blue robe. . . . If he has passed all stages and stations of the mystic Path . . . and if a ray has shone upon him from the lights of the mystical states, he shall wear a robe of different colors.[29]

One unusual use of the garment occurs in the context of the ritual gathering called the audition (*sama'*). Abu Najib Suhrawardi (d. 1168), in his manual of Sufi discipline, *The Book of Conduct of Seekers* (*Kitab adab al-muridin*), describes the practice of casting off the mantle during the ceremony, either as an expression of ecstasy or to show solidarity with fellow Sufis who have entered into ecstatic states. The mantles thus thrown become the property of the group and are torn, so that the pieces can be shared and used for patching. These patches confer blessing on those who receive them for they belonged to the ecstatic members of the group. Suhrawardi observes that there are various opinions about how the garment should be divided. One group insisted that the principle of preference should govern the process, as in cases of inheritance and in dividing the spoils of battle. Another held that if the shaykh divided the garment, he had the option of making unequal shares; but if the Sufis undertook the division themselves, they were bound to do so in equal parts. Suhrawardi adds:

> That which is not suitable for making patches should better be given without tearing it to a deserving poor man. As for the clothes of the lay members [which were thrown off in the sama'], it is better to sell them or give them to the reciter rather than to tear them to pieces.[30]

In religious practices, both those prescribed for all Muslims and those especially recommended to members of confraternities, emphasis falls on proper attentiveness. One adab text says this about reciting Qur'an:

> When you read therein a description of the true believer take a look at how you yourself measure up to that description, and how far you fall short of

it, thanking Allah for such measure of it as you possess, and purposing to attain what you lack. Similarly when you read [therein] descriptions of the hypocrites and unbelievers, take a look at whether or not these descriptions fit you yourself.[31]

PATRONAGE AND THE ARTS

Nontextual sources are considered more difficult to "read" than textual ones; however, texts do not always reveal their secrets so readily, and artistic modes of nonverbal communication are sometimes more articulate than words. From an examination of visual materials and documents about them, three kinds of information emerge: the interrelationships among religion, the arts, and political power; the religious functions of architecture; and the relationship between the arts and the spirituality of artists and their patrons.

Patronage

A most vexing issue for non-Muslim observers of Islam is the relationship between faith and ideology. This complex matter tends to be reduced especially, but not exclusively, in media coverage to a handful of hackneyed oversimplifications that make a sensational headline. There is at least one other side to the story. As Samir Khalil observes in *The Monument*, Islamic history can afford even an avowedly secular political leader a wide array of religiously suggestive imagery with which to manipulate the public. Khalil describes how Saddam Hussein exploited public religious sentiment by commissioning massive public works rich in imagery associating himself with Shi'i Islam's most important heroes. But not all institutionally mandated religious art has been so cynically employed.[32]

The arts, and architecture in particular, communicate a ruler's message of dominion and legitimacy in several ways. In this chapter I delve further into the public, institutional values embodied in the various arts, among them, the royal tomb and miniature paintings depicting scenes of rulers or their royal progeny consulting with persons who clearly represent Islamic religious or mystical values, or both.

The institutional aspects of a spectacular example of funerary architecture offer several insights. Funerary architecture has long been associated with political power. Furthermore, a number of such monuments have communicated as much a sense of present and future power as of past glory. Some monarchs have planned ahead and built their own final resting places, and some have even reserved special places for their descendants. Others

Figure 26.   Humayun's tomb (1565), Delhi, India, showing niches in the platform and the outward facing iwan and arcades that served as a model for the Taj
Mahal (Fig. 24). Note the decorative six-pointed stars on the pishtaq.

have had their burials provided by their immediate heirs, with or without
a view to dynastic use and symbolism.

Funerary architecture that not only boasts a royal patron but is also conceived of as a dynastic tomb, makes a dual contribution to a study of Islamic
institutions. One excellent example of such a foundation is the tomb of the
Mughal emperor Humayun in Delhi, built by his son Akbar between 1561
and 1572. Humayun's tomb is set on a square platform over 18 feet high
and 300 feet on each side, containing a series of fifty-six niched cells designed to hold burials. The tomb building itself has four corner rooms clustered around the central chamber, each also evidently meant as a funerary
space. (See Fig. 26.)

Akbar's use of a double dome set on a high drum (the cylindrical form
just beneath a dome's semicircle) provides the added symbolism of a visual
association with the Gur-i Mir, the tomb of Timur, an important political
forebear of the Mughal rulers. But the monument to Humayun looks forward as well as backward. Akbar used every detail of his father's tomb symbolically, from its plan and elevation to the building materials. Red sandstone, commonly used in Hindu architecture for centuries, and white marble

are revived here as structural and decorative media after falling into disuse through much of the fifteenth century. Akbar thus associates himself and his line visually with the earliest days of Muslim rule in India. A six-pointed star theme around the drum of the dome and on the grating that allows light into the tomb chambers in effect replaces calligraphy in this monument. The imagery recalls Humayun's preoccupation with astrological matters, suggests a connection with his innumerable descendants and the dynasty's growing association of its rule as world illuminating, and underscores Akbar's claims to at least semidivine lineage.[33] Other funerary monuments, such as that of Timur in Samarkand (1404), have become burial places for many members of a ruling family even though they were not originally intended for that purpose. In addition, numerous rulers founded funerary complexes not only for themselves but also for their families.

Two types of miniature painting popular among Mughal royal patrons provide variations on the theme of dynastic continuity and legitimacy. The first comprise allegorical images that depict an emperor, notably Akbar's son Jahangir (whose name appropriately means "world grabber"), dominating all space and time. One famous painting suggests the monarch's global power by showing him overshadowing a map of the Mughal world. Another depicts Jahangir sitting majestically atop a cosmic hourglass granting an audience to the world. Attending to an unassuming old man, the emperor snubs several world leaders who have traveled from as far away as Europe to seek an audience. His majesty prefers receiving a famous Indian Sufi shaykh over entertaining such lesser lights as the Ottoman sultan or King James of England.[34] (See Fig. 27.)

This last symbolic image belongs formally to the genre of visual allegory, but its religious allusion connects it with another important theme in miniature painting. The theme of a prince or sultan consulting or discussing matters of the soul with shaykhs or other Friends of God appears in Persia and Turkey, but is especially prominent in India. Sometimes the royal personage has the wisdom figure—often several of them, including representatives of more than one religious wisdom tradition—brought to the palace. Akbar, for example, was especially fond of sponsoring debates among Jesuits, Hindu gurus, and representatives of Indic religious traditions. But more frequently miniatures show the prince or ruler meeting with the saintly character in neutral territory; often the supplicant seeks out the sage in a mountain cave, far removed from city life. Scenes of the royal hero consulting a wisdom figure appear both as illustrations to a wide range of literary works, from Firdawsi's *Book of Kings* to Jami's mystical works, and as pictures without text, commissioned to adorn a royal album.[35]

Figure 27.   An allegorical album painting (c. 1625)
showing the Mughal emperor Jahangir, son of Akbar,
enthroned on a cosmic hourglass. He attends to a
dervish while appearing to snub his more politically
influential guests, the Ottoman sultan and the king
of England. The painter, Bichitr, is at lower left. Washington, D.C.: Courtesy of the Freer Gallery of Art,
Smithsonian Institution.

A related type of imagery, more indirect and subtle in its message, appears in a number of Mughal manuscripts. When visual allusions to a mystical poem are placed in the margins of a miniature painting within an illuminated manuscript, they function as a kind of gloss on the poetic text of
the manuscript. Though the margins of a painting or calligraphic panel usu-

ally serve as decoration, sometimes they may be the perfect place for patron and artist to make a statement about the regime's religious legitimacy. Standing in the margins of paintings in several sixteenth-century Indian manuscripts are figures who obviously represent either religious scholars or dervishes. Generally shown in profile, as though facing the action within the picture frame, their attitude of prayerful attentiveness and reverence suggests strongly that the patron wanted to display the support of such highly visible religious figures.[36]

Building Community

In addition to the formally public and functionally more private, tomb, a number of other important structures contribute to an understanding of community among Muslims. Among the public structures, the sabil, sabil-kuttab, and madrasa have been created for the unrestricted use of a relatively wide cross section of society. These structures either offer refreshment to all passersby or serve educational functions. The more private zawiya, *ribat*, and khanqah or tekke generally serve a residential function. Mosques and mosque complexes also have a place within the financial and social scheme.

A small institutional form the sabil, a public fountain, has played a surprisingly important role in several societies, especially in those of the arid Middle East. Although quite unimposing on first sight, the sabil both supplies an essential service and offers an occasion for reflection on several themes in Islamic spirituality. By contrast with similar public services provided in various ancient pre-Islamic societies, the sabil has taken on noteworthy symbolic significance. The Arabic word usually denotes "road, way, or path"; but because of frequent Qur'anic usage, it connotes in addition the context of acts performed with the Creator in mind. In other words, any action undertaken *fi sabil allah* (literally, "in the way of God") presupposes a religious motive. It appears, therefore, that both the sabil and the sabil-kuttab, a variation that combines a school with a water source, owe their existence at least partly to a spiritual or charitable impulse. In addition, a source of running water bears natural symbolic affinities with the ritual function of ablution before prayer, even though the sabil itself is not designed for that purpose.

But why did the kindly provision of water lead to the development of elaborate architectural settings? In addition to direct Qur'anic reminders of the importance of providing sustenance, a saying attributed to Muhammad appears to recommend the practice indirectly: "One who excavates a well, from which the thirsty among the jinns, mankind and birds cannot quench their thirst, God will render that person thirsty on the Day of Resurrection."[37] One contemporary explanation suggests that the patrons "sought to build, not just a source of water, but a holy building suitable for divine revelation, since water was regarded as a divine and not a mundane gift. It is God who makes rain to fall as a mercy, and it is God who gives it to the thirsty. Water symbolizes Creation. The sabil is therefore one of God's houses."[38] At least one such facility is known to have included a mihrab; one of its staff also acted as imam when the site served as a *musalla* (location for salat). In some instances the fountains are incorporated into larger architectural structures such as mosques or mausoleums. The ultimate symbolic referent here is the image of Paradise, with its springs of living water. The functions of bodily refreshment and spiritual nourishment mingle still more clearly in the sabil-kuttab, typically situating a Qur'an school for orphans on a second-story level above the fountain, which in turn sits over a cistern.[39] (See Fig. 28.)

Thus, certain scriptural verses have come to play both an inspirational and an emblematic role in the development of the sabil and other architectural manifestations of Islamic spiritual values. The two verses immediately following the Qur'an's celebrated Verse of Light (24:35) have often inspired and legitimated the construction of religious buildings such as the madrasa and khanqah (as well as the mosque). Qur'an 24:36–37 reads:

> [The Light of God shines] in houses God allows to be raised up and in
> which His name is recalled; therein praise Him, morning and evening,
> people whom neither buying nor selling distract from the remembrance of
> God or from the ritual prayer or from giving to the poor, people who fear
> [only] the day on which hearts and sight will be turned about.

These verses set the reflective tone for the activities that the building is meant to foster. A prominent example of this use is that on the monumental facade of the Mamluk sultan Hasan's madrasa complex in Cairo (1356–1363). (See Fig. 22.)

The madrasa, or college of law, became part of the Islamic architectural repertoire especially during and after the eleventh century. With its emphasis on education in religious law, the madrasa produced scholars steeped in the principles of one of the four Sunni schools of jurisprudence. In a number of important instances, madrasas offered instruction and housing to members of more than one law school, as in the Mamluk Sultan Hasan complex in Cairo and the Sulaymaniye complex in Istanbul. But the institution originally functioned as an instrument for the spread of Sunni law in areas previously under significant Shi'i influence.[40] Eventually the institution's mis-

Figure 28.   Sabil-kuttab (1744) of the Ottoman administrator ʿAbd ar-Rahman Katkhuda in Cairo, with water facility below and Qurʾan school above.

sion of intra-Islamic apologetics diminished, while the Shiʿi legal schools developed their own versions of the madrasa as well. The royal mosque of Shah ʿAbbas I in Isfahan, for example, provides two facilities flanking its prayer hall.

Mosques are the most important of public religious institutions. As a venue of prayer, the mosque has served primarily as a space for the gathering of the local community. A hierarchy of mosque types developed in many Muslim societies. Ideally, each large urban area has one congregational mosque, called in Arabic a *masjid al-jamiʿ* or simply *jamiʿ*, spacious enough to accommodate the city's entire population. In practice, many bigger cities boasted more than one such mosque. Still, at the level of major institutions are those mosques that occupy a wing or vaulted alcove of a madrasa, or a residential or funerary facility. Neighborhoods or villages usually have their own mosques, freestanding (or at least separate) structures usually called simply masjid. Finally, the generic term *musalla* (place of ritual prayer) has been applied to both ends of the spatial spectrum. On one end, smaller places of ritual prayer have often been incorporated into royal residences, serving in effect as private chapels or oratories. On the other, a musalla can be a huge open air space identified by nothing more than a mihrab.

In contrast to the relatively accessible institutions of sabil, sabil-kuttab, and madrasa, others serve a narrower public. Several important endowed institutions providing for the residential and other communal needs of a smaller segment of the population are the ribat, the zawiya, and, most importantly, the khanqah and its kindred form, the tekke. These structures did not always remain neatly distinct in either form or function, so the terms have been used synonymously at times; still, their original functions had several clear and significant variations. The ribat began as a frontier outpost designed to house Muslims engaged in spreading the religion into new territory. By around the year 800, the function of the institution had shifted; now its inhabitants were spiritual warriors engaged in the Greater Jihad and bent on the conquest of their own inner negative tendencies. These bands of spiritual combatants had much in common with the Sufi orders that developed formally later; hence, the ribat is associated with Sufism. While in the ribat, residents occupied themselves extensively with religious observances. Some ribats, founded for the exclusive use of women, offered protection to virtuous elderly women or those who had been abandoned or divorced.

The ribat as a separate institution gradually gave way to the zawiya. As an architectural term, *zawiya* (literally, "corner," used mostly in Arabic documents) often refers to a portion of a building, dedicated to the instructional use of a single shaykh and his disciples. Some separate structures also called zawiyas functioned as residences for a particular shaykh and his family, often with facilities for a gathering of followers. In some instances shaykhs were buried in their zawiyas, thus transforming the structure into a place of religious visitation. A shaykh's disciples often facilitated the organization's spread by founding new zawiyas elsewhere. Shaykhs frequently enjoyed the patronage of wealthy members of the princely class, who both endowed the institutions and availed themselves of the shaykh's counsel. Unlike the ribat, the zawiya was usually associated with a particular shaykh and Sufi tariqa; even so, life in a zawiya tended to be less regulated than that in the khanqah. In general neither the ribat nor the zawiya achieved the architectural significance of the khanqah.[41]

Various regimes throughout Islamic history have used the endowment of institutions such as the khanqah in the interest of greater political control, by sponsoring those religious groups they believed would be most likely to support their political program—or least likely to resist it. Since the khanqah often represented a more moderate form of Sufi practice than that of the zawiyas and ribats, regimes like that of the Egyptian Mamluks naturally preferred to support khanqahs. Among their more prominent functional features (though not necessarily combined in any particular instance) are residential quarters, kitchens, bathhouses, facilities for the shaykh, funerary chambers, madrasas, and prayer halls with associated facilities for ritual ablution.

Several important features distinguish the khanqah from the zawiya. Admission to the former was controlled, whereas the latter tended to be more open, welcoming women as well as non-Sufis. Second, khanqahs have not typically been commissioned in the name of a specific shaykh, nor has their membership been limited to a single tariqa as in the case of zawiyas. Finally, since the deed of endowment stipulated in detail both acceptable behavior and the terms of a resident's livelihood in a khanqah, the individual khanqah Sufi was far more independent of the shaykh than was the zawiya resident. In other words, the allegiance of residents of a khanqah was more institutional than personal.[42]

Salah ad-Din introduced the khanqah to Egypt in 1173, and under the Mamluks the practice of official patronage of Sufi institutions led to the religious establishment's (i.e., the 'ulama') acceptance of the relatively new institution. Sultan Baybars I built his foundation in the middle of Cairo (1306–1310). His purpose in doing so was both to take advantage of an explicit association with that great defender of Sunni Islam, Salah ad-Din, and to hasten public acceptance of a foundation linked directly to Sufism. The waqf dedicating the complex with its khanqah, ribat, and mausoleum, says that the facility will be available to all Sufis of whatever race, legal school, or confraternity, so long as they "conform to their own rules of conduct (adab)." It stipulates that the foundation will serve the poor and those who are passing through. In addition, the endowment distinguishes between the khanqah's function as residence for a more stable population, and the ribat's availability to temporary residents; each of these two main wings of the foundation had its own shaykh and administrative staff. This is a good example of the persistence of the term *ribat* in reference to part of a larger institution rather than to a separate entity.[43]

Figure 29.   Seen from one of the two minarets that frame the entry facade (on the west side), the central courtyard of the khanqah of the Mamluk Faraj ibn Barquq (1410), Cairo, showing the ablution fountain, the prayer hall with its sermon-repeater's platform (*dikka*), and the smaller dome over the mihrab. To the right is the drum of one of the twin domes of the burial chambers that flank the prayer hall. The shaykh's residence was along the right wall, and Sufi cells were along the left. The roofless burial enclosures of Cairo's northern cemetery are in the background.

A number of khanqahs built in Mamluk Cairo rank as outstanding architectural works. The early fifteenth-century complex of Faraj ibn Barquq in Cairo's northern cemetery is an excellent example. Its two elaborately detailed multistaged minarets set this foundation apart from the other monuments in the cemetery. Within the roughly square perimeter is a courtyard centered on a fountain. On the qibla side, a prayer hall open to the courtyard is flanked by two domed funerary chambers in which the founder and members of his family are buried (see Fig. 29). Around the other three sides of the courtyard are multistoried residential and service facilities, including special quarters for the shaykh and his assistants, smaller cells for resident Sufis, and a public kitchen. Placement of this complex in the midst of a necropolis might seem odd, but it is a reminder that in some cultures death has not been segregated from life.[44] Few active khanqahs still provide a full range of services today, and Sufi groups gather now where they can find available space. (See Fig. 32.)

Throughout the Ottoman lands, especially from the latter half of the fifteenth century on, the Turkic parallel to the khanqah, the tekke, played an important role in the diffusion of Sufism. The first Bosnian foundation, for example, dating to the 1460s and surviving into the twentieth century, appeared on the present site of the city of Sarajevo. Until recent outbreaks of civil conflict in the former Yugoslavia, a number of Bosnian tekkes continued to witness regular Sufi rituals. It appears that in more recent times these foundations, once devoted mostly to housing male members of religious orders, regularly offered hospitality to travelers and also included facilities for women. Thus, the tekke shares some of the functions of the ribat. As elsewhere in the Islamic world, these tekkes often enclose the tombs of founders and their successor shaykhs.[45]

In the context of the Ottoman empire, the terms *tekke* and *khanqah* are the most generic, referring to a range of institutional foundations. *Asitane* refers to a given confraternity's principal facility or grand lodge. *Zawiya* originally referred to the domicile of a saintly recluse but gradually came to denote a hostel for itinerant dervishes.[46] Zawiya-mosques served as both places of prayer and hostels. A dergah was generally a tekke with the tomb of a founding figure adjacent to it. An order's asitane often included a prayer hall; a space for engaging in the order's distinctive paraliturgical practice (*semahane*), such as the circular prayer ritual of the Mevlevi whirling dervishes; a facility for various devotional rites (*tevhithane*); and residential facilities for members and their families as well as for unmarried members.

Other urban forms included former Byzantine churches given to the orders by the sultan, preexisting mosques or madrasas, mosque complexes including social-service facilities such as soup kitchens and shaykhs' residences. Turkish tekkes in Istanbul tended to be far less spectacular architecturally than most mosques and madrasas.[47] According to Raymond Lifchez, "The received opinion is that monumental architecture indicates a society's dearest values—for here it has expended its greatest resources. But the tekkes of Istanbul point to another way of thinking: that monumentality can be said to reflect access to wealth and political power but not necessarily what people cherish most in their lives."[48] The unpretentious appearance of many Sufi residences is a reminder of the call to simplicity that, at least in the past, gave rise to Sufism. At its best, Sufism teaches that some of the most remarkable spiritual experiences occur in the most unremarkable settings.

As for its architectural scale, the Ottoman tekke ranks between the imperial and the more ordinary modes. Tekke architecture provides clues to the relative importance of a particular dervish institution. In general, tekkes appeared in cities, while zawiyas played an Islamizing role outside villages and along trade routes. Mid-nineteenth century Istanbul, with a population of some 750,000 people, had nearly three hundred tekkes representing around twenty of the thirty-seven well-established orders in Turkey. During the nineteenth century in Turkey, tekke membership averaged from 4 to 7 dervishes, with some housing up to 30 and a few with as many as 50 to 100.[49]

In medieval India, the khanqah provided an essential link in the establishment and impact of Sufi orders. In the early fourteenth century, khanqahs and similar residential facilities, such as the smaller and more austere *jama'at khana* (an assembly hall that sometimes formed a portion of a khanqah as well), numbered some two thousand in Delhi. One classic source widely used in India says that the construction of khanqahs provides three benefits: "it offers shelter for mystics who have no home of their own; it provides the setting for fostering a communitarian discipline; and in that setting the residents can offer both support and mutually constructive criticism."[50]

The best-known medieval Indian khanqah was that of the early fourteenth-century Chishti shaykh Nizam ad-Din Awliya'. The jama'at khana stood at the center of the complex, flanked by individual cells and opening into a courtyard surrounded by a portico or veranda. Across the courtyard from the jama'at khana stood a vestibule with access through the main gate; adjacent to that was the kitchen. The shaykh lived in second-floor quarters, over the jama'at khana, where he would receive disciples for consultation. Not all such facilities enjoyed the support of endowments, and in this instance the residents also relied on charitable donations. Virtually anyone could seek refuge there. Residences of the Suhrawardi Sufi tariqa used a different organizational model. While the abstemious Chishtis withdrew unambiguously from public life as far as possible, the Suhrawardis lived more comfortably and cultivated the patronage of bureaucrats and the princely class.

As the wide range of architectural developments suggests, Muslims have evolved ways of responding to the religious obligation of fostering community life and to the opportunities for celebrating community while acknowledging a plurality of human needs. Islamic institutional diversity reflects, at the same time, the ways in which the Islamic tradition has adapted to tremendously varied cultural settings.

Spirituality of Artist and Patron

Although the sincerity and personal motivation of a religious individual is difficult to assess, professions of faith buried in chancery caches and chiseled on monumental facades provide an entrée into an often neglected dimension of Islamic spirituality. Deeds of charitable endowment frequently note that the work arises out of a desire to seek God's favor, to reap a heavenly reward, and generally to secure the donor's nearness to God.[51] There is no doubt that the waqf offered a tax advantage to the wealthy, secured much endowed property against the threat of confiscation, and gave the donor the right to pay salary to relatives. Still, the value of the donors' stated claims to loftier goals than money can buy are not to be entirely discounted. In fact, from the earliest times Muslim sources on the topic have acknowledged the virtual inevitability of mixed motivation on the part of donors. One such source says that endowment provisions in the law are meant to allow the giver "to secure spiritual advancement in the life to come and also popularity in this life in the same way as by [outright] gifts and bequests but in a higher degree."[52]

Mustafa 'Ali, a shrewd Ottoman bureaucrat of the late sixteenth century, offers a perspective from within the system. In the mirror for princes he wrote for Sultan Murad III (r. 1574–1595), he makes two forthright comments about royal patronage of architecture. First, rulers who build mosques, tekkes, or madrasas in their already well-accoutered capital cities clearly do not do so out of a desire to gain spiritual merit. As any thoughtful person can tell, "[T]hese are pious deeds performed in order to accomplish being a leader and to make a good reputation." To provide such services to remote areas where people are truly in need, on the other hand, is a spiritually meritorious act. Second, even when a sultan wishes to construct edifices to serve authentically charitable purposes, religious law prohibits the use of public funds; the money must come either from private wealth or from booty seized in military campaigns.[53]

Patrons have sometimes been tempted to play God by insinuating themselves into the creative process. An artist who wants to make a living needs to maintain the quality of the objects he or she produces. In a letter to his premier calligrapher, the Timurid patron Sultan Husayn Mirza reminds the artist whence came the bread on his table:

> May the best of scribes, Master Nizamuddin Sultan-Ali, realize that the favor and patronage of the patron's all-solving mind that have attached to him are more apparent than the sun, and the royal good opinion of his art is more obvious than yesterday. We have written the page of his hopes with the pen of affection, drawn the pen of abrogation [a Qur'anic theme] through the calligraphy of former masters, and consider him above all others in that art. However, in the royal divans that have been scriven by his miraculous pen, many mistakes and errors are to be seen, and scratching and corrections in such enchanting calligraphy are unforgivable.[54]

Here the patron's concern over how the artist's work might reflect adversely on the patron is clearly paramount. For the calligrapher, the admonition must have been a keen reminder of his own fallibility.

The religious dimensions of the cultural systems of art and patronage that have flourished in the great capitals of the Islamic world must be placed in context of the worldview of the artists and their patrons. Artistic creation is always an expression of a particular worldview. Muslims living in more traditional societies have often pictured the world as an ordered, harmonious whole suffused with meaning by a sovereign creator. In such a world, the human creative process is always to some extent an expression of religious sentiment, a humble cooperation in and mimesis of God's own creativity.

Ottoman texts dedicated to chronicling the architectural efforts of certain master builders and their patrons invariably set their subject within a thoroughly religious context, sometimes reaching back to creation itself. Even if the language is stylized, referring to God's work as "a world palace that resembles a rose garden," it nevertheless reflects a religiously informed model of reality. Jale Erzen explains the situation with a theatrical metaphor. The patron is the producer, and the artist is the playwright-director. According to Erzen, one can detect in both miniature painting and architecture, a "clearly theatrical atmosphere . . . which may be rooted in the artist's world-view: he is there to perform on an already ordered stage and to match and relate his creation to an already perfect organization handed down to him. God is watching, as is also the Sultan."[55]

For a sultan to initiate, for example, a renovation of the sacred precincts of Mecca and Medina was a certain sign of power, wealth, and prestige, but it was more. And for the artist, a commission from the sovereign to undertake such a task was more than a mere occasion to display virtuosity. To be so engaged was above all to move one tentative step closer to the source of that harmony that is God's original creation and that sanctity to which all of creation's signs advert. Sinan, Sulayman the Magnificent's chief architect, was sent to Mecca to assess the state of the Ka'ba and determine how extensive its repairs would be. A classic source records the personal effect the experience had on him. As Sinan gazed on the holy place, the "blessed building appeared here and there to lean and incline like the figure of an ascetic. And its four sides, the lower parts of the honored walls and towers of happy sign, had in some places spread a bit into the rose garden of the Noble Sanctuary and were arranged and ordered like the stringing together of a pearl necklace."[56] This was no ordinary job for Sinan, nor for those who assumed his duties after his death; it was a singular honor and grace.

According to anecdotal evidence, patronage of the arts has often arisen out of a patron's desire for religious merit. The Egyptian historian Maqrizi (1364–1442), for instance, recounts how Sultan an-Nasir Muhammad experienced severe abdominal distress while hunting. He vowed that if God delivered him, he would commemorate his healing by constructing a khanqah in that place.[57] On the whole, however, royal patrons of architecture seem to have been moved by a desire to associate themselves with the holy places. This motive underscores the importance of the religious legitimation of political power. One document tells how the Safavid shah ʿAbbas I felt as he contemplated his elaborate design for the city of Isfahan. Though he had built wondrous gardens designed to rival Paradise itself,

> still his mind was troubled by, and his heart dwelled on, the thought that just as that paradise-like city was the envy of the country . . . so that noble presence [i.e., the shah] wanted the sublime mosque, the madrasas and the holy spots to be the finest of mosques and spots of Iran and to resemble in beauty and purity the Bayt al-Maʿmur [the Kaʿba] and the Masjid al-Aqsa [in Jerusalem].

Not long afterward, a hitherto unknown marble quarry was discovered nearby, confirming the shah in his convictions:

> Surely those stones had been deposited there by the powerful eternal hand which had hidden them from the eyes of man for the purpose of beautifying and adorning this noble place of worship. . . . From this, one can infer that this discovery is a clear sign from God and a manifest token of the veracity of the intention and pious devotion of the builder as well as the power and status of this constructor in the court of the World-Adorning Creator.[58]

Statements like this may be read skeptically, but the anecdote attests to the pervasive influence of religious culture.

Artists, too, have their reasons for choosing one or another medium of creative activity. One of the Ottoman empire's most famous architects, Mehmed Aga (fl. c. 1600), is said to have chosen architecture as a result of ongoing consultation with a spiritual guide, a shaykh of the Halveti Sufi order (a spiritual forebear of the shaykh in Fig. 30). Conferring his blessing on the future builder, the shaykh said:

> Son, this art and work were seen fit and worthy for you because for the most part it is the work of architects to build noble Friday mosques, and fine small mosques, and medreses [madrasas], and bridges, and tekyes [tekkes] . . . and all sorts of charitable and pious buildings. In accord with the blessed Tradition . . . if one builds a blessed mosque, even if it is like the nest of a tiny bird, in reward for it, God—may He be glorified and His name exalted—makes a room in heaven for that person. . . . Now what a

great blessing it is if a man who is involved with this sort of art attending unremittingly, to the limit of his strength, to prayer and witnessing, thus arrives at his final end! And what a joy of the two worlds it is that while in the manner described you prosper in this life, in truth you also obtain the other world. You must master this art without delay![59]

A ruler does not want to risk loss of authority by undercutting the religious legitimation upon which rule depends, at least to some degree. But powerful religious figures and movements have often tugged at the allegiance of Muslims in many cultures, thus increasing the likelihood of divided loyalties among a ruler's subjects. Efforts to use such forces to advantage have often materialized in royal support for the institutions that serve the followers of charismatic religious leaders. From Morocco to Indonesia, enormous sums of money have gone into the endowment, building or renovation, and general financial support of holy places associated with holy persons.

Some tomb-shrines have become centers of entire towns. Those of Mulay Idris I (d. c. 793) on Mount Serhun near Fez, Morocco, and of Mulay Idris II (d. 828) in Fez are two such sites. Since devotion to these two Friends of God and descendants of Muhammad runs deep among the people, for centuries Moroccan governments have contributed to the maintenance of these holy sites.

Further to the east is an example of a different sort of shrine. An important study of Timurid architecture in Iran and central Asia notes that "although social and economic reasons may account in part for the preponderance of 'charitable works' within the roster of known monuments, the degree of deep religious commitment on the part of the patrons should not be underestimated. Among the ruling classes this genuine spiritual feeling was closely linked to the popular veneration of holy men."[60] Timur was so taken with the spirit of the already long-deceased Shaykh Ahmad Yasawi (d. 1166) that he undertook a major architectural project to honor the shaykh; in 1397, he built a glorious new tomb at the site of the original grave. Timur became personally involved in the project, even stipulating the central dome's height of 126 feet. Highly visible near an oasis along a pilgrimage and caravan road, this splendid work is a statement of Timur's devotion as well as a monument to the shaykh. Questions of religious motivation are complex and subtle. The motives of an individual patron may vary from one type of project to another. Especially in the case of funding the more public (mostly architectural) enterprises, a patron must consider what constituency a project is meant to serve.

Political motives do not obliterate genuine devotion; they can merely cast doubt on the sincerity of a ruler's claim of religious motivation. Commenting on the widespread construction and renovation of shrines and tombs in the Ottoman context, Baha Tanman attributes the activity to "a genuine popular devotion to the saints. . . . Such veneration is known to have persisted even at times when the civil authorities took stiff measures to suppress it, actually forcing it underground."[61] Rumi's tomb in Konya (see Fig. 12) was originally built under a Saljuqid ruler, a predecessor of the Ottomans. But under Sulayman's rule, the tomb, already a popular place of pilgrimage for generations, was renovated and the facilities expanded. Now Rumi's final resting place provides a stunningly ironic example of the enormous power of such holy places. When Mustafa Kemal Ataturk (d. 1938) officially proclaimed the secular Turkish Republic early in this century, he suppressed the Sufi orders because they represented too great a potential force for disruption in his experiment in governing a Muslim nation. Members of the Mevlevi tariqa were officially disbanded and no longer allowed to gather publicly. But the Turkish Ministry of Culture continues to subsidize Rumi's tomb as a "museum," and pilgrims continue to visit it as a shrine. A striking tribute to the enduring spirit of Rumi (and indirectly of scores of other holy persons) appears on a 5,000 Turkish lira currency note in use until inflation rendered it virtually worthless: one side depicts a sternly serious Ataturk in profile; the other, a benignly smiling Rumi next to the fluted green dome beneath which three dervishes whirl.

While many Friends of God lived, they became well known both as teachers and as accomplished mystics. However, holy men and women whose burial places have grown into institutional foundations generally acquire greater fame in death than they had known in life. For centuries Friends of God have provided much religious focus and emotional energy within the greater Muslim community, and the holiness and spiritual ideals they represent have given the impetus for building some of Islam's most important institutions and monuments.

6 Pedagogy
Fanning Spark into Flame

LEARNING FOR LIFE

Aristotle observed that human beings by nature desire to know. The consistent pursuit of knowledge, however, comes less naturally than the desire. The attainment of practical knowledge that promises relatively immediate rewards is hard enough for human beings; and when the results of the work of learning are slow in coming, the challenge is far greater. The prospect of deferred gratification makes any learning curve seem impossibly steep. Here is where the spiritual guide, the shaykh or pir, assists the seeker as the path becomes more difficult. The demands of the so-called Greater Jihad are implicit in all aspects of Islamic practice. Every true seeker must finally delve into the inner mysteries of individual spiritual discipline and the struggle to know the whole truth about life.

Much of the textual material already discussed has included an obviously pedagogical aspect. Books on how to recite Qur'an, manuals outlining the pilgrimage ritual, stories of exemplary figures, treatises on the spiritual requirements of great calligraphy, didactic poetry, and instructions in the behavior expected of members of religious organizations—these and many similar texts have performed important teaching functions.

Like followers of any religious tradition, Muslims are susceptible to the subtle divisiveness and evident stratification that can result from spiritual elitism. In virtually every society some individuals choose, for a variety of reasons, to devote themselves entirely to a spiritual quest. Muslims have given institutional shape to that concern by providing services that foster a sense of community among devoted spiritual seekers. The increasingly arduous inner path of the individual Muslim seeker, however, has been mapped out, often by trial and error, by Islam's spiritual professionals.

Issues and Questions

In this chapter I assume four underlying issues: individual spiritual needs, pedagogical resources produced to address those needs, pedagogical strate-

Figure 30.   (*Opposite*) The shaykh of the Halveti-Jerrahi Sufi order teaching after the group performed its communal sama' ceremony (1988), Istanbul.

gies to make those resources available, and the literary forms designed to communicate those strategies. What are the deepest spiritual needs of the individual, and how may they be discerned accurately? Every spiritual way-farer willing to attempt the quest implicitly accepts the challenge of a life-long call to conversion. What are the principal pedagogical resources available to the seekers? The most important resources are always other persons who have struggled to find their way along the path, and who are willing to share the wisdom of experience. What pedagogical strategies have proved most effective? Centuries of experience have given Muslim spiritual guides a solid tradition from which to choose the most appropriate strategies. Finally, what modes of communication have proven most effective in conveying this wealth of insight? Muslim scholars of the spiritual life have adapted several existing literary forms to the purposes of this higher pedagogy; here I provide a closer look at these adaptations. Islam's theorists and spiritual guides have also created several important new genres for explaining to seekers the demands of the interior life.

Islamic instructional works are almost entirely in prose, have rarely been illustrated, and are generally unrelated directly to any commonly produced visual artifacts. They comprise the more technical and theoretical writings, and those intended to instill devotion or hand on the charism of the teacher, or both. I use the terms *instructional* and *pedagogical* in the broad sense that all of these works are designed to pass along the essential teachings and values of individual spiritual guides and their disciples. But this is decidedly advanced pedagogy in the finer points of the path (*tarbiya*) rather than the more generic kind of religious education implied in the imparting of knowledge (*ta'lim*). In this chapter and the next, I emphasize a progressive movement toward more demanding material, and a development from the public to the intimate, from the ordinary to the arcane.

Sufism's Great Books

Every cultural and educational tradition eventually formulates its canon—books considered essential to the formation of a liberally educated person. Although a single definitive list is difficult to compile in the case of Islam's mystical tradition, I propose a tentative one. Muslim mystics have sometimes taken a dim view of books and of the intellectual inquiry necessary to produce them. Sayings such as "Break the inkpots and tear up the texts" suggest an unambiguous suspicion of reliance on the rational mind. Despite this attitude, however, I suggest that Islam has produced a considerably greater wealth of written material on the mystical sciences generally than either Judaism or Christianity. Whole libraries of sources, which range over an extraordinary breadth of questions, exist in over a dozen languages. These materials have only begun to become available in reliable editions and translations.

The sources fall into two large categories. First are those gathered and edited works whose individual components were originally delivered orally or in writing to individuals and groups of diverse background. These include public addresses by famous saintly teachers on various spiritual topics; that distinctive genre that brings together sayings, utterances, or informal discourses originally delivered orally, and later transcribed and collected by a teacher's disciples; and epistolary forms, both those originally written and sent, and those that employ the form as a literary conceit.

The second large category comprises works intended for a generally more limited public consisting of individuals who are often further advanced in their understanding of the issues and better able to consider increasingly subtle questions of spiritual growth. This distinction is not hard and fast, for the addressees of letters and members of audiences at the lectures and discourses that make up the first category are not invariably neophytes.

As for content, the texts in the second group tend to be more theoretical and technical. Some of these materials include poetry as an essential element. There are works designed to help aspirants begin their journeys along the spiritual path; these function as descriptions of the itinerary. Other sources afford the traveler a bigger picture, much as a detailed map might; these are the sometimes voluminous handbooks of Sufi teaching. And another genre helps the wayfarer negotiate new territory the way a Berlitz pocketbook of foreign phrases might assist a traveler; these are dictionaries and glossaries of specific terms that have taken on special meanings for spiritual seekers.

FROM THE GREAT TEACHERS

A great teacher is rare. Students fortunate enough to encounter one often attempt to preserve for posterity some of what they have learned. Nowadays teachers are encouraged to publish their best insights in books and articles they write themselves. In the past, students have often taken up the task of preserving an influential teacher's most worthwhile reflections for the benefit of others.

Two similar types of literature—that originally delivered orally, and that written down, edited, and collected only later—have kept alive the words of some of Islam's master teachers. Sometimes the formal public lecture or sermon is difficult to distinguish from the conversational and seminarlike discourse. A subtle difference in tone, along with the elements of give-and-take that have survived the editing process of some of the discourses, nevertheless warrants a distinction. These works are mostly prose but often contain poetry, usually illustrative citations of other authors but sometimes creations of the teaching shaykh. The letters of shaykhs and spiritual guides addressed to smaller groups and to individuals also preserve important teachings. Even when treating technical matters of mystical theology, these writings usually respond to specific questions that have arisen within the community assembled around a spiritual guide, whether the recorder has actually been in the presence of the guide or is communicating by letter.

Between Sermon and Seminar

Desire to know more about the spiritual life has always brought crowds, whatever their religious affiliation, to hear speakers renowned for their distinctive insights. For centuries a type of lecture-sermon has played a significant role in educating Muslims interested in spiritual issues beyond what they hear in their local Friday sermon. ʿAbd al-Qadir al-Jilani is among the teachers most famous for his legacy of public exhortations. The *Revelations of the Unseen* (*Futuh al-ghayb*) and *The Sublime Revelation* (*Al-Fath ar-rabbani*) are two large collections of addresses attributed to him. These apparently originated as formal and integrally crafted exhortations addressed to an audience that rarely interacted with the speaker. They share these two features with the classic khutba. The difference between such material and khutba is that these addresses typically discuss themes that presuppose a more advanced level of religious sophistication on the part of their audience.

Beginning around 1127, in Baghdad, the fifty-one-year-old Jilani began to lecture three times a week—at the hostel on Wednesday mornings, in the madrasa on Tuesday nights, and at the open-air prayer space called an ʿidgah (literally, "feast place") on Friday mornings. The shaykh himself recounts that for a while his audiences were quite small; but word spread, so that the crowds became too large to fit in a mosque, even when he spoke at night: "My chair was then carried to the main street, then to the outskirts of the city, which became the new gathering place. People would come on foot, on horses, mules, mares, and camels. You could see them standing in a huge circle numbering nearly seventy thousand at some meetings."[1] In his own written introduction to the collected *Revelations of the Unseen*, Jilani sums up the genesis and purpose of the lectures:

> So now, from among such statements as the tongue is enabled to utter, the power of speech to express, the fingers to record, and the eloquence of

language to explain, here are some words that arose and emerged from me as "Revelations of the Unseen." They alighted within my being and occupied its inner space, till the energy of the experience brought them forth and made them outwardly apparent. Then the kindness of the Benefactor and the mercy of the Lord of mankind took care of their publication in the proper literary format, for the benefit of students and seekers of the truth.[2]

Technically known as utterances (*maqalat*), Jilani's eighty lectures discuss various aspects of a seeker's relationship to God, and of the spiritual discipline required to progress in that relationship. One of Jilani's methodological principles is that all mystical questions must be treated within the context of Islamic law. One example in which he distinguishes between obligatory and additional observances makes his concern clear. He quotes a saying attributed to 'Ali: "The likeness of one who performs the supererogatory prayers before the obligatory ones is that of a woman who gets pregnant, carries until the time of delivery is near, and then has a miscarriage, losing both the foetus and the experience of childbirth." The shaykh adds his own conclusion: "Thus the worshipper finds that his supererogatory prayer is not acceptable to God as long as he has not performed the obligatory worship."[3] Ultimately purity of heart allows the individual to discern God's signs in the innermost recesses of the self.

A prominent theme running through Jilani's discourses amounts to a sociology of the spiritual universe. Time and again the teacher speaks of the various levels of spiritual authority or attainment—messenger (*rasul*), prophet (*nabi*), Friend of God (*wali*), shaykh, seeker (*murid*), "substitute" (*badal*), trusted one (*siddiq*), martyr-witness (*shahid*)—as a pedagogical structure for illustrating some central principle, for example:

> God is always testing His believing servant in proportion to his faith. Thus if a person's faith is great and steadily increasing, his trial will be great as well. The trial of a Messenger is greater than that of a Prophet, because his faith is greater. The trial of a Prophet is greater than that of a *Badal*, and the trial of a *Badal* is greater than that of a *Wali*.[4]

His treatment of the concept of an elaborate spiritual hierarchy presupposes a fairly advanced level of religious education. Here the teacher has moved beyond the classic tripartite division of seekers into the categories of beginners, the more advanced, and the fully accomplished. The more expansive structure of this cosmic hierarchy offers the teacher a ready supply of paradigmatic figures who represent varying degrees of proficiency in the spiritual disciplines.

The shaykh's sixty-two lectures collected in the work called *The Sub-*

lime Revelation are generally much longer than those of the *Revelations of the Unseen*. The compiler includes at the beginning of each a note about the time, and sometimes the place, of its delivery. These speeches also convey a much more vivid sense of the teacher's style, punctuated as they are with rhetorical addresses such as "O my people!" or "O young man!" According to the student-editor, the teacher used to launch into his addresses quite spontaneously, without text or notes, in response to whatever "revelation" happened to descend upon him in that moment.[5]

Borrowed Notes

As a result of the complex editorial process by which the teachings of the great spiritual guides have survived, it is often difficult to draw a clean line between the public lecture and the more conversational discourse. One cannot always tell whether or when a compiler has deleted elements of give-and-take between speaker and audience. The works attributed to Jilani are rare good examples of both types of literature. His *Utterances (Mulfuzat)* offers a picture of the teacher surrounded by disciples whom he allows to eavesdrop on his thoughts and peer through a window into his soul to observe how he works through important issues. Typically someone asks a question; then the teacher either responds briefly and discourses at length on a related topic, or elaborates on the implications of the question. The following example makes it clear that the teacher encouraged frank and open exchange: One day after the shaykh had finished a lesson in which he responded vigorously to a particular listener, another student said to Jilani, "You were quite extreme in your admonition, and you spoke to him very harshly!" The teacher said in reply, "If my words have had any effect upon him, he will surely come back for more." The compiler of the work observes that the student not only continued to attend the seminars but often came to see the shaykh privately.[6]

The discourse or conference form (*malfuz;* pl., *malfuzat*, literally, "expressions, utterances") survives in several languages and occurs in a number of historical and cultural contexts, but the most important examples are in Persian. Recorded in disparate segments sometimes called assemblies, the genre seems to have become a major literary vehicle sometime in the late twelfth or early thirteenth century, providing much fuller information about shaykhs from that period on than exist for almost any earlier figures. The genre often includes short narrative sections, didactic poetry and sapiential sayings (wisdom literature), and the predictable citation of the Qur'an.

Malfuzat fall into two main categories. Some bear dates, and were recorded and collected shortly after the death of the shaykh. In a few cases the master collaborated in and approved the final edition. Somewhat less reliable are collections made by disciples or descendants many years after the shaykh's death. Such works often embrace several subgenres, including biographical sketches, compendiums of the shaykh's essential doctrine, and accounts of the teacher's wondrous deeds and characteristic spiritual disciplines. An early collection of malfuzat recorded long after the death of its subject is that of Abu Saʿid ibn Abi ʾl-Khayr.[7] Among other examples of the genre are Rumi's, *Discourses (Fihi ma fihi,* literally, "In it what is in it," therefore, a miscellany) and a spate of sibling works from the Indian subcontinent, written in the fourteenth and fifteenth centuries, such as Nizam ad-Din Awliya's *Morals for the Heart (Fawaʾid al-fuʾad)* and Sharaf ad-Din Maneri's *Table Laden with Good Things (Khwan-i pur niʿmat).* This genre also spread to Southeast Asia.

Rumi's *Discourses* is one of the earliest works of its type. A disciple compiled these discourses delivered toward the end of Rumi's life. In the nearly six dozen segments, ranging in length from half a page to several pages, Rumi covers a broad spectrum of topics, often treating several disparate issues in a single session. His patron, Muʿin ad-Din, *parvana* (chief minister) of the Saljuqid sultanate of Rum, figures prominently in the discourses. The first piece begins with a justification of Rumi's occasional visits to the *parvana.* Rumi uses a bit of intriguing logic to wrest a favorable interpretation from a saying of Muhammad's that appears to condemn outright the visitation of princes by religious scholars. Muhammad said, "The worst scholar is one who visits princes, but the best prince is one who visits scholars." Rumi reads the hadith metaphorically: "Its true meaning is that the worst scholar is one who receives support from princes, whom he must fear in order to gain his livelihood."[8] He then offers the prime minister the sort of counsel one finds, in a more general form, in the mirror for princes. Indeed one feature that seems to distinguish Rumi's malfuzat from those of many later spiritual authorities is that some of his discourses occur in the palace rather than in the shaykh's own meeting place.

Rumi's discourses frequently cite the Qurʾan and occasionally quote his own poetry as well as that of other authors. On the whole, the teacher attempts to bring to light the esoteric meanings of issues raised, including exegeses of scriptural texts and hadiths. Rumi's discourses retain occasional indications of the original dialogue form. Sometimes he responds in detail to an initial "someone said," or to a query from the ruler or another in attendance. In several cases, much of the discourse is an extended conversation.

Here someone asked whether or not there is harm in putting one's hopes in God and expecting a good recompense for having done good and good works.

Yes, one must have hope and faith, or, expressed another way, fear and hope. Someone asked me, since hope itself is a good thing, what fear is. "Show me fear without hope," I said, "or hope without fear, for these two are inseparable." Since you ask, I'll give you an example. When someone plants wheat, he of course hopes that it will grow. At the same time, however, he is fearful that some blight or disaster may befall it. . . . A sick man takes a bitter medicine and gives up ten sweet things he enjoys. If it weren't for the hope he has of getting well, how could he tolerate such a thing?[9]

Nizam ad-Din Awliya''s early fourteenth-century *Morals for the Heart* was one of many of a genre especially popular among members of the Chishti tariqa, serving as a primary means of passing on the order's distinctive manner of dealing with everyday issues. Compiled by the disciple Amir Hasan Sijzi, the collection became a model for similar works by members of virtually all the other major Sufi fraternities of the Indian subcontinent. Like Rumi, Nizam ad-Din uses parable and anecdote to address concerns indirectly rather than head-on. The effect of his response is both gentle and, to the receptive listener or reader, striking. Nizam ad-Din emphasizes service to one's fellows, total dedication to God, self-discipline, nonviolence, profound self-knowledge in one's relationships, and the maintenance of proper order within the Chishti organization.[10]

Morals for the Heart represents a complex communication process, as do most other works of its kind. As Bruce Lawrence observes, several factors converge here. The spiritual teacher's own relationship with God is essentially noncommunicable. Nevertheless, the teacher strives to communicate something of that experience orally. Then the disciple labors to preserve that communication in writing. In the unique instance of Nizam ad-Din's malfuzat, the shaykh's personal intervention in the disciple's editing confers on the final work the character of a deliberate literary product. According to Lawrence, "Perhaps nothing can better illustrate the compatibility verging on symbiosis between the saint and the recorder than the special role of verse throughout [the work]." The editor-compiler Amir Hasan not only translated several existing poems from Arabic into Persian but even composed others on the topic at hand and included them—with the teacher's approval—in the final text.[11]

On 6 November 1308, this conversation occurred between Amir Hasan and Nizam ad-Din:

Figure 31.   Tomb of Shaykh Salim Chishti (d. 1572) inside the Mughal emperor Akbar's mosque in the palace-city of Fatehpur Sikri, India. This monument was constructed over a period from the sixteenth to the seventeenth centuries. Salim was a spiritual descendant of Nizam ad-Din Awliya', and was Akbar's spiritual guide. Akbar named his first son after the shaykh and built his new "victory-city" (Fatehpur) on the site of the shaykh's home village of Sikri. The white marble facing was laid over the original red sandstone by Shah Jahan, Akbar's grandson and builder of the Taj Mahal.

I obtained the blessing of kissing the master's feet. He began to discuss spiritual progress (and backsliding). "The traveler is constantly on the way to perfection," he explained, "that is, so long as he is progressing in the Way, he is in hope of perfection."

"There is the traveler, the standstill, and the retreater," he later noted. "The traveler is the one who treads the Path; the standstill is the one who stops along the Way."

At this point I interjected, "Can the traveler become the standstill?" "Yes," replied the master. "Every time that the traveler lapses in his obedience, he becomes stationary. If he quickly resumes his work and repents, then he may again become a traveler. If, God forbid, he remains a standstill, then he may become a retreater or backslider."

He went on to enumerate the seven stages of spiritual backsliding.[12]

By Nizam ad-Din's death, Sharaf ad-Din Maneri (d. 1381) had risen to prominence in the Firdawsiya lineage (silsila) further to the east, in the Indian region of Bihar. Scholars have attributed to Maneri at least nine collections of discourses of the malfuz genre. The most famous and accessible of those is the *Table Laden with Good Things,* a condensed record of forty-seven assemblies. The compiler is careful to note in his introduction that "either the very words themselves or their meaning have been utilized in the course of this book so that people might derive some profit from the study of its contents and be enabled to translate it into action." He hopes that "every perplexed person in need of the comfort of religion might be enabled to catch hold of the Lord of strength and attain the blessing of tranquility, for this is a tray laden with blessings."[13]

Maneri's discourses are among the most conversational in tone. Their themes run the gamut from rudimentary to esoteric:

> Maulana Karimuddin asked: "What is meant by 'Tradition?'" He said: "Revelation is either manifest or hidden. Manifest revelation is that which occurred through Gabriel as an intermediary. That is the Qur'an, for the entire Revealed Qur'an came to the Apostle through Gabriel. On the other hand, hidden revelation is that which descended upon the Apostle without any intermediary and was related by him. This type is called 'Tradition.'"[14]

Slightly more esoteric topics treated in the course of one assembly of Maneri include: the limits of a Friend of God's power to work miracles, the ability of a Friend of God to recognize his or her own sanctity, the need of discernment as to the veracity of one's dreams and of the persons that appear and speak in them, the impossibility of having a vision of God in this world, and whether someone engaged in religious seclusion (retreat) may simultaneously engage in a trade.[15] A theme of great importance to many Muslim writers over the centuries is Muhammad's status among the prophets. In one of Maneri's shortest assemblies a participant asks why, if Muhammad is superior to all other prophets, people commonly said, "O God, bless Muhammad as You have blessed Abraham." Surely Muhammad ought to be compared with someone superior to him. Maneri responds:

> The comparison is with the essence of compassion [i.e., God], not with the soul of the deceased [Abraham]. The intention is that, to the extent and degree that Abraham had been shown mercy, to the very same extent and degree Muhammad should also be granted mercy. Thus there is no harm as far as excellence is concerned.

Another listener then asks what point there is in comparing Muhammad with Abraham, if all the prophets received a special gift of divine mercy. The teacher says,

Because Abraham was the prophet who had attained the stage of friendship with God, while our prophet had attained that of love[,] and . . . friendship and love are one and the same. Hence the comparison is more apt with him [Abraham] than with others.[16]

An intriguing text whose translator has titled it *The Admonitions of Seh [Shaykh] Bari* comes from Southeast Asia. The sixteenth-century Javanese document purports to be the work of a teacher of the school of religion (*pesantren*) in Karan, noted for its instruction in the mystical tradition. Seh Bari claims to have taken three teachers of questionable authority to visit Ghazali, so that the great eleventh-century Sufi of Baghdad might point out to the three the errors of their understanding of mysticism. *Admonitions* thus presents itself as a doubly authoritative pedagogical work, cast in the form of a question-and-answer encounter between the teacher and his disciples characteristic of the malfuz genre. Within that framework, Seh Bari gives an account of his session with Ghazali, making the work a dialogue within a dialogue. Tradition then accords the document a third claim to credibility by suggesting that the disciple who recorded Seh Bari's teaching was the Javanese religious hero Sunan Bonan, one of the *wali songo* (nine Friends of God). What distinguishes this work from the more authentic malfuzat is that *Admonitions* is a literary conceit rather than a disciple's compilation of actual sessions with the master. It begins with an apparent monologue by the teacher, then moves into a question-and-answer mode.

The text covers a wide range of issues in the interpretation of an otherwise unknown work, *Principles of Mysticism* (*Usul suluk*), and provides an important testimony to the assimilation of the Islamic mystical tradition in an Indonesian context. By identifying itself directly with the authority of Ghazali, the document espouses a moderate form of Sufism. The teacher spends a great deal of time pointing out the unacceptable doctrines of a number of religious factions and of individuals who go to extremes in their religious practice. But he is evenhanded, never exempting himself from his own critique. He has a low opinion of individuals whose ascetical practices are mere show.

Earlier in life he found himself tempted to believe that his godly life had put him beyond reproach. But God made him aware of his own hypocrisy and self-centeredness, and he realized that he had fallen victim to his own erudition:

> My friend! I have no respect for people who possess learning and great knowledge but lack sincerity of heart.
> Once I had accumulated great learning and masterly knowledge and I thought to myself: It seems that I am now well-versed in the most difficult

and intricate rules of the law. Then I heard a voice saying: "Seh Bari! Of all
the servants of the Lord you are perhaps the most blind, deaf and dumb."

By virtue of the mercy and help of the Lord I no longer heeded learning
and knowledge. Then I heard a voice saying: "Now you will be elevated in
rank by the Lord and restored to your scholarly position, if you do not
strive after acts of devotion and have no ulterior designs."[17]

Seh Bari has learned that knowledge is a gift; it must be pursued energetically, but pride is to be avoided; devotions must be performed for the sake
of God alone, without calculating possible rewards.

The seminar genre stands at the midpoint of the spectrum that runs from
popular and public to professional and private. Another form, correspondence, offers a still closer look at the issues that occupied the minds of these
great teachers.[18]

Keeping in Touch

Letters of important religious figures constitute one of the most plentiful
and widespread pedagogical genres. Some letters (*rasa'il* and *maktubat*) were
created as a literary conceit, whereas others were actually sent to an individual and preserved by devotion or historical accident. Letters arise out of
several kinds of concrete circumstances and settings. Some are a product of
an ongoing correspondence between two people who communicate as peers;
some result from a seeker's request for help from a spiritual guide; and others record the relationship between a prominent religious figure and a political ruler.

With respect to content, these letters range from advice on intimate personal domestic matters to refined analyses of spiritual experience to smaller
versions of the mirror for princes genre.[19] Some letters presuppose only the
desire to make progress in the spiritual life and then move on to sources designed for more seasoned travelers. Ghazali addressed a number of letters
both to individual religious and political leaders of his time, and to groups
of influential persons, such as notable theologians. Ghazali's missives provide a glimpse of the personal conviction and values of this self-possessed
and competent man. Willing to confront the high and mighty without flinch-
ing, Ghazali "gave his wise advice to kings, governors and other government officials and brought down heavens of wrath and invective upon
exploiters, un-sympathetic rulers and corrupt officials . . . and others employing improper use of power and position."[20] His letters exemplify a spirituality founded on the conviction of God's sovereignty in all things and of
the consequent need for human beings to set their political priorities accordingly. In one letter to a Saljuqid sultan, Ghazali writes:

May it please your most excellent Majesty, I realize that for an ambitious man it is very hard to lead a pious life. As I find you very honest and careful, I would have you do this out of wisdom and kindness to yourself. Our Holy Prophet . . . has said: "A day spent in administering justice by a God-fearing monarch is equal to sixty years spent by a holy man in devotion and prayers." . . . This world is a pitcher made of earth, while the next is a pitcher made of gold. Would you not condemn the folly in a person who holds that the former is superior to the latter? If you live a good life and fix your hopes on Heaven, a day of your life would be worth sixty years spent by others in worship, and God would certainly open to you sources of happiness to which you are a stranger.[21]

Another sort of epistolary writing, a response to specific requests for advice, comes from the western end of the Islamic world. In one such instance the recipient has asked for personal spiritual advice from Ibn ʿAbbad of Ronda (1332–1390), a member of the Shadhiliya Sufi order. The Iberian-born shaykh, who spent most of his life in Morocco, left two collections of letters of spiritual direction. Written largely in response to questions his correspondents posed about their own struggles, Ibn ʿAbbad's fifty-four letters seek to allay ordinary fears about the suitability of certain means of livelihood. The writer encourages his addressees in such disciplines as mindfulness of God, recitation of the Qurʾan, and the habit of reading the most helpful spiritual classics. He seeks not so much to impart arcane mystical theory as to adapt the Islamic tradition to the everyday needs of lay seekers.

One correspondent expresses concern over the difficulty of searching for just the right spiritual director. Ibn ʿAbbad responds that one has finally to leave the matter to God's providence; one can expend only so much effort in that quest. In fact, even difficulty in finding a spiritual guide is itself a means of divine guidance, for it throws one back entirely on God's care. For a person who cannot find a living guide, help is available in the works of outstanding shaykhs of the past:

If the seeker does not find such a guide, or has a hard time doing so, he should rely on the writings of the Sufi authorities, especially the books of al-Muhasibi [e.g., *The Book of Self-Scrutiny*], as-Sulami [e.g., *The Generations of the Sufis*], al-Qushayri [*Treatise on Sufism*], Abu Talib al-Makki [*The Food of Hearts*], Abu Hamid al-Ghazali [*Revivification of the Sciences of the Faith*], and as-Suhrawardi's *The Benefits of Intimate Knowledge*. These are the primary sources from which people have taken advice and derived every kind of knowledge and understanding. . . . [Of these] I know of none more likely to quench the thirst, cure illness, and lead to the Path than the works of . . . Makki and Ghazali. They have incorporated in these two books such mysteries of knowledge and marvels of understanding as will provide both delight and comfort.

Ibn 'Abbad then offers more specific suggestions about how a less experienced seeker might derive maximum profit from those classic works.[22]

Maneri was contemporary with Ibn 'Abbad but lived toward the eastern end of the Islamic world. As spiritual guide of the Firdawsiya order of India, Maneri has left a treasury of Persian letters that share features of the epistolary writings of both Ghazali and Ibn 'Abbad. Maneri's principal correspondent is a government official who initiated the relationship; many of his *Hundred Letters* (*Maktubat-i sadi*) respond to requests from a nearby governor, Qazi Shams ad-Din, for instruction in the spiritual life. According to Maneri's scribe and compiler, Zayn Badr 'Arabi, the teacher's letters discuss

> the ranks and states of the travelers [i.e., on the spiritual path], the states and affairs of the disciples, such as repentance, discipleship, belief in the Unity of God, mystical knowledge, passionate and affectionate love, turning back and going ahead, attraction and effort, servitude and service, solitude and seclusion, security and blame, spiritual guides and novices . . . as well as stories of our predecessors that could serve both to verify and render palatable this teaching.[23]

Lawrence suggests that Maneri's letters bear more apt comparison to the earliest Persian formal treatise on Sufism, 'Ali ibn 'Uthman al-Hujwiri's (d. c. 1071) *Unveiling the Hidden* (*Kashf al-mahjub*), than to other collections of letters. He bases his observation on the scope and content of Maneri's epistles. However, Hujwiri's work is composed as a unitary piece, whereas at least two separate collections of Maneri's letters come together in integral documents as a result of his disciples' devotion.[24]

Some two centuries later and a little further to the west lived the famous Indian Naqshbandi Sufi Ahmad Sirhindi (d. 1624). Most of his 534 Persian letters were written for broad circulation with only a few addressed to individuals. He addressed nearly six dozen to bureaucrats and officials in the Mughal government,[25] often confronting them boldly. Since most of Sirhindi's letters function as treatises rather than as missives, they provide one of the more comprehensive overviews of a single spiritual authority's thought expressed in correspondence. M. Ansari has translated a selection of Sirhindi's letters that offers an excellent cross section of his central themes. They retain only hints of an epistolary style. Here and there Sirhindi calls his correspondent "my dear" or "my son"; and several pieces have preserved elements of what was presumably their original form, as in the following example with its rather brusque tone. The opening remarks suggest that it was written with a group of correspondents in mind:

I got your letter wherein you have put some questions. Normally a question that reflects arrogance and prejudice does not deserve an answer. But I will ignore it and try to reply. If it does not benefit one, it may benefit another.

Your first question was: "How come the early Sufis wrought a lot of miracles, but the Sufis of our age hardly show any?" If by this question you want to deny the merits of present-day Sufis, because they work few miracles, as it appears from your question, God may save us from the insinuation of Satan.

Sirhindi then discusses the theoretical aspects of wonderwork that apply to the questioner's inquiry.[26]

Concerned with instructing his readers in the underlying significance of the mystery of God's relationship with humankind, Sirhindi emphasizes the need to maintain adherence to the revealed law, Shariʿa, as the ultimate standard of spiritual authenticity. In a letter whose tone is much warmer than that of the earlier example, Sirhindi writes to an unidentified individual:

My dear! you have time, and you are in good health and free from worries. Engage yourself all the time in the *dhikr* of God. Remember that everything you do according to the *Sharʿ* [Sharʿa] is *dhikr* even if it is so ordinary as buying and selling. Observe, therefore, the rules of the *Sharʿ* in all activities so that the whole of life becomes *dhikr*.[27]

Constant remembrance of God is not only possible but well within reach of the average seeker, so long as all his or her actions are pursued within the context of divine revelation.

Most of the letters already discussed are intended to assist Muslims struggling through the initial stages of the mystical quest. In addition, numerous important Sufis have left illuminating correspondence with other mystics whom they seem to have regarded as their peers and companions on the path. Junayd of Baghdad composed several letters to fellow mystics of late ninth- and early tenth-century Baghdad. His collected Arabic *Letters* (*Rasaʾil*) are an important source of early so-called sober Sufism. One interpreter observes that "what Ash-Shafiʿi did for jurisprudence in his *risala* [treatise], al-Junayd did for sufism in his *Rasaʾil*. Ash-Shafiʿi [founder of one of the four Sunni legal schools], by his synoptic comprehension and vast learning, was able to initiate principles of Muslim jurisprudence which were so fundamental that later generations of jurists were happy to elaborate them, but unable either to add to them or change them. It is in this sense that al-Junayd is the father of sufism."[28]

Five pieces included in Junayd's *Letters* are cast in the form of actual letters, with attention to issues apparently raised in earlier exchanges with the correspondent. The rest belong to more formal kinds of treatise than the malfuzat genre. A letter Junayd wrote to another famous mystic, 'Amr ibn 'Uthman al-Makki, conveys the tone of Junayd's correspondence in general. It treats a theme of great importance to Junayd, that of mystical knowledge and the role of the accomplished mystic in passing it on to seekers. The entire letter is therefore an instruction to an instructor. Beginning with a series of prayerful wishes, Junayd underscores his correspondent's lofty responsibility as a teacher. He then elaborates on the process of learning from a master teacher. His emotionally reserved tone emphasizes the role of knowledge and avoids the language of ecstasy, a hallmark of the sober mystics:

> When the ignorant individual hears the discourse of the learned, he thinks he understands his point, but in reality (the learned one is also) in utter darkness and does not fully appreciate the subject of his discourse. In the midst of his discourse he is impelled by the essential truth of his subject and draws the listeners' attention to attempting to understand the words he uses and to follow out the verbal positive commands and observe the prohibitions. But this is only part of knowledge. . . . Beware, you who have donned the garb of learning, whom his fellow men point out as a scholar, but who falls short of knowledge in its pure reality. Be aware of what I have said and be wary of public fame. This is but the bitter death of the type of scholar I have described.[29]

Junayd's tone is characteristically sober, much more restrained and matter-of-fact than poets like Hallaj and Rumi. For Junayd there is ecstasy, but he regards the steady awareness of the "second sobriety" to which one returns as the test of the true mystic.

REQUIRED READING FOR MYSTICS

The first part of this chapter deals with material pitched to a wide spectrum of listeners and readers. Most of what remains in anthologies—whether lectures, discourses, or letters—the primary audience would have experienced either by listening to the teacher in person or by reading fairly short written documents. A range of sources, however, differ in several ways: From the start, they were intended to be read in the form of books and are narrower in focus. Although the various genres identified here represent a broad variety of pedagogical purposes, they are arranged here according to their primary emphases.

Advice for Inexperienced Travelers

'Abdallah Ansari's *One Hundred Fields* (*Sad maydan*) and *Resting Places of the Wayfarers* (*Manazil as-sa'irin*) are excellent early examples of the use of mnemonic devices for teaching key aspects of the spiritual journey. *One Hundred Fields* provides a series of elaborate definitions, typically supported and illustrated by a Qur'anic citation. Though the entries make no use of narrative or anecdote of any sort, they do use the mnemonic device of breaking a given concept down into its principal features in groups of three. For example, there are three essential elements of, three varieties of, three signs of, three reasons for, three circumstances under which one must cultivate the quality or attitude in question, and so forth. The tripartite structure recalls the traditional distinction among the three principal levels of spiritual attainment already mentioned: the generality of believers, persons closer to God and progressing spiritually, and the most advanced individuals who are the "elite of the elite." *One Hundred Fields* also uses other traditional teaching devices, such as the condensed expression of aphorism and adage, and the kind of internal and final assonance or consonance found in the rhymed prose (*saj'*) of the Qur'an.

One Hundred Fields shares features of other spiritual typologies, such as the various listings of stations and states devised early on in the history of Sufism; but it develops the form more fully than most such typologies, without insisting on any distinction between stations and states or any other larger organizing categories. The work begins, as do most other such progressive lists, with repentance and proceeds through the less demanding spiritual prerequisites to the most lofty conditions such as unveiling, intimacy, dread, vision, and survival (*baqa'*). Ansari uses a cumulative teaching method, since each "field" presupposes the preceding one and prepares for the following. This work simplifies the systematic analysis of the spiritual quest.

A good example of Ansari's pedagogy is his treatment of the ninety-seventh field, contemplation (*mushahada*). He defines contemplation as the "removal of obstacles between the devotee and God," and says that one gets there by way of three paths, each of which has three sources. One achieves wisdom (hikma) by revering God's commands and by following Muhammad's example; one attains wisdom's discursive knowledge (*'ilm*) by good use of knowledge; one achieves purity and its characteristic patience by means of avoiding strife, refraining from directing oneself spiritually, and regarding contentment as essential; and one attains reality through the intimate knowledge achieved by revering God in solitude, self-reproach for inadequate service to God, and putting one's friends above oneself.[30]

Ansari's *Resting Places of the Wayfarers* uses a form superficially similar to that of *One Hundred Fields*, but it represents a more advanced level of understanding and thus serves a different function. S. de Beaurecueil calls

Figure 32. A gathering of Sufis during the mawlid celebration of Sayyida Zaynab, inside the complex of the Mamluk Amir Sirghitmish (1356), Cairo, as seen from the minaret of the adjacent mosque of Ibn Tulun (879). Note the banners of two Sufi tariqas hanging on left and right walls.

One Hundred Fields a "rough draft in Persian" of the later Arabic *Resting Places*. Comparison of the two works reveals the difference between the more glossarylike form of the earlier *One Hundred Fields* and the fuller explication of the spiritual journey in *Resting Places*. The later work adds a structural device, in that it arranges the one hundred "resting places" in groups of ten. There are thus ten beginnings, doors, deeds, virtuous habits, principles, valleys, mystical states, custodial bonds, mystical realities, and destinations.

Ansari writes in the preface to *Resting Places* that a number of pupils had long besought him to provide a key to the signposts that mark the mystical journey: "They have asked me to present these resting places arranged in such a way as to suggest their order of progress and to demonstrate their implications; (they ask me) to leave out of my treatment the sayings of others and to be succinct, so that the explanation will be pleasant to repeat and easy to remember." As any good teacher, he wishes to avoid boring his pupils by loading his explanations with unnecessary verbiage.[31]

In chapter 2, I mention a group of three thirteenth-century pedagogical texts by Nasir ad-Din of Konya, and connect the most basic (*The Easy Roads of Sayf ad-Din*) with fundamental instruction in the ways of faith and devotion (a form of ta'lim). Two more demanding and more detailed pieces of that trilogy are intended for individuals slightly more advanced in learning. The shorter text, *The Rising Places of Faith* (*Matali'-i iman*), uses imagery from astronomy/astrology to describe three principles of belief (faith in God, in prophecy, and in the last day) as "rising places," within each of which the author describes the ascension of two or three "stars," each representing a particular aspect of the principle in question. These stars also symbolize guidance for the wayfarer, focusing on various inner aspects of faith, knowledge of God, adherence to the Prophetic teachings, and preparedness for the next life as journey's end.

In his preface, Nasir ad-Din explains the impetus for his pedagogical effort: "With the remoteness of the era of prophecy, God's carpet was rolled up and the foundation of religion destroyed. Hence the sun of faith turned toward eclipse, the light of Islam hid in the corner of exile. . . . The fog of error filled every direction and the darkness of innovation and sectarian caprice spread." In a world dark with unbelief the teacher offers glimmers of seemingly distant but eternal illumination meant to "bring dead souls to life and to incite seeking spirits with the desire to follow" the prophetic revelation.[32] And at the end, the teacher reminds the reader that there is no substitute for a competent shaykh who can assist the seeker in spiritual discernment of the various lights "shining down from the horizon of the dominion upon the tablet of his heart."[33]

In the longer and more detailed *Clarification for Beginners and Reminders for the Advanced* (*Tabsirat al-mubtadi*), Nasir ad-Din uses a similar tripartite metaphor of illumination. In each of three "lamps" he extols an essential aspect of religious knowledge, but with each the level of subtlety increases. Each lamp explores, in two or three "gleams," knowledge of the Creator, of spiritual friendship and prophecy, and of the two worlds (the present and that to come). The text, title notwithstanding, actually presumes that its readers have made considerable progress on their spiritual journeys and are now searching for more. Nasir ad-Din prays that his writing might bless him as well, by helping him to come to the "furthest limit of my heart's aspiration—arriving at the encounter with God and being consumed by the witnessing of His majesty and beauty."[34]

Sprinkled with Sufi poetry and lore, this treatise points out that although the religious scholars ('ulama') and jurists enjoy some access to the truths in question, those whom God invites to journey along the mystical path are led to a still higher and deeper awareness of their mysteries. In this special type of pedagogy "the sciences of unveiling can only be grasped by way of wayfaring and tasting [i.e., experience], not through investigation and reflection."[35]

Another genre that bridges the more informal and less theoretical forms of letters and discourses has been called isharat (literally, "allusions, hints, or indications"). As a technical term, the word evidently referred originally to paradoxical or enigmatic statements made by mystics about their relationships with God or about the nature of the spiritual life in general. To a concise question concerning some important issue, such as the meaning of death, the text answers with a sometimes lengthy explanation combined with useful advice. In the *Principles of the Path* (*Usul at-tariqa*), by an early Indian Chishti Sufi, Hamid ad-Din Suwali (d. 1276), a pedagogical item on the meaning of death employs the imagery of illumination used in Nasir ad-Din's *Rising Places* and *Clarification*. To the question "What is the goal?" the teacher answers:

> That you recite daily the Qur'anic verse: "Everything perishes except His face" (Q 55:26) and apply to yourself the following quatrain:
>
> There is a work beyond all knowledge. Go and have it.
> Don't go after the gem. Go and have the mine.
> The heart is a temporary abode. Leave it and come.
> The soul is the last destination. Go and have it.
>
> He has put a path before you. It is both narrow and long. He has given you a life. It is both dark and short. And in this short life He has commanded you to tread this long path. The night of the world may be dark . . . yet in this darkness for your sake He has created the moon to shine. He created mankind in darkness but then He caused the light of the heavens and the earth to shine upon them, and He illuminated the earth with the light of its Lord.
>   Arise and hasten. . . . Count yourself as already among the dead, and if you are not dead, then know yourself to be subject to death.[36]

The question-and-answer format is characteristic of one isharat form, although not all responses are as complete as this one. Whereas malfuzat record live sessions, isharat are written works that do not set down an actual dialogue.

The Admonitions of Seh Bari, discussed earlier, has appended to it a shorter text in catechism form, made up of brief questions and answers that summarize the material in the larger document. While the larger report of question-and-answer sessions suggest malfuzat, the catechism style of the later section belongs in the category of isharat. The Javanese document answers succinctly some fifty-six questions on the central themes of mysticism and the exemplary behavior of prophets and saints. Themes include the meanings of the most subtle concepts such as annihilation (fana') and survival (baqa'), love, and various distinctions within the notion of intimate knowledge (*ma'rifa*). The document is a curious mixture of basic and complex concepts, usually given in response to simple questions with concise formulaic answers. In several instances, the question asks what one is to think about a certain controversial statement; the answer in those cases is that the statement is erroneous or that one who holds it is an infidel, or both.

An example of an advanced issue addressed is: "What is the meaning of: *tawhid* is a mere 'yes'? (Answer:) It is a concentrated vision which no longer envisages anything else, as its outcome is the insight that devotion and sin equally spring from the same source. This is the meaning of: *tawhid* is a mere 'yes.'"[37] The dense and deceptively simple questions and answers attempt to get at a profound reality: a total acceptance and acknowledgment of God's absolute transcendent unity (tawhid) obliterates all other human choices. Tawhid effects a radical focusing of one's life, so that one can no longer answer either no or maybe to the question of God's reality and presence. To a person who sees God as the one reality, it becomes clear that God is the source of *everything*.

Most entries are even more terse and condensed, but many are also slightly easier to grasp: "What is the perfect mystic like?" Answer: "(The goal attained by) the perfect mystic is God alone." The tantalizing, often paradoxical, nature of the typical "allusion" appears in this question: "Does faith go with ritual prayer or does it not? (Answer:) If it does, the ritual prayer is idolatrous; if it does not, one is an infidel."[38] This concise entry is meant to summarize and recall a complicated discussion; it presupposes that the reader has already been exposed to the more complete treatment of the topic in the *Admonitions of Seh Bari,* where the puzzled disciple requests a clarification of the teacher's cryptic response. The teacher obliges and says:

> The reason why the ritual prayer of saints and true believers (*mu'min*) is neither polytheism nor unbelief is that according to the tradition of the Prophet—peace be upon him—, they are carried away. Therefore it is neither polytheism nor unbelief, as the tradition of the prophet should not be taken in a figurative sense. So their being has vanished completely without leaving a trace . . . it is overpowered and replaced by the all-pervading love of the Being which imparts being.[39]

A final mode of written pedagogy is the glossed treatise or poem, using commentary to explain an already classic work, making it intelligible to relative newcomers. Many great classics of Islamic spirituality have been transcribed, translated, and commented on at length. One common method of elucidating a text is to gloss, interlinearly or marginally, the sayings of some great master. For example, Kemas Fakhr ad-Din of Palembang, an eighteenth-century Sumatran scholar, helped to further the popularity in Southeast Asia of an Arabic classic of spiritual pedagogy, Wali Raslan's *Treatise on Divine Unity* (*Risala fi, 't-Tawhid*). His work is a superb example of how Islamic teaching has traveled across the globe.

G. W. J. Drewes has translated, under the title *Directions for Travellers on the Mystic Path*, several works that developed out of interest in a twelfth-century treatise on God's unity by Shaykh Wali Raslan of Damascus. Zakariya al-Ansari's (d. 1520) Arabic commentary on Wali Raslan's *Treatise on Divine Unity* served as a vehicle by which Wali Raslan's influence, and that of the more sober Junaydi school of Sufism, spread to Southeast Asia. Kemas then created a Malay adaptation of the original work, with excerpts from Ansari's commentary. Throughout the work, Kemas recalls the classic tripartite analysis of human beings into those just beginning, those progressing on the path, and those who have become spiritually accomplished, but he writes especially for the first group. In his preface, Kemas says:

> This is a concise tract by Shaykh Wali Raslan of Damascus. . . . I have translated this tract into Malay in order to make it easily understandable to beginners, adding a few things taken from the commentary named *Revelation of the Merciful* (*Fath al-Rahman*) by Shaykh Zakariyya' al-Ansari and from that named *Wine from the Inn* (*Khamrat al-khan*) by Shaykh 'Abd al-Ghani b. Isma'il, and other things to the extent to which novices should know these, and I hope that God may cause me and all my brethren on the mystic path to profit by it in this world and the world to come.[40]

The work repeatedly warns of the dangers of "hidden polytheism," all the subtle ways in which, while falling short of outright idolatry, seekers fail to cleanse themselves entirely of polytheism's pollution. Evidently aimed at rooting out perceived improprieties in Sufi views and practices then common in the Indonesian archipelago, Kemas's effort emphasizes a return to the basics of Junaydi spirituality. Of utmost importance are the discipline of the inner struggle (the Greater Jihad) as integral to the purgative way, and the cultivation of the art of spiritual discernment and vigilance over one's every interior movement. The commentary on the allusive statement "If you are with Him, He screens you from self, and if you are with self, He brings you under bondage" is typical of this teaching method. The gloss explains:

> If you are with Him, He certainly will screen you from self; that is to say, He will prevent you from looking upon yourself, so that you will be protected from hidden polytheism. This state [*hal*] is called "passing away [fana'] in tawhid," and "union" [*al-jam'*]. If, however, you are occupied

with self on account of your not concentrating on Him, He certainly will demand worship of you; that is to say, you were created for worship. . . . This is the state of separation [*farq*], in which the servant is back to the performance of religious service.[41]

In this passage, as in the poetry of Hallaj and other mystics, the dilemma is the nature of the self or personality in relationship to God. If the self is truly annihilated, there is no longer a danger of one's worshiping oneself in even a subtle way; but there is a danger that one's statements about the divine-human relationship might verge on blasphemy. In a state of clear separation of the two personalities—the divine and the human—one is challenged to worship God alone.

Mystical Geography

Works that lay out the basic itinerary for the seeker are supplemented by more comprehensive writings that function like maps that are both broad in coverage and very detailed. All display the same overall landscape, and all lead to the same destination. But there is some variation in the precise routes they recommend. These manuals function as one- or two-volume encyclopedias of classical Sufi teaching. They combine elements of various other genres, such as the biographical dictionary and the lexicon of technical terms. Several examples of the genre are arranged here according to their various structural models. The chief organizational principles the authors use are epistemological, historical, and theological or cosmological, or some combination thereof.

Two of the most important theoretical works in Arabic are those of Abu Nasr as-Sarraj (d. 988) and Abu Bakr al-Kalabadhi (d. 990). Both works are theoretical in that they aim to place Sufism within mainstream Islamic belief and practice. Critics of Sufism since at least the eighth century complained that too many Sufis were casual about the religious obligations incumbent on all Muslims. In Sufism's defense, Sarraj and Kalabadhi argue that those criticisms are unfounded. Sarraj's *Book of Light Flashes (Kitab al-luma' fi 't-tasawwuf)* preserves the sayings of many Sufis whose works have been lost, and many authors after Sarraj relied heavily on his work. Although Sarraj begins with conspicuous attention to the Qur'anic and Prophetic roots of Sufism, he spends less time on the fundamentals of Islamic religious practice than do several of the other manuals and proportionately more on the esoteric dimensions of mysticism.

Sarraj divides his 152 chapters into twelve books. The first serves as a sociology of Islamic learning, attempting to establish that Sufism represents as valid a way of knowing as the sciences of the traditionists (*ashab al-hadith*) and legal scholars (*fuqaha'*). As custodians of knowledge of the spiritual life, Sufis rank as the third group of traditional religious scholars (*'ulama'*). Sarraj boldly affirms that the province of Sufism extends far beyond those of the other religious scholars, for Sufis know the truth emotionally as well as intellectually, and translate their knowledge into action.

After defending Sufi claims to esoteric knowledge, Sarraj explains the various stages on the mystic path. He discusses mystical interpretation of the Qur'an and Hadith; the imitation of Muhammad; and the laudable qualities of Muhammad's Companions, the latter two topics paralleling segments found in several hadith collections. The longest book by far, over a quarter of the entire work, is devoted to the manners (adab) of those who wish to be Sufis. This section includes much material on how Sufis ought to behave—how to dress, eat, relate to others—except that here the author is describing rather than prescribing.

Sarraj's final five books deal with musical sessions (sama'), ecstasy (*wajd*), prophetic miracles (*mu'jizat*) and saintly marvels (karamat), technical terms (*mushkilat*), and ecstatic expressions (*shathiyat*).[42] From the perspective of pedagogy, Sarraj's treatment aims at a relatively sophisticated public, but other compendiums seem to have been assembled with slightly different constituencies in mind.

Kalabadhi's *The Book of Doctrines of the School of Sufism* (*Kitab at-ta'arruf li madhhab ahl at-tasawwuf*) treats, in seventy-five short chapters, a broad range of material. Unlike works that situate their discussion in the context of knowledge, Kalabadhi's uses a historical model. A preface and four opening chapters provide a summary background for the work. Explaining his motive for writing the book, the author points to the lamentable spiritual entropy that has characterized Islamic history since the Prophet's day. Those few perceptive individuals who have maintained a grasp of spiritual values have of necessity parted company with the masses hypnotized by change. Speaking of the general state of spiritual values and truth, he observes:

> He who knew not (the truth) pretended to possess it, he who had never so much as described it adorned himself with it: he who had it much upon his tongue denied it with his acts, and he who displayed it in his exposition concealed by his true conduct. . . . But he who had experienced (the truth [i.e., the genuine Sufi]) drew apart, being jealous for it: he who had described it was silent, being envious for it. So the hearts (of men) fled from it . . . ; science [i.e., knowledge] and its people, exposition and its practice, vanished; the ignorant became the scientists, and the scientists became guides.[43]

Kalabadhi then explains how the doctrines of the Sufis "will serve as a guide to those who desire to tread God's path, and have need of God for the attainment and realization of this."[44] He examines in some detail the meaning of the term *Sufi* and lists famous Sufis, with special attention to those who wrote books.

Part 2 addresses the matter of Sufism's place within mainstream Islam as defined by the essential elements of the creed. A third major section focuses on mystical knowledge and analyzes the various mystical states, carefully noting that all mystical science is rooted in that of jurisprudence. Properly understood, therefore, these states represent a development out of, rather than an aberration from, basic Islamic themes. His fourth section comprises an explanation of Sufi technical terms.

In the last twelve chapters Kalabadhi describes several observable aspects of the Sufis' relationships to God and to their fellow human beings. Kalabadhi's book ends, as do Sarraj's and Hujwiri's, with a discussion of the practice of audition (sama'); but Kalabadhi's reasons are different. Kalabadhi calls sama' "a resting after the fatigue of a (spiritual) moment, and a recreation for those who experience (spiritual) states," so that it seems to him a fitting conclusion to his book.[45]

Midway between the theoretical and the practical come the works of Hujwiri and Abu 'l-Qasim al-Qushayri (d. 1074). Hujwiri, who lived in what are now Afghanistan and Pakistan, wrote the earliest work of mystical pedagogy in Persian, *The Revelation of the Veiled* (*Kashf al-mahjub*). Hujwiri indicates in his preface that he composed the work in response to questions from a friend during his days in Lahore. A seeker named Abu Sa'id made this request:

> Explain to me the true meaning of the Path of Sufism and the nature of the
> "stations" (maqamat), and explain their doctrines and sayings, and make
> clear to me their mystical allegories, and the nature of Divine Love and
> how it is manifested in human hearts, and why the intellect is unable to
> reach the essence thereof, and why the soul recoils from the reality thereof,
> and why the spirit is lulled in the purity thereof; and explain the practical
> aspects of Sufism which are connected with these theories.[46]

In his initial response, Hujwiri laments how the works of great Sufis of the past have been little appreciated and allowed to serve only as wrappings for the bawdy lyrics of Abu Nuwas (d. c. 810) or the witticisms of al-Jahiz (d. 869)—neither classical Arabic author was noted for his piety. Hujwiri resolves to try one more time to restore some authentic understanding of the spiritual life.

Combining epistemological and historical methods, Hujwiri begins his work with a chapter on knowledge ('ilm) as the foundation of striving on the path. He wants to persuade skeptics that Sufism stands on solid ground. He first considers a broad range of concepts, practices, and theories, and offers several dozen short biographical sketches of famous spiritual guides down to his own time. Then he analyzes the mysteries beneath the eleven veils, the removal of which provides the metaphor of his book's title.

Hujwiri's eleven central chapters show no obvious theoretical progression, but just beneath the surface a carefully conceived plan is suggested. For the most part these chapters discuss practices of universal importance to Muslims such as the Five Pillars. Only under the first and last two veils does the author reveal matters potentially controversial, namely, mystical knowledge of God, the idiosyncratic terminology of the Sufis, and the practice of musical recital and its attendant dancing (sama'). As Hujwiri pulls back the first veil, he discloses intimate knowledge of God (ma'rifa) as an advanced variety of the foundational knowledge to which he devotes the opening chapter. He distinguishes between two types of mystical knowledge: discursive ('ilmi) and nondiscursive or affective (hali). The former is the object of theological and jurisprudential endeavors; the latter, that of all mystical questing. Hujwiri thus explains that a simple awareness of this distinction could obviate controversy over divergent epistemologies.

In conclusion the shaykh removes the last veil from a matter of still greater potential for controversy, namely, Sufi recourse to musical sessions. Once again the teacher situates the issue in the context of knowledge. In a pedagogical turn reminiscent of the Thomistic dictum "nothing gets to the intellect except through the senses," Hujwiri recalls that God has provided five avenues of human knowing. He argues from the auditory nature of divine revelation to the primacy of hearing, through a reference to a hadith that seems to speak favorably of listening to poetry, and then on to the analogous benefits of listening to instrumental and vocal music. He concludes by sandwiching a discussion of ecstasy between sections on the principles and rules of sama', probably in hopes of addressing the reservations of critics who regarded all loss of control as unseemly or even blasphemous.[47]

Qushayri's *Treatise on Sufism* (*Risala ila's-Sufiya*) has been one of the most influential and popular works of its kind. Numerous writers on Sufism in the two or three centuries after him felt a duty to acknowledge him, and many quoted him at length. Though in one modern Arabic edition the book runs nearly eight hundred pages, Qushayri called it his letter to the Sufis of his day. Like several other authors of such compendiums, Qushayri was concerned not only with providing a reliable treatment of the high points in the mystical tradition but also with exonerating Sufism from any suspicion of heterodoxy.

He begins with a chronological collection of eighty-three hagiographical sketches of famous Sufis and ends with a treatment of various aspects of Sufi practice and discipline. At the heart of the work are its two middle sections. One discusses a number of specialized terms, some taken individually and some as related clusters, a segment that belongs technically to the genre of mystical lexicon described at the end of this chapter. The other examines the inner meanings of various stages the wayfarer experiences on the spiritual path. Unlike Hujwiri, Qushayri uses no overarching metaphor or theoretical structure. As a teacher, he is interested in providing a broad survey of the Sufi tradition grounded in a solid appreciation of influential figures and basic concepts. His two segments on technical terminology and the stations and states, however, suggest basic structural concerns. In the section on the various stages of the path, Qushayri arranges the stations and states in a generally progressive order, beginning with repentance and culminating in love and union. He describes the beginnings of the quest:

> Repentance is the first degree among the degrees of the wayfarers and
> the first station among the stations of the seekers. The inner meaning of
> repentance in Arabic is "return." . . . So repentance is to return from what
> is blameworthy in the law of Islam to what is praiseworthy in it. . . . Sahl b.
> 'Abdallah declared, "Repentance is giving up procrastination." Al-Harith
> [al-Muhasibi] asserted, "I never say, 'O God, I ask you for repentance.' I
> say, 'I ask You for the longing for repentance.'"[48]

Qushayri thus sets the appropriate tone for the wayfarer who would journey farther. The seeker's first priority is to pray for the desire to receive whatever quality is required for a given stage of the quest.

Other compendiums emphasize practice slightly more than theory. Among these works is Abu Talib al-Makki's (d. 996) *The Food of Hearts*, whose full title continues: *in One's Conduct toward the Beloved, and the Description of the Path of the Seeker toward Divine Unity (Qut al-qulub fi mu'amalat al-mahbub wa wasf tariq al-murid ila maqam at-tawhid)*. As the title suggests, the author plunges into questions of practice. He devotes over half of part 1 to ritual and devotional prayer, before moving into more subtle matters of the seeker's inner consciousness and discernment. Makki eventually takes up the matter of knowledge, as do most manuals, but he postpones his discussion of 'ilm, one of his most extensive, until the penultimate section of part 1. Once he has defined the nature of the spiritual science of the heart in relation to traditional religious learning, he begins a careful study of the various mystical stations (*maqamat*). Part 1 ends in the midst of a discussion of the station of asceticism (*zuhd*).

Part 2 of *The Food of Hearts* continues with a lengthy commentary on the station of trust (*tawakkul*) and on the Five Pillars. Makki concludes by treating various dimensions of Islam—faith and tradition; sincerity of intention in practice; and a variety of practical questions related to poverty, travel, marriage, personal hygiene, livelihood, and basic ethics. Unlike the authors of several other manuals, Makki does not discuss his subjects in an ascending order of subtlety, importance, or spiritual sophistication.[49]

Abu Hafs 'Umar Suhrawardi's (d. 1234) *The Benefits of Intimate Knowledge* (*'Awarif al-ma'arif*) devotes sixty-three chapters to topics considerably more circumscribed than Makki's, but his overarching concern is similarly practical. Associating Sufism with the most fundamental and essential forms of knowledge in chapter one, the teacher focuses in early chapters on various aspects of Sufism as a socio-religious institution, discussing the origins of the name "Sufi," and various aberrant forms and disreputable claimants to membership in Sufism. Suhrawardi then moves into a cluster of broad considerations of institutional life, especially the regime of shaykhs, general characteristics of life in dervish residences (ribat), means of livelihood, and manner of affiliation of married or unmarried seekers to a Sufi institution.

Much of the book is a discussion of various aspects of the Sufi practices of sama' and the forty-day retreat (*chilla, khalwa*); manners and morals, the proper discipline and behavior for all basic practices, from ritual prayer and purification to eating and dress; and comportment in the presence of the shaykh. The final chapters turn to more subtle questions of personal spiritual discernment, explanations of the stations and states and of the subtle allusions and technical expressions of the great shaykhs. Suhrawardi clearly intends his work for a more advanced and well-defined public.[50]

Najm ad-Din Daya Razi's (d. 1256) *Path of [God's] Servants* (*Mirsad al-'ibad*) moves across the imaginary line between pedagogy and the analysis of mystical experience. This work begins with a careful explanation of the author's method and reasons for writing. A number of friends had been asking him for some time to write a compendium "that should be slight of girth and rich in content; set forth the beginning and end of creation, the start of wayfaring and the finish of voyaging; and treat of the goal and the destination, the lover and the beloved. It should be a world-displaying goblet[51] and a mirror to God's beauty; it should both benefit the deficient beginner on the path and profit the perfect drawing near to the goal."[52] No small task, to be sure; and the result is hardly slight of girth. Ehsan Yarshater believes that Razi's work "strikes a middle course between those mystics who concentrated on ecstacy [*sic*] and spiritual raptures and neglected or made light of religious observances and rituals, and the ascetic Sufis who emphasized worship through meticulous or excessive performance of religious duties."[53]

Razi's compendium utilizes much material similar to Suhrawardi's *Benefits of Intimate Knowledge* but structures it quite differently. Razi explains that he has arranged the work in five sections, in recognition of Islam's Five Pillars. The work's forty chapters recall the forty nights Moses communed with God, as well as Muhammad's recommendation that seekers worship devoutly for forty days. Razi's unique contribution to the literature of spiritual pedagogy lies not so much in the kind of information he passes along or in some striking new theory he claims to advance, but in his use of a cosmological setting for his discussion of the tripartite traversing of the path. After three ample prefatory chapters explaining his rationale and method, Razi devotes his central sections to analyses of human origin, life, and return to humanity's heavenly source.

Parts 3 and 4 constitute one of the most important systematic critiques of spiritual experience ever written. Part 5 then explores, from a religiously elite perspective, what the sapiential or counsel genres examine from a less esoteric point of view. Therein lies one of the most interesting aspects of Razi's manual; its concern with translating lofty principles into everyday morality for people who are not professional seekers sets it apart.

In those final eight chapters Razi characterizes the spiritual striving (i.e., "wayfaring") appropriate to the seven social strata: royalty, government bureaucrats, scholars, the wealthy, farmers, merchants, and those who work in trades and crafts. Razi writes with admirable clarity and pedagogical organization, classifying and enumerating the various elements of his analysis in such a way that one can envision an outline from which he might have worked. He concludes his fifth and final section by saying that all these classes of persons can be sure of a heavenly reward if they follow his spiritual teaching. But, he goes on, if they seek to have a fuller measure of nearness to God, "[t]hey should also follow the means for the refinement of the soul, and the adornment of the spirit we have explained in previous chapters, in accordance with their capacity. They should know for certain that the greater their exertions, the greater shall be their reward." He explains further that one can make much better progress by engaging the services of a spiritual guide.[54] Razi does not think of spiritual seekers as a separate social category. All are called to explore God's intimate invitation to the fullest of their capacity and to follow the path that God opens up before them.

Languages of the Spirit

Like travelers in a foreign land wayfarers in the land of the spirit must also learn a new language. Responding to the need, Islam's teachers devised a pedagogical tool, the elucidation of technical terms or conventional usages (*bayan al-istilahat*, sometimes simply *istilahat*) or clarification of ambiguities and obscurities (*bayan al-mushkilat*). This glossary of terms is employed especially by Sufi organizations and shaykhs. It differs in tone from works of the catechism (isharat) or instructional dialogue described earlier, in that the glossary tends to be more dispassionate and detached. However, the isharat can also sometimes tend toward a highly technical and metaphysical tone. Principles of organization vary, but terms are generally clustered (as in Ansari's *One Hundred Fields* and *Resting Places*) in groups of two, three, or four on the basis of similarity of word derivation or meaning or phrasing, opposite meanings, or grammatical form. "It is possible," Ernst observes, "that a core list of Sufi mystical terms was widely used in oral teaching, and later became the basis for the similarity of sequence in different texts."[55]

There are four main types of spiritual lexicography: lexicons included within larger works to serve as general references to Sufi literature; glossaries composed by Sufis to help readers understand their works; separate or freestanding works meant as general reference tools; and finally, more complex works in which the concepts defined are part of a more elaborate pedagogical structure.

Glossaries are often included as parts of mystical compendiums, partly out of a concern to defend their usage as rooted in and consistent with that of the Qur'an, partly with the intention of providing information to insiders about an important but easily misunderstood aspect of Islamic spiritual teaching, and partly to cloak the mystical meaning from the uninitiated. Kalabadhi, Sarraj, and Hujwiri, for example, provide listings of terms, each followed by definitions. The tone of glossaries of this type tends to be technical and disinterested, striving for objectivity. If the author has a theoretical structure in mind in his choice and order of terms, it is often difficult to discern. These early examples of the bayan al-istilahat genre exercised enormous influence on later works that further developed the form for teaching purposes. Kalabadhi, like Sarraj and Hujwiri, has a distinct approach to his material. His *Doctrine of the Sufis* begins his fourth section this way:

> Now the Sufis have certain peculiar expressions and technical terms
> which they mutually understand, but which are scarcely used by any
> others. We will set forth such of these as may be convenient, illustrating

Figure 33.   Graves of the Mevlevi chelebis, successors to Jalal ad-Din Rumi (from the thirteenth century on), Konya, Turkey. On the wall are the names "Allah" and "Muhammad," along with those of Muhammad's first four successors, "Abu Bakr," "'Umar," "'Uthman," and "'Ali." (See also Fig. 12.)

their meanings. . . . In this we merely aim at explaining the meaning of the several expressions, not the experience which the expression covers: for such experience does not come within the scope even of reference, much less explanation. The real essence of the spiritual states of the Sufis is such that expressions are not adequate to describe it: nevertheless these expressions are fully understood by those who have experienced these states.[56]

He discusses approximately twenty terms in some detail, usually beginning each section with his own definition and supporting it with citations of various Sufis. Kalabadhi deals sometimes with single terms, such as *ecstasy*, sometimes with pairs of complementary or contrasting terms, such as *passing away* (fana') and *survival* (baqa'). One definition reads: "Passing-away is a state in which all passions pass away, so that the mystic experiences no feelings towards anything whatsoever."[57] Kalabadhi follows no readily apparent conceptual development or pedagogical strategy.

Sarraj elaborates on 155 terms in his manual's section entitled the "Book of the Explanations of Obscurities." Like Kalabadhi, he cites sayings of famous Sufis, but Sarraj's entries are briefer. He uses several organizational principles meant to facilitate a student's learning the concepts. For example, he sometimes pairs words with opposite meanings, such as *sobriety/intoxication* (*sahw/sukr*) or *contraction/expansion* (*qabd/bast*), and sometimes groups terms in semantic clusters, that is, words that refer to similar aspects of mystical experience, such as *state* (hal), *station* (*maqam*), and *place* (*makan*).[58] Sarraj defines these words in terms that refer to levels of spiritual progress: *State* refers to an experience of, for example, contentment that descends briefly upon a servant of God and enters the heart, then departs. *Station* corresponds to a more lasting experience of, say, trust or patience, that occurs in relation to the servant's deeds and spiritual struggle. Finally, *place* refers to a level of experience attained by only the most advanced; it transcends both state and station, as suggested in the poet's expression "Your place in my heart is the whole of my heart, so that there is in my heart no room for anything but you."[59]

In his *Revelation of the Veiled*, Hujwiri explains that Sufis, no less than any other specialized social groups, naturally develop their own technical jargon for "expressing the matter of their discourse and in order that they may reveal or disguise their meaning as they please." Then he classifies terms into four categories. He begins with full discussions of eleven pairs of terms, either complementary or opposite in meaning, used to conceal the underlying meaning of Sufi discourse. He proceeds through two sparsely annotated lists, one of terms used metaphorically and another of terms used nonmetaphorically. Then he concludes with a number of terms, again more fully described, that are "commonly used by the Sufis in a mystical sense that is not familiar to philologists."

Hujwiri adds to Sarraj's definitions of *state, station,* and *place.* Hujwiri associates the experience of a state with the notion of a mystical moment or time (*waqt*), which is in reality an experience of timelessness, of living purely in the now. A state defines or qualifies a time, for that mystical moment must be an experience of *something,* such as satisfaction or ecstasy; and that something is the state. A station is a more enduring spiritual quality that best characterizes a person's inner condition during a particular period of his or her life. Each prophet, for example, can be identified by a particular station—Adam's is repentance; Jesus', hope. Individuals move in and out of various stations but typically return to the one that is most characteristic. Finally, Hujwiri refers to *place* (*tamkin,* a cognate of *makan*) as the "residence of spiritual adepts in the abode of perfection and in the highest grade . . . (stations) are stages on the way, whereas *tamkin* is repose within the shrine."[60]

Shorter collections of terms provided by an author assist readers as they work their way through a complex larger work. Ghazali's *Book of Clarification of the Ambiguities of the "Revivification"* (*Kitab al-imla' fi ishkalat al-ihya'*) offers one of the earliest examples of such glossaries. Writing in response to a particular individual's request, Ghazali defines briefly some fifty terms, describing many in only a few words, then addresses a number of questions he has been asked to clarify. His definitions of state, station, and place, for example, are close paraphrases of Sarraj. Ghazali even includes in slightly altered form the citation of the anonymous poet with which Sarraj illustrated his entry on *place*. Apparently Ghazali was satisfied with already well-known definitions, judging them adequate reference material for readers of his chief work on the spiritual life.[61]

The mystical poet Ibn 'Arabi also wrote two reference aids for readers of his monumental *Meccan Revelations* (*Al-Futuhat al-Makkiya*). One is tucked away in that work itself, while the other stands as a short separate piece. The first presupposes considerable knowledge on the part of the reader who has managed to wade through an enormously difficult text on divine knowing before arriving at the lexicon. Each of the nearly two hundred terms is integrally linked to the one that follows. As Ernst notes, "This linkage of terms is certainly no accident; it suggests that they all share an essential relationship beyond their purely lexical connotations. . . . It is, in addition, expressed in a teaching formula ('If you say . . . then we say') characteristic of the Islamic religious sciences."[62]

Ibn 'Arabi also produced an example of the third type of lexicon, namely, the freestanding dictionary. Unlike the glossary just described, Ibn 'Arabi's separate booklet is meant for beginners. It defines nearly all the same terms but in reverse order and more simply. Responding to the individual who asked him to produce the work, Ibn 'Arabi says he has included only the most important terms. He adds, "I have avoided mentioning those which may be understood by anyone who gives the slightest attention to their metaphoric and analogical character."[63] His definitions of the terms *state* and *place* are quite similar to Sarraj's or Hujwiri's; but he defines *station* (maqam) in relation to proper behavior this way: "An expression for complete fulfillment of the demands of the protocol." In other words, a station is a level of spiritual experience attained as the seeker's life is increasingly characterized by right behavior (adab), the concept whose definition immediately precedes that of station.[64]

Further clarification of Ibn 'Arabi's cryptic definition is available in one of the largest and most comprehensive glossaries, that of 'Abd ar-Razzaq al-Kashani (d. 1330). His definition of station (maqam) reads:

This is the fulfillment of one's prescribed duties, for whoever has not fulfilled the requirements of the Stations is not fit to progress to a higher level. Thus, anyone who has not verified the reality of Abstemiousness until he has made it his own, is not fit for the stage of Trust; whoever has not verified Trust is not fit for Submission—and so on. . . .

The word "fulfillment" does not imply that none of the steps of the lower stage may be left incomplete before one is able to proceed to a higher one. The greater part of what has not been completed in the lower stage and its finer gradations will be rectified in the higher. Rather the intention is that one should become so solidly grounded in that particular stage that one actually becomes part of it, and that the name associated with one's [station], such as abstinent or trusting, is an exact description [of the seeker's condition].[65]

Kashani's definition of *place* adds nothing to those of earlier lexicons; but he clarifies the notion of state by adding that "[w]hen it appears, the characteristics of the Self go into abeyance, and the State may or may not do likewise; but if it endures and becomes a permanent characteristic, then it is called" a station.[66] Kashani's is the most extensive of the classical freestanding lexicons. He defines some 516 terms for the use of scholars with some philosophical background, who might be working in fields other than Sufism. But he also says in his introduction that he composed the glossary to help readers of his commentary on Ansari's *Resting Places of the Wayfarers*.

This genre has retained its interest for segments of the contemporary Muslim (especially Persian-speaking) world as well. A large one-volume dictionary-style work by Ja'far Sajjadi arranges over a thousand terms alphabetically, with variant or related expressions clustered under the main terms. Sajjadi includes numerous illustrations from classical Persian Sufi poetry to support his basic definitions. For example, he defines the word *ocean* (*bahr*) as "the limitless place of God's essence and attributes, and all existent beings are the waves of the infinite ocean." He follows with definitions of the related terms *ocean without shore, ocean of generosity,* and *ocean of existence,* among others.[67] Poets and commentators often use the metaphor of voyaging upon, and drowning in, the ocean of divine reality as a description of mystical experience.

Javad Nurbakhsh's multivolume dictionary entitled *Sufi Symbolism* sets out the various inner meanings of thousands of terms, supplying illustrative citations from mostly Persian-writing Sufi poets. His treatment of the term for *wine jar* recalls Ibn al-Farid's "Wine Ode" and the drinking/begging bowl, and is related to the concept of mystical moment (waqt) as defined by Hujwiri. Explaining that the term *qadah* symbolizes the timeless moment, he says it "alludes to the moment and occasion of mystical illumination ... [whose occurrence] depends upon the mystic gambling himself away to the Beloved and obliterating from his heart all mental influences and visual responses, as well as all types of control exercised by the senses and the imagination."[68]

Another variant of the genre differs in overall structure, but includes similar content and maintains the individual entry form of the glossary. This type often includes additional anecdotal illustrative material or employs a clearly pedagogical structure. It stands midway between the simple lexicon and the more elaborate treatises describing the intricacies of the spiritual journey. Some such works arrange the key concepts in a progressive order of importance, thus suggesting a series of steps by which to measure spiritual development.

Ahmad Ibn 'Ajiba's (1746–1809) *Book of the Ascension in Perceiving the Realities of Sufism (Kitab al-mi'raj at-tashawwuf ila haqa'iq at-tasawwuf)* is essentially a glossary of key concepts arranged, more or less as in Ansari's works, in ascending order of importance. Its general content owes a great deal to Qushayri's *Treatise on Sufism*, but the method differs considerably. In its original form, this Moroccan work included 100 terms but gradually grew to 143. The author likens his work in general to the explication of technical expressions that Qushayri provides at the beginning of his *Treatise*. Employing imagery reminiscent of Muhammad's mystical experience of ascension, Ibn 'Ajiba composed a work that is both a handy reference and a blueprint of the more advanced spiritual quest: "let one who wishes assistance in understanding the expressions of the Sufis study it carefully."[69]

Preparing the reader for a steady upward climb, the author begins with an examination of the term *Sufism (tasawwuf)*, which he defines as

> the science by which one comes to know the modalities of the journey to the King of kings; it is also an interior cleansing from vice and an inward adornment with all the virtues; in other words, the effacement of the creature so that it might be engulfed in the vision of the Truth.[70]

In the first third of the book Ibn 'Ajiba discusses the virtues that lead to the farther reaches of the mystical path, starting with repentance (*tawba*) and ending with poverty of spirit (*faqr*). He devotes by far the largest portion to a wide range of basic mystical, cosmological, and metaphysical concepts. He outlines a demanding upward journey, starting with recollection (dhikr, followed immediately by moment, state, and station) and ending with the three components of the metaphor of intoxication, namely, wine, cup, and the act of drinking (*khamr, ka's, sharab*). Ibn 'Ajiba explains that Ibn al-Farid sang of the wine of divine self-manifestation. The cup is the heart, especially that of the shaykh who teaches other seekers. And the act of drinking is the presence (or concentration) of the heart as it imbibes love, to the point of losing itself in the reality of God.[71]

Finally, he describes the upper levels of the spiritual universe. Ibn 'Ajiba lines up the various ranks in the mystical hierarchy, from novice (murid) to cosmic axis (qutb). He has thus set up a three-level structure, within which he distinguishes among the traditional three degrees of realization of each level or concept, and relates each level to the tripartite composition of the person as body, psyche, and spirit.[72]

All Islam's great teachers point out that what is written on paper serves a useful purpose only if it helps the seeker understand what God has written in the human heart. Pedagogical books have always been important tools, but even today most spiritual instruction occurs within the personal relationship between journeyer and guide, the living experience at which books can only hint.

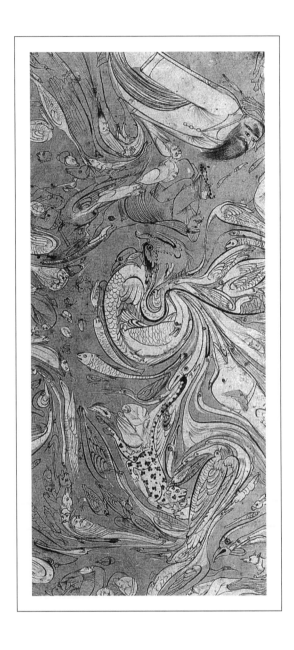

7 Experience
Testimony, Paradigm, and Critique

Nothing captivates the imagination like stories of personal experience. More than that, accounts of the wonders and adventures of a celebrated personality can assume mythic proportions; the subject of such a story becomes larger than life and functions as an inspiration and goal to be attained. That is one reason why the tales of Islam's religious heroes have played such an important role as exemplars for millions of Muslims. The hagiographical tales of prophets and Friends of God described earlier emphasize how God works through the intermediacy of human beings but seldom reveal much of the heart and soul of the heroic figure. Several other kinds of literature, however, break the surface of external action and marvelous deeds. These experiential narratives speak not of the heroic figure's instrumental role but of the individual's personal relationship to the goal of the journey, God. First-person accounts of spiritual journey, often modeled on that of Muhammad, offer a glimpse of a more intensely personal realm, suggesting the essence of what it is to be, from a religious perspective, truly human.

Religion and Experience

A spiritual tradition offers its followers ways to describe and evaluate a broad spectrum of experience. Islamic sources present an enormous variety of concerns, from the daily performance of basic religious duties to the discipline of ongoing vigilance over subtler personal motivation to breathing the rarified atmosphere of mystical insight and union. Some of those sources have translated these religious concerns into a blueprint for sustaining the Islamic spiritual tradition's original impulse.

Islam's religious heritage is multifaceted. The all too common identification of Islamic spirituality with mysticism alone, or with an arcane wis-

Figure 34.   (*Opposite*) A whimsical ink and watercolor painting of a mystical journey from Safavid Persia (c. 1650). Cambridge, Mass.: The Harvard University Art Museums. Grace Nichols Strong, Francis H. Burr Memorial, and Friends of the Fogg Fund.

dom accessible only to the elect, distorts the tradition. But even among the most reflective active practitioners of any religious tradition, relatively few will be both able and willing to speak openly and articulately about their deepest religious experience. Persons who have recorded such reflections *in writing*, either those who have had such experiences or their spiritual descendants, are therefore an even smaller minority. In this chapter I consider some textual forms that articulate the most subtle hints about the nature of the divine-human relationship, as described by a number of gifted Muslim authors. These writers offer a view of the meaning of, in the words of Thomas Aquinas, "an experiential knowledge of God."

Articulation of that experience occurs principally in three broad categories of written sources. (I have arranged the material in this chapter so as to reflect the progressive movement toward ever more profound mysteries that Muslim authors have experienced and described.) The first major type is a narrative account by or about individuals who have claimed, or were perceived, to have experienced an extraordinary level of intimacy with God. Individual life stories often come under the guise of autobiographical or biographical accounts (often called sira). Some others also take the form of first-person accounts either of actual specific experiences or of imaginatively embellished occurrences. These are sometimes disjointed and episodic but still narrative recollections, similar to diary entries, with no imposed narrative structure to hold them together. Authors who speak of their own mystical experiences have created a form of auto-hagiography.[1]

The visionary recital (hikayat) is an imaginative and literarily cohesive narrative patterned on Muhammad's paradigmatic experience. The recital generally speaks in the first rather than the third person, which distinguishes it from stories of Muhammad's own journey. Even though the recital may arise out of an author's intensely personal spiritual experience, it is quite different from autobiographical recollections.

Finally, a variety of works either describe or presuppose the experience of Muhammad as paradigm of the mystical quest. They are like episodic spiritual biographies of the Prophet, since they take as their models peak moments in the Prophet's life, such as his reception of revelation, his combined experience of Night Journey (*isra'*) and Ascension (mi'raj), and his ongoing spiritual function of illumination. Unlike the visionary recital, these works do not employ an obviously allegorical structure. Since these narratives purport to give accounts of the experiences of actual persons, whether of Muhammad or of some mystic who claims to have had an experience like Muhammad's, they are written from either a first- or third-person point of

view. In the history of Islamic spirituality these account have played principal roles as models and touchstones for the experience of later Muslim
seekers.

The second major type, often called allusive speech or symbolic expression, includes shorter statements or collections of statements. These allusions take the form of either general references to some aspect of mystical
experience (*ishara*) or of first-person exclamations arising out of personal
experience (often called *shath*, "ecstatic utterance or mystical paradox"). The
mystical aphorism (*hikma*; pl., *hikam*) lies between these two forms. It shares
both the pedagogical tone of the ishara and the intensely personal quality
of the shath while utilizing a form somewhere between poetry and prose. I
also include in this category works that analyze or comment upon these usually cryptic and often doctrinally controversial utterances of ecstatic mystics. Commentary on mystical expressions can be either a fairly dispassionate
analysis or a dedicated attempt to rehabilitate a mystic whose public statements have been considered blasphemous by religious scholars.

Works of or about spiritual direction constitute the third major type. An
important dimension of Islamic spiritual writing is the unrelenting concern
of spiritual guides for complete honesty and freedom from all forms of self-
deception on the part of disciples. These works are models and tools for in-
trospective analysis. The literature of the "science of hearts" belongs technically to the broader category of pedagogy, and comes in a variety of forms;
but because of its specialized purpose, it merits explicit attention here. How
is one to know when such rarified talk of otherworldly experience is credible, and when it represents merely the ravings of an overworked psyche or
an underaffirmed ego? The theme of spiritual discernment runs through a
number of discrete literary forms, some of which have already been discussed
in slightly different contexts. In the wisdom literature, the disciplinary stric-
tures, and instructional works, there is an underlying wariness of a treacherous human capacity for mendacity.

HEART SPEAKS TO HEART

Stories of intensely personal experience take many forms. Predictably they
occur in autobiography, but they also appear in diaries, letters, dream jour-
nals, and even poetry. They can be organized in a number of ways. Chronological accounts move temporally from beginning to middle to end; space
sometimes provides an organizational metaphor in which the storyteller
moves from place to place. Stories can also move by free association from

one feeling or mood to another until the teller has ranged the full emotional spectrum of an experience; time and place are of no consequence. Whatever the form, however, these accounts represent the disclosures of the inmost heart.

Soul on Pilgrimage

Most readers can identify readily with the literary form known as autobiography. A life story holds the promise of a frank firsthand account, concrete and immediate, of an individual's journey. Ghazali's *Deliverance from Error (Al-Munqidh min ad-dalal)* is probably the most famous, although not the earliest, spiritual self-portrait written by a Muslim. Sometimes compared to Augustine's *Confessions,* Ghazali's fascinating account describes his lifelong quest for certitude in which he ventured to ask even the most dangerous and probing of questions:

> The thirst for grasping the real meaning of things was indeed my habit and wont from my early years and in the prime of my life. It was an instinctive, natural disposition placed in my makeup by God Most High, not something due to my own choosing and contriving. As a result . . . inherited beliefs lost their hold on me when I was still quite young. For I saw that the children of Christians always grew up embracing Christianity, and the children of Jews always grew up adhering to Judaism, and the children of Muslims always grew up following the religion of Islam. . . . I felt an inner urge to seek the true meaning . . . of the beliefs arising through slavish imitation of parents and teachers.[2]

Ghazali relates how a series of psychosomatic difficulties led him to question his occupation as an academician. An unexpected loss of his ability to speak persuaded him that he no longer truly believed in what he was teaching. Leaving his position, he went in search of certitude, inquiring after it among various groups of intellectual seekers: philosophers, theologians, mathematicians. At length he became convinced, through a revelatory event in which God cast the light of certainty into his heart, that only the Sufi emphasis on intensely interiorized spiritual experience or taste (*dhawq*) could lead to knowledge without doubt. Only the Sufis, he concluded, pursued a sound approach to spiritual truths, combining the theoretical with the practical: "The aim of their knowledge is to lop off the obstacles present in the soul and to rid oneself of its reprehensible habits and vicious qualities in order to attain thereby a heart empty of all save God and adorned with the constant remembrance of God."[3]

Ghazali's story is remarkable, revealing his tenacity in pursuing such a variety of ways to the truth. He explored every avenue, from the more objective, example and authority, and proof through rational argument to the more subjective, personal experience that was so intimate and intense he could barely talk about it. He organizes much of his account "around the recurrent topos of sickness and health, in which, broadly speaking, sickness or disease represents error, ignorance, skepticism . . . while health and healing conveys notions of truth, knowledge, and certainty."[4] Ghazali discovered that he could not continue his relatively comfortable but sterile life of unquestioning conformity to tradition. But letting go of that consoling certitude left him temporarily without moorings. He could easily have given in to cynicism any number of times, but his conviction that he was meant to discover a way to truth kept him searching. His experience of doubt and confusion were an index of the times in which he lived. He listened to the rhetoric of social and intellectual revival, but looked upon a world in which reality and rhetoric did not coincide. Ghazali knew his share of disillusionment, but he remained faithful to his conscience.

Ghazali was not the first Muslim to tell of a personal search. Muhammad ibn 'Ali al-Hakim at-Tirmidhi's (d. c. 932) short autobiography represents one of the earliest statements of its kind by a Muslim mystic. Tirmidhi, most famous for his *Seal of the Friends of God* (*Khatm al-awliya'*), describes his earlier life quite straightforwardly. He began his studies in traditional religious disciplines at the age of eight. As a young man he traveled through Iraq in search of Prophetic hadiths while en route to pilgrimage in Mecca. In that holy city he found authentic repentance and devotion to God. Tirmidhi's pilgrimage was not precisely a conversion experience, but it was a significant turning point for him. At the age of twenty-seven he began to memorize the Qur'an. On his return to central Asia, he experienced great frustration because he was unable to find a suitable spiritual director. He had to settle for guidance from a book on self-discipline.

Extended periods of seclusion eventually led to a series of revelatory events that transformed Tirmidhi; but there followed a time of spiritual distress during which he was falsely accused of various doctrinal and moral lapses. He reports that he was vindicated when his accusers fled at the outbreak of social upheavals in the region. Dreams or visions that his wife and some friends reported having about him form an important element in Tirmidhi's story. This is unusual, because when mystics record dreams as significant events in their lives, they ordinarily refer to their own.

The people in Tirmidhi's story recount their dreams in such a way that their experiences sound much like visions that function as initiations into the farther reaches of the spiritual path. Latter sections of the account offer a picture of the various levels in Tirmidhi's journey. For example, Tirmidhi sees Muhammad entering a mosque and follows him right up the steps of the pulpit, where he sits at the Prophet's feet. In another dream, his wife sees a tree, which she tends, so that many birds come to nest in it, and which then turns green all the way to its top. This has been interpreted as a reference to her husband's spiritual stature, but it also suggests that Tirmidhi's wife regarded herself as contributing to his development. Her other dreams likewise imply that Tirmidhi attained the loftiest rank among the saints.[5]

Another autobiography is 'Ayn al-Qudat al-Hamadhani's (b. 1098) *Complaint of the Exile (Shakwa 'l-gharib)*. It takes the form of an apologia, a defense of his religious beliefs. 'Ayn al-Qudat composed the work in prison just before he was executed. He speaks of himself initially in the third person, describing the suffering of one exiled from his home. Then he shifts to a first-person defense of the controversial positions for which he had incurred the displeasure of the religious establishment of Baghdad—he was accused of claiming to be divine.

'Ayn al-Qudat addresses the list of charges against him. He has been falsely accused by detractors who have badly misinterpreted his statements. The theologians do not understand the inner meanings of Sufi technical terminology and are therefore incapable of plumbing the true depths of their mystical reflections. Just as a person whose knowledge of jurisprudence extends no further than an ability to recite a list of technical terms could scarcely claim credibility as a jurist, so those who know only superficially of the mystical path are hardly qualified to judge its adherents. In this context one can readily appreciate why so many Sufi authors produced dictionaries to clarify the terms of their discussions.

'Ayn al-Qudat is one of a number of now-famous Muslims who have been similarly misinterpreted and slandered. "Why," he asks, "should I consider it so curious that the theologians of the present age should disapprove of me, seeing that the greatest scholars of every age have always been the object of envy, and have been the targets of every kind of persecution. . . . Victims of the same hostility have been the Sufi shaikhs such as al-Junaid [Junayd]."[6] Lives of individuals of substance, he observes, are impenetrable to the scrutiny of those whose social status alone persuades them that they are licensed to sit in judgment. In this case, he writes, the critics claim to disagree intellectually, saying they are merely protecting the truth of Islam; but in fact they secretly covet his celebrity status. Among the other renowned Sufis harassed for their mystical utterances were Hallaj, Abu Yazid (Bayazid) al-Bistami (d. 874), and Yahya Suhrawardi Maqtul, "the one killed" (d. 1191).

A more recent example of a large-scale autobiography is *The Chronicle*

(*Fahrasa*) of Ahmad Ibn 'Ajiba, the eighteenth-century Moroccan Sufi of the Darqawi order whose *Book of the Ascension* was discussed earlier. He wrote *The Chronicle's* nineteen autobiographical chapters to celebrate God's goodness, and he covers a remarkable range of experiential issues and themes. After a genealogical introduction, Ibn 'Ajiba describes his childhood and his student years in considerable detail. As a child, he could sense precisely the moment of ritual prayer and would badger his mother until she performed the prescribed salat. While he was still in Qur'an school, the boy would arise at midnight and go to the mosque. Even before Ibn 'Ajiba could read, God inspired in him a love of solitude. His studies in jurisprudence (*fiqh*) and of Hadith won him certificates from renowned teachers.

In his seventh chapter the author says that any worthwhile knowledge bears fruit in action. His meditation on Ibn 'Ata' Allah's (d. 1309) *Aphorisms* (*Hikam*) and on Ibn 'Abbad of Ronda's commentary on that book, encouraged him to put his convictions into action. He then describes the transition, not from unbelief to belief, but from a complacent attitude toward his slice of reality to a more incisive critique of his place in the larger world. The chapter is a variation on the conversion story genre, reminiscent of Ghazali's *Deliverance from Error*. Like Ghazali, Ibn 'Ajiba speaks of forsaking the prestige of his academic position and his celebrity status as a jurist, in favor of the more marginal life of a dervish. Both men describe a conversion from a life of relative social conformity, externally laudable but interiorly less than satisfying, to one in which inner values finally outweigh external criteria. Both came to redefine the meaning of success. No longer a matter of prestige or power, success now meant being at peace with self and trusting entirely in God.

Ibn 'Ajiba wanted to exchange his books for a life of prayer, but his teacher, Sidi Talha, advised him against such a move. Although he continued his studies for four more years, mindfulness of God so absorbed him that he was oblivious to what his teacher said. Ibn 'Ajiba's conversion was the final stage of an ongoing process. It was also a startling departure from his accustomed public demeanor, which one famous teacher had likened to Junayd of Baghdad's, the paragon of sober self-discipline and private piety.

In chapters 9 through 16 Ibn 'Ajiba describes many experiences: his relationship to his shaykh; his own activities as spiritual teacher; his travels and experience of imprisonment; his various supports during the course of the journey—including that of a dream-vision of the Prophet himself; the numerous miraculous wonders he witnessed; and the results of his initiating various individuals in the spiritual path. He provides one of the most complete and integrated chronicles available of a Muslim's spiritual odyssey.

Its themes reflect concerns shared by Muslim seekers across the globe over many centuries. But it also provides valuable insights into the culturally and geographically unique aspects of the life of this early-modern Moroccan Sufi.[7]

Letters, diaries, and discourses of the great mystics also provide information about their personal lives. These sources usually contain shorter recollections of individual spiritual high points. One important recurrent theme in their stories is the ongoing search for a spiritual guide to assist them on their quest.

An impressive story from the life of Shaykh ʿAbd al-Qadir al-Jilani tells of how as a youth he heard the ox with which he was plowing reveal that he was not meant to spend his life at such tasks. He then set out toward Baghdad, carrying only the forty pieces of gold his mother had sewn into his tunic, and fortified with her injunction that he always be truthful. Accosted by bandits who inquired about his possessions, Jilani divulged his secret. The chief bandit was so shamed by his honesty that he repented his ways and brought all sixty of his henchmen into Islam. As Jilani approached Baghdad, the prophet Khizr appeared and told him he must remain in a desert ruin outside the city for seven years. With Khizr reappearing each year to strengthen the young man's resolve, his spirit was put to the most strenuous of trials. In an account reminiscent of tales of the trials of the Christian desert father Anthony, Jilani tells how Satan marshaled every conceivable ally to seduce him. Through severe mortification he kept his enemies at bay and his own baser natural proclivities in check. Austerities were his only sustenance.

Seven years later Khizr gave Jilani permission to enter Baghdad. But the evil and injustice there were so pervasive that within days he headed back toward the city gate to seek peaceful seclusion. Again there came a voice ordering him to stay and serve the people, and assuring him nothing in the city could harm his faith. At that point Jilani found himself slipping into a meditative state that lasted until the next day. He prayed intensely that God would grant him clarity. He continues his story:

> The next day, as I was wandering through a neighbourhood called Muzaffariyya, a man whom I had never seen opened the door of his house and called to me, "Come in, ʿAbdul-Qadir!" As I came to his door, he said, "Tell me, what did you wish from Allah? What did you pray for yesterday?" I was frozen, with amazement. I could not find words to answer him. The man looked at my face and slammed the door with such violence that the dust was raised all around me and covered me from head to foot. I walked away, wondering what I had asked from Allah the day before. Then

I remembered. I turned back to tell the man, but I could find neither the house nor him. I was very worried, as I realized he was a man close to Allah. In fact, later I was to learn that he was Hammad al-Dabbas, who became my shaykh.[8]

This narrative belongs to a subgenre of stories about how an individual is led to find a spiritual guide. The theme of difficulty in identifying the guide is not uncommon.

An Indian Muslim half a millennium later describes his most intense spiritual experience, interpreted with the help of his shaykh. Ahmad Sirhindi's Persian epistles contain a number of reports of his encounters with God. He tells how God led him to one of the prominent spiritual teachers of his day, who instructed him in the subtleties of self-effacement. As Sirhindi progressed, he experienced what his shaykh identified as one level of annihilation of the ego (fana') and eventually the passing away of that experience too (the fana' of fana'). Wonder is essential to the experience. Recalling the words of the martyr-poet Hallaj, Sirhindi recounts his further inner movements and his conversations with the teacher:

> After that I saw a light that comprehended everything. I thought it to be God. This light was black. I reported to the Shaykh. He said: "You have seen God, but under the veil of light." He further said: "The expansion of light that you see is in the realm of knowledge, it appears due to the contact of Divine Essence with innumerable things, high and low; but it should be negated." After that, that all-comprehending black light started contracting till there remained just a point. The Shaykh said: "You should negate that point too, till you reach the state of wonder (hayrat)." I did as he said, and that imaginary point . . . disappeared from there and wonder set in, wherein God was visible by Himself through Himself. When I reported it to the Shaykh he said: "This presence (hudur) is the presence which the Naqshbandiyah aim at, and this is what the nisbat [a name that indicates a relationship, in this case to a social group, a Sufi tariqa] of Naqshbandiyah means. It is also called the presence (of God) without concealment . . . , and herein lies the inclusion of the goal in the commencement. . . . In our order one acquires this nisbat as others acquire adhkar [mantralike phrases] and awrad [litanies] from their preceptors in other orders.[9]

Sirhindi notes that it is most unusual for an individual to reach this point so rapidly, and that he proceeded to a still subtler experience of psychic annihilation (fana'). His perceptions of reality began to change dramatically. All things merged into one another, and his sense of wonder and bewilderment escalated. His anxiety level also increased, and his shaykh advised him that he clearly had more hard work to do. Gradually Sirhindi realized three truths: the distinction between reality and illusion; the sole reality of God;

and the nonexistence of all acts and attributes that proceed from the realm of illusion.

Thus far in his reminiscence, the author has noted how at each stage the shaykh helps him to name the specific level at which he has arrived, using the terminology of a classical Sufi typology of spiritual development. At this point Sirhindi sums up his experience, with alternating moments of wonder and clarity as the keynote. After the fana' of intoxication, God returns him to the baqa' of sobriety. He can see only God, and that again induces in him a state of wonder. Again God brings him back to his senses, so that he discerns God's presence in every fiber of his being. And again he experiences wonder, and again his return to sobriety is accompanied by still greater insight and still more intense bewilderment: "At this time I was informed that the object of my vision (*mashhud*) . . . was not God. It was rather the symbolic form of His creative relation."[10] The farther the mystic advanced, the more vividly he understood the infinite distance between himself and his Creator.

Autobiographical narratives have continued to provide information about definitive experiences in the lives of influential Muslims. Although not all these seekers have gained world renown, their stories are valuable. Some began as oral narratives and were then written down by the person to whom the story was first told. From Malaysia comes one such account, the story of 'Abd al-Qadir of Johore, a shaykh of the Qadiri order who had migrated from Malabar in India. He was working as a truck driver in 1945, when an unexpected event changed his life. In a manner less spectacular than that of his namesake, the earlier 'Abd al-Qadir al-Jilani, this modern Muslim also found a spiritual guide. He recalls:

> I used to leave my home and family for weeks to resign myself to the solitude of the Pasir Pelangi mosque in Johore Bahru, where I met then a certain Haji Fadil, who was a well known teacher of several *Tariqahs*. The mosque belonged to the Sultan of Johore, and Haji Fadil lived there by the Sultan's permission. . . . I went to this mosque and devoted myself to religious duties for about two years before the Haji, one day, approached me to set before me a cup of tea. Without a word the Haji left me to my devotions. But very soon after this incident he used to approach me with tea and some cakes as well. Then the Haji began to invite me to his room in the precinct of the mosque where there was more privacy, and there used to talk to me for long sessions. After about two years . . . he disclosed to me his intention to initiate me into the (Sufi order).

Haji Fadil then bestowed on the initiate the special dhikrs he was to recite as a murid. For the next two years the new initiate observed his devotional duties, after which Haji Fadil summoned him again to confer the authority to initiate other seekers as members of the Qadiri order. Though he possessed no formal education, the new shaykh now had the inner knowledge required of a spiritual guide.[11]

Dream accounts known technically as oneiric autobiographies are another important genre of experiential narrative. Usually incorporated into larger works, these dream stories are an important subgenre of autobiography, especially in North Africa. By means of these dream-visions or conversations, the subject of the narrative lays claim to an intimate relationship with the Prophet, gaining spiritual stature and even salvific power through that association. Some dream accounts describe how Muhammad and a retinue that might include Companions, wives, or angels visit the subject's house. In some cases the visitors bring food. The ensuing conversation confers a special legitimacy on the work and life of the narrator by placing him close to the sources of holiness. Sometimes the account confirms the narrator's rights against the claims of his critics and enemies. Other dreams depict the dreamer visiting a paradisal garden, taking stories of Muhammad's own journey through the heavens as their model.

Personal accounts of life experiences need to be read critically, especially if the narrator claims to have had a visionary experience. Though dream accounts appear the most intimate self-revelations, they can be blatantly political or self-aggrandizing. As a form of religious expression, nevertheless, these documents open another window into the spiritual experience of individuals within the Islamic tradition.[12]

Narrative and Imagination

The visionary recital, or hikayat, is a most unusual genre of narrative literature. It serves as a thematic bridge between the authentically first-person accounts of experience and the more dispassionate analyses of the seeker's spiritual progress. The hikayat belongs formally to the category of first-person accounts, because it often uses the literary conceit of the personal recollection. It functions, however, more as an analysis in that it describes in highly symbolic language the intricacies of the most private spiritual or mystical experience. The deeper an individual delves into the mysteries of the experiencing self, the more he or she relies on metaphor to express the mystery. Two influential figures, Ibn Sina and Yahya Suhrawardi Maqtul, have written marvelous metaphorical visionary recitals.

Ibn Sina (980–1037), also known as Avicenna, composed in Arabic three of the earliest hikayats. Some scholars argue that the form belongs to philosophy rather than spirituality. These recitals do sometimes speak the language of the philosophical treatise, but they are also meditations on the ultimate goals which the Creator offers to humankind. They therefore clearly move beyond purely rational analysis and into the realm of mystery. As Henry Corbin observes, Ibn Sina's three recitals allow the author to locate himself spiritually within the cosmos that he had elsewhere described in philosophical terms: "By substituting a dramaturgy for cosmology, the recitals guarantee the genuineness of this universe; it is veritably the place of a personally lived adventure . . . [the recitals reveal] something, indeed, of the secret of Avicenna's personal experience."[13] Ibn Sina describes a spiritual universe "living *in the soul,* and no longer a world *into which* the soul is cast as a prisoner because it has not acquired consciousness of it."[14]

Ibn Sina explains the soul's return to its origin as a threefold project. First it recognizes life's purpose, then it learns how to achieve that purpose, and finally it arrives at the goal. Ibn Sina regards mythic discourse as a valid alternative to philosophic analysis and employs it in his recitals. In Ibn Sina's *Alive, Son of Awake (Hayy ibn yaqzan),* the storyteller recounts his meeting with a traveling wisdom figure named Hayy ibn Yaqzan, who describes the cosmic terrains across which he has ventured. The great eastern, western, and middle regions with their various climes and inhabitants represent the full range of human experience. The seeker must go through various trials and tests, and face both victory and defeat. At the eastern extreme of the world dwells the great king. All humankind journeys toward the vision of that monarch, but few attain it. The recital ends with Hayy inviting the seeker to accompany him toward a vision of the king.[15]

In his second work, *The Recital of the Bird (Risalat at-tayr),* Ibn Sina describes how the soul accepts Hayy's invitation to fly across the cosmic landscape toward the Orient. He must journey beyond discursive reason and into the dazzling beauty of the divine countenance. At the end the journeyer observes wryly how his friends will surely advise him on how to cure his manifest bewilderment. Get plenty of rest and maintain a curative diet, they will say, unaware that his experience has taken him beyond earthly remedies.[16]

Ibn Sina brings the experiential cycle to a consummation in the third piece, *Salaman wa Absal,* the recital of the brothers Salaman and Absal, "depicting the psychological struggle that spiritual reorientation can provoke."[17] Here the author shifts to a third-person narrative whose plot centers on family intrigue. Salaman's wife covets Absal, who is married to her own sister. She pursues Absal, eventually compassing his death; Salaman finds her out and has her killed. A complex allegorical interpretation reads the story as an interaction among the rational and animal souls (Salaman and his wife) and the acquired intellect (Absal). In the end, the rational soul overcomes the animal soul but only with the help of the acquired intellect— and at the price of submission to it.[18]

Shihab ad-Din Yahya Suhrawardi Maqtul followed in Ibn Sina's foot-steps with a series of short Persian works of the same type. As Wheeler Thackston notes, the Persian genre "did not become popular as a literary vehicle. It may be that it was too intimate and confining; it certainly did not offer the immediate adaptability to the facile exploration and juxtaposition characteristic of poetry."[19] These works provide an essential link between the more factual concerns of autobiography and biography, and the more imaginative mode of allusive speech.

Suhrawardi's favorite metaphor is that of the soul's quest for its origi-nal abode. The traveler moves either "upward" through the macrocosm and beyond, or "inward" through the microcosm of the self; in either case the journey moves beyond the world of ordinary experience. In the macrocos-mic journey, the seeker rises through the various (as many as eleven) spheres. For example, each sphere is described as a person the seeker meets or as a mountain range to be crossed, on the way to liberation from mate-riality. The metaphor of the microcosmic or inward journey describes an ex-ploration through and among the various spiritual faculties. In order to bring to consciousness the temporarily lost memories of his or her origin, the seeker must submit to what a psychotherapist might call a helpful form of regression. By retrieving those primordial experiences the seeker "purifies the corporeal shell that contains the divine spirit." Through that purifica-tion the wayfarer rides the steed of nostalgic longing to return to a forgot-ten place of origin. Yearning for home thus transports the traveler "across the celestial barriers to the City of the Soul, where he is bathed in the liv-ing waters that confer the immortality of divine wisdom."[20]

Within the context of the inward journey, Suhrawardi employs the clas-sic dichotomy of city and wilderness. In order to achieve liberation from the enslaving power of reason, the seeker must escape to the wild, venturing into a domain as unsettling as it is exhilarating. There the seeker at last comes to know the authentic truth of experience. Akin to what Ghazali calls "tast-ing," this experience transcends mere intellectual assent. In every case the seeker meets a guide, the spiritual director, who provides the clues neces-sary for negotiating the rigors of the journey. In the third recital, *The Red Intellect* (*'Aql-i surkh*), the questing soul is portrayed as a falcon. Suhrawardi describes the seeker's encounter with the guide. Speaking in the first person, the falcon tells how he greets a figure he sees coming toward him. The per-son has a reddish complexion, and the falcon concludes he must be young.

When the falcon addresses him as "young man," the mysterious individual responds that he is in fact the first person ever born.

Responding to the falcon's questions, the Red Intellect explains the nature of his present plight and the way to liberation from it:

> Then I [the falcon] said, "Elder, where do you come from?"
>
> He replied, "From beyond Mount Qaf, where my residence is. Your nest too was there, but you have forgotten it."
>
> "What are you doing here?" I asked.
>
> "I am a traveller," he said. "I continually wander about the world and look at marvelous things." [After enumerating seven marvels, the guide goes into greater detail concerning the ultimate goal, Mount Qaf.] "First of all," he began, "Mount Qaf surrounds the world and consists of eleven mountains. When you are delivered of your bondage you will go there, for you have been brought from there, and eventually everything that exists returns to its initial form."
>
> I asked how to get there.
>
> "The way is difficult," he said. "First of all there are two mountains in the way, one hot and the other cold. The heat and cold of these two are beyond measure."
>
> "That is easy," said I. "I shall cross the hot mountain during the winter and the one that is cold during the summer."
>
> "That would be a mistake," he said, "because the climate of that realm never changes."
>
> "What is the distance of this mountain?" I asked.
>
> "However you go," he replied, "you can only reach the first stage—like a compass, one leg of which rests on the center of the circle and the other on the line of the perimeter. No matter how much it revolves it still comes back to the place it started."

The falcon asks whether he might drill a small tunnel through the mountains. No, the guide explains, but a "certain quality," which he likens to the ability of balsam oil to seep through the palm to the back of the hand when the sun warms it, will allow the falcon to make progress. He then describes in symbolic cosmological imagery the balance of the journey yet to be made. The trek ends at the Spring of Life in the Land of Darkness. When one knows truly, one has reached that spring and has achieved the penetrating power of balsam oil.[21]

Henry Corbin insists that the recital "is not a *story* that happened to others, but the soul's own story, its 'spiritual romance.' . . . The soul can tell it only in the first person." He sums up the meaning of these works of Ibn Sina and Suhrawardi with an observation about the former's *Recital of the Bird* and the latter's *Recital of Occidental Exile:* "both recitals testify to the fact that their narrators, each in the measure of his own spiritual experience, reproduced the case of the Prophet, relived for and by themselves the exemplary condition typified in the *Mi'raj*. By experiencing this in their turn, they have performed the *ta'wil*, the *exegesis* of their soul."[22] *Ta'wil* means interpreting a foundational revelation; but here revelation is assimilated experientially by the seeker, rather than contained in a scriptural text external to the seeker.

Muhammad as Mystical Model

Muslims have always measured their actions against the Prophetic model of Muhammad, even to emulating his use of a toothpick. Among narrative accounts of higher levels of spiritual discovery, some texts describe the mystical experience of Muhammad as an exemplar. These works also develop that paradigmatic narrative as a medium of literary and personal expression. As discussed earlier, awareness of the Muhammadan paradigm has been an important, if implicit, element in several other narrative forms as well.

A variety of literary and visual forms that celebrate the life and mission of Muhammad are central to certain ritual observances, as well as entertaining, exhortatory, and aesthetic. Another kind of writing focuses more directly on the Prophet's intimate relationship with God and on Muhammad as model for mystics. Authors have naturally been attracted to the three signal dimensions of the Prophet's experience: God's transmission of the message to the messenger; the messenger's journey to the divine presence; and the medium of Muhammad's ongoing relationship with creation, namely, his "light." All three aspects contribute equally to the imagery that ranges the spectrum of the articulation of mystical experience.[23]

Ibn 'Arabi's short treatise *The Cosmic Tree* or *Tree of Existence* (*Shajarat al-kawn*) provides insight into one cosmological schema of Muhammad's mystical journey and its paradigmatic implications for Muslim mystics. The cosmic tree appears often in world religious literature as an organizing metaphor. In Islamic cosmology the tree functions as an axis, rooted in the heavens and growing downward into the material world.[24] Using technical terms, Ibn 'Arabi describes the Prophet's passage through four stations (maqamat). First, Muhammad enters into existence and responds to God's command to arise and warn humankind. In the "praised station" the Prophet receives the office of intercessor for humankind at Judgment Day. The third station is Muhammad's eternal dwelling in Paradise and his visit to each abode therein. And finally the Prophet reaches the station in which he is but "two bows' length" from God (an allusion to Q 53:9). Muhammad is thus the ultimate fruit of the cosmic tree.

At this point Ibn 'Arabi begins a fascinating description of the Night Journey and Ascension, through which five "steeds" carry Muhammad. The first, Buraq (see Fig. 35), takes him to Jerusalem; on the second, the ladder (mi'raj), he mounts to the lowest heaven. Then angels' pinions bear the Prophet up to the seventh heaven. And on Gabriel's wing Muhammad rides to the tree beyond which even Gabriel cannot pass. Finally, he floats on a flying carpet to God's throne. There God sums up the Prophet's mission:

> Now what is demanded of a witness is truthfulness about that to which he bears witness, and it is not permissible for him to bear witness to something he has not seen, so I shall show you my Paradise that you may see what I have prepared for my friends, and I shall show you my Hell that you may see what I have prepared for my enemies. Thus shall I have you witness my majesty, and uncover for you my beauty, that you may know that I in my perfection am far removed from anything [in ordinary experience].[25]

Ibn 'Arabi offers four varying descriptions of the Night Journey and Ascension, ostensibly referring to the experience of Muhammad. But all the key features of the terrain, as well as the various personalities the journeyer meets, correspond to aspects of the human heart. In fact, Ibn 'Arabi comes surprisingly close to saying outright that *he* is the journeyer who meets different prophets in each of the seven heavens. In other words, he experiences different aspects of revelation within himself. A key feature of the experience is that the wayfarer enjoys the services of a guide appropriate to each level of the journey. In several instances, that guide appears to be Muhammad himself. Ibn 'Arabi thinks of the experience as the confirmation of his own mission in life once he returns from the journey: "So now I am teaching what I learned and transmitting to these (disciples and readers) what I came to know."[26]

Ibn 'Arabi was not the first to describe Muhammad's mystical experience as a model. An early untitled Arabic document that R. A. Nicholson calls "a handbook for those seeking mystical union" gives an account of Abu Yazid (Bayazid) al-Bistami's peak experience. This Sufi's dream-vision of mystical ascent (mi'raj) is clearly patterned on Muhammad's experience. As the mystic travels upward through the seven heavens, he passes a series of tests of the authenticity of his motivation and the depth of his desire.

In each heaven a phalanx of angels offers the journeyer a kingdom; the formulaic account repeats nearly verbatim at each level the mystic's steadfast refusal of the offer. Arriving at the seventh heaven, the dreamer is transformed into a bird capable of traversing the whole cosmos, but the mystic has to pass yet another test of his God centeredness and then another. At

Figure 35. A Persian painting of the mi'raj of Muhammad (1514), showing the Prophet, led by a crowned Gabriel, rising heavenward on Buraq. This image is unusual because it suggests that the three men in the mosque are experiencing the upper scene in a vision or ecstatic trance. Note the fiery illumination produced by the Qur'an on its stand in the mihrab. New York: The Metropolitan Museum of Art, Bell Fund and Astor Foundation Gift.

last God, satisfied as to the purity of the journeyer's intention, introduces him to the spirits of all the prophets. The Spirit of Muhammad then tells him he must return to earth with his new experiential knowledge to encourage the Prophet's people to continue their quest for God.[27] This narrative is reminiscent of the classic hero's journey to another world and subsequent return to his people with a boon for them. But above all, Muhammad serves as a model precisely because he is a human being.

Well into the twentieth century the model of Muhammad's journey has exercised an active fascination upon Muslim poets. Muhammad Iqbal (d. 1938) is one of Pakistan's most famous authors and thinkers. His *Book of Eternity* (*Javid-nama*) describes a seven-tiered spiritual odyssey. The wayfarer passes through the planetary spheres of the Moon, Mercury, Venus, Mars, Jupiter, Saturn, and beyond, to the very presence of God. As Dante chose the poet Virgil as his guide in the *Divine Comedy*, Iqbal asks Rumi to lead him. At the pinnacle of the experience, the poet exclaims:

> Suddenly I beheld my world,
> that earth and heaven of mine,
> I saw it drowned in a light of dawn;
> I saw it crimson as a jujube-tree:
> out of the epiphanies which broke in my soul
> I fell drunk with ecstasy, like Moses.
> That light revealed every secret veiled
> and snatched the power of speech from my tongue.
> Out of the deep heart of the inscrutable world
> an ardent, flaming melody broke forth.[28]

In form, structure, and imagery, Iqbal's work places him in the tradition of the classical authors. More to the point, he expresses a kinship of feeling and mood with his spiritual forebears that marks his work as Islamic.

BEYOND STORYTELLING

Some experiences are too intense to talk about. The poet E. E. Cummings called them "beyond any experience . . . things which enclose me, or which I cannot touch because they are too near."[29] They range from the most joyful to the most painful. Poets and mystics have given voice to these moments that, according to Islam's mystics ultimately define our humanity. But communicating these core realities still strains conventional language. The term *ishara* (indicator or pointer) is used in connection with catechismlike instructional works. The term is also applied to another type of literature, briefer statements, hints or allusions of mystical teachers concerning subtle aspects of spiritual experience.

I consider three forms of expression as more or less independent modes of experiential discourse. The first is the mystical allusion. One early definition of *ishara* suggests that it refers to a form of intimate knowledge that becomes more obscure the more one attempts to express or explain it.[30] The second is the mystical aphorism, for which the Arabic term *hikma* (pl., *hikam*) is used. (This form can also be classified as a subcategory of the allusion.) Finally, the mystical paradox or ecstatic utterance, called shath in Arabic, is in many ways the most intriguing form of allusive speech. A formidable body of literature is devoted to interpreting, and in some cases defending, these three ways of saying the unsayable.

Saying the Unsayable

Abu Hamid al-Ghazali's younger brother, Ahmad Ghazali (d. 1126), wrote a book called *Sparks (Sawanih)* in response to requests from a friend. The younger Ghazali opens his splendid Persian essay on mystical love by describing its manner and level of communication. He refers to his entire work as a form of ishara and then elaborates:

> the ideas of love are like virgins and the hand of words cannot reach the edge of the curtain of those virgins. Even though our task here is to marry the virgin ideas to the men of words in the private chambers of speech, yet outward expressions (*'ibarat*) in this discourse cannot but be allusions to different ideas. Moreover, this indefiniteness (of words) exists only for those who have no "immediate tasting" (dhawq [i.e., direct experience]). From this idea originate two roots: the allusive meaning (ishara) of an outward expression ('ibara) and the outward expression of an allusive meaning. However, in the innermost heart of words is concealed the sharp edges of a sword, but they can be perceived only by inner vision (basira). Hence, if in all of the chapters (of this book) something is said which is not comprehended, then it must be one of these (esoteric) ideas.[31]

Ghazali's thoughts on love share the composite literary form of Sa'di's *Rose Garden*, except that much of the poetry Ghazali quotes he borrows from other authors. *Sparks* also recalls the wisdom literature partly because of its occasional aphoristic tenor. What is critical in this context is Ahmad's distinction between allusion and expression.

Throughout the seventy-seven short segments of *Sparks*, Ghazali unveils deeper and deeper meanings of the experience of mystical love. Beneath the surface of his reflections run a subtle metaphysics and epistemology of spiritual experience. The former focuses ultimately on the ontological status of the lover in relation to the beloved, turning on the controversial question of whether the lover continues to exist as a distinct entity when united with the beloved.

Ahmad Ghazali, like many Muslim authors on mystical subjects, employs a classic tripartite model to organize the key epistemological issues. Three degrees of certainty (*yaqin*) describe three levels of experience. First, faith in the beloved on the basis of traces or indirect manifestations (the knowledge of certainty, *'ilm al-yaqin*) indicates initial awareness. Then a more direct sense experience of the beloved (the essence [literally, "eye"] of certainty, *'ayn al-yaqin*) is characterized by belief or conviction. Finally there is a loss of identity in the beloved (the truth of certainty, *haqq al-yaqin*), equivalent to the status of servanthood. Ironically, though the experiencing self remains a discrete entity at the first two levels, attainment of the pinnacle of mystical experience brings with it the annihilation of the self.[32]

The ishara mode of communication is characterized by paradox and oxymoron. Love is an inebriation that both heightens and dulls one's perceptions:

> Love is a kind of intoxication, the perfection of which prevents the lover from seeing and perceiving the beloved in her perfection. This is because love is an intoxication experienced by the organ of (inner) perception, hence it is a prevention to perfect perception. However, there is a fine secret beyond this; namely, while the reality of the lover's essence is wholly dedicated to perceiving the beloved's essence, how could he recognize the attributes and affirm them? And yet, even if he perceives them, he cannot perceive this perceiving. This is the meaning of the saying: "The inability to perceive the perceiving is a perception."[33]

Fakhr ad-Din 'Iraqi (1213–1289) develops a number of Ahmad Ghazali's insights further in the poetic *[Divine] Flashes (Lama'at)*. 'Iraqi's twenty-eight "flashes" recall the structure of another classic work, representing the author's meditation on the chapters or "facets" of Ibn 'Arabi's *Bezels of Wisdom (Fusus al-hikam)*.[34] In that work, Ibn 'Arabi uses the metaphor of a succession of prophets from Adam to Muhammad as the structure, with each prophet a different setting of the divine gemstone. 'Iraqi explains his overall scheme in his prologue, evoking an image of pilgrimage to Mecca:

> But now to our intent: a few words explaining the way-stations of Love in the tradition of *The Sparks*; in tune with the voice of each spiritual state as it passes, I shall dictate them as a mirror to reflect every lover's Beloved. But how high is Love, too high for us to circle the Kaaba of its Majesty on the strength of mere understanding, mere words.[35]

'Iraqi describes his allusions to a reality beyond description as reflections of light from the various facets of the precious stone of wisdom:

> In each mirror, each moment the Beloved shows a different face, a different shape. Each instant reflections change to suit the mirror, image follows image in harmony with the situation.[36]

'Iraqi chooses a number of traditional metaphors, from wine and intoxication to drowning in the ocean of divinity, as he circles around the mystery of the lover-beloved relationship. The elements of the complex metaphysical system of Ibn ʿArabi with its multileveled spiritual cosmos lie just below the surface of ʿIraqi's work. In flash 28, the last of the series, ʿIraqi speaks of the latter stages of the seeker's spiritual odyssey; but even this marks yet another juncture in the journey:

> When the Beloved would exalt the lover, He first strips from him the garments collected from all worlds, and clothes him in the robe of His own Attributes. Then the Beloved calls him by all His own Names, and seats him in His own place. Now He may either keep the lover here in this Station of stations, or send him back to the world to the still-imperfect ones. If He sends him back, He will clothe him not in the world's colors, which He has stripped away, but in His own Divine hues. . . .
>
> Now he knows the meaning of "Everything is perishing but its face" [Q 28:88], and he will know why the pronoun "its" here must refer to "everything"; because everything perishes in its form but subsists in its meaning, its "face." He will grasp that in one respect this "face" is the Self-Manifestation of God; for "The face of thy Lord remains" [Q 60:27]. Dear reader, when you yourself have realized that the meaning and reality of things is identical with this Divine Countenance, you will pray, "Show us things as they are," and by this come to see with inward vision that in everything there is a sign, a clue to "He is One."[37]

Citing a hadith popular among Sufis, ʿIraqi alludes here to the final stages of mystical experience in which the seeker is given that intimate knowledge that discerns the presence of God in all things.

Wisdom sayings (hikam) comprise a second form of mystical utterance. A kind of ishara, hikam manifest a greater formal affinity with the proverb-like popular aphorism. The mystical hikam tend to employ less description and explain themselves less than the isharat just discussed. A famous example is the *Book of Wisdom* (*Kitab al-hikam*) of Ibn ʿAtaʾ Allah of Alexandria. This short work became one of the most influential of its kind across North Africa. It consists of three main sections: the aphorisms, four short treatises (similar in content to the malfuz genre), and a selection of intimate conversations of prayer (munajat). Ibn ʿAtaʾ Allah dictated the aphorisms, probably his first work, sometime between 1276 and 1288. I locate hikam here because the mystical aphorism serves a significantly different function than does the proverb coined for more general consumption.

Ibn ʿAtaʾ Allah's hikam are meant for reflection by seekers attuned to the subtlest of inner experiences. For example:

> Sometimes He opens the door of obedience for you, but not the door of acceptance; or sometimes He condemns you to sin, and it turns out to be a cause for union with God.

He expanded you so as not to keep you in contraction; He contracted you so as not to keep you in expansion; and He took you out of both so that you not belong to anything apart from Him.[38]

Here Ibn 'Ata' Allah touches upon an issue of special interest to Sufi guides and seekers of the Shadhiliya order, to which he belonged: how is the subject to interpret experiences at least superficially manifested as either fearfulness, sadness, or desolation on the one hand, or as hopefulness, elation, or consolation on the other? Ibn 'Ata' Allah maintains, as do subsequent commentators on his work, that an individual ought not to become overly concerned with conditions that appear either positive or negative, since both are passing phenomena. God uses both types of experience, as well as a state of balance between the two, as elements of a comprehensive divine pedagogy designed to lead the seeker beyond attachment to ephemeral conditions and ultimately to perfect reliance on the initiator of those conditions.

Paradox is the principal mode of expression in this genre. Ibn 'Ata' Allah wants the seeker to know that God has nothing but surprises in store for the committed seeker. Human beings naturally hunger for a measure of predictability and familiarity in their lives. Just when the seeker decides it is safe to settle comfortably into one or another way of feeling and being, God introduces an unexpected turn in the path. God is not toying with the seeker. This is in fact the gift of divine honesty bestowed on individuals whom God judges ready for the hard truth.

Mystical aphorisms have continued to be an important mode of communication into the twentieth century. The Algerian Sufi shaykh Ahmad al-'Alawi (d. 1934) left a collection of them as part of his legacy. His sayings provide excellent examples of the use of enigma as well as paradox. Paradox parallels two ideas that appear oppositional, even totally contradictory. The notion that God's greatest gift to a seeker is often the very thing the seeker wants least is a paradox. From God's perspective, at least, paradox follows the rules of a certain logic. Paradox works like a gentle nudge, an invitation to change one's way of thinking.

Enigma, however, is "a challenge to the soul; the need to knock more than once at the door of the formal expression is a reminder that the content also needs to be penetrated, and that it is not merely a surface that can be lightly skimmed."[39] At the same time, one cannot "figure out" an enigma, for it seems to defy logic at every level. Its purpose is partly to dissolve whatever need for logic the seeker clings to, partly to stun that person into moving beyond intellectual complacency.

The Zen Buddhist koan "What is the sound of one hand clapping?" is a classic example of the use of enigma. From a strictly logical point of view there is no simple answer. Take Shaykh Ahmad al-'Alawi's aphorism "Neither abandon [your] soul, nor oppose it, but go along with it and search for what is in it."[40] Replace the words "your soul" with "an enigma," and the aphorism captures succinctly the appropriate response. Ahmad al-'Alawi's aphorisms are enigmatic in their own right. For example, he says, "[Whoever acts] upon knowledge before its time [has] come [forfeits] that knowledge." He then quotes the Qur'anic text in which God counsels Muhammad not to anticipate the revelation: "Hasten not with the [Qur'an] until its revelation [has] been perfected unto [you], and say: Lord, increase me in knowledge." But the shaykh follows that with advice that seems to nullify it: "To demand increase [shows] ignorance in a disciple."[41]

The third type of mystical utterance is *shath*.[42] Its prototype appears in Islamic tradition initially as Sacred Hadith (hadith qudsi) or sayings attributed to God. Enigmatic utterances describe various aspects of the divine-human relationship. They underline the fundamental paradox of divine immanence and transcendence, and bring to the fore the central matter of human perceptions of God's communication to human beings. Here the mystics have taken their cue especially from the famous sacred hadith in which God suggests that he becomes the ear, eye, hand, and foot of the servant who approaches through ceaseless works of devotion. Mystical reflection on vivid Qur'anic conversations between God and Moses flowered into *shath*, a characteristic expression of spiritual experience. The speaker in every instance is God himself, giving voice to the reality of union through the human being who can no longer control what emerges in the ecstatic moment.

Abu Nasr as-Sarraj, the author of the late tenth-century *Book of Light Flashes*, explains the etymology of the term *shath*. It means "movement" and can connote "agitation," as in the movement required to sift flour, which is so vigorous that some flour naturally falls outside the receptacle. *Shath* has therefore come to refer to that experience of spiritual energy that causes an ecstatic overflowing. That fullness in turn expresses itself willy-nilly in utterances that either make no obvious sense or render the speaker religiously suspect.[43]

Early examples of shath include Abu Yazid (Bayazid) al-Bistami's "Glory be to me! How exalted am I!" The same Bayazid who wrote of a heavenly ascent modeled after Muhammad's was not merely boasting, nor was he necessarily guilty of blasphemy, as some claimed. He was giving expression to an experience of union with God that had obliterated the mystic's sense of self: Bayazid no longer existed as a separate being. A well-known story tells how a man who had been looking for Bayazid once came and knocked at the mystic's door. "For whom are you looking?" asked Bayazid. "For Bayazid," replied the man. "Bayazid has been looking for Bayazid for thirty years and has not caught sight of him; how can you expect to see him?"[44] Many Muslims then and since have heard his words as the height of blasphemy.[45]

Hallaj is perhaps best known for his statement "I am the Truth," in which "Truth" is expressed by a term ordinarily reserved for reference to God. Three lines from one of his most famous poems recall the experience of union with God:

> In the erasure of my name and physical traces I asked about myself and said: You.
> My inmost being pointed to You until I became nothing to myself, while You lived on.
> You are my life and the secret of my heart; so wherever I am, You are.[46]

Two longer, integrated works that belong to the category of shath are Muhammad Ibn 'Abd al-Jabbar an-Niffari's (d. 965) books entitled *The Book of Stayings* (*Kitab al-mawaqif*) and *The Book of Addresses* (*Kitab al-mukhatabat*). These unusual works are a variation on the theme of shath. Although texts usually identified as shath tend to be terse, arresting statements, sometimes even explosive outbursts, Niffari's books are extended and editorially integrated segments. Furthermore, none of the seventy-seven "stayings" and the fifty-six "addresses" seems to represent a spontaneous outpouring; each is without doubt consciously and carefully crafted. But Niffari's works embody the energy and paradox characteristic of more compact forms of ecstatic utterance. They therefore stand midway between the category of ishara, with its often more extended comment on experience, and that of ecstatic statements spoken—from the perspective of the selfless mystic—by God.

Niffari's *Book of Stayings* recounts a series of moments in which God gives the seeker pause between any two mystical moments or experiences, variously described as state (hal), station (maqam), stage (*manzil*), abode (*munazila*), or realm of spiritual presence (hadra). Before the seeker can move on, God must supply the appropriate preparation for a higher level of intimate knowledge. Without the pause, the wayfarer would be ill equipped to experience fully the next step of the way.

Staying (*waqfa*) is the source of knowledge ('ilm) and the spirit of mystical experience (ma'rifa), and thus transcends both; it is akin to a state of spiritual suspended animation, a moment out of time characterized by a specific psychic or emotional quality and symbolizing a particular aspect of the seeker's relationship to God. In waqfa the mystic belongs entirely to God, so that the individual is no longer self-conscious. Each staying begins with a formulaic first-person statement such as "He stayed me in [then the name of the staying is given], and said to me." There follows a statement, placed in the mouth of God, from a paragraph to several pages long, sometimes interrupted by another first-person statement from the mystic. This mystic places islam (surrender) toward the end of his list; he makes it the second last of the stayings. A seeker does not achieve the state of surrender merely by claiming to have become a Muslim. In the staying of surrender (i.e., islam), the mystic and God engage in dialogue:

> He stayed me in Surrender, and said to me: It is my religion: desire only that, for I will accept nothing else. It is this, that you surrender to Me what I have decreed both for you and against.
>
> I said: How shall I surrender to you?
>
> He answered: Do not gainsay me with your way of thinking, and do not look to yourself for guidance to My truth; for your self [nafs] will never guide you to the truth of Me in obedience.
>
> I said: How shall I not oppose You?
>
> He answered: Be a follower, not an innovator.
>
> I said: How will I not look to myself for guidance to your truth?
>
> He answered: When I tell you, "This is yours," you will reply, "This is mine"; and when I tell you, "This is mine," you will reply, "This is yours."[47]

The *Addresses* consist entirely of God's first-person characterizations of his relationship to the mystic. Niffari's language is dense and difficult. In this work, his discourse resembles shath: "Nothing is closer to you than I; there is no between. Though I am closer to you than even your self [nafs], still you cannot take me in"—that is, the mystic is unaware of any duality, any separation between the knower and what is known.[48] Several addresses recall the Qur'an's command to the Prophet to "say" or "proclaim," and then tell the mystic what to say. The passage quoted below echoes the Verse of the Throne. God instructs the servant to proclaim:

> My Lord inclined me towards Him, and said to me: "Be elevated to the Throne." And I was elevated and above it I saw only knowledge ['ilm]; and I perceived everything as though in a wave. And He said to the wave, "Roll back." Then I saw the Throne; and He obliterated the Throne, so that I saw knowledge above and below. And He elevated knowledge, so that it was elevated above and below. A knower remained and He stretched out knowledge, established the Throne, and rolled back the wave. . . . And He made me go around the Throne, so that I could see that the knowledge above and the knowledge below were one and the same. Then I wrote down

the knowledge and knew all things; I gained insight into it so that I grasped all things. Then He said to me, "You are one of the knowers, so teach, and study no more."[49]

Such a paradoxical mode of expression remains current. Many mystics since the days of Bayazid, Hallaj, and Niffari have found it useful. The nineteenth-century Algerian-born author Amir 'Abd al-Qadir (d. 1883 in Damascus, not to be confused with the men from Baghdad and Malaysia of the same name) wrote a book also titled *The Book of Stayings*. This modern 'Abd al-Qadir was a follower of Ibn 'Arabi, and he understood Niffari's concepts as Ibn 'Arabi interprets them. Several of the stayings refer to visions in which Ibn 'Arabi teaches his disciple special lessons. The overall teaching of the stayings is that the spiritual voyager must await further instructions from God as to the proper demeanor to be observed in the next station or state on the itinerary. In one of his stayings 'Abd al-Qadir makes reference to Hallaj's statement "I am the Truth" and relates it to his own experience:

> God has carried me away from my [illusory] "me" and brought me together with my [true] "me"; the disappearance of earth [body, the world of sense] has compassed that of heaven [spirit, the hidden world] as well. The whole and the part have been mingled. Vertical and horizontal have been abolished. Acts of supererogatory devotion have become once again obligatory, and colors have been reduced to their original pure whiteness. The journey is at an end, and all that is not He has ceased to exist. . . . Then was spoken for me the saying of Hallaj, except that he himself spoke it, while it was spoken for me without my having to express it myself. Those who are worthy accept this saying and understand its meaning; those who value ignorance pay it no heed and reject it.[50]

Once the mystics had attempted to put into words experiences no words could contain, the task of attempting to explain them was left for the commentators of subsequent generations.

Explaining the Unexplainable

Sufi authors have been producing detailed commentaries on the most influential works of their esteemed predecessors for over a millennium. Among the earliest efforts to analyze the phenomenon of shath is that of Abu Nasr as-Sarraj. He discusses the topic in his *Book of Light Flashes* (see chapter 6). Sarraj devotes the entire last book of his compendium to a forthright defense of various early mystics whose statements had subjected them to what he considered unjustifiable condemnation by religious authorities. He agrees that some individuals and groups have deserved the name "heretic" for their positions on certain sensitive matters; but the mystics he cites are not among those people. They have, in Sarraj's opinion, been misunderstood. He bases his defense, not surprisingly, on a theory of knowledge that does not limit human knowing to the purely discursive and rational operations of the jurists and philosophers.

Use of shath, Sarraj notes, is characteristic of mystics well along on the spiritual path but not quite fully accomplished. Those who have reached the ultimate goal no longer resort to the paradoxical utterance. Ernst suggests that Sarraj's assessment here, inconsistent with his overall view of the matter, may be "intended to offer a ready excuse in cases where otherwise heresy would be suspected." In other words, a mystic's relative spiritual immaturity might excuse the speaker for not knowing better.[51]

Ruzbihan Baqli (d. 1209), the most famous commentator on shath, devoted an entire work to the subject. His *Commentary on Ecstatic Utterances (Sharh-i shathiyat)*[52] examines historically nearly 200 sayings of some forty-five mystics from the eighth to the eleventh centuries, with fully a third of the work dedicated to Hallaj's 45 utterances. Ruzbihan prefaces his analysis with a word about his motives for writing. Convinced that a patient study of the complexities of mystical speech will exonerate the speakers in question, he emphasizes the need to understand the subtleties of their language.

> Language becomes manifest in the form of *shathiyat* particularly for those intoxicated ones who are drowned in the waves of eternity, on account of the thundering clouds experienced in the moment of profound sighs, in the reality of overwhelming raptures. From each of their words, a world of learned men is filled with consternation. The deniers have drawn forth the sword of ignorance from the scabbard of envy, and from foolishness are wielding it themselves. . . . God's jealous ones cried out from the wombs of the hidden world, "O witness of secrets and niche of lights! Free the holy spirits from denial by the bankrupt, show forth the long past of those who kill and crucify in sacrifice [an allusion to the martyrdom of Hallaj in 922]! Say the secret of the *shath* of the lovers, and the expression of the agitation of the intoxicated, in the language of the people of the inner reality and the outer law! Say every subtlety in the form of knowledge connected with a spiritual state, and the guidances of Qur'an and hadith. (Say all this as) a subtle and marvelous commentary."[53]

In short, Ruzbihan attempts to vindicate those unjustly condemned because of the misunderstanding of the authorities and unenlightened religious scholars. The experience of the divine presence, he explains, overwhelms the mystic. The individual becomes intoxicated and loses control altogether, and is therefore beyond culpability. (See Fig. 36.) In any case, Ruzbihan argues further, there is precedent for such enigmatic speech in the Qur'an and

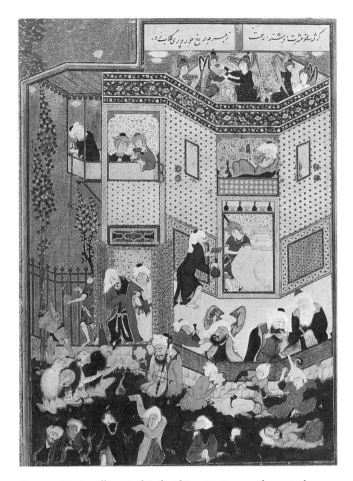

Figure 36. An allegorical Safavid Persian image of mystical intoxication, signed by Sultan Muhammad in the panel over the doorway, with angels passing around the elixir above, and Sufis and courtiers in ecstatic dance below, from *Diwan*, by Hafiz, folio 135r, (c. 1527). The panel of text at upper right contains the verse: "The angel of mercy sprinkled sips from the drinking goblet as rosewater onto the cheeks of houris and angels." Cambridge, Mass.: The Harvard University Art Museums. Promised Gift of Mr. and Mrs. Stuart Cary Welch, Jr.: partially owned by the Metropolitan Museum and the HUAM, Cambridge, Mass.

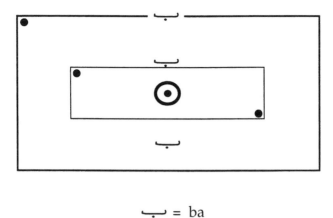

ب = ba

Figure 37. *Ta-Sin of the Circle,* from *Kitab at-tawasin,* by Hallaj
(early tenth century), Baghdad. Computer drawing by David Vila.

Hadith. He takes his stand on the Qur'an's reference (3:7) to the existence
of both plain and symbolic verses, insisting that mystics and Friends of God
are those "rooted in knowledge" to whom the scripture gives license to exercise esoteric interpretation (ta'wil).[54]

Ruzbihan's style and concerns are evident in his commentary on an intriguing text of Hallaj. Although Hallaj was a poet, creator of lyrics both intense and formally simple, he also produced an important short work called
The Book of Ta-sins (*Kitab at-tawasin*). He fashioned the curious title by
creating a plural of *tasin,* a compound of the Arabic letters *ta* and *sin,* which
are among the "mysterious letters" that occur at the beginnings of several
Qur'anic suras (in this case, beginning Suras 26, 27, and 28). The letters symbolize two words whose initial letters they are, namely, the *tahara* (purity)
of pre-eternity and the *sana* (glory) of post-eternity; the final *n* in the letter *sin* stands for the *nawal* (gift) God bestows on the lover.

Ten *ta-sins* are structured like short chapters composed of verses that
range from five to thirty-five in number, each chapter developing a particular theme. In the first three, Hallaj reflects indirectly on his own mystical
experience in relation to that of Muhammad and then of Moses. Chapters
4 through 10 then introduce a feature rare in the literature of mystical experience, namely symbolic visual diagrams to accompany Hallaj's observations. They use elements of the Arabic alphabet in conjunction with geometric forms (circles and rectangles). For example, chapter 4 is called the
"Ta-sin of the Circle," although as the diagram in Figure 37 indicates, two
of Hallaj's enclosing figures are rectangular.

The Arabic letter *ba* represents the word for *door* (*bab*), indicating the entries through which the traveler arrives at the innermost circle, within which the Truth (God) resides. A caption explains that "this is an image of the Truth and of those who seek it, and of its doors, and of the ways of attaining it." Hallaj then says that the first *ba* represents the person who arrives at the Truth; the second, one who arrives in the vicinity but whose way is blocked; and the third, one who wanders in the desert of the Truth of the Truth.[55]

Ruzbihan approaches Hallaj's ta-sin of the circle this way. Hallaj's symbolism is not accessible to beginners and therefore requires explanation. The door (*ba*) above the enclosure represents the divine action that causes God's signs to appear in creation. Below that, inside the larger enclosure, a second door stands for the glory of God's attributes. The door just beneath the inner enclosure symbolizes the light of the ultimate Truth, from which the attributes emerge. A point at the upper left-hand corner of the larger enclosure is the wise person's zeal for the divine attributes. The smaller, inner enclosure symbolizes knowledge of the divine essence, far superior to knowledge of the attributes. Within that enclosure, the point on the right is the mystic's eagerness to approach the divine essence. To the left of the central circle, a dot stands for the perplexity of the seeker wandering in the desert of divine power. In the middle stands the circle of knowledge of the innermost essence of God, and within that is the dot of pre-eternity and absolute essence.[56] Even in a world of strange and difficult writings, Hallaj's work stands out as unique. Hallaj is not only a poet of great power and sensitivity, but he has also allowed his fertile imagination further play in the symbolism of letters and geometric forms.

The Indian shaykh Ahmad Sirhindi also makes some significant observations on the proper interpretation of mystical paradox. He composed several letters entirely on this subject. In his discussion of this controversial material, he maintains a cautious tone. Some of the oft-cited sayings attributed to Sufis of the classical period Sirhindi condemns outright, insisting that a devout Muslim can in no way defend them. As for others, he admits that they point to an important truth, but their choice of words is unacceptable because it is so vulnerable to misinterpretation.

Sirhindi has an overriding theological concern: if taken literally, shath statements amount to a blasphemous obliteration of the distinction between the divine and the human, between Creator and creature. Ecstatic utterances, the shaykh warns, must be taken metaphorically. They mean that although the mystic is granted an apparent experience of *actual* unity with God (*wahdat al-wujud*), the sights and sounds are not authentically those of the divine being and voice. Sirhindi thus manages to find an acceptable way of interpreting many of these mystical paradoxes, as expressing an experiential unity (*wahdat ash-shuhud*) rather than a metaphysical unity. In other words, the mystic experiences *God's* oneness so profoundly that the existence of all else—including that of the experiencing self—is obliterated from consciousness. The mystic therefore experiences an *apparent* unity with God, but that is a far cry from actually becoming one with God. One needs always to understand, Sirhindi cautions, that the ecstatic statement emanates from an intoxicated mystic. In other words, the speaker has become disengaged from ordinary thought processes and discourse, and is therefore no longer speaking ordinary language. Sirhindi states repeatedly that spiritual sobriety is preferable to ecstasy, since ecstatic states are so difficult to interpret in a theologically acceptable manner.[57]

EVALUATING EXPERIENCE

Sufi authors have been justifiably concerned about the various perils of venturing toward the outer or inner limits of the spiritual universe. The more intense an experience, the more difficult it is for an individual to understand and explain it. Human beings, always susceptible to self-deception, are more vulnerable to that weakness as they advance spiritually. The most insidious temptation is to imagine that one's attainment of great heights obviates the need of further guidance. To yield to that would be to lose touch with the reality of one's permanently fallible humanity. In response to the ongoing need for guidance, Sufi writers have articulated the science of hearts.

The Science of Hearts

In the broadest sense, the literature of spiritual guidance functions as pedagogy. At the same time, the science of hearts constitutes such a specialized variety of pedagogy that it bears separate consideration. Although a good deal of this material is found in various textual forms, only a handful of works are devoted solely to spiritual direction. Much material that relates directly to the topic appears in three types of books: works that record the actual interchange between teacher and pupil (shaykh and murid); handbooks that explain the technical intricacies of the science to future guides; or do-it-yourself manuals intended for seekers who have not been able to find a suitable guide.

A study of the compendiums and collections of letters and malfuzat, of the Sufi adab works, and of some works of didactic poetry reveals a number of important themes: the notion of self-scrutiny; the need for and role of the shaykh as spiritual guide; traditional analyses of the various species of interior stimuli the seeker is likely to experience; and the elaboration of models of spiritual development as primary interpretative devices for the guide's use. Here I consider only the methods of analysis and critique of the most subtle aspects of human experience as employed in Islamic mystical literature.

Four principal interpretative foci emerge from the classic texts in their analyses of the movements of soul. Some authors refer to the interior movements of mystical experience as "provisions" for the spiritual journey that God provides the seeker. Important features in the analysis of those inner movements include the following: the immediate source of the movement, its duration and relation to the seeker's initiative, its content, and its emotional tone.

A key scriptural source for the development of the science of hearts is Sura 114 of the Qur'an:

> Proclaim: I seek refuge in the Lord of humankind, the King of humankind, the God of humankind, against the evil of the one who whispers and slinks away, who whispers into human hearts, among jinns and humankind.

The "whisperer" is usually taken to be a diabolical force, but the tradition has analyzed the matter further. Among the earliest detailed analyses of spiritual experience, it is generally agreed that there are six principal sources of the random thoughts (*khawatir;* sg., *khatir*) processed in the human heart, though the lists of different authors vary. Random thoughts can originate from the lower self (nafs), Satan, the world, reason, a good angel, and God.

When given over to its most negative proclivities, the lower self (nafs, or soul) can send the individual on a sometimes frantic search for whatever he or she is persuaded will satisfy his or her lusts. The Enemy, Satan or Iblis, seeks to cast doubt on God's faithfulness and mercy, thereby fostering a sense of hopelessness and futility. In both of these instances, the world functions as bait. Working against these destructive tendencies, the good angel (or the spirit) works to turn the heart toward confidence in God, who meanwhile reinforces that movement with the inner experience of the certitude of faith. Reason, finally, is capable of urging the heart in either direction and must be tutored in constructive habits.[58]

Discerning more precisely the nature of these interior movements, Sufi theorists eventually formulated various models that could allow seekers and their guides to name and analyze the least obvious manifestations of experience and thereby to monitor spiritual progress. One criterion for distinguishing among various levels of interior experience is duration. Some inner movements, either positive or negative, come and go in rapid succession, while others remain. Fleeting negative movements may, even after being banished, return to badger the seeker and cause great confusion; more welcome movements that continue ordinarily exert a much gentler influence. God's suggestions tend to come and go, while demonic whisperings frequently "slink away" only to return with renewed vigor. To describe more positive movements, theorists devised the distinction between states (*ahwal*), which tend to be highly charged, fleeting, and of divine origin; and stations (maqamat), which typically arise from human effort and last for some time.

A movement's origin may often be discerned by its content and emotional tone. The lower self can generate on its own, so to speak, desires for wealth, power, reputation, and so forth. When one's lower self has been gaining the upper hand for some time, the devil can more readily insinuate suggestions prompting desires for ease and comfort, since the lower self hates the Greater Jihad. Under those same circumstances, a suggestion from God will characteristically engender turmoil, for it runs contrary to the prevailing mood of the heart. As suggested earlier, in connection with Ibn 'Ata' Allah's *Book of Wisdom*, experiences of "expansion" and "contraction" (consolation, desolation, etc.) must be interpreted with great caution, for negative and positive emotional responses do not necessarily betoken evil and good sources respectively.

The science of hearts developed into a sophisticated set of methods for categorizing and evaluating spiritual experience.[59] Islamic spiritual guides have counseled and assisted seekers to know their Lord by first knowing themselves intimately; however, genuine self-knowledge is an elusive goal. To achieve it the seeker needs both determination and help from a spiritual guide.

Traveling Companions

According to a popular Sufi tradition, "one who has no spiritual guide has the devil for spiritual guide." The saying arises out of the conviction that although a certain amount of solitude is helpful—even essential—in any person's quest for God, none ought to attempt the journey without help. Islam's rich literature of spiritual direction offers an excellent picture of the role of the shaykh as companion on the long journey. But a guide is not the same as a friend. The shaykh's role is to offer a reasonably objective assessment of the seeker's progress now and then, including well-placed challenge or criticism. I close this chapter with a look at how one important spiritual guide fulfilled his responsibilities. The literature on the subject is enormous, and this glimpse represents only a hint of its richness and sophistication.

Najm ad-Din Daya Razi's famous compendium, *The Path of [God's] Servants,* offers a comprehensive and integrated treatment of the subject. This beautiful work was written to serve as an aid in critical analysis of the seeker's inner life, a touchstone against which wayfarers and mystics

> can strike the coin of their state. If they find within themselves some sign and indication of the stations we describe, they will be fortified and may hope that their feet are planted on the highway of the Truth and that they are progressing along the straight path. If, on the other hand, they find no such indication, they will not be deceived by the wiles of Satan and the oglings of the soul [i.e., nafs]; they will expel all arrogant fancies from their minds, . . . refusing to be deceived by stale verbiage.[60]

Razi situates the science of hearts first within the context of his cosmology, within which he frames his "theological anthropology," and within that, his epistemology or theory of knowledge. Progress in the spiritual quest involves removing the innumerable (seventy thousand) veils of light and darkness that constitute humanity's forgetfulness of its original condition. Razi offers as his etymological foundation the derivation of the Arabic term for human being (*insan*) from a root that means "intimacy" (*uns*). Thus, he hints that through their spiritual nature, human beings have an important link with the Creator. Razi likens the traces of familiarity with the divine source to the seed of faith: to uncover the first is to cultivate the second and vice-versa. He plays further on the similarities between the terms for humankind (*nas*) and forgetful person (*nasin*) to set up the problem: human beings are inherently and fundamentally forgetful, and their memory must be restored. Spiritual guidance therefore seeks to foster the penetrating recollection of the self's complete history. God equips some individuals with nearly seamless memory, virtually unspoiled by the ravages of denial and repression, so that they serve as models of ideal self-knowledge and as proofs of God's power.[61]

Razi says that there are four sources of difficulty in the human struggle to remain in touch with the truest self, according to the most widely accepted traditional analysis: the lower self (nafs), the devil and his minions, the world, and unbelievers. Working against those are the countervailing forces of God and the angelic messengers, who use dreams and visions among their most potent revelatory media. The critical human experiential faculties—soul or lower self (nafs), heart (for which a number of technical terms are used in addition to *qalb*), and spirit (*ruh*)—exhibit several important features. Struggling against the negative forces, a person must maintain in equilibrium the lower self's inherent passion on the one hand, which energizes the quest for good, and anger on the other, which fends off harmful influences. The lower self represents enormous potential but can too easily lose its balance and turn its considerable energy to destructive ends.

Purifying itself by constant vigilance over its own inner five senses, the multifaceted faculty called the heart can become the seat of the divine quality of compassion. With those five inner senses the heart perceives the realities of the unseen world. That perception is at the core of the phenomenon called spirituality. Hence the goal of the science of hearts is to provide means and motives for maintaining the utmost clarity in one's spiritual perceptive faculties. Meanwhile, the spirit needs to be nurtured and guided like an infant with infinite potential for attachment. Spirit nurses at the breasts of the Path (tariqa) and Ultimate Reality (haqiqa). From the Path, Spirit drinks the milk "of severance of attachment from all that is familiar to instinctual nature"; from Ultimate Reality, the "milk of intimations [waridat] from the unseen world, of flashes and rays from the lights of the Divine Presence." Referring to the end result of this spiritual nurturance, Razi remarks that "when the spirit has emerged from the garment of humanity and become safe from the harmful effects of fantasy and imagination . . . it contemplates the clear signs of God in all the atoms of the universe and in the mirror of the soul. . . . In this state, even though the spirit looks out through the window of the senses, it observes a trace of God's signs in all that it looks upon."[62]

Razi continues his remarkable description with images of human intimacy. Moving toward greater maturity, the spirit's relationship to the divine source becomes that of lover to beloved. Intent on the goal of intimacy with God, the seeker must utter the triple formula of divorce from things of the world. This, says the shaykh, is a lengthy process: "If one waits for a thousand years unnoticed at the threshold [of the beloved], one must not weary nor turn away from the court."[63]

In the next twelve chapters Razi describes three aspects of the practice of spiritual guidance: the role of the shaykh; the various practices in which the seeker must engage; and the four modalities of actual spiritual experience leading to one's ultimate arrival before the Creator. Razi lists ten reasons why the seeker must have assistance along the path, all of which are variations on the theme of insufficient ability to interpret properly the data of deeper experience. One hundred and twenty thousand prophets have walked this path, but they have left no footprints. In addition, the road is the haunt of highway robbers (the self, lust, the devil). Perhaps the most telling reason is the sixth: At one point God strips away significant remnants of human deceitfulness from the heart. The seeker begins to discern in the polished mirror of the heart a reflection of spirit so attractive that the seeker might mistake this condition for the final goal. At this juncture the danger of self-deception is at its height, and only a guide can keep the seeker on the path.

Razi then describes five experiential characteristics of the full-fledged and accredited guide, all deriving in some way from the guide's attainment of virtually immediate access to the ultimate source of truth, the divine presence. These qualities turn the guide into a midwife who can assist at the seeker's second birth. Razi then develops the metaphor of the seeker as an egg incubated under the wing of the hen (shaykh). An egg endowed with the appropriate gifts may also eventually become a hen and be able to continue the process of nurturing spiritual growth in others. Razi fashions a full-scale allegory out of the chicken-and-egg imagery. After listing twenty further moral and spiritual attributes of the shaykh, the author similarly enumerates twenty prerequisites of the promising murid, and discusses the centrality of the twin practices of dhikr, duly transmitted only by the guide, and khalwa (seclusion, retreat).

Razi does not analyze in detail the various types of events that transpire within the subject—thoughts, intimations, passing suggestions. But he makes great use of visual metaphors to describe the media of spiritual experience: dreams and visions; the witnessing of lights; unveiling; and the manifestation of divine qualities. Visions occur either in total wakefulness or just between sleeping and waking; dreams occur only in sleep. Visions do not originate in the individual imagination; they derive instead from the unseen world, though they may be manifest through the imagination. Dreams can be either mediated by the imagination while originating in the lower self or the devil; or of divine origin, as in the case of dreams granted to prophets. Razi makes some fascinating observations about how to interpret one's dreams, which always communicate some potential insight into one's spiritual condition. He continues the imagery of the vision until the final chapter of his analysis of experience; there he deals with attainment to divine presence, which transcends vision. Throughout his discussion Razi carefully distinguishes among various levels of experience and describes the various criteria by which one can determine an experience's authenticity. In the end, the experiencing self is no more, its identity lost in the divine presence.[64]

Each chapter of this book has highlighted a particular aspect of the Islamic tradition's enormous wealth of spiritual wisdom. Muslim authors have attended to the minutest details of religious experience. Their concerns encompass everything from the appropriate interior disposition of one who recites Qur'an or utters a personal prayer, to the role of creative genius in praise of the divine beauty, to the invitation mystics accept when they risk losing everything to find the source of all things. Together these insights open up a panorama of heart and soul much too broad to be contained in a survey. The heart of Islamic spirituality and religious life is located in personalities and personal relationships, never in books. Focusing on the prophet Joseph, the reprise that follows suggests something of that personal dimension.

Reprise:
Joseph of the Seven Doors

Few characters have captured the imagination and hearts of generations of Muslims across the world as the prophet Joseph has. The Islamic tradition's long love affair with this prophet has made Joseph a unique paradigm of the spiritual life. Joseph provides the most comprehensive reminder of the various aspects of that tradition. Joseph's story in the Qur'an begins and leads the way on a return journey through the seven doors.

JOSEPH IN THE QUR'AN

What the Qur'an calls "the most beautiful of stories" has also been one of the most popular in Islamic life and thought. It has been the inspiration for some lovely mystical and didactic poetry, especially in Persian, which has in turn provided occasion for a number of dazzling illustrated manuscripts. The Qur'anic account of the prophet Joseph in Sura 12 offers an excellent opportunity to enter into a unified dramatic narrative, as well as to appreciate one aspect of the Islamic scripture's relationship to Jewish and Christian traditions. Unlike many other prophets, Joseph appears virtually nowhere else in the Qur'an. Despite his popularity, Joseph is only mentioned in a handful of hadiths.

In the story Joseph dreams that the sun and moon and eleven stars bow before him. His father, Jacob, warns him not to reveal this dream to his half brothers lest they envy him. Meanwhile the brothers are already convinced that their father prefers Joseph over any of them, and they plot to do away with Joseph. They throw him into a well and sell him to some traders who are on their way to Egypt. The brothers take his bloodstained shirt back to

Figure 38.   (*Opposite*) Bihzad's painting of Yusuf fleeing through the seven locked doors of Zulaykha's palace, Timurid Persia (1488). The text throughout the work's various panels is *Bustan*, by Sa'di. Courtesy of Egyptian National Library, Adab Farsi 908, folio 52b. Photograph by Peter Brenner, reproduced by permission of Los Angeles County Museum of Art.

Jacob to prove that a wolf has devoured Joseph. (The shirt is not a source of jealousy in the Qur'an as it is in the Bible.) Upon seeing the shirt, Jacob weeps himself blind with grief. The merchants then sell the slave to an Egyptian bureaucrat who bears the title 'Aziz (the lofty one), whose wife seeks to seduce the handsome youth. Discovering that his wife was the aggressor, the official tells her to ask Joseph's forgiveness. When the women of Egypt criticize the behavior of 'Aziz's wife, she throws a party for them; just as they are about to peel their dessert oranges, she brings Joseph into the hall. The women are so distracted by his beauty that they cut their hands, now persuaded that the seductress can hardly be blamed for her actions.

'Aziz's wife, whom later tradition identifies as Zulaykha, nevertheless contrives to have Joseph imprisoned, and the prophet decides prison would be a relief. Joseph's two cellmates tell him their dreams, and he interprets them. One is later released to work for the pharaoh. When the monarch reports a dream that none of his own courtiers can explain, the former prisoner seeks Joseph's help. When 'Aziz's wife finally admits in the presence of the king that she, not Joseph, had been the aggressor, the ruler releases Joseph and elevates him to a position of authority.

During a time of famine in their country of Canaan, Joseph's brothers come to Egypt to buy grain. Joseph decides to keep his identity secret until they have brought their youngest sibling, Benjamin. Then Joseph delays the revelation further and contrives to detain young Benjamin by having his assistants slip a royal goblet into Benjamin's bag. When Joseph's guards discover the cup, the other brothers add insult to injury by protesting that this is no surprise, for they once had another brother (Joseph) who was also a thief. One brother remains behind with Benjamin while the others return to explain the situation to their father. The grief-stricken Jacob sends them back to Egypt to inquire after Joseph and Benjamin until they know the truth.

The brothers return and ask Joseph, whose identity is still hidden, to show kindness and leniency. Then Joseph asks what only he could have asked, for no one else in Egypt knows the story of their violent act: were they not aware of what they had done to Joseph? He then forgives them all. At that the brothers realize Joseph's true greatness, for he has not only been favored by God but has also forgiven them in spite of their treachery. Joseph then sends them back home to cast his shirt over Jacob's face, so that he might recover the sight his grief has cost him. Joseph's scent heals Jacob's eyes, and the whole family returns to Egypt. They acknowledge Joseph's high estate (thus fulfilling his dream of the heavenly lights bowing before him), and he receives them gladly. Joseph's prayer sums up the story: "My Lord, you have granted me a share in authority and have schooled me in the interpretation of events/dreams. . . . Let me die as one who surrenders [to you (literally, "as a muslim")] and set me among the righteous" (Q 12:101).[1]

There are several ways to discuss the Qur'an's version of the Joseph story. One contemporary Muslim interpretation of the Qur'an observes that it is "less a narrative than a highly spiritual sermon or allegory explaining the seeming contradictions in life, the enduring nature of virtue in a world full of flux and change, and the marvelous working of God's eternal purpose in His Plan as unfolded to us on the wide canvas of history";[2] and some of Islam's greatest poets have read the story similarly. Non-Muslim readers may be tempted to interpret the story primarily as a retelling of the biblical account in Genesis 37–46. Comparative study can indeed shed important light on both traditions, but ceding authority or definitive form to the earlier tradition may diminish the value of the later. The two accounts arise out of very different circumstances, differ in tone, and communicate different messages; each must be read on its own terms.

As a number of recent studies of Sura 12 demonstrate, the Qur'anic tradition demands a unique interpretation. One way is to read the story with an eye to plot, theme, and character. According to Mustansir Mir, the plot turns on three axes. First, the story builds tensions during its first half (Q 12:1–44), then resolves them in reverse order in the second half (Q 12:45–100). The king's dream-dilemma is interpreted, Joseph is released from prison, Joseph is exonerated before the Egyptian women and 'Aziz's wife, Joseph's brothers are repaid for their conniving, and Joseph's dream is fulfilled. Second, the sura parallels certain events, sometimes antithetically. For example Joseph in the well is paired with his imprisonment in Egypt; and the brothers' attempts to capture their father's love parallels 'Aziz's wife's attempt to win Joseph's love. Third, dramatic elements—such as the dream, Joseph's secrecy, and the foreshadowing of one event by another—heighten the story's effect.

In Sura 12 the treatment of the image of God emphasizes God's attributes of transcendence and sovereignty, graciousness and subtlety, and omniscience and wisdom, all to demonstrate the inevitability of the divine design. Within that larger theme several subordinate themes emerge: Joseph's embodiment of the chief qualities of a prophet, namely, knowledge, trust, and uprightness; a balance between God's initiative and human responsibility; and the pattern of trial, recompense, and repentance. As for the function of character, the Qur'anic story emphasizes both the positive moral model of laudable figures such as Jacob and Joseph, and the virtues they exemplify (patience, trust, shrewdness, and veracity); and the negative model of reprehensible characters such as the brothers and ʿAziz's wife, who exemplify the qualities of recklessness, mendacity, and lustful exploitation.[3]

JOSEPH AND ISLAMIC DEVOTION

Although Joseph has never been precisely an object of devotion in Islam, he does figure prominently in the literature and lore associated with a theme of great importance in Shiʿi devotional tradition: the redemptive suffering of prophets and Friends of God. All God's prophets suffer at the hands of unbelieving people, and their endurance is a mark of their friendship with God. Joseph's story is especially poignant in that the opposition comes from his own family; and patience in adversity is Joseph's special virtue.

In the taʿziya plays commemorating the martyrdom of Husayn, the tribulations of Joseph and his father, Jacob, become a touchstone of redemptive suffering for Shiʿi Muslims. The scenes that depict the story of Joseph generally embellish the Qurʾanic account. They heighten the emotional effect by emphasizing the torment that the prophet and his father suffered. Jacob reflects on the trauma of seeing the bloodstained coat of his son. As he looks into the future, Jacob wonders how much greater will be the pain of the mother of Husayn when she sees the shirt of her son who has been so brutally slain. Jacob prays that a thousand like himself and Joseph might be Husayn's ransom and then asks Gabriel to show him the scene at Karbala still so many centuries in the future.

A surprising twist toward the end of this tale of redemptive suffering again features Jacob and Joseph. In the final scene of the taʿziya, Jacob and Joseph are the first to appear after the trumpet of resurrection sounds. But both Jacob and Joseph have by now forgotten their ancient care for each other; each now pleads only for his own salvation. Their story becomes a foil to underscore both the torment suffered by the family of Muhammad and their unfailing altruism. Even prophets like Jacob and Joseph can experience a falling out, but the Prophet's family remain in harmony. Husayn recalls that though Jacob lost his son Joseph, Joseph was eventually found; Husayn, on the other hand, lost his beloved son ʿAli Akbar for good. When Jacob rehearses his grief at how Joseph, the most beautiful of creatures, was thrown into the well, Husayn retorts that ʿAli Akbar was far more handsome than Joseph. Jacob was indeed fortunate to have lost his sight from grief, for Husayn's good eyes were forced to watch his son's slaughter. Never did Joseph suffer as Husayn did, and in any case Jacob only heard the story from others. In short, Joseph and his father function here as the standard against which all beauty, grief, and redemptive suffering are to be judged—until the story of Muhammad's family raises that standard.[4]

JOSEPH AS MODEL OF VIRTUE AND WISDOM FIGURE

Joseph's qualities and values made him a model even for Muhammad. Most obvious, Joseph had a gift for dream interpretation that initially prompted Pharaoh to place the young man in a position of leadership, and he showed a strong administrative capability in the high office to which Pharaoh had assigned him. But more significant in this context is Joseph's capacity for forgiveness. In his Sufi manual, *The Book of Light Flashes,* Sarraj describes the personal qualities Muhammad exhibited when he returned to conquer Mecca. Even though the Meccans had plotted against the Prophet, heaped injury on him and punished his family and Companions to the point of driving them away, Muhammad rose to address the Meccans with a message of forgiveness on the day of conquest. According to Sarraj, the Prophet praised and glorified God and said, "I speak to you as did my brother Joseph, peace be upon him, 'You bear no reproach this day, for God has forgiven you.'" This close paraphrase of Qur'an 12:92 recalls how Joseph received, and was reconciled with, his once treacherous brothers.[5]

Since even Muhammad emulated Joseph, ordinary leaders have greater cause to do so. Nizam al-Mulk's mirror for princes, *Treatise on Government,* tells a story of Joseph in its chapter "On recognizing the extent of God's grace towards kings":

> Tradition tells that when Joseph the prophet . . . went out from this world,
> they were carrying him to Abraham's tomb . . . to bury him near his
> forefathers, when Gabriel . . . came and said, "Stop where you are; this
> is not his place; for at the resurrection he will have to answer for the
> sovereignty which he has exercised." Now if the case of Joseph the prophet
> was such, consider what the position of others will be.[6]

Tradition has it that Joseph "was detained for five hundred years at the gates of paradise and not admitted so that the pollution of worldly kingship might be fully removed from him."[7]

Joseph models forgiveness for everyone. In a discourse, Sharaf ad-Din Maneri discusses the meaning of sin and forgiveness in the context of the Joseph story. When Joseph first reveals his identity to his brothers, they fear wrathful vengeance for their perfidy. But Joseph instead forgives them unconditionally after the model of God's infinite mercy, refusing even to mention their injustice to Jacob at their eventual reunion. Joseph sees in that reunion the final meaning of his dream; he has refused to dwell on the evil he had suffered, preferring to recall only the good.[8]

Joseph is also an exemplar for young Muslim men, especially in his virtue of chastity, which can only be built on complete trust in God. In one of his discourses 'Abd al-Qadir al-Jilani asks his listeners when they will begin to appreciate that only the jealousy of God can keep them chaste. He explains that it was the divine jealousy that prompted Joseph to leave Zulaykha's presence. He quotes Qur'an 12:24, "So it was, that We might ward off from him evil and lewdness; he was one of Our devoted servants," and then explains further that his listeners must emulate the virtue of Joseph in this respect. God gave Joseph the virtue during his confinement in the well and in prison, where he learned total reliance on God's sustenance.[9]

Far from the Middle East this prophet's example remains equally potent. In Southeast Asia the story of Joseph survives in an indigenized adaptation, a poem called *The Story of Joseph (Serat Yusup)*. This "most representative pre-modern poem of rural East Java" is still performed ritually on special occasions. In Java, Joseph also became a model for village youth through his exemplary heroism, faith, prophetic power, chastity, and familial devotion. Here Joseph's multifaceted character represents a model of virtue for every situation in which an exemplar is needed.[10]

Joseph also holds an important place as the embodiment of wisdom. Sharaf ad-Din Maneri includes in his *Table Laden with Good Things* a discourse devoted almost entirely to Joseph as wisdom figure. He reflects on the sagacity of Joseph's instructions to his brothers that they "fling" his shirt over Jacob's face, rather than merely "take it to him"; for Jacob's joy at hearing news of his lost son would have naturally overwhelmed the old man and would have made him forget to rub the tunic on his eyes. In addition, since it was the shirt that caused his father's blindness in the first place, Joseph knows that only the shirt can restore sight. Post-Qur'anic tradition holds the shirt as a prime symbol of Joseph's relationship to Jacob. Maneri further interprets this aspect of the story as an indication of mystical love. The scent of Joseph reaches his father but not the rest of the family, because Jacob is a true lover passionately seeking the beloved. The others do not attend to that fragrance, for they do not appreciate the consummate value of its source as their father does. After all, the brothers do not recognize Joseph even when he stands before them. Normally it is appropriate that a son come to his father, not vice-versa; but because Jacob is a lover and Joseph the beloved, Maneri finds it not at all strange that Joseph instructs his brothers to bring his father to him in Egypt. Besides, Maneri continues, even from the juristic perspective, it would not be fitting for Joseph to leave his position of authority, and risk disorder in his absence.[11]

JOSEPH AS THE BEAUTY OF GOD

According to an ancient saying, "God created goodness and beauty in ten parts; he gave nine parts to Joseph . . . and one part to the rest of the world."[12] On a popular level, Joseph's beauty has naturally been associated with physical attractiveness. Local folk tradition in some Muslim communities still recommends the use of spells to tap into the spiritual power of Joseph's comeliness. On the Indonesian island of Sumatra, for example, the Gayo people use spells that feature Joseph when they wish to enhance their general attractiveness to members of the opposite sex. One popular invocation requests that "[j]ust as Sitti Zulaika [Potiphar's ('Aziz's) wife] was attracted to the prophet Yusuf, so let [insert name] be attracted to me."[13] But classical tradition has also found much deeper meanings in Joseph's beauty. Joseph is both the image of God's irresistible splendor understood as the goal of the soul's journey, and the symbol of that for which all artists strive in their creative endeavors.

Joseph's beauty has inspired numerous imaginative works of literature. Some reflect on the scriptural text of Sura 12 and then develop a meditative tale to explain it, much the way medieval rabbis elaborated their Midrashic commentaries on the Hebrew scriptures. Yahya Suhrawardi Maqtul's charming recital "On the Reality of Love, or The Solace of Lovers" is a fine example of such a meditative tale. It describes how three brothers—Beauty, Love, and Sorrow—are born of the pearl of God's first creature, Intellect. Kingly Beauty, the eldest of the three, waits long for a person on whom he might bestow his sovereignty. On hearing of the birth of Joseph, Beauty races to him, with the brothers in pursuit. Beauty becomes so united with Joseph that when the heavenly brothers Love and Sorrow catch up with their older sibling, they can see no difference between Beauty and Joseph. Beauty has no further interest in Love and Sorrow, and the two depart as if exiled. They decide that they will journey in different directions in quest of self-discipline, seeking out guidance from the seven sages of this created world.

Love heads for Egypt; Sorrow, for Canaan. Sorrow becomes inseparable from Joseph's father, Jacob, so that the old man surrenders his sight to Sorrow at the loss of Joseph. Meanwhile Love, in search of the perfect person, finds his way to Zulaykha's apartment. She is immediately smitten and asks Love to tell her his story. Love explains how he and his brothers were separated, and how Zulaykha built a house for him, in which she had hoped she might persuade him to stay. There Love remained as her only prize—until word arrived that Joseph had come to Egypt. Seeing Joseph, Zulaykha was beside herself with longing and gave up everything to be with him.

Meanwhile Jacob in Canaan hears that his son has appeared in Egypt, so he and Sorrow travel there with his other sons. "When Sorrow saw Love he knelt in servitude to Beauty and placed his face on the ground. Jacob and his sons did as Sorrow had done and all placed their faces to the ground. Joseph turned to Jacob and said, 'Father, this is the interpretation of my vision I related to you: I saw in my dream eleven stars, and the sun and the moon; I saw them make obeisance unto me" (Q 12:4).[14] Suhrawardi's allegory belongs to the genre of visionary recital (hikayat), for it depicts Joseph as a symbolic type of the mystical seeker.

Perhaps the most famous literary creation that praises and meditates on Joseph as divine beauty is the fifteenth-century Persian poet Jami's didactic epic *Joseph and Zulaykha*. Tradition has thoroughly exonerated Zulaykha of guilt in her attempted seduction of Joseph, and she has come to be regarded as the epitome of the lover beside herself at the sight—even the mere thought—of the beloved. The transformation had occurred long before the eleventh-century writer Abu 'l-Qasim al-Qushayri chose to describe Zulaykha as a prime example of preferring another to oneself—a prime characteristic of true love.[15] Jami took that sympathetic view of Zulaykha and fashioned around it a romance. In his preface, the poet writes, "Never was there a beloved to compare with Yusuf, whose beauty exceeded that of all others; when we wish to describe an exceptionally handsome youth, we call him 'a second Yusuf.' Among lovers none was ever the equal of Zulaykha, whose ardent passion was quite unique. She loved from childhood to old age, both in omnipotence and in destitution. She never ceased to devote herself to love: she was born, she lived, and she died—in love."[16]

In one of Jami's most enchanting scenes, Zulaykha schemes to have Joseph to herself. Acting on the suggestion of a handmaiden, Zulaykha enlists the services of a master architect to build a special palace just for the occasion. Within the edifice he builds seven adjoining apartments, each of a different kind of stone. This palace is to mirror on earth the seven heavens. Everywhere the artist places images of Joseph and Zulaykha in amorous poses. When Joseph accepts her invitation to the palace, Zulaykha entices him through the first door and locks it behind him. Then she pours out her heart to him and lures him into the second chamber, again locking the door. At last she manages to bring Joseph, against his better judgment, through the seventh door, locking it with an iron bolt and a golden chain. (See Fig. 38.)

Here Jami offers advice to the spiritual wayfarer: "One must never lose heart on the path: the pitch darkness of the night always gives way at last to daylight. Even if a hundred doors should stay closed to your hopes, there is still no need to eat your heart out: knock at one more door, and suddenly it will open; and the way to your goal will be clear."[17] To no avail the lover begs her beloved to stay. Putting all his trust in God, Joseph flees, each door flinging itself open before him. Zulaykha is left feeling like the fabled spider who labors to entangle the king's hunting falcon in her delicate web, only to watch heartbroken as the bird effortlessly breaks free to return to the king. The metaphor of the prophet as a royal falcon was already ancient in Jami's day and had been a favorite of earlier mystics like Rumi, for nothing can prevent this great bird from returning to the one who sent it on its mission.

As a result of his refusal, Joseph endures imprisonment; but Zulaykha is still more painfully imprisoned in her unrequited longing. As his life improves after his release, hers disintegrates. She grows old living in a hut along the roadside, hoping only for a glimpse of Joseph. One day he sees her as she glorifies God for reducing royalty (herself) to slavery and for making this former slave (Joseph) into a king. News of his interest restores Zulaykha's youth; at last the two are to be married. After they live a long and happy life together, Joseph dies. Not many days later the inconsolable lover plucks out her eyes and perishes from grief. Zulaykha's action recalls the blinding sadness of Jacob. Jami sums up her plight this way: "First she made herself blind to all that was not the beloved; then she laid down life itself for him. May a thousand graces be showered on her; and may the eyes of her seeing soul be bright with the sight of the beloved."[18]

Joseph is associated with other aspects of the visual arts as well. Baba Shah Isfahani's classic work on calligraphy, *Manners of Practice*, offers a good example of the second aspect of Joseph's aesthetic significance, his role as symbol of creative beauty. God, the first calligrapher, wrote on the heart of Adam and thus gave him the gift of knowledge. "The gleam of the sparks of that writing's light cast a glimmer of the sun of Joseph's beauty into the heart of Zulaykha, and made her famous through the world as a lover."[19] Within the broader contexts both of God's cosmic creativity and of Joseph's place in the history of prophetic revelation, Joseph is a symbol of divine radiance.

At the pinnacle of human perfection, of course, stands the Prophet. According to a prominent mystical interpretation, all creation exists for, and as a result of, Muhammad's being. A classic historian of Persian culture, Dust Muhammad, makes explicit connections between Muhammad and Joseph.

In Dust Muhammad's preface to a sixteenth-century album of calligraphy and miniature paintings, he includes a poetic encomium of Muhammad. Dust Muhammad interprets the Prophet's virtually cosmic splendor as a fulfillment of Joseph's beauty. He begins with praise of the Creator's painterly accomplishments, inserts a note of moral exhortation reminiscent of the earlier homiletical poetry of Sana'i of Ghazna, and meditates on the relationship between physical and spiritual beauty.

> Hail to the Creator who, without assistance, clothed being with existence by the command "Be!"
>
> . . . .
>
> He quickened thousands of charming forms; neither did he use a magic incantation nor did he mix colors.
>
> . . . .
>
> If a form is not worthy of astonishment, it is not worth the touch of the brush.
> Why are you perplexed by this master painting when you know that it is necessary to amend your conduct?
> If conduct is not pure and charming in essence, what is the use of a beautiful form?
> When a man is ignorant in his being, he cannot be called human simply because of his form.
> O God, I am that handful of dust that previously was void of my form and conduct.
> Since you gave me human form first, make me share intrinsically in humanity.
> Especially he who is the final goal of the world [Muhammad]: the final goal of the creative fiat is he.
> In form he perfected Joseph's beauty; in conduct he quickens Gabriel's soul.[20]

A short prose interlude explains further how even those whose vision of Joseph's beauty has already taken them to the limit of astonishment are moved beyond that with one glimpse of the Prophet.

Dust Muhammad observes further that beauty is not all joy. He would perhaps have agreed with the words of the German poet Rainer Maria Rilke, "Beauty is only the first touch of terror we can barely stand. And it awes us so much because it so coolly disdains to destroy us."[21] The wondrous comeliness of Joseph, like the presence of the fascinating mystery of Holiness, is also terrifying. "By Joseph was much agony created, but this beauty [that of Muhammad] has stirred up a different tumult." After tracing prophetic glory from Adam to Muhammad, the author descends, in classic Shi'i fashion, following a line of magnificence toward the realm of mere mortals, from Muhammad through the twelve imams, "for were the hand of destiny to reopen the gate of prophecy, it would be opened to none other than their prophet-like beauty." At last, Dust Muhammad places his own patron, the Safavid prince Bahram Mirza, in this most exalted company; for it is only the patron's own magnificence, "his Saturnian exaltedness," and sensitivity to beauty that inclines him to decree "that the scattered folios of past and present masters should be brought out of the region of dispersal into the realm of collectedness."[22] This poem is a superb illustration of the interplay of Joseph imagery with the doctrine of prophetic revelation and patronage of the arts.

JOSEPH AND PATRONAGE OF THE ARTS

Even though Joseph is not described precisely as a patron of the arts, he possesses many qualities of such a patron. And a number of artists have praised their patrons as latter-day Josephs. One of the most splendid Safavid illustrated manuscripts is Jami's *Seven Thrones* (*Haft awrang*), commissioned by Prince Sultan Ibrahim Mirza and produced between 1556 and 1565. Jami's story of Joseph and Zulaykha is one of seven Persian mathnawis in that collection. Sultan Ibrahim Mirza apparently identified with Joseph. Several sections of the illustrated manuscript of Jami's poetry that Ibrahim Mirza had commissioned were completed in the year he was married and appointed to a governorship. In one section completed that year a miniature painting depicts the prophet Joseph's "bachelor party" on the eve of his wedding to Zulaykha. Lest the association escape the viewer of the painting, the artist inscribed the name Sultan Ibrahim Mirza prominently over the flame-haloed head of the prophet. The art historian Marianna Shreve Simpson concludes that this may be "a direct allusion to Sultan Ibrahim Mirza's own marriage, and perhaps even a portrayal of the prince in the idealized form of another, legendary groom."[23]

Najm ad-Din Daya Razi provides another example of praise of a patron by association with Joseph. He dedicates the second version of his *Path of [God's] Servants* to the Saljuqid Sultan Kay Qubad. Razi evidently intended to present the work as a gift to the sultan, in the hope that the ruler would take the author under his beneficent patronage. In his explanation of his reasons for writing the book, Razi pays the sultan the supreme compliment of comparing him to Joseph. God, says the author, noticed how fine a creation this new book was. God then told him to "[t]ake as a gift a necklace of these precious jewels . . . and present them to that servant whom We have chosen, that monarch whom We have raised up; who in Our Potiphar-like presence is like Joseph raised to honor from the well." (Kay Qubad had suffered imprisonment and mistreatment at the hands of his envious brother Kay Kawus.)[24]

JOSEPH AS TEACHER AND INTERPRETER OF DREAMS

The great eighteenth-century Indian Muslim Shah Wali Allah of Delhi composed a fascinating short work entitled *The Interpretation of Tales* (*Ta'wil al-ahadith*). He took the title from Qur'an 12:6, in which Joseph's father, Jacob, tells his son that God will bestow on the youth this special gift. Shah Wali Allah interprets a later remark by Joseph (Q 12:101, "My Lord, to me You have given an authority and have instructed me in the interpretation [ta'wil] of events, You who have created the heavens and the earth") as an indication that the prophet was a Friend of God, like the author himself. He goes a step further and concludes that he, like Joseph, has been granted the ability to interpret tales.

Shah Wali Allah explains that Joseph received "associative perspicacity," which he defines as "the capacity of visualizing basic concepts through images arising from the individual unconscious (*tabi'a*), inasmuch as such is postulated by the collective unconscious (*at-tabi'at al-kulliya*) when effusing an archetypal truth into an individual."[25] Najm ad-Din Daya Razi makes a similar connection between Joseph and the teaching shaykh. He quotes the same Qur'anic text (12:101) with its references both to authority and the ability to interpret mysteries. The seeker needs a shaykh "to explain the visions" of the seeker and "unveil his states to him, gradually teaching him the language of the unseen, and acting as his teacher and translator."[26]

Finally, the anonymous mirror for princes called *The Sea of Precious Virtues* records a reference to the prophet Joseph as a model of the Greater Jihad, the ongoing discipline of the spiritual life. The book cites Qur'an 12:52, which refers to the moment in which it becomes known that Zulaykha, not Joseph, was the aggressor: "This discovery has been made so that my lord (Pharaoh's minister) might know that I was not unfaithful to him in his absence." The book then explains that just when that truth becomes known, the angel Gabriel appears to the prophet. Though Joseph found himself attracted to Zulaykha, the angel explains, it was God who showed him a sign and kept him from sinning. At that moment Joseph speaks the following verse (Q 12:53), "Every soul is prone to evil," meaning according to *The Sea of Precious Virtues*, "without God's grace and protection this erring soul would never turn away from sin."[27]

JOSEPH AS MODEL FOR MYSTICS

The Qur'anic story mentions more than once that God chose to bestow on Joseph the gift of "the interpretation of stories/events" (*ta'wil al-ahadith*, 12:6, 21, 101). With that special quality he models not only the shaykh as teacher but the mystic who has the gift of articulating his own experience as well.

As a prophet, Joseph was granted a lofty spiritual state, and his story provides imagery for analyses of profound religious experience. Many spiritual writers have discerned in Joseph qualities that parallel many of the stations and states that they consider markers along the spiritual path. Describing for his hearers an aspect of progress on that path, 'Abd al-Qadir al-Jilani speaks of the importance of the virtues for which Joseph was renowned: patience, contentment, reflective silence, and modesty. God will lead the seeker whose conduct is characterized by these qualities upward along the path, and the seeker will hear the words once spoken to Joseph, "You are today in our presence established and worthy of trust." The shaykh explains that although outwardly it was the pharaoh who thus rewarded Joseph with high authority, in reality it was God who spoke those words. To all appearances Joseph was given the kingdom of Egypt, but the inner meaning is that God gave Joseph the kingdom of the spirit. Jilani reads the scripture metaphorically as a reference to the spiritual power of which Joseph's temporal authority is but a shadow. In this way Joseph's experience is a model for the mystic.[28]

Joseph is also used as a model of mystical experience in a letter from the eighteenth-century Moroccan mystic Ahmad ibn Idris to his follower Muhammad al-Majdhub. Ahmad counsels Muhammad to write down all the good news (*mubashshirat*) that descends upon him, then recalls the example of the Prophet, who

> used to ask his companions after morning prayer: "Those of you who have had a vision (tonight), let them tell it!" It is counted as an instance of revelation, and one should not disregard revelation, for God, glory to Him, does not cause it to no purpose. Think of the story of Joseph, peace be with him: he preserved his vision, together with his father, for long years; and when its true meaning became evident in the world of senses he said immediately—for throughout this long time he had always kept it in mind: "O my father! this is the fulfillment of my vision of old! My Lord hath made it come true!"[29]

The major prophets have long been associated with specific heavenly spheres as well. For the Indian mystic Shah Wali Allah, Joseph represents the fourth of seven "regions" through which a mystic must pass on the journey toward God. In that capacity Joseph, along with Abraham, possesses special insight into creation. On the other hand, Joseph's love for the minister's wife also underscores the prophet's humanity and need of divine protection.[30]

The Joseph story has offered renowned Muslim writers a way to interpret the most mundane difficulties they experienced at the hands of their critics and detractors. No prophet has felt more deeply than Joseph the sting of rejection by those close to him, those on whose support he thought he could depend. The martyred Sufi 'Ayn al-Qudat al-Hamadhani likens himself to the prophet Joseph, whose brothers' envy prompted them to attack Joseph and even to accuse their father of error. He concludes that if "the sons of prophets dared to act thus towards their brother and their father on account of envy, it is not surprising if men like ourselves should commit wrongs many times as great against total strangers."[31] Rumi too saw in his own experience a reflection of Joseph's trials. Rumi's family were so jealous of his friendship with his mystical alter ego, Shams of Tabriz, that they plotted to kill Shams.[32]

Islam's poets have also found in the various critical moments of Joseph's life symbols through which mystics might interpret and describe equally critical experiences in their quest for God. The well and prison into which Joseph is thrown refer to all forms of adversity through which one must live in patience and trust. Allusions to Joseph's shirt have come to mean any experience that restores the blinded seeker's sight. The expression "to cut one's hand," an allusion to the guests at Zulaykha's dinner party, has become a coded reference to the seeker's experience of stark bewilderment in the presence of the Beloved. And Joseph's necessary separation from, and eventual reunion with, his father offers a perfect pattern to console the lover of God who seems to experience God's absence. Most of all, Joseph's beauty keeps the poets enthralled as the most apt image for the deepest of all experiences, the ever-present yearning for the source of all life and being. As Rumi writes of his own experience of longing for the Beloved, "Like Jacob I am crying alas, alas; the fair visage of Joseph of Canaan is my desire."[33]

These are only a few of the countless examples of Joseph as a symbol of so many dimensions of the spiritual life of Muslims. As the Qur'an concludes its "most beautiful of stories": "In their tales is instruction for people of insight. This is no newly concocted story, but a verification of its precursors, an explanation of all things, and a source of guidance and mercy for people of faith" (12:111).

Notes

ABBREVIATIONS

AO   Ars Orientalis
BSOAS   Bulletin of the School of Oriental and African Studies
EI2   Encyclopedia of Islam, 2d ed.
IA   Islamic Art
IC   Islamic Culture
IJMES   International Journal of Middle East Studies
ISF   Islamic Spirituality I: Foundations (ed. S. H. Nasr)
ISM   Islamic Spirituality II: Manifestations (ed. S. H. Nasr)
JAOS   Journal of the American Oriental Society
JNES   Journal of Near Eastern Studies
JRAS   Journal of the Royal Asiatic Society
KO   Kunst des Orients
MW   The Muslim World
SI   Studia Islamica
WI   Die Welt des Islams
ZDMG   Zeitschrift der Deutschen Morgenlaendischen Gesellschaft

PREFACE

1. Ewert Cousins, ed., *World Spirituality: An Encyclopedic History of the Religious Quest*, vol. 19 (New York: Crossroad Publishing, 1987), xiv.

2. Several methodological issues arise at the outset. First, relationships between form and function are not constant, neither in literature nor in the visual arts, nor at the points of contact between textual and visual sources.

A second issue is the utility of a form-based typology. In the study of Islamic literatures, one soon finds that the basic formal distinction between prose and poetry is of limited use, in view of the number of forms that freely intersperse the two. The same distinction may be made between narrative and didactic forms. Literary studies rarely attempt to deal with genre in a comprehensive manner, usually preferring to focus on one form or a few related genres.

Third, what advantages might a function-based approach offer? A distinction between theoretical and practical works can be stretched to include a great deal of important material, but it also leaves out a number of important genres, while others that do seem at first to fit do not fit very neatly.

Finally, the inclusion of related visual materials as well as textual increases the difficulty of choosing a structure. Treating the nontextual objects as equal to documents in importance, not merely as illustrative material, raises the matter of emphasis and priority: where does one start in describing the sources? With the texts, with the objects, with texts on objects, or with objects that have functioned as illustrations to texts? I opt here for a combination of several approaches as a partial solution to the shortcomings of each but retain a textual bias only because texts are so often relied upon for interpretations of nonverbal artifacts.

Each of the seven chapters treats textual sources first and then incorporates the related visual material. I could as easily have folded the visual data together with the textual but chose not to do so in the belief that it is more effective pedagogically to be exposed to a concept or phenomenon twice under slightly different guises. Therefore, some chapters revisit, from a slightly different angle, certain aspects of sources that are formally or functionally multivalent, or both.

Some material for further reading has been included in endnotes, but in the interest of concision and utility these are limited largely to recent scholarship in English. I have used a simplified transliteration scheme. Technical terms in Arabic, Persian, and other languages are italicized on first occurrence but not thereafter, except for the term *jihad*, whose Islamic meaning is distinct from that found in many American dictionaries. Unless otherwise specified, all dates are Common Era (C.E.).

A companion anthology of text and pictures is now in preparation and will be published by the University of California Press.

ONE. FOUNDATIONS: PROPHETIC REVELATION

1. See Majid Khadduri, trans., *Islamic Jurisprudence: Shafi'i's Risala* (Baltimore: Johns Hopkins Press, 1961), 123–45; also John Burton, *The Sources of Islamic Law: Islamic Theories of Abrogation* (Edinburgh: Edinburgh University Press, 1990). For a different approach, see S. H. Nasr, "The Quran as the Foundation of Islamic Spirituality," and A. K. Brohi, "The Spiritual Significance of the Quran," in *ISF,* ed. S. H. Nasr (New York: Crossroad Publishing, 1987), 3–23.

2. Jane Dammen McAuliffe, "Ibn al-Jawzi's Exegetical Propaedeutic: Introduction and Translation," *Journal of Comparative Poetics* 8 (spring 1988): 108, see also 101–13.

3. Mahmoud Ayoub, *The Qur'an and Its Interpreters,* 2 vols. (Albany: State University of New York Press, 1984, 1992), 1:6.

4. For further discussion, see Kenneth Cragg, *The Event of the Qur'an* and *The Mind of the Qur'an* (London: Allen and Unwin, 1971, 1973).

5. Quoted in Jane Dammen McAuliffe, "Qur'anic Hermeneutics: The Views of al-Tabari and Ibn Kathir," in *Approaches to the History of the Interpretation of the Qur'an,* ed. Andrew Rippin (Oxford: Oxford University Press, 1988), 61, see also 46–62.

6. Ayoub, *Qur'an and Its Interpreters,* 1:24.

7. Sahl at-Tustari (d. 896), Abu 'Abd ar-Rahman as-Sulami (d. 1021), Abu 'l-Qasiam al-Qushayri (d. 1074), and Ibn 'Arabi (d. 1240), among others.

8. Gerhard Böwering, *The Mystical Vision of Existence in Classical Islam* (Berlin and New York: Walter De Gruyter, 1980), 135.

9. Ibid., 157. I omit the translator's parenthetical insertion of certain Arabic technical terms.

10. Ayoub, *Qur'an and Its Interpreters,* 1:35.

11. Helmut Gätje, *The Qur'an and Its Exegesis* (Berkeley: University of California Press, 1976), 244; for samples of mystical and Shiʿi exegesis, see 228–47. See also Abdurrahman Habil, "Traditional Esoteric Commentaries on the Quran," in *ISF*, 24–47.

12. See, for example, Hebrews, 11:26, in which "[Moses] considered abuse suffered for the Christ greater wealth than the treasures of Egypt, for [Moses] looked to the reward"; summary from Ayoub, *Qur'an and Its Interpreters*, 1:20–40; Böwering, *Mystical Vision*, 135–42; and Gätje, *Qur'an*, 1–44.

13. Qur'an 14:35–36, 40–41. See also Abraham's prayer for himself and his father in the middle Meccan text Qur'an 26:83–87 and Moses' prayer for the worshipers of the golden calf in the late Meccan Sura 7:151–57.

14. Qur'an 3:191, see also 193–94. For more complete analysis of the subject, see Ary A. Roest Crollius, "The Prayer of the Qur'an," *Studia Missionalia* 24 (1975): 223–52.

15. The powerful parable of the blighted garden (Q 68:17–33) tells of people who jealously guard their produce to prevent the poor from sharing it; the next day they return to find that their crop had vanished. On these themes see M. Watt, *Muhammad at Mecca* (Oxford: Clarendon Press, 1953), 66–71.

16. For these and other important Qur'anic issues, see Fazlur Rahman, *Major Themes in the Qur'an* (Minneapolis and Chicago: Bibliotheca Islamica, 1980); Toshihiko Izutsu, *God and Man in the Koran* (Tokyo: Keio Institute of Cultural and Linguistic Studies, 1964); and idem, *Ethico-Religious Concepts in the Quran* (Montreal: McGill University Press, 1966).

17. *Sayings of Muhammad*, trans. Ghazi Ahmad (Lahore: Sh. Muhammad Ashraf, 1972), 34. On hadiths on particular themes, see ʿAʾisha ʿAbd ar-Rahman at-Tarjumana, trans., *Islamic Book of the Dead* (San Francisco: Diwan Press, 1977); and Barbara Stowasser, *Women in the Qur'an, Traditions, and Interpretation* (New York: Oxford University Press, 1994).

18. James Robson, trans., *Mishkat al-Masabih*, 2 vols. (Lahore: Sh. Muhammad Ashraf, 1975), 1:273.

19. Ibid., 1:133.

20. William Chittick, ed. and trans., *A Shiʿite Anthology* (Albany: State University of New York Press, 1981), 7.

21. See S. M. Jafery, trans., *Nahjul Balagha of Hazrat Ali* (Elmhurst, N.Y.: Tahrike Tarsile Quran, 1977).

22. Chittick, *Shiʿite Anthology*, 29–30. Arabic technical terms that the translator supplies parenthetically have been omitted.

23. See William Graham, *Divine Word and Prophetic Word in Early Islam* (The Hague: Mouton, 1977); also *EI2*, s.v. "Hadith" and "Hadith Kudsi."

24. Mustansir Mir, "The Qur'an as Literature," *Religion and Literature* 20, no. 1 (1988): 51, see also 49–64.

25. Summary from Mustansir Mir, "Qur'an as Literature," 53–63; idem, "Dialogue in the Qur'an," *Religion and Literature* 24, no. 1 (spring 1992): 1–22; and idem, "Humor in the Qur'an," *MW* 81, nos. 3–4 (1991): 179–93.

26. Paraphrase of Qur'an 81:1–14. The following Sura (82) uses a similar device, as do Suras 75:26–30, 84:1–6, and 99:1–4.

27. Similar texts reminiscent of the form are Suras 37:1–4, 51:1–6, 77:1–7, 79:1–14.

28. Similarly, Qur'an 92:1–4 and 93:1–3. More generic series of objects or occurrences may also be the subject of oath-takings, as Qur'an 85:1–8 and 95:1–4; see W. Montgomery Watt, *Bell's Introduction to the Qur'an* (Edinburgh: Edinburgh University Press, 1970), 75–80. Another category of adjurations begins, "I call to witness . . . "; on adjurations,

see *The Holy Qur'an: English Translation of the Meanings and Commentary,* (Madina: King Fahd Holy Qur'an Printing Complex, 1410/1988), 2004–2008.

29. Further examples in Suras 26 and 54.

30. Sayings used as examples here taken passim from the translations mentioned above in notes 17–18; and M. Khan, trans., *Sahih al-Bukhari,* 9 vols. (Lahore: Kazi Publications, 1979).

31. For more examples, see Robson, *Mishkat al-Masabih,* 1120–386.

32. Sahir El Calamawy, "Narrative Elements in the Hadith Literature," in *Arabic Literature to the End of the Umayyad Period,* ed. A. F. Beeston et al. (Cambridge: Cambridge University Press, 1983), 311, see also 308–16.

33. See also R. Marston Speight, "The Function of *Hadith* as Commentary on the Qur'an, as Seen in the Six Authoritative Collections," in Rippin, *Approaches,* 63–81.

34. The uppercase letters indicate the three radicals or consonants of the triconsonantal root, with *Dh* representing one consonant that is pronounced like the *th* in *this.*

35. Roest Crollius, "Prayer of the Qur'an," 227–32.

36. Quoted in Ayoub, *Qur'an and Its Interpreters,* 1:8–9.

37. Ibid., 1:9.

38. A fully indexed compact-disc version of the whole Qur'an in tartil, by Shaykh Muhammad A. bin Muhammad Yusuf, has been published by Cipa SA, Switzerland; unindexed selections in tajwid, by Shaykh ʿAbd al-Basit ʿAbd as-Samad, on compact disc from Duniaphon, Beirut.

39. Kristina Nelson, *The Art of Reciting the Qur'an* (Austin: University of Texas Press, 1985), 58.

40. Ibid., 99.

41. See Ibn ʿAbbad of Ronda's citation of the texts for purposes of encouraging a correspondent, in *Letters on the Sufi Path by Ibn ʿAbbad of Ronda,* trans. John Renard (Mahwah, N.J.: Paulist Press, 1986), 160. Ibn ʿAbbad does, however, counsel his correspondent that it is more important to keep reciting Qur'an, regardless of whether one achieves such a level of emotional consolation; see also Frederick M. Denny, "Qur'an Recitation Training in Indonesia: A Survey of Contexts and Handbooks," in Rippin, *Approaches,* 288–306; Frederick M. Denny, "The Adab of Qur'an Recitation: Text and Context," *International Congress for the Study of the Qur'an,* ed. Anthony Johns and S. H. M. Jafri (Canberra: Australian National University, 1981), 143–60; William Graham, "Qur'an as Spoken Word: An Islamic Contribution to the Understanding of Scripture," in *Approaches to Islam in Religious Studies,* ed. R. Martin (Tucson: University of Arizona Press, 1985), 23–40.

42. Wayne E. Begley, "The Myth of the Taj Mahal and New Theory of Its Symbolic Meaning," *The Art Bulletin* 61, no. 1 (March 1979): 7–37; for a complete inventory of inscriptions around the Taj, see idem and Z. A. Desai, comp. and trans., *Taj Mahal: The Illumined Tomb* (Cambridge: Harvard University and Massachussetts Institute of Technology, 1989), 195–244.

43. Sheila S. Blair, "The Epigraphic Program of the Tomb of Uljaytu at Sultaniyya: Meaning in Mongol Architecture," in *IA* 2 (1987), 44, 55; see also 43–96.

44. See Salah M. Hassan, *Art and Islamic Literacy among the Hausa of Northern Nigeria* (Lewiston, Maine: Edwin Mellen, 1992).

45. Mir, "Qur'an as Literature," 51–52.

46. For examples, see Annemarie Schimmel, *Calligraphy and Islamic Culture* (New York: New York University Press, 1984); idem, *Islamic Calligraphy* (Leiden: Brill, 1970); idem, *Islamic Calligraphy* (New York: Metropolitan Museum of Art, 1992); Martin Lings, *The Quranic Art of Calligraphy and Illumination* (London: Festival of the World of Is-

lam, 1976); S. H. Nasr, *Islamic Art and Spirituality* (Albany: State University of New York Press, 1987); Erica C. Dodd and Shereen Khairallah, *The Image of the Word* (Beirut: American University, 1981); Esin Atil, *Renaissance of Islam: Art of the Mamluks* (Washington, D.C.: Smithsonian Institution Press, 1981); and idem, *The Age of Sultan Süleyman the Magnificent* (New York: Harry N. Abrams, 1987).

TWO. DEVOTION: RITUAL AND PERSONAL PRAYER

1. Vernon Schubel, *Religious Performance in Contemporary Islam: Shiʿi Devotional Rituals in South Asia* (Columbia: University of South Carolina Press, 1993), 1–6; and Frederick M. Denny, "Islamic Ritual: Perspectives and Theories," in Martin, *Approaches to Islam*, 63–77.

2. Quoted in Constance Padwick, *Muslim Devotions* (London: SPCK, 1961), 54. I owe much of the following section to her.

3. Mukhtar Holland, trans., *Al-Ghazali: Inner Dimensions of Islamic Worship* (Leicester: Islamic Foundation, 1983), 27–28.

4. Padwick, *Muslim Devotions*, 10.

5. William Chittick, *Faith and Practice of Islam* (Albany: State University of New York Press, 1992).

6. Ibid., 118.

7. W. Montgomery Watt, trans., *The Faith and Practice of Al-Ghazali* (London: George Allen and Unwin, 1953).

8. Chittick, *Faith*, 132.

9. Michel Reeber, "A Study of Islamic Preaching in France," *Islam and Christian-Muslim Relations* 2, no. 2 (December 1991): 275–94; Patrick D. Gaffney, "The Changing Voices of Islam: The Emergence of Professional Preachers in Contemporary Egypt," *MW* 81, no. 1 (January 1991): 27–47; and Abu ʿUmar ibn ʿAbd Rabbihi, *Adab al-minbar* (from his *ʿIqd al-farid*), trans. Arthur Wormhoudt, 2 vols. (Oskaloosa, Iowa: William Penn College, 1988, 1989).

10. Richard Antoun, *Muslim Preacher in the Modern World* (Princeton: Princeton University Press, 1989), 155–57.

11. D. R. Marshall, "Some Early Islamic Sermons," *Journal of the Faculty of Arts, Royal University of Malta* 5 (1972): 94–95, see also 91–110. Marshall translates from Ibn Qutayba's *Sources of Information* (*ʿUyun al-akhbar*). The reference to the questioner may refer either to judgment or to the interrogation of the angels in the tomb, to which I return later in this chapter.

12. S. H. Nasr, "Sacred Art in Persian Culture," in idem, *Islamic Art and Spirituality*, 64–83.

13. Roger Joseph, "The Semiotics of the Islamic Mosque," *Arab Studies Quarterly* 3, no. 3 (1981): 286–87, see also 285–95. Joseph offers an initial proposal for the study of the mosque's use of space as a distinctive language, acknowledging the critical element of cultural diversity in regional inspiration in architectural design. See also idem, "Toward a Semiotics of Middle Eastern Cultures," *IJMES* 12 (1980): 312–29.

14. See Dodd and Khairallah, *Image of the Word*; also Sheila Blair, "Legibility vs. Decoration in Islamic Epigraphy," in *World Art: Themes of Unity in Diversity*, Acts of the XXVIth International Congress of the History of Art, ed. I. Lavin, 3 vols. (University Park: Pennsylvania State University Press, 1989), 2:329–35. For theory that promises some application across religious traditions, see Gerard Lukken and Mark Searle, *Semiotics and Church Architecture* (Kampen, Netherlands: Kok Pharos Publishing House, 1993).

15. For a useful survey of the major forms and functions, see Doǧan Kuban, *Muslim Religious Architecture* (Leiden: Brill, 1982).

16. Richard Ettinghausen, "The Early History, Use and Iconography of the Prayer Rug," in *Prayer Rugs* (Washington, D.C.: Textile Museum, 1974), 10–25.

17. Color plates in Atıl, *Age of Sultan Süleyman,* 65; see also Carol G. Fisher and Alan Fisher, "Illustrations of Mecca and Medina in Islamic Manuscripts," in *Islamic Art from Michigan Collections,* ed. Carol G. Fisher and Alan Fisher (Lansing, Mich.: Kresge Art Gallery, 1982), 40–47, ills. 98–101; and photographs in F. E. Peters, *The Hajj* (Princeton: Princeton University Press, 1994).

18. Barbara D. Metcalf, "The Pilgrimage Remembered: South Asian Accounts of the Hajj," in *Muslim Travellers: Pilgrimage, Migration and the Religious Imagination,* ed. Dale F. Eickelman and James Piscatori (Berkeley: University of California Press, 1990), 88, see also 85–107.

19. Ibid., 97–98.

20. Kurt Erdmann, "Kaʿbah-Fliesen," *AO* 2 (1959): 192–97; and Richard Ettinghausen, "Die Bildliche Darstellung der Kaʿba im islamischen Kulturkreis," *ZDMG,* n.s., 12 (1934): 111 ff.

21. Joseph Pitts says he observed "many Moors who get a beggarly livelihood by selling models of the temple unto strangers." Quoted in William Foster, ed., *The Red Sea and Adjacent Countries* (London: Hakluyt Society, 1949), 39.

22. Juan Campo, *The Other Sides of Paradise* (Columbia: University of South Carolina Press, 1991), 139–65.

23. William Chittick, trans., *The Psalms of Islam* (London: Muhammadi Trust, 1988); and idem, trans., *Supplications* [of ʿAli] (London: Muhammadi Trust, 1987).

24. Kojiro Nakamura, trans., *Ghazali on Prayer* (Tokyo: Institute of Oriental Culture, 1973), 109, 117.

25. Ibid., 117–18. I omit the translator's parenthetical insertion of Arabic technical terms.

26. Ibid., 35–36. I have modified the second translation, replacing "invoked" with "remembered" to reflect the word *dhakara* in the original.

27. On various forms of dhikr, see Annemarie Schimmel, *Mystical Dimensions of Islam* (Chapel Hill: University of North Carolina Press, 1975), 167–78, and passim.

28. Padwick, *Muslim Devotions,* 14.

29. Chittick, *Psalms of Islam,* 245.

30. Wheeler Thackston, trans., *Intimate Conversations* (Ramsey, N.J.: Paulist Press, 1978), 176.

31. Ibid., 190, 193, 198.

32. Annemarie Schimmel, "The Prophet Muhammad as a Centre of Muslim Life and Thought," in *We Believe in One God,* ed. Annemarie Schimmel and Abdoldjavad Falaturi (New York: Crossroad Publishing, 1979), 43–44; see also F. Lyman MacCallum, trans., *The Mevlidi Sherif* (reprint, London: John Murray, 1957).

33. Jan Knappert, *Swahili Islamic Poetry,* 3 vols. (Leiden: Brill, 1971), 3:289–91; see also 1:41–60, 1:102–44, 3:276–365.

34. Ibid., 3:227.

35. Ibid., 3:251.

36. Litanies (*durud*) are also important, invoking blessings upon the Prophet, used both in the dhikrs of mystical groups and in the daily prayer of other Muslims as well. Three related genres are called signs or proofs (*dalaʾil*), ornament (*hilya*), and excellent qualities (*shamaʾil*). Hybrid of biography and litany, these forms catalogue the Prophet's

evidentiary miracles. Two eleventh-century works, both entitled *Proofs of Prophethood* (*Dala'il an-nubuwwa*), one written by Abu Nu'aym al-Isfahani (d. 1037) and the other by Bayhaqi (d. 1066), represent the beginnings of the genre. The term *hilya*, with its visual connotations of ornament or adornment, was readily transferred to the practice of using calligraphic renderings of Muhammad's unique qualities both as decoration and as talismanic devices for Muslim homes; see Annemarie Schimmel, *And Muhammad Is His Messenger* (Chapel Hill: University of North Carolina, 1985), 33, 94 ff., and passim; and idem, *As through a Veil: Mystical Poetry in Islam* (New York: Columbia University Press, 1982), especially chapter 5 on poetry in honor of the Prophet.

37. Padwick, *Muslim Devotions*, 279.

38. M. U. Memon, trans., *Ibn Taymiya's Struggle against Popular Religion* (The Hague: Mouton, 1976), 302.

39. Padwick, *Muslim Devotions*, 241–42.

40. In Muhammad M. Shams ad-Din, *The Rising of al-Husayn*, trans. I. K. A. Howard (London: Muhammadi Trust, 1985), 49. See also F. De Jong, "The Cairene *Ziyara*-Days: A Contribution to the Study of Saint Veneration in Islam," *WI* 17 (1976–1977): 26–43.

41. Carl Ernst, "An Indo-Persian Guide to Sufi Shrine Pilgrimage," in *Manifestations of Sainthood in Islam*, ed. Grace Martin and Carl Ernst (Istanbul: Isis Press, 1993), 63, see also 43–67. Lamentation poetry called *marthiya* is also important; in Arabic, Persian and Urdu, especially, the form distills the feeling and mood of the ziyara.

42. For a helpful survey, see Frederick M. Denny, "God's Friends: The Sanctity of Persons in Islam," in *Sainthood: Its Manifestations in World Religions*, ed. R. Kieckhefer and George Bond (Berkeley: University of California Press, 1988), 69–97.

43. L. Pelly, trans., *The Miracle Play of Hasan and Husain* (1879; reprint, Gregg International, 1970), 2:347–48.

44. Antoun analyzes five sermons on this topic (*Muslim Preacher*, 219–34).

45. Ibn al-Jawzi, *Kitab al-qussas wa 'l-mudhakkirin*, trans. Merlin L. Swartz (Beirut: Dar al-Mashriq, 1986), 96–97, 113; see also J. Pedersen, "The Criticism of the Islamic Preacher," *WI*, n.s., 2 (1952): 215–31.

46. Carter V. Findley, "Social Dimensions of Dervish Life as Seen in the Memoirs of Asci Dede Ibrahim Halil," in *Dervish Lodge*, ed. Raymond Lifchez (Berkeley: University of California Press, 1992), 179–80, see also 175–86.

47. Sheila S. Blair, "Sufi Saints and Shrine Architecture in the Early Fourteenth Century," *Muqarnas* 7 (1990): 35–49; Caroline Williams, "The Cult of 'Alid Saints in the Fatimid Monuments of Cairo, Part 2: The Mausolea," *Muqarnas* 3 (1985): 39–60; and Oleg Grabar, "The Earliest Islamic Commemorative Structures, Notes and Documents," *AO* 6 (1966): 7–46.

48. James Dickie, "Allah and Eternity: Mosques, Madrasas and Tombs," in *Architecture of the Islamic World*, ed. George Michel (New York: William Morrow, 1978), 45, see also 15–47.

49. On that of 'Abdallah Ansari in Herat, see Lisa Golombek, *The Timurid Shrine at Gazar Gah* (Toronto: Royal Ontario Museum, 1969).

50. Baha Tanman, "Settings for the Veneration of Saints," in Lifchez, *Dervish Lodge*, 130–71, especially 133–35.

51. Abbas Daneshvari, *Medieval Tomb Towers of Iran* (Lexington, Ky.: Mazda Publishers, 1986), 9–64.; also Begley, "Myth," 7–37.

52. Tanman, "Settings," 166–67.

53. Samuel R. Peterson, "The Ta'ziyeh and Related Arts," in *Ta'ziyeh: Ritual and Drama in Iran*, ed. Peter Chelkowski (New York: New York University Press, 1979), 64–87.

54. Schubel, *Religious Performance*, 109–12.

55. Caroline Williams, "The Qur'anic Inscriptions on the *Tabut* of al-Husayn," *IA* 2 (1987): 3–13; on the Seven Pillars, see Farhad Daftary, *The Isma'ilis* (Cambridge: Cambridge University Press, 1990), 250.

56. Louis Massignon, "La Rawda de Médine: Cadre de la méditation musulmane sur la destinée du prophète," in *Opera minora de Louis Massignon*, 3 vols., ed. Y. Moubarac (Paris: Presses Universitaires de France, 1969), 3:286–315. See also Fisher and Fisher, "Illustrations" (in note 17 of this chapter); on the talismanic use in Africa of stylized images of Medina, see René Bravmann, "A Fragment of Paradise," *MW* 78, no. 1 (January 1988): 29–37; and color plates in Atil, *Age of Sultan Sulëyman*, 65.

THREE. INSPIRATION: EDIFICATION AND ETHICS

1. I do not consider a third important source, namely, universal histories, which include stories of the great models of sanctity within the larger story of world history.

2. On these major heroic types, see John Renard, *Islam and the Heroic Image* (Columbia: University of South Carolina Press, 1993).

3. Carl Ernst, *Eternal Garden* (Albany: State University of New York Press, 1992), 85, 88; see also Marcia K. Hermansen, "Interdisciplinary Approaches to Islamic Biographical Materials," *Religion* 18 (1988): 163–82.

4. R. Steven Humphreys, "Qur'anic Myth and Narrative Structure in Early Islamic Historiography," in *Tradition and Innovation in Late Antiquity,* ed. F. M. Clover and R. Steven Humphreys (Madison: University of Wisconsin Press, 1989), 278, see also 271–90.

5. The order is analogous to Jesus' lineage to Adam as traced by the evangelist Luke (cf., Luke 3:23–38).

6. *The Life of Muhammad: A Translation of Ibn Ishaq's "Sirat Rasul Allah,"* trans. A. Guillaume (Oxford: Oxford University Press, 1955), 181–82.

7. Ibid., 690–91. See also Josef Horovitz, "The Earliest Biographies of the Prophet and Their Authors," *IC* 1, no. 4 (October 1927): 535–59; 2, no. 1 (January 1928): 22–50; 2, no. 2 (April 1928): 164–82; 2, no. 4 (October 1928): 495–526.

8. Zeren Tanindi, *Siyer-i nebi* (Istanbul: Hurriyet Foundation, 1974), 10.

9. Richard Winstedt, *A History of Classical Malay Literature* (Kuala Lumpur: Oxford in Asia Historical Reprints, 1969), 103; for summaries of many of these Malay works, see chapter 7; on the merit of reading, see page 102.

10. See Ismail Hamid, *Arabic and Islamic Literary Tradition* (Kuala Lumpur: Utusan Publications, 1982), especially chapters 6 and 7.

11. Abu 'l-Hasan ad-Daylami, *Sirat-i Abu 'Abdullah Ibn Khafif ash-Shirazi*, ed. Annemarie Schimmel (Ankara: Turk Tarih Kurumu Basimevi, 1955), 36; see also Annemarie Schimmel, "Zur Biographie des Abu 'Abdallah ibn Chafif ash-Shirazi," *WO* 2, no. 1 (1955): 193–99; and idem, "Ibn Khafif: An Early Representative of Sufism," *Journal of the Pakistan Historical Society* 6 (1958): 147–73.

12. Mahmud ibn 'Uthman, *Firdaws al-murshidiya fi asrar as-samadiya*, ed. Fritz Meier (Leipzig: F. A. Brockhaus, 1948); Fritz Meier, *Die Vita des Abu Ishaq al-Kazaruni* (Leipzig: F. A. Brockhaus, 1948); A. J. Arberry, "The Biography of Shaikh Abu Ishaq al-Kazaruni," *Oriens* 3 (1950): 163–72; and Hamid Algar, "Kazaruni," *EI2* 4:851–52.

13. Muhammad ibn-i Munawwar, *Asrar at-tawhid*, trans. John O'Kane (Costa Mesa, Calif.: Mazda Publishers, 1992), 63.

14. Ibid., 68.

15. Ibid. For material on the life story of another famous Sufi, see Fritz Meier, "Zur Biographie Ahmad-i Gam's und sur Quellenkunde von Gami's Nafahatu'l-uns," *ZDMG* 97 (1943): 47–67; and Vladimir Ivanow, "A Biography of Shaykh Ahmad-i Jam," *JRAS* (1917): 291–365.

16. Wheeler Thackston, trans., *The Tales of the Prophets of al-Kisa'i* (Boston: Twayne Publishers, 1978), 3. On historical prophetology as one of several approaches to the subject, see John Renard, *All the King's Falcons: Rumi on Prophets and Revelation* (Albany: State University of New York Press, 1994), 2–5.

17. For example, Abu Ishaq an-Nisaburi ath-Tha'labi, *Qisas al-anbiya'* (Cairo: Dar Ihya' al-Kutub al-'Arabiya, n.d.).

18. Ahmad Bahjat, *Anbiya' Allah* (Cairo: Dar ash-Shuruq, 1975).

19. Abd ar-Rahman as-Sulami, *Kitab tabaqat as-Sufiya,* ed. Johannes Pedersen (Leiden: Brill, 1960).

20. Summarized from Farid ad-Din 'Attar, *Muslim Saints and Mystics,* trans. A. J. Arberry (London: Routledge and Kegan Paul, 1966), 12, see also 11–12. Jami's fifteenth-century contribution to the genre, *Warm Breezes of Intimacy (Nafahat al-uns)* relied on Ansari's Persian reworking of Sulami.

21. Saiyid Athar Abbas Rizvi, *A History of Sufism in India,* 2 vols. (New Delhi: Munshiram Manoharlal, 1978), 1:9–10.

22. Ernst, *Eternal Garden,* 92.

23. Ibn 'Arabi, *Sufis of Andalusia,* trans. R. W. J. Austin (Berkeley: University of California Press, 1971), 143–44.

24. Shams ad-Din Aflaki, *Legends of the Sufis,* rev. ed., trans. James W. Redhouse (London: Theosophical Publishing House, 1976), 17.

25. See selections in Bernard Lewis, ed. and trans. *Islam from the Prophet Muhammad to the Capture of Constantinople,* 2 vols. (New York: Harper and Row, 1974), 1:180–83.

26. Ann K. S. Lambton, "Islamic Mirrors for Princes," in *La Persia nel medioevo* (Rome: Accademia Nazionale dei Lincei, 1971), 420, see also 419–42.

27. A. H. Dawood, "A Comparative Study of Arabic and Persian Mirrors from the Second to the Sixth Century A. H." (Ph.D. thesis, University of London, 1965).

28. The Saljuqids were descendants of a central Asian Turkic leader whose people converted to Islam in the early eleventh century. Moving west across Persia, they took the city of Baghdad in 1055. The Saljuqids left the Muslim caliph in his place, but reduced his authority to the religious sphere and established the parallel institution of the sultanate with effective political authority.

29. Nizam al-Mulk, *The Book of Government, or Rules for Kings,* trans. Hubert Darke (London: Routledge and Kegan Paul, 1978), 2, 13.

30. *Ghazali's Book of Counsel for Kings,* trans. F. R. C. Bagley (London: Oxford University Press, 1964), 44.

31. Ibid., 136.

32. Julie S. Meisami, trans., *The Sea of Precious Virtues: A Medieval Islamic Mirror for Princes* (Salt Lake City: University of Utah Press, 1991), vii, xiv.

33. Ibid., 72.

34. Ibid., 83.

35. Other important examples of this genre are Kay Ka'us Ibn Iskandar, *A Mirror for Princes, the Qabus Nama,* trans. Reuben Levy (London: Luzac, 1951); Mustafa Ali Gelibolu, *Mustafa Ali's Counsel for Sultans of 1581,* trans. Andreas Tietze (Vienna: Verlag der Osterreichischen Akademie der Wissenschaften, 1979); and Yusuf Khass Hajib, *The*

Wisdom of the Royal Glory, trans. Robert Dankoff (Chicago: University of Chicago Press, 1983).

36. Nasir ad-Din Tusi, *The Nasirean Ethics*, trans. G. M. Wickens (London: Allen and Unwin, 1964).

37. Dimitri Gutas, "Classical Arabic Wisdom Literature: Nature and Scope," *JAOS* 101, no. 1 (January–March 1981): 52, see also 49–87.

38. Ibid., 68

39. Rizvi, *Sufism in India*, 1:146–48.

40. See J. Rypka, *History of Iranian Literature*, ed. Karl Jahn (New York: Humanities Press, 1968), 37–38; and S. Shaked, "Andarz Literature in Pre-Islamic Iran," in *Encyclopedia Iranica*, ed. E. Yarshater (London: Routledge and Kegan Paul, 1987), 2:11–16.

41. Saʿdi, *Gulistan*, ed. Nurallah Iranparast (Tehran: Danish-i Saʿdi, 1348/1969), 156.

42. David Pendlebury, trans., *The Abode of Spring* in *Four Sufi Classics*, ed. I. Shah (London: Octagon, 1980), 199–200; older but fuller translation is E. H. Rehastek, *The Abode of Spring* (Benares: Kama Shastra Society, 1887). These writings of Saʿdi and Jami differ from other instructional works in that they exist in illustrated versions.

43. Ibn al-Jawzl, *Kitab al-qussas*, 96–97.

44. Another important dimension of storytelling is the use of various song forms by, for example, Qawwali of south Asia and Munshidin of Egypt. Singing has not always enjoyed acceptance from Islam's religious establishment. Ibn al-Jawzi warns of the dangers of breaking into song in response to storytellers. See, for example, Ali Asani, "Music and Dance in the Work of Mawlana Jalal al-Din Rumi," *IC* 60, no. 2 (April 1986): 41–55; D. B. MacDonald, "Emotional Religion in Islam as Affected by Music and Singing," *JRAS* (1901–1902): 1–28, 195–252, 705–48; Earle Waugh, *The Munshidin: Their World and Their Song* (Columbia: University of South Carolina Press, 1985); and articles by Earle Waugh, I. Markoff, and R. Qureshi, in Smith and Ernst, *Manifestations of Sainthood*.

45. Peter Chelkowski, "Narrative Painting and Painting Recitation in Qajar Iran," *Muqarnas* 6 (1989): 98–111.

46. Samuel Peterson, "The Taʿziyeh and Related Arts," in *Studies in the Art and Literature of the Near East*, ed. Peter Chelkowski (Salt Lake City: University of Utah Press, 1979), 64–87.

47. M. Masmoudi, *La Peinture sous-verre en Tunisie* (Tunis: Ceres Productions, 1972), 41.

48. For examples of images, see Penny Williams, "Through a Glass Brightly," *Aramco World Magazine* 29, no. 4 (July–August 1978): 2–5.

49. See Annemarie Schimmel, "Calligraphy and Mysticism," in idem, *Calligraphy and Islamic Culture*.

50. Perween Hasan, "The Footprint of the Prophet," *Muqarnas* 10 (1993): 335–43; and Schimmel, *Muhammad Is His Messenger*, 40–43.

51. William L. Hanaway, Jr., "The Symbolism of Persian Revolutionary Posters," in *Iran since the Revolution*, ed. Barry Rosen, (Boulder: Social Science Monographs, 1985), 48, see also 31–50.

52. See Ernst Grube, "The Siyar-i Nabi of the Spencer Collection in the New York Public Library," in *Atti del Secondo Congresso Internazionale di Arte Turca* (Naples: Istituto Universitario Orientale Seminario di Turcologia, 1965), 149–76; and for color images, Tanindi, *Siyer-i nebi*.

53. Miguel Asin Palacios, *Islam and the Divine Comedy* (London: Frank Cass, 1968); for color plates, see also Marie Rose Seguy, *The Miraculous Journey of Mahomet* (New

York: George Braziller, 1977); see also Richard Ettinghausen, "Persian Ascension Miniatures of the Fourteenth Century," *Accademia Nazionale dei Lincei* 12 (1957): 360–83;
and Priscilla Soucek, "The Life of the Prophet: Illustrated Versions," in *Content and Context of Visual Arts in the Islamic World*, ed. idem, (University Park: Pennsylvania State
University Press, 1988), 193–209 (see illustrations).

FOUR. AESTHETICS: FROM ALLEGORY TO ARABESQUE

1. See S. A. Bonebakker, "*Adab* and the Concept of *Belles-lettres*" in *'Abbasid Belles
Lettres*, ed. J. Ashtiyani et al. (Cambridge: Cambridge University Press, 1990), 16–30.

2. Francesco Gabrieli, "Religious Poetry in Early Islam," in *Arabic Poetry: Theory and
Development*, ed. G. E. von Gruenebaum (Wiesbaden: Otto Harrassowitz, 1973), 7, see
also 5–17.

3. The Khawarij were a faction that separated from the early supporters of 'Ali (the
Shi'a); they believed that 'Ali had wrongly agreed to submit to human arbitration after
an apparent military stalemate during the Battle of Siffin against Mu'awiya, the Umayyad
governor of Damascus in 657.

4. Michael Sells, trans., *Desert Tracings* (Middletown, Conn.: Wesleyan University
Press, 1989), 35.

5. Safa Khulusi, "Arabic Literature," in *ISM*, ed. S. H. Nasr, (New York: Crossroad
Publishing, 1991), 320, see also 319–27.

6. Quoted in Schimmel, *Mystical Dimensions of Islam*, 40.

7. Schimmel, *As through a Veil*, summary from 11 ff.

8. My translation. Hallaj, *Diwan*, in Louis Massignon, ed., *Journal Asiatique* (January–July 1931): 45, poem no. 17; the second hemistich of the last line could have been
rendered: "and in my annihilation you come to be." That line is built around an alliter-
ation: "fa-fi fana'i fana' fana'i / wa-fi fana'i wujidta anta." The verb *to find* (*wajada*) is
related to the Arabic noun most commonly used for mystical ecstasy (wajd).

9. For more on these two poets, see Schimmel, *As through a Veil*, 34–48; also Martin
Lings, "Mystical Poetry," in Ashtiyani, *'Abbasid Belles Lettres*, 235–64.

10. R. A. Nicholson, trans., *The Tarjuman al-Ashwaq* (London: Royal Asiatic Society, 1911), 82–83.

11. Ibid., 58–59.

12. See also, S. H. Nasr and J. Matini, "Persian Literature" in Nasr, *ISM*, 328–49.

13. The Sindhi *ghinan* is a prime example of Islamic mystical poetry in vernacular
languages; other such genres include the Gayo *syair* and the Urdu *charkhi nama*. See
articles on Turkish, Indo-Muslim, Malay, and African literatures in Nasr, *ISM*, 350–92;
and Schimmel, *As through a Veil*, 135–69.

14. For a comparative study, see Michael Sells, *Mystical Languages of Unsaying*
(Chicago: University of Chicago Press, 1994).

15. Sana'i of Ghazna, *The First Book of the Hadiqatu'l-Haqiqat, or The Enclosed Garden of the Truth*, ed. and trans. Major J. Stephenson (New York: Samuel Weiser, 1971),
13–14; Persian text, 8–9.

16. Peter Heath, *Allegory and Philosophy in Avicenna* (Philadelphia: University of
Pennsylvania Press, 1992), 193.

17. Ibid., 197, see also 194–98.

18. Farid ad-Din 'Attar, *The Conference of the Birds*, trans. Afkham Darbandi and Dick
Davis (New York: Penguin Books, 1984), 36–37.

19. A. El Tayyib makes a case for putting the qasida in a class by itself, since it ranges from polemic to rhetorical to epic and even sapiential material. But he is speaking of the pre-Islamic genre; in the present context, the form has clearly undergone important adaptations; see El Tayyib's "Pre-Islamic Poetry," in *Arabic Literature to the End of the Umayyad Period*, ed. A. F. L. Beeston et al. (Cambridge: Cambridge University Press, 1983), 27–113, especially 38 ff.

20. M. M. Badawi, "Abbasid Poetry and Its Antecedents," in Ashtiyani, *'Abbasid Belles Lettres*, 151, see also 146–166.

21. El Tayyib, "Pre-Islamic Poetry," 39 ff. See Michael Sells, "Bewildered Tongue: The Semantics of Mystical Union in Islam," in *Mystical Union and Monotheistic Faith*, ed. M. Idel and B. BcGinn (New York: Macmillan, 1989), 87–124, especially 90–93, on the mystical adaptation of elements of the qasida.

22. Suzanne Stetkeyvich, "Structuralist Interpretations of Pre-Islamic Poetry: Critique and New Directions," *JNES* 42, no. 2 (1983): 85–107; and idem, "The Su'luk and His Poem: A Paradigm of Passage Manqué," *JAOS* 104, no. 4 (1984): 661–68.

23. For further discussion of feminine imagery of the Ka'ba, see William C. Young, "The Ka'ba, Gender, and the Rites of Pilgrimage," *IJMES* 25, no. 2 (May 1993): 285–300.

24. R. A. Nicholson, *Studies in Islamic Mysticism* (Cambridge, England: University Press, 1967), 184–88. See also Issa Boullata, "Verbal Arabesque and Mystical Union: A Study of Ibn al-Farid's *Al-Ta'iyya Al-Kubra*," *Arab Studies Quarterly* 3 (1981): 152–69; and Th. Emil Homerin, *From Arab Poet to Muslim Saint: Ibn al-Farid, His Verse, and His Shrine* (Columbia: University of South Carolina Press, 1994).

25. J. T. P. De Bruijn, *Of Piety and Poetry* (Leiden: Brill, 1983), 173, vv. 3–7 (verse numbers deleted).

26. See Schimmel, *As through a Veil*, 172–76; see also above, p. 79.

27. Arthur Jeffery, ed. and trans., *A Reader on Islam* (The Hague: Mouton, 1962), 619; full translation, 604–20. Brackets enclose the translator's insertions. See also Schimmel, *As through a Veil*, chapter 5; and idem, *Muhammad Is His Messenger*, chapter 10.

28. Hj. Muhammad Bukhari Lubis, *Qasidahs in Honor of the Prophet* (Bangi, Selangor: Penerbit Universiti Kebangsaan Malaysia, 1983), 3.

29. See Gilbert Lazard, "Le Langage symbolique du *ghazal*," in *Poesia di Hafez* (Rome: Accademia Nazionale dei Lincei, 1978), 59–71.

30. My translation. Rumi, *Diwan-i Shams*, ed. B. Furuzanfar (Tehran: University of Tehran Press, 1349/1970), 702, poem no. 1861.

31. Kermani, *Heart's Witness*, trans. Brend M. Weischer and Peter L. Wilson (Tehran: Imperial Iranian Academy of Philosophy, 1978), 116–19, poem nos. 77, 79, 80.

32. G. W. J. Drewes and L. F. Brakel, ed. and trans. *The Poems of Hamzah Fansuri* (Dordrecht, Netherlands: Foris Publications, 1986), 59, poem 6, vv. 1–8. I have deleted verse numbers and enclosed original technical terms in brackets.

33. Ibid., 123. See also Syed Naguib al-Attas, *The Origin of the Malay Sha'ir* (Kuala Lumpur: Dewan Bahasa dan Pustaka, 1968); and idem, *Concluding Postscript to the Origin of the Malay Sha'ir* (Kuala Lumpur: Dewan Bahasa dan Pustaka, 1971).

34. Abu Hamid al-Ghazali, *The Alchemy of Happiness*, quoted in Richard Ettinghausen, "Al-Ghazzali on Beauty," in *Art and Thought*, ed. K. Bharatha Iyer (London: Garland Publishing, 1974), 160–65. Ettinghausen suggests four of the following levels of interpretation; I add a fifth and elaborate on two of his. See Richard Ettinghausen, "Decorative Arts and Painting: Their Scope and Character," in *The Legacy of Islam*, ed. J. Schacht and C. E. Bosworth (Oxford: Oxford University Press, 1974), 284–91, see also 274–91.

35. Qadi Ahmad, *Calligraphers and Painters*, trans. V. Minorsky (Washington, D.C.: Freer Gallery of Art, 1959), 51–52, 22.

36. Kufic is a style named after the Iraqi city of Kufa where the early supporters of 'Ali had an important center. This style is characterized by broad, angular forms as distinguished from the more vertically extended and rounded forms of the so-called cursive scripts; see Figure 3.

37. L. Binyon, J. V. Wilkinson, and B. Gray, *Persian Miniature Painting* (New York: Dover Publications, 1971), 183–84.

38. *Discourses of Rumi*, trans. A. J. Arberry (New York: Samuel Weiser, 1972), 164; and Rumi, *The Masnavi*, trans. R. A. Nicholson (London: Luzac, 1925–40), book 4: 476, 753; book 6: 861 ff, 4672.

39. Qur'an 68:1, 96:3–4; see also Schimmel, *Islamic Calligraphy*, 1.

40. Qadi Ahmad, *Calligraphers and Painters*, 41, 50.

41. Ettinghausen, "Decorative Arts and Paintings," 287–88.

42. Rumi, *Selected Poems from the Divani Shamsi Tabriz*, ed. R. A. Nicholson, (Cambridge: Cambridge University Press, 1977), 135.

43. For similar use of Ka'ba imagery in a Persian source from the eastern part of the Islamic world, see *Sharafuddin Maneri: "The Hundred Letters,"* trans. Paul Jackson, S.J. (Mahwah, N.J.: Paulist Press, 1980), 134–35.

44. Rumi, *Selected Poems*, 135; Annemarie Schimmel, *The Triumphal Sun* (London: Fine Books, 1978), 168, 175.

45. A. Papadopoulo, *Islam and Muslim Art* (New York: Harry N. Abrams, 1979), 114 ff.

46. Carl Ernst, "The Spirit of Islamic Calligraphy: Baba Shah Isfahani's *Adab al-mashq*," *JAOS* 112, no. 2 (1992): 284, see also 279–86.

47. History and visual analysis in Ernst Kuehnel, *The Arabesque*, trans. Richard Ettinghausen (Graz: Verlag für Sammler, 1977).

48. See Lois Ibsen al-Faruqi's chapters on the arts in Lois Ibsen al-Faruqi and Ismail R. al-Faruqi, *A Cultural Atlas of Islam* (New York: Macmillan, 1986), 162–81, 354 ff; also Lois Ibsen al-Faruqi, *Islam and Art* (Islamabad: National Hijra Council, 1985); idem, "Islam and Aesthetic Expression," in *Islam and Contemporary Society* (London: Longman, Islamic Council of Europe, 1982), 191–212; and idem, "An Islamic Perspective on Symbolism and the Arts," in *Art and the Sacred*, ed. Diane Apostolos-Cappadona (New York: Crossroad Publishing, 1984), 164–78. Marshall Hodgson agrees but for different reasons: "the introduction of any other symbols beside the Qur'an, however much they may point to other aspects of divinity, must necessarily, in the nature of symbols, share in, channel away, and finally dissipate devotional energies," in "Islam and Image," in *History of Religions* 3 (1964): 241, see also 220–60.

49. Nader Ardalan, *The Sense of Unity* (Chicago: University of Chicago Press, 1973); Titus Burckhardt, *Art of Islam: Language and Meaning* (London: World of Islam, 1976); and Nasr, *Islamic Art and Spirituality*.

50. Ardalan, *Sense of Unity*, 21 ff.

51. Oleg Grabar, *The Mediation of Ornament* (Princeton: Princeton University Press, 1992), 5.

52. Ibid., xxiv.

53. Ibid., 77–78.

54. Ibid., 111.

55. Gulru Necipoğlu, "The Suleymaniye Complex in Istanbul: An Interpretation," *Muqarnas* 3 (1985): 92, see also 92–117; my description summarizes the article's findings. Useful surveys of architecture are Henri Stierlin, *Architektur des Islam* (Zurich:

Atlantis, 1979); Michel, *Architecture;* John Hoag, *Islamic Architecture* (New York: Harry N. Abrams, 1977); and Godfrey Goodwin, *History of Ottoman Architecture* (Baltimore: Johns Hopkins University Press, 1971).

56. Jale Nejdet Erzen, "Aesthetics and Aisthesis in Ottoman Art and Architecture," *Journal of Islamic Studies* 2, no. 1 (1991): 17, see also 1–24.

57. Texts listed in Necipoğlu, "Suleymaniye Complex," 109–11.

58. Other famous buildings took on similar symbolic associations; see, for example, Caʿfer Effendi, *Risale-i Miʿmariyye,* trans. Howard Crane (Leiden: Brill, 1987), especially 64–75, 104–9. Erzen observes that "[a]rchitecture as *text* is an idea which constitutes the basic theme of the Selimiye Risalesi, written on Sinan's Mosque Selimiye. The book is an attempt to understand and interpret the building, through dialogues; but the story of the man who had devoted all his life, as a lover, to the study of the edifice, makes the point explicit. Architecture as text expresses the decisive attitude of Ottoman culture towards art or architecture, namely the importance it accords to experiential quality. Architecture is valued as a performed art, whose qualities are not fixed but variable in time and according to orientation" ("Aesthetics," 9–10).

59. See, for example, Oleg Grabar, *The Alhambra* (London: Allen Lane, 1978).

60. See James Dickie, "The Mughal Garden: Gateway to Paradise," *Muqarnas* 3 (1985): 128–37; Elizabeth Moynihan, *Paradise as a Garden* (London: Scolar Press, 1979); Elizabeth MacDougall and Richard Ettinghausen, eds., *The Islamic Garden* (Washington, D.C.: Dumbarton Oaks, 1976); Donald Wilber, *Persian Gardens and Pavilions* (Tokyo and Rutland, Vt.: Charles E. Tuttle, 1962); also Sheila S. Blair and Jonathan Bloom, eds., *Images of Paradise in Islamic Art* (Hanover, N.H.: Hood Museum of Art, 1991).

61. See Nasr, "Sacred Art."

62. L. I. al-Faruqi, passim in works cited above. For a different approach, see Terry Allen, "Aniconism and Figural Representation in Islamic Art," in idem, *Five Essays on Islamic Art* (Manchester, Mich.: Solipsist Press, 1988), 17–37.

63. Deborah Klimburg-Salter, "A Sufi Theme in Persian Painting: The Divan of Sultan Ahmad Galair in the Freer Gallery of Art," *KO* 11 (1976–1977): 43–84.

64. King Khusraw Parwiz's wife, Shirin, had a taste for milk from a herd that grazed in distant mountains. Khusraw hired Farhad to chisel a tunnel through the mountain rock that could carry the milk from the pasture to the palace. One day Shirin went to see how Farhad's work was progressing, and Farhad was smitten with love for her. Learning of this, the jealous king told Farhad that Shirin was dead, and the despondent sculptor flung himself off the mountain to his death.

65. Anthony Welch, *Shah ʿAbbas and the Arts of Isfahan* (New York: Asia Society, 1973), 71, image on 57. On a series of candlesticks apparently depicting scenes of Sufi dancers performing a dhikr, see Eva Baer, "Aspects of Sufi Influence on Iranian Art," *Acta Iranica* 12 (1977): 1–12. Inscriptions support the interpretation; Baer cites one quatrain that reads: "With one's lover a (mystic) dance [samaʿ] is worth a life; The face of a candle is worth a gold mine. A butterfly (or moth), a candle, the *shahid* (beloved youth), a dance and ecstasis with the sound of a flute are worth a Kingship over the world" (4).

66. Toby Falk, ed., *Treasures of Islam* (London: Phillip Wilson, 1985), catalogue item 298, see also items 299 and 300.

67. For a discussion of the celestial symbolism of another type of candlestick, see A. S. Melikian-Chirvani, "The Light of the World," in *The Art of the Saljuqs in Iran and Anatolia,* ed. R. Hillenbrand (Costa Mesa, Calif.: Mazda Publishers, 1994), 146–53.

68. A. S. Melikian-Chirvani, "From the Royal Boat to the Beggar's Bowl," *IA* 4 (1991): 7, 8, 9; see also 3–111.

69. Ibid., 26.

70. Ibid., 32.

71. Ibid., 33.

72. Ibid., 31. For plate and description, see also Falk, *Treasures of Islam*, catalogue item 297.

FIVE. COMMUNITY: SOCIETY, INSTITUTIONS, AND PATRONAGE

1. Oleg Grabar slices the patronage pie somewhat differently, using Ibn Khaldun's more sociological categories—caliphal, urban, and communal: "In a sense the communal patronage operated with the caliphal one as centripetal forces vying to unify among other ways by writing, geometry, or other types of ornament. Local urban patronage may well have been more centrifugal as it sought to emphasize the pride and achievement of an area or person as different from some other one. The tensions between the two are still present today within the Muslim world and they could be as creative now as they have been in the past" ("Patronage in Islamic Art," in *Islamic Art and Patronage*, ed. Esin Atil (New York: Rizzoli International, 1990), 33, see also 27–39).

2. Ira M. Lapidus, "Mamluk Patronage and the Arts in Egypt: Concluding Remarks," *Muqarnas* 2 (1984): 173–81.

3. Ibid., 178.

4. Oleg Grabar, "Reflections on Mamluk Art," *Muqarnas* 2 (1984): 8, see also 1–12; for color plates, see Atil, *Renaissance of Islam*.

5. Erzen, "Aesthetics," 17.

6. Color plates in Atil, *Age of Sultan Süleyman;* J. M. Rogers and R. M. Ward, *Suleyman the Magnificent* (Seacaucus, N.J.: Wellfleet, 1988); Aptullah Kuran, *The Mosque in Early Ottoman Architecture* (Chicago: University of Chicago Press, 1968); and Yanni Petsopoulos, ed., *Tulips, Arabesques and Turbans* (New York: Abbeville Press, 1982).

7. See Thomas Lentz and Glenn Lowry, *Timur and the Princely Vision* (Los Angeles: County Museum of Art, 1989); and Rachel Milstein, "Sufi Elements in the Late Fifteenth Century Painting of Herat," in *Studies in Memory of Gaston Wiet*, ed. Myriam Rosen-Ayalon (Jerusalem: Hebrew University, 1977), 357–69.

8. See Marianna Shreve Simpson, "The Production and Patronage of the *Haft Aurang* by Jami in the Freer Gallery of Art," *AO* 13 (1982): 93–104. Surveys of Safavid art in Welch, *Shah 'Abbas;* and idem, *Artists for the Shah* (New Haven: Yale University Press, 1976).

9. Surveys of Mughal works in Milo C. Beach, *The Grand Mogul: Imperial Painting in India, 1600–1660* (Williamstown, Mass.: Clark Art Institute, 1978); Emmy Wellesz, *Akbar's Religious Thought as Reflected in Mughal Painting* (London: Allen and Unwin, 1952).

10. Leonor Fernandes, "The Foundation of Baybars al-Jashankir: Its Waqf, History, and Architecture," *Muqarnas* 4 (1987): 28–29, see also 21–42; and idem, *The Evolution of a Sufi Institution in Mamluk Egypt: The Khanqah* (Berlin: Klaus Swarz Verlag, 1988), 3–4.

11. See George Makdisi, *The Rise of Colleges* (Edinburgh: Edinburgh University Press, 1981), 35–74; and idem, "Muslim Institutions of Learning in Eleventh-Century Baghdad," *BSOAS* 24, no. 1 (1961): 1–56.

12. See, for example, Renard, *All the King's Falcons*, 46.

13. R. D. McChesney, *Waqf in Central Asia* (Princeton: Princeton University Press, 1991), 7.

14. George Makdisi, "On the Origin and Development of the College in Islam and

the West," in *Islam and the Medieval West,* ed. K. I. Semaan (Albany: State University of New York Press, 1980), 26–49, especially 37, note 47; also George Makdisi, "The Madrasa in Spain: Some Remarks," *Revue de l'occident musulman et de la Méditeranée* (1973): 153–58.

15. Summarized from John R. Barnes, *An Introduction to Religious Foundations in the Ottoman Empire* (Leiden: Brill, 1987), 5–20; see also Doris Behrens-Abouseif, *Egypt's Adjustment to Ottoman Rule: Institutions, Waqf and Architecture in Cairo* (Leiden: Brill, 1994).

16. Makdisi, "Origin and Development," 36. Islamic law makes a distinction between private familial (*ahli*) and public charitable (*khayri*) endowments: the generally smaller, less stable ahli supports family beneficiaries, while the khayri type designates revenues as "endowments to benefit religious or charitable ends" (Gaffney, "Changing voices," 30).

17. Fernandes emphasizes how the introduction of a teaching function into the khanqah setting gave Sufis a measure of respectability among the 'ulama' (*Evolution,* especially 47–95 and passim): "The final integration of Sufism into the official religious sphere would only come, however, with the incorporation of the khutba in the khanqah" (39).

18. Begley and Desai, *Taj Mahal,* 183–84.

19. Wayne E. Begley, *Monumental Islamic Calligraphy from India* (Villa Park, Ill.: Islamic Foundation, 1985), 43.

20. Ibid., 116.

21. Sheila S. Blair, *The Monumental Inscriptions of Early Islamic Iran and Transoxiana* (Leiden: Brill, 1992), 80–81.

22. Nurhan Atasoy, "Dervish Dress and Ritual: The Mevlevi Tradition," in Lifchez, *Dervish Lodge,* 253–68.

23. Klaus Kreiser, "Dervish Living" in Lifchez, *Dervish Lodge,* 53. On various major *dargahs* in India, see Christian Troll, S. J., ed., *Muslim Shrines in India* (Delhi: Oxford University Press, 1989).

24. Lineage matters in the arts also, particularly among calligraphers, as in Wheeler Thackston, ed. and trans. *A Century of Princes* (Cambridge, Mass.: Agha Khan Program for Islamic Architecture, 1989), 340.

25. Fernandes, "Foundation," 25.

26. For example, Abu Najib Suhrawardi's *Sufi Rule for Novices* (*Adab al-muridin*), 'Abdallah Ansari's *Essentials of Sufi Conduct* (*Mukhtasar fi adab as-Sufiya*), Ibn al-'Arabi's *Treatise on Mandatory Comportment for the Aspirant* (*Risala fi kunhi ma la budda minhu li 'l-murid*), Muhammad Chishti's *Conduct of the Seekers* (*Adab at-talibin*), and Sulami's *Comportment for [Spiritual] Companionship* (*Adab as-suhba*).

27. Such as Abu Nasr as-Sarraj's *Book of Light Flashes* (*Kitab al-luma'*), Hujwiri's *Unveiling the Hidden* (*Kashf al-mahjub*), Qushayri's *Treatise on Sufism* (*Risala*), Abu Hafs 'Umar Suhrawardi's *Benefits of Intimate Knowledge* (*'Awarif al-ma'arif*), and Najm ad-Din Daya Razi's *Path of [God's] Servants* (*Mirsad al-'ibad*).

28. Gerhard Böwering, "The Adab Literature of Classical Sufism: Ansari's Code of Conduct," in *Moral Conduct and Authority,* ed. Barbara D. Metcalf (Berkeley: University of California Press, 1984), 79–80, see also 62–87.

29. Ibid., 75.

30. Abu Najib Suhrawardi, *A Sufi Rule for Novices,* trans. M. Milson (Cambridge: Harvard University Press, 1975), 66.

31. Ibn al-'Arabi, "Instructions to a Postulant," in Jeffery, *Reader on Islam,* 645.

32. Samir Khalil, *The Monument: Art, Vulgarity, and Responsibility in Iraq* (Berkeley: University of California Press, 1991).

33. Glenn D. Lowry, "Humayun's Tomb: Form, Function, and Meaning in Early Mughal Architecture," *Muqarnas* 4 (1987): 133–48; see also Dickie, "Mughal Garden," 128–37.

34. See S. C. Welch, *Imperial Mughal Painting* (New York: George Braziller, 1978), plates 21, 22.

35. Ibid., plates 31–32, 36.

36. Amina Okada, *Mughal Miniatures* (New York: Harry N. Abrams, 1992), plates 36, 40.

37. Begley, *Monumental Islamic Calligraphy,* 31.

38. Saleh L. Mostafa, "The Cairene Sabil: Form and Meaning," *Muqarnas* 6 (1989): 35, see also 33–42.

39. Summarized from ibid.

40. See Gary Leiser, "The *Madrasa* and the Islamization of the Middle East: The Case of Egypt," *Journal of the American Research Center in Egypt* 22 (1985): 29–47; and idem, "Notes on the Madrasa in Medieval Islamic Society," *MW* 76, no. 1 (1986): 16–23.

41. Fernandes, *Evolution,* 10–16; see also J. Spencer Trimingham, *The Sufi Orders in Islam* (Oxford: Oxford University Press, 1971). In Malaysia the analog to the Middle Eastern zawiya is the *surau,* a house designed especially for religious rituals; see R. A. Kern, "The Origin of the Malay Surau," *Journal of the Malayan Branch of the Royal Asiatic Society* 19 (1956): 179–81. Muhsin Kayani's study of the khanqah in Iran, *Tarikh-i khanqah dar Iran* (Tehran: Tahouri Books, 1369/1990), gives general background on the khanqah elsewhere in the Islamic world, as well; describes the various permutations of the institution and its relationships to ribats, zawiyas, and other related structures; and discusses foundations belonging to particular orders or associated with individual holy persons.

42. Fernandes, *Evolution,* 16–19.

43. Fernandes, "Foundation," 25.

44. See Saleh L. Mostafa, *Kloster und Mausoleum des Faraj ibn Barquq in Kairo,* Abhandlungen des Deutschen Archäologischen Instituts Kairo, Islamische Reihe, Band 2 (1968); and for a survey of the three types of building, Donald Little, "The Nature of Khanqahs, Ribats, and Zawiyas under the Mamluks," in *Islamic Studies Presented to Charles J. Adams,* ed. Wael Hallaq and Donald Little (Leiden: Brill, 1991), 91–105.

45. See, for example, Hamid Algar, "Some Notes on the Naqshbandi Tariqat in Bosnia," *WI,* n.s., 13, nos. 3–4 (1971): 168–203.

46. On the zawiya of Sadr ad-Din Konawi, a student of Ibn 'Arabi's and contemporary of Rumi, see Suraiya Faroqhi, "Vakif Administration in sixteenth Century Konya" *Journal of the Economic and Social History of the Orient* 17 (1979): 145–72.

47. Godfrey Goodwin, "The Dervish Architecture of Anatolia" in Lifchez, *Dervish Lodge,* 57–69.

48. Raymond Lifchez, "The Lodges of Istanbul," in idem, *Dervish Lodge,* 126, see also 73–129.

49. Lifchez, *Dervish Lodge,* 2–5.

50. Cited in Khaliq A. Nizami, "Some Aspects of Khanqah Life in Medieval India," *SI* 8 (1957): 51–70.

51. For example, McChesney, *Waqf in Central Asia,* 142.

52. Cited in Makdisi, *Rise of Colleges,* 39.

53. Cited in Necipoğlu, "Suleymaniye Complex," 99, 113.

54. Thackston, *Century of Princes,* 332.

55. Erzen, "Aesthetics," 5–6.

56. Ca'fer Effendi, *Risale-i Mi'mariyye,* 53–54.

57. Fernandes, *Evolution*, 29.

58. Robert McChesney, "Four Sources on the Building of Isfahan," *Muqarnas* 5 (1988): 111–12, see also 103–34.

59. Ca'fer Effendi, *Risale-i Mi'mariyye*, 32.

60. Lisa Golombek and Donald Wilber, *The Timurid Architecture of Iran and Turan* (Princeton: Princeton University Press, 1988), 1:57.

61. Tanman, "Settings," 167.

SIX. PEDAGOGY: FANNING SPARK INTO FLAME

1. 'Abd al-Qadir al-Jilani, *The Endowment of Divine Grace and the Spread of Divine Mercy (Al-Fathu Rabbani)*, trans. M. Al-Akili (Philadelphia: Pearl Publishing House, 1990), 1:viii.

2. 'Abd al-Qadir al-Jilani, *Revelations of the Unseen*, trans. Muhtar Holland (Houston: Al-Baz Publishing, 1992), 7.

3. Ibid., 121.

4. Ibid., 56–57.

5. 'Abd al-Qadir al-Jilani, *The Sublime Revelation*, trans. Muhtar Holland (Houston: Al-Baz Publishing, 1992), xiii.

6. *Utterances of Shaykh 'Abd al-Qadir al-Jilani*, trans. Muhtar Holland (Houston: Al-Baz Publishing, 1992), 56.

7. Rizvi, *Sufism in India*, 1:3–8.

8. Rumi, *Signs of the Unseen*, trans. Wheeler Thackston (Putney, Vt.: Threshold, 1994), 1.

9. Ibid., 79. See also *Discourses of Rumi*, 87.

10. See K. A. Nizami, introduction to *Nizam ad-Din Awliya: Morals for the Heart*, trans. Bruce Lawrence (Mahwah, N.J.: Paulist Press, 1992), especially 5–15.

11. Ibid., 65–67.

12. Ibid., 98.

13. Sharaf ad-Din Maneri, *Khwan-i pur ni'mat: A Table Laden with Good Things*, trans. Paul Jackson, S. J. (Delhi: Idarah-i Adabiyat-i Delli, 1986), 1.

14. Ibid., 20.

15. Ibid., 101–108, examples from assembly 29.

16. Ibid., 98.

17. G. W. J. Drewes, ed. and trans., *The Admonitions of Seh Bari* (The Hague: Martinus Nijhoff, 1969), 97.

18. Similar material from a twentieth-century West African figure in Louis Brenner, *West African Sufi: The Religious Heritage and Spiritual Search of Cerno Bokar Saalif Taal* (Berkeley: University of California Press, 1984), 142–86, where Cerno Bokar's teaching discourses are discussed and translated.

19. See J. D. Latham, "The Beginnings of Arabic Prose Literature: The Epistolary Genre," in Beeston et al., *Arabic Literature*, 155–64.

20. Abdul Qayyum, *The Letters of al-Ghazzali* (Lahore: Islamic Publications, 1976), ix.

21. Ibid., 27–28.

22. *Ibn 'Abbad of Ronda: Letters on the Sufi Path*, trans. John Renard (New York: Paulist Press, 1986), 125–26. On modern North African figures, see *Letters of a Sufi Master: The Shaikh Al-'Arabi ad-Darqawi*, trans. T. Burckhardt (London: Perennial Books, 1969); and *The Letters of Ahmad ibn Idris*, ed. E. Thomassen and B. Radtke (Evanston, Ill.: Northwestern University Press, 1993).

23. Sharaf ad-Din Maneri, *The Hundred Letters*, trans. Paul Jackson (New York: Paulist Press, 1980), 10. On letters of analogous context in Turkey, see William Chittick, "Sultan Burhan al-Din's Sufi Correspondence," *Wiener Zeitschrift für die Kunde des Morgenlandes* 73 (1981): 33–45.

24. Bruce Lawrence, foreword to Maneri, *Hundred Letters*, xviii–xix.

25. Schimmel, *Mystical Dimensions of Islam*, 367–69.

26. Muhammad Abdul Haqq Ansari, *Sufism and Shariʻah: A Study of Shaykh Ahmad Sirhindi's Effort to Reform Sufism* (Leicester: Islamic Foundation, 1986), 244–45.

27. Ibid., 233.

28. A. H. Abdel-Kader, *The Life, Personality and Writings of al-Junayd* (London: Luzac, 1976), xvii–xviii.

29. Ibid., 27–28.

30. A. G. Ravan Farhadi, "The *Hundred Grounds* of ʻAbdullah Ansari (d. 448/1056) of Herat: The Earliest Mnemonic Sufi Manual in Persian," in *Classical Persian Sufism from Its Origins to Rumi*, ed. Leonard Lewisohn (London: Khaniqahi Nimatullahi Publications, 1993), 388–89, 396–97; see also 381–99. Also ʻAbdallah Ansari, *Sad Maidan: Hundred Fields between Man and God*, trans. Munir Ahmad Mughal (Lahore: Islamic Book Foundation, 1983).

31. Serge de Beaurecueil, *Ansari: Chemin de dieu* (Paris: Sindbad, 1985), 154.

32. Chittick, *Faith*, 35–36.

33. Ibid., 55.

34. Ibid., 59.

35. Ibid., 103.

36. Bruce Lawrence, *Notes from a Distant Flute* (Tehran: Imperial Iranian Academy of Philosophy, 1978), 36–37.

37. Drewes, *Admonitions*, 115.

38. Ibid., 117.

39. Ibid., 91. The translator notes: "Perhaps the meaning of this passage is that ritual prayer is incumbent on the true believer at every stage of his spiritual progress: dogmatic belief, faith, confession of unity, and mystical knowledge. If, however, the believer has not proceeded to the stage of tawhid, then he may be considered a polytheist, as the uniqueness of the Supreme Being is not yet fully understood. . . . On the other hand, should iman [faith] be lacking, then the person in question is an unbeliever" (91).

40. G. W. J. Drewes, ed. and trans. *Directions for Travellers on the Mystic Path* (The Hague: Martinus Nijhoff, 1977), 107.

41. Ibid., 117.

42. *"Kitab al-lumaʻ fi 't-tasawwuf" of Abu Nasr al-Sarraj*, ed. R. A. Nicholson (London: Luzac, 1963).

43. Abu Bakr al-Kalabadhi, *The Doctrine of the Sufis*, trans. A. J. Arberry (1935; reprint, Cambridge: Cambridge University Press, 1978), 3.

44. Ibid., 4.

45. Ibid., 166.

46. ʻAli ibn ʻUthman al-Hujwiri, *Kashf al-mahjub*, trans. R. A. Nicholson (London: Luzac, 1976), 6–7.

47. Ibid., 267–277, 393–420.

48. *"Principles of Sufism" by Al-Qushayri*, trans. Barbara von Schlegell (Berkeley: Mazda Press, 1990), 1–2, 7.

49. Arabic text used is Abu Talib al-Makki, *Qut al-qulub* (Cairo: Al-Matbaʻat al-Maymaniya, 1306/1889).

50. Arabic text in Abu Hamid al-Ghazali, *Ihya' 'Ulum ad-Din* (Beirut: Dar al-Kutub al-'Ilmiya, n.d.), 5:51–342.

51. A magical cup that allowed the Iranian king Jamshid to view all of reality at a glance.

52. Najm ad-Din Daya Razi, *The Path of God's Bondsmen from Origin to Return,* trans. Hamid Algar (Delmar, N.Y.: Caravan Books, 1982), 38. I have translated the title of this work as *Path of [God's] Servants.*

53. Ehsan Yarshater, preface to ibid.

54. Razi, *Path of God's Bondsmen,* 490–91.

55. Carl Ernst, "Mystical Language and the Teaching Context in the Early Lexicons of Sufism," in *Mysticism and Language,* ed. Steven Katz (New York: Oxford University Press, 1992), 187, see also 181–201.

56. Kalabadhi, *Doctrine of the Sufis,* 104.

57. Ibid., 120.

58. Ernst, "Mystical Language," 199.

59. "*Kitab al-luma',*" 335 (Arabic text, 333–74).

60. Hujwiri, *Kashf al-mahjub,* 366, 387, 371; see also 366–92. Qushayri borrows freely from Sarraj for his 102 terms (apart from those scattered elsewhere in the work); see Qushayri, *Risala* (Cairo, 1967), chapter 2, 21–151. Abu Hafs 'Umar Suhrawardi's *Benefits of Intimate Knowledge* (*'Awarif al-ma'arif*) includes both descriptions of terms illustrated by citations of earlier Sufi shaykhs and shorter one-line definitions of individual concepts and clusters of related terms (such as *intoxication* and *sobriety*); text of *Benefits* in A. H. Ghazali, *Ihya' 'Ulum ad-Din,* chapter 62, 5:330–334.

61. From Arabic text in *Ihya',* 5:18, see also 15–49.

62. Ernst, "Mystical Language," 185.

63. Ibn 'Arabi, *What the Seeker Needs,* trans. Rabia Terri Harris (London: Threshold, 1992), 89.

64. Ibid., 91.

65. 'Abd ar-Razzaq al-Kashani, *A Glossary of Sufi Technical Terms,* trans. Nabil Safwat (London: Octagon Press, 1991), 49.

66. Ibid., 26.

67. Ja'far Sajjadi, *Farhang-i lughat va istilahat* (Tehran: Tahouri Books, 1369/1990), 92.

68. Javad Nurbakhsh, ed., *Sufi Symbolism,* 10 vols. (London: Khaniqahi-Nimatullahi Publications, 1984–), 1:134–35.

69. Jean-Louis Michon, ed. and trans. *Le Soufi marocain Ahmad ibn 'Ajiba et son mi'raj: Glossaire de la mystique musulmane* (Paris: J. Vrin, 1973), 139.

70. Ibid., 179.

71. Ibid., 261–62.

72. Ibid., 140–47; for French translation of 'Ajiba's glossary, see 175–269.

SEVEN. EXPERIENCE: TESTIMONY, PARADIGM, AND CRITIQUE

1. Cemal Kafadar, "Self and Others: The Diary of a Dervish in Seventeenth Century Istanbul and First-Person Narratives in Ottoman Literature," *SI* 69 (1989): 128, see also 121–50.

2. Richard McCarthy, S. J., trans., *Freedom and Fulfillment* (Boston: Twayne Publishers, 1980), 63. This work comprises translations of several works by Abu Hamid al-Ghazali.

3. Ibid., 89–90. On other aspects of the spiritual life story, see Ira M. Lapidus, "Adulthood in Islam: Religious Maturity in the Islamic Tradition," *Daedalus* 105, no. 2 (1976): 93–107.

4. Eric Ormsby, "The Taste of Truth: The Structure of Experience in al-Ghazali's *Al-Munqidh min al-Dalal*," in Hallaq and Little, *Islamic Studies*, 134, see also 133–52.

5. Text of Tirmidhi's *Bad' Sha'ni* in Osman Yahya, ed., *Khatm al-awliya'* (Beirut: Imprimerie Catholique, 1965), especially 14–33; see also Nicholas L. Heer, "Some Biographical and Bibliographical Notes on Al-Hakim al-Tirmidhi," in *The World of Islam: Studies in Honor of Philip K. Hitti*, ed. James Kritzeck and R. Bayly Winder (London: Macmillan, 1960), 121–34; and Muhammad al-Geyoushi, "Al-Tirmidhi's Theory of Saints and Sainthood," *Islamic Quarterly* 15 (1971): 17–61, especially 50–51.

6. *A Sufi Martyr: The Apologia of 'Ain al-Qudat al-Hamadhani*, trans. A. J. Arberry (London: Allen and Unwin, 1969), 69.

7. J. -L. Michon, ed. and trans., "L'Autobiographie *(fahrasa)* du soufi marocain Ahmad ibn 'Ajiba (1747–1809)," parts 1–4, *Arabica* 15 (1968): 225–69; 16 (1969): 25–64, 113–54, 225–68.

8. Tosun Bayrak, introduction to 'Abd al-Qadir al-Jilani, *The Secret of Secrets (Sirr al-asrar)* (Cambridge, England: Islamic Texts Society, 1992), xv–xvii.

9. M. Ansari, *Sufism and Shari'ah*, 203.

10. Ibid., 205–6, summary from 203–5.

11. Syed Naguib al-Attas, *Some Aspects of Sufism as Understood and Practiced among the Malays* (Singapore: Malaysian Sociological Research Institute, 1963), 52–55.

12. Jonathan Katz, "Visionary Experience, Autobiography, and Sainthood in North African Islam," *Princeton Papers in Near Eastern Studies* 1 (1992): 85–118; on dream accounts in the Ottoman context, see Kafadar, "Self and Others," 130.

13. Henry Corbin, *Avicenna and the Visionary Recital*, trans. Willard R. Trask (New York: Pantheon Books, 1960), 4–5. Corbin notes that "[i]t appears that henceforth we must cease to separate the history of philosophy from the history of spirituality. Philosophy itself is only a partial symptom of the secret that transcends all rational statements and that tends to express itself in what we may comprehensively term a spirituality, which includes all the phenomena and expressions of the religious consciousness" (16).

14. Ibid., 15.

15. Ibid., 123–64, with translation of text 137–50, and of commentary thereon, 282–380; and Heath, *Allegory*, 35–48.

16. Translation in Corbin, *Avicenna*, 186–92; see also Heath, *Allegory*, 176–79.

17. Heath, *Allegory*, 94.

18. For summary and analysis, see Corbin, *Avicenna*, 204–41; and Heath, *Allegory*, 94–96.

19. *The Mystical and Visionary Treatises of Suhrawardi*, trans. W. M. Thackston (London: Octagon, 1982), 5.

20. Ibid., 10.

21. Summarized and quoted in ibid., 35–43.

22. Corbin, *Avicenna*, 33, 166.

23. Ibn Sina's Persian *Mi'rajnama* is a commentary on a narrative of Muhammad's Ascension, whereas the present works either retell that story or reinterpret it as a paradigm of the narrator's own experience; see Heath, *Allegory*, 109–43.

24. See, for example, Noble Ross Reat, "Tree Symbolism in Islam," *Studies in Comparative Religion* 9 (1975): 164–82.

25. Arthur Jeffery, "Ibn al-'Arabi's *Shajarat al-Kawn*," *SI* 10 (1959): 43–77; 11 (1959): 113–60, especially 136–58 (quotation from 158).

26. James W. Morris, "The Spiritual Ascension: Ibn 'Arabi and the Mi'raj," parts 1–2, *JAOS* 107, no. 4 (1987): 629–52; 108, no. 1 (1988): 77, see also 63–77.

27. R. A. Nicholson, "An Early Arabic Version of the *Mi'raj* of Abu Yazid al-Bistami," *Islamica* 2 (1926): 402–15; and Earle Waugh, "Following the Beloved: Muhammad as Model in the Sufi Tradition," in *The Biographical Process,* ed. Frank Reynolds and Donald Capps (The Hague: Mouton, 1976), 63–85. Waugh observes that the "shape of his [the Sufi's] inner experience is cast by an internalization of the mythic pattern, interpreted through existential categories and, in turn, making new kinds of demands" (75).

28. Muhammad Iqbal, *Javid-Nama,* trans. A. J. Arberry (London: Allen and Unwin, 1966), 140. The title plays on the name of Iqbal's son, Javid.

29. E. E.Cummings, *Complete Poems, 1913–1962* (San Diego:Harvest Books, 1963), 366.

30. "*Kitab al-luma',*" 337.

31. Ahmad Ghazali, *Sawanih: Inspirations from the World of Pure Spirits,* trans. Nasrollah Pourjavady (London: KPI, 1986), 15; see also *Ahmad Ghazzali: Gedanken über die Liebe,* trans. Richard Gramlich (Mainz: Akademie der Wissenschaften und der Literatur, 1976), 7.

32. Nasrollah Pourjavady, commentary on A. Ghazali, *Sawanih,* 89–90.

33. A. Ghazali, *Sawanih,* 65.

34. Since Ibn 'Arabi's chapters number twenty-seven, the correspondence is not perfect; see *Ibn al-'Arabi: "The Bezels of Wisdom,"* trans. R. W. J. Austin (New York: Paulist Press, 1980).

35. *Fakhruddin 'Iraqi: "Divine Flashes,"* trans. William Chittick and Peter Lamborn Wilson (New York: Paulist Press, 1982), 70–71.

36. Ibid., 81.

37. Ibid., 124–26. "Show us things as they are" is a saying of Muhammad's popular among Sufis.

38. *Ibn 'Ata' Allah: "The Book of Wisdom,"* trans. Victor Danner (New York: Paulist Press, 1978), 71, 68.

39. Martin Lings, *A Sufi Saint of the Twentieth Century* (Berkeley: University of California Press, 1973), 206.

40. Ibid., 213. I have changed "thy" to "your."

41. Ibid., 208–9. Again I have taken the liberty of modifying the translator's more archaic forms.

42. For helpful comparative discussion of these forms, see Carl Ernst, *Words of Ecstasy in Sufism* (Albany: State University of New York Press, 1985), 133–45.

43. "*Kitab al-luma',*" 375–76.

44. Story cited in Ernst, *Words of Ecstasy,* 26.

45. See Hellmut Ritter, "Die Aussprüche des Bayezid Bistami," in *Westöstliche Abhandlungen,* ed. Fritz Meier (Wiesbaden: Otto Harrassowitz, 1954), 231–43.

46. My translation. *Hallaj, Diwan,* 45, poem no. 17, lines 6–8.

47. My translation. *The "Mawaqif" and "Mukhatabat" of Muhammad ibn 'Abdi'l-Jabbar an-Niffari with Other Fragments,* trans. A. J. Arberry (London: Luzac, 1935), from Arabic text, 138.

48. My translation. Ibid., from Arabic text, 148.

49. My translation. Ibid., from Arabic text, 200–201.

50. Emir Abd el-Kader, *Ecrits spirituels,* trans. Michel Chodkiewicz (Paris: Editions du Seuil, 1982), 45. My translation is from Chodkiewicz's French, including the terms in brackets; an English translation of the work was published in 1995.

51. "*Kitab al-luma',*" 375–435; Ernst, *Words of Ecstasy,* 13.

52. Henry Corbin, ed., *Commentaire sur les paradoxes des soufis* (Paris: Adrien-Maisonneuve, 1966).

53. Translation in Ernst, *Words of Ecstasy,* 16.

54. Ibid., 18–20; Corbin, *Commentaire,* introduction and 8–19. In chapter 1, I discuss the various levels of interpretation and meaning in the scripture.

55. Hallag: *"Kitab al-tawasin,"* ed. Paul Nwyia *Mélanges de l'Université Saint-Joseph* 47 (1972): 197–98, see also 185–237; diagrams on 197, 200, 211, 212, 213, 214, 215. See also *The Tawasin of Mansur al-Hallaj,* trans. 'A'isha 'Abd ar-Rahman (Berkeley: Diwan Press, 1974).

56. Louis Massignon, ed., *Kitab al-tawasin* (Paris: Librairie Paul Geuthner, 1913), 81–83.

57. M. Ansari, *Sufism and Shari'ah,* 188–200.

58. See Peter Awn, *Satan's Tragedy and Redemption: Iblis in Sufi Psychology* (Leiden: Brill, 1983), 64 ff.

59. See Paul Jackson, S.J., "Spiritual Guidance in the Islamic Tradition, I," and John Renard, "Spiritual Guidance in the Islamic Tradition, II," in *Traditions of Spiritual Guidance,* ed. Lavinia Byrne (London: Geoffrey Chapman, 1990), 188–210.

60. Razi, *Path of God's Bondsmen,* 52.

61. Ibid., 124–31.

62. Ibid., 225–26.

63. Ibid., 231.

64. Ibid., 235–332. For a contemporary Muslim's description of the experience of spiritual guidance, see Frances Trix, *Spiritual Discourse: Learning with an Islamic Master* (Philadelphia: University of Pennsylvania Press, 1993); for a detailed analysis of an early modern Iranian Shi'i spiritual guide, see Michel de Miras, *La Méthode spirituelle d'un maître du soufisme iranien Nur 'Ali-Shah* (Paris: Les Editions du Sirac, 1974).

REPRISE: JOSEPH OF THE SEVEN DOORS

1. For a useful pedagogical approach to the story, see James Morris, "Dramatizing the Sura of Joseph: An Introduction to the Islamic Humanities," in Maria Eva Subtelny, ed., *Journal of Turkish Studies: Annemarie Schimmel Festschrift* 18 (1994): 201–24.

2. A. Yusuf Ali, trans., *An Interpretation of the Holy Qur-an* (Lahore: Sh. Muhammad Ashraf, 1975), 313.

3. Mustansir Mir, "The Qur'anic Story of Joseph: Plot, Themes, and Characters," *MW* 76, no. 1 (January 1986): 1–15; see also Anthony H. Johns, "Joseph in the Qur'an: Dramatic Dialogue, Human Emotion, and Prophetic Wisdom," *Islamochristiana* 7 (1981): 29–51; M. S. Stern, "Muhammad and Joseph: A Study of Koranic Narrative," *JNES* 44, no. 3 (July 1985): 193–204; Marilyn Waldman, "New Approaches to the 'Biblical' Materials in the Qur'an," *MW* 75, no. 1 (January 1985): 1–16; Gary A. Rendsburg, "Literary Structures in the Qur'anic and Biblical Stories of Joseph," *MW* 78, no. 2 (April 1988): 118–120; for a more explicitly comparative approach, see M. A. S. Adel Haleem, "The Story of Joseph in the Qur'an and the Old Testament," *Islam and Christian-Muslim Relations* 1, no. 2 (1990): 171–91; John Macdonald, "Joseph in the Qur'an," *MW* 46, no. 2 (1956): 113–31; and for a study of Moses from a similar comparative perspective, see Muhib O. Opeloye, "Confluence and Conflict in the Qur'anic and Biblical Accounts of the Life of Prophet Musa," *Islamochristiana* 16 (1990): 25–41.

Though the Qur'anic account has naturally provided the most widely known version of the Joseph story throughout the Islamic world, other variants demonstrate the importance of the story far from the land of Islam's Arabic roots. Wherever the story has been told, elements that represent regional influences have been included. The Malay counterpart, called the *Story of Joseph* (*Hikayat Yusof*), includes a number of biblical details not found in the Qur'anic account. In the Malay version the biblical name "Potiphar" appears, not "'Aziz" as in the Qur'an, and Potiphar's wife is called and Asnath instead of Ra'il or Zulaykha (as in most later Islamic texts). In the Malay version the brothers tell Jacob his beloved son has been devoured by a tiger rather than by a wolf; see Hamid, *Arabic and Islamic Literary Tradition*, 125, 150. There is also a famous Swahili epic dedicated to the story of Joseph, *Utenzi wa Yusupu*, see Jan Knappert, *Four Swahili Epics* (Leiden: Drukkerij "Luctor et Emerigo," 1964), 9–58.

 4. Pelly, *Miracle Play*, 1:1–18, 2:326–46.

 5. "*Kitab al-luma*'," Arabic text, 100–101.

 6. Nizam al-Mulk, *Book of Government*, 12.

 7. Razi, *Path of God's Bondsmen*, 228.

 8. Maneri, *Khwan-i pur ni'mat*, 84–86.

 9. *Utterances of Shaikh 'Abd al-Qadir al-Jilani*, 53.

 10. A. Day, "Islam and Literature in South-East Asia," in *Islam in South-East Asia*, ed. M. B. Hooker (Leiden: Brill, 1983), 157–59.

 11. Maneri, *Khwan-i pur ni'mat*, 66–71.

 12. Meisami, *Sea of Precious Virtues*, 313.

 13. John Bowen, *Muslims through Discourse: Religion and Ritual in Gayo Society* (Princeton: Princeton University Press, 1993), 89.

 14. *Mystical and Visionary Treatises*, 71, summary from 62–75.

 15. "*Principles of Sufism*," 339–40.

 16. Jami, *Yusuf and Zulaykha*, trans. David Pendlebury (London: Octagon, 1980), 7–8.

 17. Ibid., 81.

 18. Ibid., 136.

 19. Ernst, "Spirit of Islamic Calligraphy," 282; see also 279–86. See also Hortense Reintjens, "Der Schoene Joseph," *Journal of Turkish Studies: Annemarie Schimmel Festschrift* 18 (1994): 225–38.

 20. Thackston, *Century of Princes*, 336–38.

 21. Rainer Maria Rilke, *Duino Elegies*, trans. David Young (New York: W. W. Norton, 1978), 19, elegy 1, ll. 4–5.

 22. Thackston, *Century of Princes*, 338.

 23. Marianna Shreve Simpson, "Production and Patronage," 100, see also 93–119.

 24. Razi, *Path of God's Bondsmen*, 12, 48–49. John Bowen notes an analogous connection between the story of an important ancestor of the Sumatran society of Isak, Merah Mege, and that of Joseph: "the youngest of seven brothers, he was cast into a pit and left for dead. . . . He was rescued, and the other brothers fled, to found kingdoms on the Achenese coast" ("Graves, Shrines, and Power in a Highland Sumatran Society," in Smith and Ernst, *Manifestations of Sainthood*, 8).

 25. J. M. S. Baljon, trans., *A Mystical Interpretation of Prophetic Tales by an Indian Muslim* (Leiden: Brill, 1973), 23. The translator shows an evident Jungian tilt in his choice of technical equivalents.

 26. Razi, *Path of God's Bondsmen*, 240.

 27. Meisami, *Sea of Precious Virtues*, 18.

 28. Jilani, *Revelations of the Unseen*, 67–68.

 29. Qur'an 12:100; and *Letters of Ahmad ibn Idris*, 133–35.

 30. J. M. S. Baljon, *Religion and Thought of Shah Wali Allah Dihlawi, 1703–1762* (Leiden: Brill, 1986), 110, 112, 119.

 31. *Sufi Martyr*, 36.

32. Annemarie Schimmel, "Yusuf in Mawlana Rumi's Poetry," in *The Legacy of Medieval Persian Sufism,* ed. L. Lewisohn (London: Khaniqahi Nimutullahi Publications, 1992), 47.

33. *Mystical Poems of Rumi,* trans. A. J. Arberry (Chicago: University of Chicago Press, 1968), 45; see further, for example, Renard, *All the King's Falcons,* 59–66; and Annemarie Schimmel, *A Two-Colored Brocade* (Chapel Hill: University of North Carolina Press, 1992), 64–68.

Select Glossary

adab	civility, good upbringing, and courtesy; took on the meaning of liberal education; also the knowledge needed to perform a certain function, especially the behavior expected of a member of a Sufi organization; and fine literature in general.
adhkar	the plural form of *dhikr*, which refers to supplication and is very similar in meaning to *du'a'*.
andarz	a Persian term for the genre commonly called sapiental literature, which can be poetry, prose, anecdote, or moralizing reflection.
asitane	Turkish, the principal facility of a particular Sufi order.
aya (*pl.,* ayat)	a sign; also a verse of the Qur'an.
ayatullah	"sign of God," an honorific title.
badal (*pl.,* abdal)	"substitute," a term of Sufi doctrine that teaches that the cosmic order is preserved by a fixed number of saints, and that therefore when a holy man dies, his place is immediately filled by a substitute. *Abdal* means "appearance" or "emergence," and refers to the emergence of new circumstances that causes a change in an earlier divine ruling.
baqa'	"survival," a Sufi technical term that refers to the mystic's eternal "abiding" with God.
baraka	God's blessing; spiritual power.
batin	interior, esoteric, or hidden meaning.
chilla	a forty-day retreat often taken by Sufis for spiritual instruction and meditation.
dede	Turkish, "elder," one of the ranks of the Mevlevi order of Sufism.
dergah	Persian, a tekke with the tomb of a founder adjacent to it.
dhawq	"taste," the direct quality of a mystic experience; insight or intuitive apprehension.
dhikr	"recollection, mentioning or remembering God," a form of prayer to God with certain fixed phrases, repeated in a ritual order, either aloud or mentally, and which is a central part of Sufi spirituality. By extension also the formal ritual ceremony that derives from the practice of "mentioning."
du'a'	literally, "calling"; calling upon God in supplication or petition. A spontaneous and personal prayer as distinct from the ritual prayer of salat.

durud	an important devotional literary form consisting of litanies on various important events in the life of the Prophet invoking blessings on him.
fana'	"passing away, extinction," a Sufi term for the annihilation of the ego or ceasing to "be" before attaining final union with God; a correlative of baqa'.
faqir	"poor person," in Sufism used to denote both physical and spiritual poverty.
faqih (*pl.*, fuqaha')	jurist, legal scholar.
gharad	the third section of the lyric literary form of qasida, put into service as a vehicle for praising God, in which the main theme of the poem is presented.
ghazal	"song, elegy of love," a lyric poetic form often used by mystics to express allegorically the mystic's intimate relation with the divine.
gunbad	the design of a dome from which a building takes its name; funerary architecture.
hadith	"report, news, event, tradition," a literary form that communicates the Sunna of the Prophet, his sayings and deeds; the sayings attributed to the imams; and Sacred Hadith, sayings attributed to God but held distinct from Qur'anic revelation.
hadra	the realm of spiritual presence.
hajj	pilgrimage to Mecca during the twelveth lunar month.
hal (*pl.*, ahwal)	a spiritual "state" along the path of spiritual maturation that is given immediately and momentarily by divine grace, and that tends to be highly charged and short-lived.
hali	"emotional, mystical." This is an adjectival cognate of *hal.*
Hanafi	the Sunni school of law named after Abu Hanifa (699–767).
Hanbali	the Sunni school of law named after Ahmad ibn Hanbal (780–855).
haqiqa	"truth, ultimate reality," the final goal of mystical journey.
hawd	the drinking trough often constructed by means of charitable endowment (waqf).
hayrat	the state of wonder experienced in the mystical contemplation of God.
hikam	maxims that embody a practical wisdom and are "lived out" in everyday life. The singular form, *hikma,* means "wisdom," specifically, wisdom that has attained maturity. *Hikma* has also come to mean "guidance for appropriate behavior, general moral exhortation."

hikaya
(*pl.,* hikayat)
: "story, narrative," often refers to shorter literary works dedicated to the tale of a single prophet, holy person, or heroic figure; also visionary recital.

hilya
: "ornament," a litany invoking blessing upon the Prophet, focusing on his extraordinary physical and spiritual attributes. This form was used in decorative calligraphic renderings of Muhammad's unique qualities.

hizb
(*pl.,* ahzab)
: a type of litany or lengthy invocatory prayer.

hudur
: the experiential "presence" of God in the life of the mystic.

hujjat waqf
: the legal document by which a person establishes a waqf.

hukm
: "legal judgment," the act by which the mind affirms or denies one thing with regard to another.

huzn
: Sadness arising from the profound and moving intimation of one's frail and mortal humanity in awe before the transcendent God, especially in recitation of Qur'an.

'ibadat
(*sg.,* 'ibada)
: "deeds of worshipfulness," the whole complex of ritual and devotional acts that describe or acknowledge the human posture of servanthood before a divine master.

'Id al-adha
: the feast of sacrifice during the Hajj season.

'Id al-fitr
: the festival celebrating the end of the month of Ramadan.

'idgah
: building or open-air space; feast place to celebrate 'Id al-adha and 'Id al-fitr.

i'jaz
: a term that refers to the uniqueness and inimitability of Qur'an in content and form.

ijma'
: consensus; one of the four roots of Islamic religious law; the general agreement of the recognized religious authorities or of the *umma* on a regulation given by God.

'ilm
: discursive "knowledge," especially that of a religious character, as distinct from experiential knowledge.

'ilm ar-rijal
: the study of persons mentioned in the isnads of the hadiths.

imam
: "leader," one who leads the community in the daily salat; for Shi'i Muslims a spiritual descendant of Muhammad.

imami
: Shi'i followers of twelve imams, called Twelvers.

injil
: Gospel, the revelation transmitted by Jesus; also extended to include the whole New Testament scriptures of Christians.

ishara
(*pl.,* isharat)
: a term used in Sufism indicating an "allusion" from a text of Qur'an to a greater reality that is inexpressible in ordinary human language.

islam	"surrender," from the root *slm*, "wholeness, completeness, integration," which Muslims believe is found only when one surrenders oneself to God.
isma'ili	Shi'i followers of seven imams, called Seveners.
isnad	the "chain of authorities" who testify to the veracity of the transmitters of the sayings of Muhammad.
isra'	Muhammad's Night Journey.
istilahat	the lexicon or glossary of mystical terminology used by the Sufis.
iwan	in medieval times, one of the halls in a madrasa or mosque.
jama'at khana	"gathering house," Sufi residential facility.
jami'	a large, congregational mosque.
jihad	"striving, exertion," all striving in the way of God; struggle both against outside injustice and for personal spiritual discipline.
jinn	"creatures of smokeless fire" who are often mischievous.
Ka'ba	"cube," the main Islamic sanctuary in Mecca.
kahin	a "soothsayer, seer," especially in pre-Islamic Arabia.
karamat	wonders worked by nonprophets, for example, Friends of God.
Karbala	a place in Iraq some sixty miles south-southwest of Baghdad, where Muhammad's grandson Husayn was killed and buried.
kashkul	a Persian word for the oval begging bowl in which dervishes put the alms and food they receive.
khalifa	caliph, leader of the Muslim community.
khalwa	isolation in a solitary place or cell for spiritual exercises; retreat.
khanqah	a building used as a residence for members of Muslim confraternities.
khatib	the preacher who delivers the sermon (khutba) at the Friday salat.
Khawarij	Kharijites (seceders), a strict sect of early Islam; early Islamic puritans.
khawatir (*sg.*, khatir)	"random thoughts," one form of inner movement to be sorted out in spiritual experience.
khirqa	the coarse woolen robe worn by Sufis as an outward sign of their poverty.
khutba	the sermon preached at the Friday midday salat.

kulah	Persian, a felt hat worn by Sufi dervishes.
kursi	A footstool, chair, or throne; in Qur'an 2:256 and 38:33, refers to the "throne" of God and a throne of King Solomon, respectively; also a stand for holding Qur'ans.
madhhab	"way of acting, procedure," came to refer to a law school or methodology for the study of Islamic law.
madih	a poem of praise directed to a living person.
madrasa	"place to study," college where Islamic law is studied.
makan	"place," a mystical term that indicates a level of spiritual experience.
maktubat	"letters," a genre of epistolary literature for communicating spiritual teaching.
malfuz (*pl.*, malfuzat)	a literary genre that consists of the collected discourses of a spiritual leader; sayings, utterances, or informal discourses originally delivered orally and later collected by a teacher's disciples.
Maliki	a school of Islamic law named after Malik Ibn Anas (715–795).
manaqib	a collection of laudatory biographical works that have become part of Islamic hagiographic literature.
mansukh	a term used by Qur'an interpreters to indicate that a text has been "abrogated."
manzil	"stage," place along the spiritual journey.
maqam (*pl.*, maqamat)	the "stations" of spiritual maturity that arise as a result of human effort and are lasting in duration.
ma'rifa	intimate mystical knowledge.
marthiya	an elegy composed to lament the passing of a loved one or to celebrate his or her merits, especially in the case of a martyr; dirge poetry.
masjid	"place of prostration," a mosque.
mathnawi	a didactic poem written in rhyming couplets whose content is generally romantic, ethical, or mystical.
matn	the body of text of a hadith. A hadith is composed of an isnad and a matn.
maw'iza	a brief section of the Friday midday sermon devoted to moral exhortation.
mawlid (*pl.*, mawalid)	the celebration of the birthday of Muhammad or a famous saint.
mihrab	the niche in the wall of a mosque that indicates the direction of Mecca.

minaret	the cylindrical or polygonal tower attached to a mosque, from which the call to prayer emanates.
minbar	a raised pulpit in a congregational mosque from which the preacher (khatib) delivers the Friday sermon (khutba).
miʿraj	"ascension," especially the Ascension of Muhammad into heaven. In a spiritual sense, also the goal of a Muslim pilgrim to transcend self-centeredness.
muʿamalat	acts governing interpersonal relations, as distinguished in Islamic law from acts of service to God.
muezzin	the person who intones the call to the five daily ritual prayers.
mufassir	one who interprets the Qurʾan.
muhip	"sympathizer," one of the ranks in the Mevlevi order of Sufism.
muhkamat	a term referring to verses (ayat) of the Qurʾan that are clear and unambiguous.
muʿjiza (*pl.*, muʿjizat)	prophetic "evidentiary miracles."
munajat	literally, "intimate conversations; whispered prayers"; a technical term of Islamic mysticism indicating personal extempore prayer.
munazila	"abode," a level of spiritual experience.
muraqqaʿa	the patched garment often worn by Sufis.
murid	"seeker, aspirant, Sufi disciple," one desiring to be guided in a spiritual path by a master.
musalla	literally, "a place for prayer"; a type of building smaller than a congregational mosque (jamiʿ), akin to an oratory.
mushahada	contemplation, attention to inner experience.
mushkilat	"technical terms," terms that are used in mystical pedagogical literature.
mutashabihat	a term that refers to verses (ayat) of the Qurʾan that are less clear and whose full understanding only God knows.
nabi (*pl.*, anbiyaʾ)	a prophet of God.
nafs	"soul" or "self," frequently used in the negative sense of "lower self."
nasib	a technical term in Arabic poetry referring to the opening segment of a qasida in which the poet laments the loss of a longtime friend or expresses grief over distance from the beloved.

nasikh	a term used by Qur'an interpreters to refer to a text that "abrogates" another.
naʿt	"qualities, attributes," a panegyric poem that extols the wonders and virtues of the Muhammad.
niyya	intention.
pir	Persian for "elder," a spiritual guide in Sufism.
pishtaq	Persian, a large rectangular facade often found in Iranian architecture.
qasida	one of the three major lyric forms, whose chief subject is the lover-beloved relationship.
qibla	the direction of Mecca, toward which Muslims orient themselves in salat.
qisas (*sg.*, qissa)	stories that recount events from the lives of prophets, as in *qisas al-anbiya*,' "stories of the prophets." Qussas: professional storytellers, especially during medieval times.
qiyas	"analogical reasoning," a legal term.
qubba	"dome; cupola," by extension, a domed structure, typically erected over the burial site of a saint.
qur'an	"recitation," especially of the Islamic scriptures. Qur'an: the Islamic scripture itself.
Quraysh	the leading tribe in Mecca at the time of Muhammad, who was a member of the Quraysh clan of Banu Hashim.
qussas	*see* qisas.
qutb	the cosmic axis of the universe; a title given to some major spiritual leader.
rahil	the second section of the classical qasida, the "journey" in search of the departed one, which can become an image of spiritual pilgrimage.
rahl	literally, "camel saddle," which refers to a Qur'an stand that resembles such a saddle.
rasul (*pl.*, rusul)	a messenger of God.
ribat	originally a military outpost or fort on the boundaries of a Muslim country; came to mean a Sufi retreat center used for spiritual enrichment and devotion.
risala	as a theological term, messengership or the mission of a prophet-messenger; as a literary term, treatise, and an imaginative and formally cohesive narrative structure. The plural form, *rasa'il*, means "letters."
ritha'	a panegyric poem in the form of a eulogy to a dead person.
rowza	miniature replicas of tombs of famous martyrs.

ruba'iyat	"quatrains," one of three major lyric forms whose chief subject is the lover-beloved relationship.
ruh	"spirit," used either of God or a faculty within a human being.
sabil	"way, path," a public fountain, often donated as an act of piety through a waqf. The term *sabil-kuttab* refers to a fountain attached to a primary school.
sabr	"patience," a virtue Qur'an associates strongly with the prophet Joseph.
saj'	rhymed prose, used in Qur'an.
sakina	God's "tranquility," which descends on his faithful servants especially when Qur'an is recited.
salat	the formal ritual prayer offered by Muslims five times daily.
sama'	"hearing, audition," in Sufism, the participation in an ecstatic spiritual recital or dhikr involving prayer, music, and dance.
sawm (siyam)	"fasting"; specifically, fasting from before dawn to after dusk during the month of Ramadan.
semahane	Turkish, paraliturgical practices particular to a specific Sufi order.
Shafi'i	a Sunni school of law named after Shafi'i (d. 820).
shahada	the profession of faith: "There is no god but God, and Muhammad is the Messenger of God."
shajara	"tree," a term used in Sufism to refer to the spiritual lineage of a particular person or Sufi order.
shama'il	"excellent qualities," a litany that extols Muhammad's extraordinary physical and spiritual qualities.
Shari'a	the Islamic revealed law based on and derived from Qur'an and sunna.
shath (*pl.*, shatahat, shathiyat)	"movement," the paradoxical expression of mystical ecstasy.
shaykh	an elder, religious scholar, or Sufi master.
Shi'a	"party"; specifically, party of 'Ali; the minority community of Muslims.

shi'r	a general literary term that refers to various forms of poetry.
silsila	"chain," the lineage of a person or group.
sira	a literary term for biography, especially of the life of Muhammad.
Sufism	a mystical expression of the Islamic faith.
sunna	"custom, tradition, way of acting," especially of Muhammad (Sunna). His Sunna is remembered and transmitted by means of the literary form known as hadith. *Sunna* is also a legal term that means "recommended."
Sunni	the popular name of Islam's majority, as distinct from Shi'i.
sura	a chapter of Qur'an.
syair	the Malay term for a short encomium; from the Arabic *sha'ir,* "poet," related to *shi'r.*
tabaqat	"classes or generations," a literary form similar to the biographical dictionaries but later in date and used for demonstrating spiritual lineage and for edification.
tabut	a burial container.
tadhkira	"recollection," a form of biographical dictionary similar to the tabaqat but with a greater emphasis on edification.
tafsir	"explanation, commentary," a category of interpretation that moves something "out of concealment into full view"; the elucidation of scripture by commenting on its historical context, relative clarity, and applicability.
tahara	"purification," including various forms of ritual means to that end; sometimes refers to circumcision.
tajwid	elaborate style of Qur'an recitation.
takhallus	the second part of the classical qasida, which takes as its major theme a search for a departed one that becomes an image of spiritual pilgrimage; also called the rahil.
takiya	building in which ta'ziya rituals occur.
ta'lim	a general term for instruction or pedagogy.
tarbiya	advanced pedagogy in the finer points of the spiritual life.
tariqa (*pl.,* tariqat, turuq)	"path," a method of spiritual discipline with specific techniques of meditation; an order or organization of Sufis; also the Sufi "way."

tasawwuf	Sufism.
tawakkul	trust.
tawba	repentance.
tawhid	maintaining God's unity; the confession that God is one and has no associates.
ta'wil	allegorical or symbolic interpretation, for example, of the Qur'an.
ta'ziya	"consolation," the Shi'i passion play that commemorates the martyrdom of Husayn at Karbala.
tekke (Arabo-Persian: takiya)	the Turkish term for a building used as a residence or retreat center for dervishes, often where the tomb of the founder and his successors is located.
turba	(*also* turbe) a domed building, typically a mausoleum.
'ulama' (*sg.*, 'alim)	the learned class of religious and legal scholars.
'umra	the lesser pilgrimage, a visit to Mecca outside the formal pilgrimage season.
umma	global community of Muslims.
'urs	"marriage festivities" commemorating the death of a holy personage whose soul is thus married to God.
wahdat ash-shuhud	a term that refers to "experiential unity," which means experience of union with God that does not imply an ontological change in the human being.
wahdat al-wujud	a term that refers to "unity of being" or "ontological unity."
wajd	literally, "finding"; "being found"; ecstasy.
wali	one who is close, a friend or relative; Friend of God.
waqf	a charitable trust dedicated to some pious or socially beneficial purpose endowed in perpetuity.
waqfa	"staying," a metaphor for a type of mystical experience.
waqfiya	the legal document by which a founder establishes a waqf.
wa'z	preaching, moral exhortation. The term *wu' 'az* refers to a class of public figures whose profession was to give moral exhortation.

wazir	a government official whose duty is to offer advice to the chief ruler; minister of state.
wird (*pl.*, awrad)	a litany of prayers strung together.
wuʿʿaz	*see* waʿz.
yaqin	certainty.
zabur	a Qurʾanic term for the revelation given to David; the Psalms.
zahir	the external or plain meaning of something.
zakat	legally enjoined almsgiving.
zawiya	a sufi retreat or cloister usually associated with a particular shaykh.
ziyara	visitation to a holy shrine such as Medina, but more popularly, to tombs of holy persons; local pilgrimage.
ziyaratkhana	visitation house, where models of martyrs' tomb-shrines are displayed.
zuhd	asceticism.

Index of Qur'anic Citations

Brackets indicate reference to verse by name (e.g., Throne, Light) rather than by number.

General Index

Aaron, 20, 84. See also Prophets

'Abbas, Shah (1588–1629), 149, 151, 170, 178

Abbasids, 146; and religious poetry, 110, 112. See also Patronage

'Abdallah Ansari of Herat (d. 1089), 55–56, 163, 198–200, 212, 216

'Abdallah ibn Ja'far (7th c.), 97

'Abd al-Ghani b. Isma'il (1641–1731), 204

'Abd al-Qadir al-Jilani (1088–1166), 97, 98, 185–88, 228–29, 230; celebration and commemoration of, 58, 61; and Joseph, 263, 271; tomb of, 61, 85, 101

'Abd al-Qadir of Damascus (d. 1883), 246

'Abd al-Qadir of Johore (fl. c. 1950), 230–31

'Abd ar-Rahman Katkhuda (18th c.), 170

Ablution, 23, 37, 38, 39–40, 47, 172–73, 210. See also Purity; Ritual; sabil

Abode of Spring (Baharistan) by Jami, 94–95

Abraham, prophet, 1, 84, 102, 126, 263, 272; and the Ka'ba, 38, 48, 50; compared to Muhammad, 192–93; and Nimrod, 80, 103, 120; prayer of, 10; as prophet-builder, 153. See also Prophets

Abrogation, 3–6, 9, 14, 176. See also Interpretation; Qur'an, interpretation of

Abstraction, 98, 129–31, 136. See also Art

Abu Bakr (d. 634), 43, 134, 213

Abu 'l-Hasan al-Bakri (fl. c. late 13th c.), 79

Abu 'l-Hasan ad-Daylami (d. c. 1000), 80–81

Abu Hurayra (d. c. 678) 14

Abu Ishaq al-Kazaruni (d. 1035), 81–82

Abu Jahl (7th c.), 80

Abu Nu'aym al-Isfahani (d. 1037), 86

Abu Nuwas (d. c. 810), 207

Abu Sa'id ibn Abi 'l-Khayr (d. c. 1049), 81–82, 189

Abu Talib al-Makki (d. 996), 209–210

Abu Yusuf (d. 798), 154–56. See also Law

Accommodation. See also Interpretation; Pedagogy, divine; Revelation, adaptation

adab as behavior, 89, 206, 215; as literature, 108, 152, 161–62, 163, 251; al-minbar, 40.

Adab al-mashq. See Manners of Practice

Adam, 78, 84, 102, 214, 240. See also Prophets

Admonitions of Seh (Shaykh) Bari, 193, 202–3

Aesthetics, 93, 104, 107, 125–28, 144. See also Art

Aflaki (d. 1356), 88

Ahmad al-Badawi of Tanta (d. 1276), 58

Ahmad Sirhindi (d. 1624), 196–97, 229–30, 250–51

Ahmad Yasawi (d. 1166), 179

'Ajiba, Ahmad Ibn (1746–1809), 217–18, 226–28

Akbar (r.1556–1605), 150–51, 165–67. See also Mughals; Patronage

Akhbari Law School, 154. See also Law

Akhlaq-i Nasiri. See Nasirean Ethics

'Alawi, Ahmad al- (d. 1934), 242–43

Alchemy of Happiness (Kimiya-yi sa'adat) by Ghazali, 125

Al Futuhat al-Makkiya. See Meccan Revelations

Alhambra, The Court of Lions, 134–35

'Ali ibn Abi Talib (d. 661), 8, 61, 66, 70, 134; and art, 97–98, 126, 141, 213; as intimate Friend of God, 28, 29; sayings of, 14–15, 187 .

Alive, Son of Awake (Hayy ibn Yaqzan), by Ibn Tufayl, 232

Allah. See God

Allegory, 8, 256, 261; and miniature painting, 166; mystical, 207; Shi'i art, 107, 248; Shi'i narrative, 114–16, 232; Shi'i poetry, 118, 137. See also Literary devices

Allusion, 134, 166, 202–3, 210, 223, 233; allegorical, 116; mystical, 238–40; in

Faithfulness of believers, 133

Fakhr ad-Din 'Iraqi (1213–1289), 240–241

fana', 111–114, 203, 204–5, 213, 240; of *fana'*, 111–12, 229; of intoxication, 229–30

faqr. See Poverty

Faraj ibn Barquq (d. 1412), 173. See also *khanqah*; Mamluks; Patronage

Farid ad-Din 'Attar (d. 1220), 86, 107, 112, 116–17, 124, 137

farq, 205

Fasting, 14, 28, 57, 81, 91; breaking of, 41; as one of the Five Pillars, 37, 39; as one of the Shi'i Seven Pillars, 70. *See also* Ritual; Ramadan

Fath ar-rabbani, al. See Sublime Revelation

Fath ar-rahman. See Revelation of the Merciful

Fatima, 61, 79, 88; tomb of, 48, 71

Fatimids, 29, 70, 131, 146. *See also* Patronage

Fawa'id al-fu'ad. See Morals for the Heart

Fear of God, 90, 96

Figural art. *See* Symbolism

Figurative images and language, anthropomorphic, 113, 136–37; metaphor, 18, 141;—, dancing and music as, 137;—, for God, 113–14;—, for mystical experience, 124, 137, 208, 216, 231;—Qur'anic, 5, 7, 271;—, in poetry, 122, 114;—, in Rumi, 122, 189; simile 18, 22; visual, 256; zoomorphic, 136. *See also* Images; Literary devices; Symbolism

Fihi ma fihi, 189–90

Firdawsi (d. 1020), 117

Firdawsiya order, 191, 196

Five Pillars, 35, 36–37, 39, 56, 208, 210–11. *See also* Almsgiving; Fasting; Pilgrimage; Ritual prayer; Seven Pillars; *Shahada*

Five Senses, 123, 208, 255

Flashes (Divine) (Lama'at), by 'Iraqi, 240

Forgiveness, 63, 123; divine, 3, 14, 17; God as [title], 10, 27–28; Joseph as model of, 260, 263; prayer for, 11, 40

Fraternities Mystical, 38, 66, 85. *See also* Sufi Orders

Freedom moral, 12

Friends of God, 'Ali as, 28–29; in art and imagery, 72, 99, 137; dedication of buildings to, 148; inspiration of, 80–82; intercession of, 63, 221; al-Jilani as, 58, 97–99; Joseph as, 262, 270; as models/heroes, 75–77, 86, 99, 180; mystical/spiritual knowledge of, 124, 249; redemptive suffering of, 262; Rumi as, 88; spiritual authority of, 91, 166, 187, 192–93; tombs of, 60, 62, 66, 179–80

Funerary, architecture, *See* Architecture, funerary; practice, 59–63; objects 67–72; rite, 59

Fusus al-hikam. See Bezels of Wisdom

Futuh al-ghayb. See Revelations of the Unseen

Futuh al-haramayn. See Openings of the Two Sanctuaries

Gabriel, 58, 192, 236–37, 262–63, 268, 270. *See also* Angels

Garden imagery of, 28–29, 71, 102, 114, 137, 231; in architectural symbolism, 68, 132–35; in poetry, 21, 56, 120

Garden of Ultimate Reality (Hadiqat al-haqiqat), by Sana'i, 114, 117

Geneaology, physical, 78; spiritual, 85. *See also* Biographical dictionary; Hadith; Tradition; *Isnad*

Generations of the Sufis (Tabaqat as-sufiya), by Sulami, 85, 195

Geography, mystical, 205–211. *See also* Journey, spiritual; Mystical path

gharad. See qasida

ghazal, 110–12, 118, 121, 122, 138. *See also* Literary genres

Ghazali, Abu Hamid al- (d. 1111), 39, 64, 67; autobiography of, 224–25; beauty and harmony in, 125–27; and *dhikr*, 53–54; letters of, 194–95; and mirror for princes, 89–91; and mystical experience, 215, 233; and prayer, 37–38, 52

Ghazali, Ahmad (d. 1126), 239–40

Ghengis Khan (d. 1227), 148–50. *See also* Mongols

Glory, 2, 41, 178, 249, 250, 268

Glossaries. *See* Lexicons, mystical

God, attributes of, 16; as beauty, 127, 136–37, 201, 210, 236; as Creator, 2, 10,

Compositor: Integrated Composition Systems, Inc.
Text and Display: Aldus
Printer and Binder: BookCrafters